Lecture Notes in Computer Science 4901

Commenced Publication in 1973
Founding and Former Series Editors:
Gerhard Goos, Juris Hartmanis, and Jan van Leeuwen

David Zhang (Ed.)

Medical Biometrics

First International Conference, ICMB 2008
Hong Kong, China, January 4-5, 2008
Proceedings

 Springer

Volume Editor

David Zhang
The Hong Kong Polytechnic University
Department of Computing
Hung Hom, Kowloon, Hong Kong
E-mail: csdzhang@comp.polyu.edu.hk

Library of Congress Control Number: 2007941380

CR Subject Classification (1998): I.4, I.5, I.3, I.2.10, I.2.1, J.3

LNCS Sublibrary: SL 6 – Image Processing, Computer Vision, Pattern Recognition,
and Graphics

ISSN   0302-9743
ISBN-10   3-540-77410-6 Springer Berlin Heidelberg New York
ISBN-13   978-3-540-77410-5 Springer Berlin Heidelberg New York

Springer is a part of Springer Science+Business Media

springer.com

© Springer-Verlag Berlin Heidelberg 2007
Printed in Germany

Typesetting: Camera-ready by author, data conversion by Scientific Publishing Services, Chennai, India
Printed on acid-free paper   SPIN: 12208487   06/3180   5 4 3 2 1 0

Preface

The past decade has seen a rapid growth in the demand for the usage of behavioral and physiological characteristics of humans for e-*security and forensics* applications. The significant advances in the biometrics techniques are increasingly incorporated in a number of other applications. In this context, medicine has emerged as the largest and most promising area. Medical biometrics primarily refers to the usage of behavioral and physiological characteristics of humans for *medical diagnosis and body care*. Thus the goal of medical biometrics is to explore solutions to the open problems in medicine using biometric measurements, technologies and systems.

The International Conference on Medical Biometrics (ICMB 2008) was the first major gathering in the world devoted to facilitating this interaction. We are pleased that this conference attracted a large number of high-quality research papers that will benefit international medical biometrics research. After a careful review process, 40 papers were accepted either for oral (17) or poster (23) presentations. In addition to these technical presentations, this conference also held a workshop on Computerized Traditional Chinese Medicine. Our efforts are focused to generating awareness among researchers, organizing researchers to foster research in this area, and providing a common platform for discussion and investigation. This conference provided a forum for discussing practical experiences in applying the state-of-the-art biometric tecnologies for medical diagnosis and body care, which will further stimulate research in medical biometrics.

We are grateful to Max A. Viergever, Heinz-Otto Peitgen, and Tadashi Watsuji for accepting our invitation to give keynote talks at ICMB 2008. In addition, we would like to express our gratitude to all the contributors, reviewers, Program Committee and Organizing Committee members who made this a very successful conference. We also wish to acknowledge the International Association of Pattern Recognition (IAPR), IEEE Computational Intelligence Society (IEEE-CIS), National Natural Science Foundation in China (NSFC), and Springer for sponsoring this conference. Special thanks are due to Jane You, Milan Sonka, Xiaoyi Jiang, Ajay Kumar, Lei Zhang, Jing Li, Vivek K., Zhenhua Guo and Liu Li for their dedication and hard work in various aspects of the conference organization. We thankfully acknowledge the partial support from the National Natural Science Foundation in China (NSFC) Key Overseas Project (60620160097).

We hope that the fruitful technical interactions during this conference will benefit your further research and development efforts in medical biometrics.

October 2007 David Zhang

Organization

General Chair

David Zhang (The Hong Kong Polytechnic University, Hong Kong)

Program Chairs

Milan Sonka (The University of Iowa, USA)
Jane You (The Hong Kong Polytechnic University, Hong Kong)
Xiaoyi Jiang (University of Münster, Germany)

Program Committee

Hong Yan (City University of Hong Kong, Hong Kong)
Prabir Bhattacharya (Concordia University, Canada)
Alejandro Frangi (Pompeu Fabra University, Spain)
Bernadette Dorizzi (Institut National des Télécommunications, France)
Chuang-Chien Chiu (Feng Chia University, Taiwan)
Dinggang Shen (University of Pennsylvania School of Medicine, USA)
Heang-Ping Chan (University of Michigan, USA)
Changen Wang (National Natural Science Foundation of China, PR China)
Jeffery Huang (Raytheon Company, USA)
Jerome Zhengrong Liang (State University of New York at Stony Brook, USA)
Kwang Suk Park (Seoul National University, Korea)
Kwang-Sup Soh (Seoul National University, Korea)
Liang-Yu Shyu (Chung Yuan Christian University, Taiwan)
Mateo Aboy (Oregon Institute of Technology, USA)
Michael Abrmoff (University of Iowa, USA)
Naimin Li (No.211 Hospital of People Liberation Army, PR China)
Nicholas Ayache (The French Research Institute of Computer Science and Automatic
    Control, France)
Opas Chutatape (Nanyang Technological University, Singapore)
Pong Chi Yuen (The Hong Kong Baptist University, Hong Kong)
Yazhu Chen (Shanghai Jiao Tong University, PR China)
Stanislaw Osowski (Warsaw University of Technology, Poland)
Ruwei Dai (Chinese Academy of Science, PR China)
Witold Pedrycz (University of Alberta, Canada)
Yanda Li (Tsinghua University, PR China)
Yang Cai (Carnegie Mellon University, USA)
Yoshiharu Yonezawa (Hiroshima Institute of Technology, Japan)
Ali Can (Woods Hole Oceanographic Institution, USA)

Table of Contents

Feature Extraction and Classification

Health Care

Medical Diagnosis

Medical Image Processing and Registration

A New Feature Selection and Classification Scheme for Screening of Oral Cancer Using Laser Induced Fluorescence

Lalit Gupta, Sarif Kumar Naik, and Srinivasan Balakrishnan

Philips Research Asia - Bangalore,
Bangalore - 500045, India
{lalit.gupta,sarif.naik,srinivasan.balakrishnan}@philips.com

Abstract. Screening for oral cancer in its early stage is of utmost importance for improving the survival rate of oral cancer patients. The current method of visual examination followed by biopsy of suspected cases is subjective with inter and intra personal variations. With a low ratio of oral-cancer experts to patients compounded by the reluctance of patients to undergo biopsy in rural India. The situation cries out for automatic screening device for oral cancer. In this context, optical spectroscopy based on Laser Induced Fluorescence (LIF) has been shown to be a promising technique in distinguishing between cancerous and benign lesions in the mouth. However, it has been observed that it is very difficult to distinguish pre-malignant spectra from malignant and normal spectra recorded *in-vivo*. Hence, obtaining the most discriminating features from the spectra becomes important. In this article a new method of feature selection is proposed using mean-shift and Recursive Feature Elimination (RFE) techniques to increase discrimination ability of the feature vectors. Performance of the algorithm is evaluated on a *in-vivo* recorded LIF data set consisting of spectra from normal, malignant and pre-malignant patients. Sensitivity of above 95% and specificity of above 99% towards malignancy are obtained using the proposed method.

1 Introduction

Oral cancer refers to the cancer of the oral cavity and pharynx. It is the sixth most common form of cancer in the world. It poses a major public health problem. The number of new cases are estimated to be 274,289 [1] per year and about two-thirds of them arise in developing countries. The Indian sub-continent accounts for more than one-third of the total number oral cancer cases in the world [2]. The incidence of oral cancer is rising in several other regions of the world such as Europe, Taiwan, Japan and Australia. Oral cancer is most often found by physicians at a later stage as a persistent ulcer with raised edges and an indurated base. Oral cancer may be preceded by pre-malignant lesions such as leukoplakia, erythroplakia, oral sub-mucous fibrosis (OSMF) etc. Some of these lesions may transform into cancer over a period of time. The cancerous lesions of oral cavity are staged depending on the size, location, the clinical aspects and

D. Zhang (Ed.): ICMB 2008, LNCS 4901, pp. 1–8, 2007.

the histopathological features of biopsy. The 5-year survival rate in oral cancer is less than 50%. However, if diagnosed at early pre-cancerous stage, the chances of survival could be greatly improved with minimal intervention.

The current method of visual examination followed by biopsy of suspected cases is subjective. With a low ratio of oral-cancer experts to patients compounded by the reluctance of patients to undergo biopsy in rural India. The situation cries out for automatic screening device for oral cancer. In recent years, various optical spectroscopy methods have been studied for the screening of oral cancer [3,4]. In general LIF spectroscopy in particular has been shown to be a promising technique for classifying oral lesions as cancerous and non-cancerous [3,4]. In the present study LIF technology has been used for screening of oral cancer. The scope of this article includes automatic classification of LIF spectra into three classes malignant, pre-malignant and normal.

Most of the algorithms reported for the classification of LIF data use traditional multi-variate statistical techniques such as principal component analysis (PCA), singular value decomposition (SVD) etc. Nayak et al.[3] used PCA for feature extraction and match no-match scheme for classification of LIF Spectra obtained in-vitro. They used PCA to obtain a feature vector for each samples. Each of these feature vectors consists of the scores from the first four principal components and the sum of squared spectral residual for each spectrum. Match no-match test is performed using Mohalanobis distance and spectral residual. Sensitivity of 99% and specificity of 95% is reported using this methods. Kamath et al.[5] have worked on the same data using K-means clustering and similar results are reported. Majumder et al.[6] reported an algorithm using support vector machine (SVM) for the development of algorithms for optical diagnosis of cancer. Recursive feature elimination (RFE) is proposed for feature selection. SVM is used for classification stage as well as for feature selection. Better results are claimed compared to PCA based feature extraction algorithms and Fishers linear discriminant (FLD)- based algorithms. Using the proposed scheme sensitivity of 95% and specificity of 96% toward cancer are reported on the training set and sensitivity of 93% and specificity of 97% toward cancer are reported on the independent validation set. In the pre-processing step of the algorithm, variance of all the spectra (training as well as testing) in the data is used for normalization. However, variation in test samples should not be considered to normalize the training samples because test samples are supposed to be blind from the training samples. Hence, the reported accuracy in sensitivity and specificity likely be far away from the actual.

Naik et al.[7] performed a comparative study of different feature extraction techniques for the classification of LIF spectra recorded from oral tissue. It is reported that discrete wavelet transform (DWT) features give better classification accuracy than other features such as PCA, linear discriminant analysis(LDA) or independent component analysis(ICA). Classification is performed using support vector machines. Apart from [3,5] and [6] other work only classify oral cancer into two classes of malignant and pre-malignant. Only Majumdar et al.[6] and [7] worked on in-vivo recorded spectra and all other work are on in-vitro recorded spectra.

In this paper, a system for classifying LIF data is proposed. In the first step features are extracted from LIF spectra using DWT [7] and then the most relevant features are selected from all the features using a new feature selection technique. Finally, classification is done using support vector machines. The rest of the article is organized as follows: A brief description of the LIF data set used for classification is discussed in Section 2. The algorithm proposed for feature selection is explained in Section 3. Results obtained using proposed algorithm are discussed in Section 4. Concluding remarks on the proposed algorithm are given in Section 5.

2 Overview of LIF Spectra

The details of LIF system used for collecting data is given in [7]. Three examples of spectra corresponding to normal, pre-malignant and malignant condition and recorded *in-vitro* are shown in Fig. 1(a). It is observed that the malignant spectrum contains only one peak due to Nicotinamide Adenine Dinucleotide (NADH) at 440nm and the normal spectrum contain two peaks one due to collagen at 400nm and the other due NADH at 440nm. Two peaks can also be seen in pre-malignant spectra. However, the difference between normal spectra and pre-malignant spectra is that he relative strength of the two peaks in case of pre-malignant spectrum is similar. Hence, to a great extent, it is possible to distinguish between normal, pre-malignant and malignant spectra easily by visual observation.

The aim of the current study is to screen oral cancer non-invasively in real time. Hence, for this study all the spectra are recorded *in-vivo*. Some examples of spectra recorded using the LIF system are shown in Fig. 1(b)-(c). However, unlike *in-vitro* data *in-vivo* data has huge variations. This can be observed from the spectra shown in Fig. 1(b)-(c). It can be observed from Fig. 1(b) that pre-malignant spectrum look like a weighted average spectrum of a normal and pre-malignant spectra, i.e., there is a peak at 440nm for all types of spectra and the peak strength at 400nm increases from malignant to normal to premalignant. Fig. 1(c) shows a set of spectra, in which it is almost impossible to differentiate between malignant and pre-malignant spectra by visual observation. In a few rare cases malignant spectrum also shows a valley at 400nm. In these cases it becomes difficult to visually differentiate between malignant and normal spectra. The

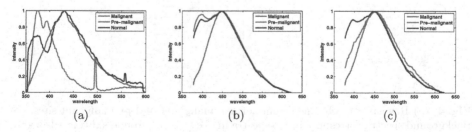

| (a) | (b) | (c) |

Fig. 1. (a) Spectrum showing LIF data recorded *in-vitro*. (b)-(c) Spectra recorded using the LIF system *in-vivo*.

possible sources of these variations are (1) subjective evaluation of malignancy of lesions by clinicians and (2) variation in thickness of the layer of tissue in different stages of malignancy.

3   Proposed Methodology

Each LIF spectra consists of 1024 sample points recorded from the wavelength of 375nm to 600nm. The steps followed in the proposed algorithm are shown in Fig. 2. The complete algorithm comprises of three steps, and each of the three steps are described below:

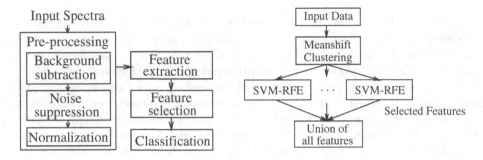

Fig. 2. Steps in the algorithm   **Fig. 3.** Steps in feature selection

3.1   Pre-processing

The first step is pre-processing. It contains three sub-steps, background subtraction, filtering and normalization. First, we subtract the background spectra to get the actual spectra information. Due to the variations in recording environment, the LIF system can induce some unwanted signal (background noise) to the spectrum. This is commonly known as plasma lines included to the original signal due to back scattering properties of the quartz window, used in the LIF system. Hence, a background spectrum is captured before each set of recordings from a patient, by exposing the probe to the blank space. By subtracting

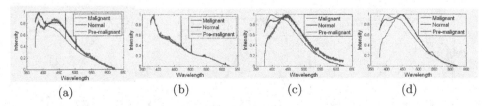

Fig. 4. (a) Raw spectra obtained from normal, malignant and premalignant sites. (b) Background spectra corresponding to spectra in (a); (c) Background subtracted spectra corresponding to spectra in (a); (d) Resultant spectra obtained by filtering the spectra in (c).

the recorded spectrum with background spectrum, the background noise is suppressed. Background subtracted spectrum is filtered using a median filter of size five (obtained empirically) to suppress noise in the spectrum.

Finally, we normalize the spectrum values between 0 and 1. Fig. 4(a) show raw spectra obtained from normal, malignant and premalignant sites. Fig. 4(b) show background spectra corresponding to spectra in (a). Fig. 4(c) show spectra obtained after background subtraction and fig. 4(d) show resultant spectra obtained after filtering using median filter.

3.2 Feature Extraction

In the second step, features are extracted from the pre-processed spectra. Due to variation in the *in-vivo* data as shown in Fig.1(b)-(c), using raw (intensity values) as features would not able to distinguish the premalignant spectra from malignant and normal. We have used DWT [8] for feature extraction. The discrete wavelet transform analyses a signal based on its content in different frequency ranges at varying scales. The DWT can be realized by iterations of filters with rescaling. The resolution of the signal, which is a measure of the amount of detailed information in the signal, is determined by the filtering operations, and the scale is determined by upsampling and downsampling (subsampling) operations. We have used four-level decomposition of Daubechies 8-tap wavelets. Empirically, we found that Daubechies 8-tap wavelet works marginally better than Haar and Daubechies 4 and 12 tap wavelets. All detailed and coarse components of DWT are finally concatenated to get a large feature vector. The coarse component of DWT captures the shape information of the spectra and detailed component captures the high frequency information which helps in classification of a few confusing premalignant spectra from normal and malignant.

3.3 Feature Selection

A desired algorithm should extract the most relevant features and eliminate the irrelevant and redundant ones. It is important because throwing away irrelevant features reduces the risk of overfitting and decreases computational complexity. The selection of an optimal subset of features can be carried out by using an appropriately designed performance measure to evaluate their ability to classify the samples. It could not be done using a brute force method, if number of features are huge. The Support Vector Machine - Recursive Feature Elimination (SVM-RFE) algorithm proposed in [6], first takes all the features for training a SVM and assess the relative importance of the features in the classifier by the feature ranking criterion. The feature ranking criterion for SVM-RFE is

$$w_r = \sum_{x_i \in S} y_i \lambda_i K(x_i, x) \tag{1}$$

where, λ_i is the lagrange multiplier, $K(.)$ is the kernel of the SVM and x is the input data. In our work, we have used linear kernel for feature selection. For more details on SVM, refer to [9]. It preserves the higher rank features and eliminates the lower rank features. The process is repeated (using only survived features) until all the features are assessed. At the end, ranks of all the features is obtained. Now the task is to decide the optimal set of features from this ranked list of features. For that, the different numbers of top-ranked features are selected to form a series of different feature subsets. The optimal set of features is decided by computing the performance of the classifier with these selected features, iteratively.

The drawback of using SVM-RFE in its original form is that it may also end up in removing a few informative features, which is undesirable [10]. We propose a modification over the SVM-RFE algorithm which processes a small subsets of data at a time to take into account small variations in the data. The block diagram of the proposed algorithm is shown in Fig. 3. The algorithm proposed in this work first clusters the data into different sub-groups using a mean-shift algorithm. The advantage of using mean-shift over other clustering techniques is that it automatically computes the number of clusters in which the data should be divided based on the properties of the data. Then potential features are selected using SVM-RFE considering the samples within the subgroup. Finally, an union of the selected features from each group is considered to form the final feature vector. In this way, the feature vectors consider the variations and also removes all irrelevant features. This feature vector is now used for classification considering all the samples together.

3.4 Classification

There are a lot of classification techniques proposed in the literature and support vector machine is one of them. SVMs are a set of supervised learning methods used for classification and regression. SVM belong to a family of generalized linear classifiers which use structural risk minimization for classification. A significant advantage of SVMs is that they look for a global and unique solution. Additionally, the computational complexity of SVMs does not depend on the dimensionality of the input space and less prone to overfitting. Therefore, in our current study, support vector machine [9] has been used for classification of LIF spectra.

4 Experimental Results

In the current study, we have used 197 spectra of normal lesions, 174 spectra of pre-malignant lesions and 169 spectra of malignant lesions. These spectra are obtained from left cheek, right cheek, lower lip, tongue bottom, left tongue lateral and right tongue lateral part of the mouth. A collection of 50 spectra from each class are selected randomly to form the training set. Rest of the data set i.e. 109, 124 and 147 from malignant, premalignant and normal spectra, respectively, are used for testing. The method is evaluated using standard measures such as sensitivity, specificity and over all accuracy of the algorithms.

Table 1 shows results of classification. Column 1 and 2 show the features used and the feature selection method used for classification, respectively. In all our

Table 1. Classification results (%)

Features	Feature Selection	Sensitivity	Specificity	Accuracy
Raw data	-	93.6	95.2	86.5
Raw data	SVM-RFE	94.0	95.3	87.0
DWT	-	94.0	99.0	88.5
DWT	SVM-RFE	94.1	99.0	88.7
DWT	Proposed technique	95.5	99.3	89.5

experiments, SVM with a polynomial kernel degree 3 has been used for classification. Empirically, we found SVM with polynomial kernel works better than Gaussian and Sigmoidal kernels. Column 3 and 4 show the sensitivity and specificity towards malignancy (i.e. considering malignant and premalignant together as positives samples and normal as negative samples). Last column shows the overall accuracy obtained by classifying the samples into three classes i.e. malignant, pre-malignant and normal. The first row of the Table 1 shows results using raw (intensity) features without using any feature selection algorithm. Second row shows results using raw features with SVM-RFE used for feature selection as used in [6]. The next two rows show results with and without using SVM-RFE on the features obtained using DWT (Daubechies 8-tap). It can also be observed from first four rows that DWT features perform superior to using just raw (intensity values) as features. The last row of the table show results obtained using the proposed method. It can be observed that there is a significant improvement in sensitivity, specificity and overall accuracy using the proposed method. The proposed method uses RFE on the DWT features extracted in smaller clusters obtained using mean-shift clustering. A sensitivity of 95.5% and specificity of 99.3% are obtained using the proposed method compared to sensitivity of 94.0% and specificity of 95.3% using method proposed in [6].

To examine the robustness of the algorithm Receiver Operating Characteristic (ROC) curves has been used for study. Fig. 5 shows the ROC curves generated using different methods by considering malignant and pre-malignant samples together in one class and normal in the other class. It can be observed that ROC curve generated using proposed method is more closer to its ideal shape compared to other methods. It can also be observed that after a particular

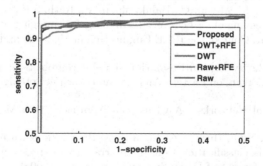

Fig. 5. ROC curves using different methods

threshold sensitivity of the system does not change significantly and specificity starts decreasing. Higher sensitivity can also be obtained at the cost of lower specificity by varying the threshold in the binary classifier as shown in Fig. 5.

5   Conclusions

In this paper, an algorithm for the classification of LIF spectra has been proposed. This algorithm includes four steps i.e., pre-processing, feature extraction, feature selection and classification. Features extracted using DWT are passed through a new feature selection method to select the best set of discriminating features in the spectra. Finally, the combined set of features are used for the classification using SVM. The proposed method is evaluated on a collection of *in-vivo* recorded LIF spectra for oral cancer screening. A sensitivity of 95.5% and specificity of 99.3% are obtained using proposed method compared to sensitivity of 94.0% and specificity of 95.3% using method proposed in [6]. Current results show that LIF system along with the proposed method of classification has potential to be used for oral cancer screening. However, the system has to be tested on more samples before using it for practical application.

References

1. International agency for research on cancer (2007), http://www-dep.iarc.fr
2. Mouth cancer foundation (2006), http://www.rdoc.org.uk
3. Nayak, G.S., Kamath, S., Pai, K.M., Sarkar, A., Ray, S., Kurien, J., D'Almeida, L., Krishnanand, B.R., Santhosh, C., Kartha, V.B., Mahato, K.K.: Principal component analysis and artificial neural network analysis of oral tissue fluorescence spectra: Classification of normal, premalignant and malignant pathological conditions. Biopolymers 82/2(6), 152–160 (2006)
4. Majumder, S.K., Ghosh, N., Kataria, S., Gupta, P.K.: Nonlinear pattern recognition for laser-induced fluorescence diagnosis of cancer. Lasers in Surgery and Madicine 33, 48–56 (2003)
5. Kamath, S.D., Mahato, K.K.: Optical pathology using oral tissue fluorescence spectra: classification by principal component analysis and k-means nearest neighbor analysis. J. Biomedical Optics 12, 14028 (2007)
6. Majumder, S.K., Ghosh, N., Gupta, P.K.: Support vector machine for optical diagnosis of cancer. Journal of Biomedical Optics 2, 024034-1–14 (2005)
7. Naik, S.K., Gupta, L., Mittal, C., Balakrishnan, S., Rath, S.P., Santhosh, C., Pai, K.M.: Optical screening of oral cancer: Technology for emerging markets. In: Proc. of 29th Annual Int. Conf. of the IEEE Engineering in Medicine and Biology Society (2007)
8. Mallat, S.G.: A theory for multiresolution signal decomposition: The wavelet representation. IEEE Tran. on Pattern Analysis and Machine Intelligence 11, 674–693 (1989)
9. Kumar, S.: Neural Networks - A Classroom Approach. Tata McGraw Hill, New Delhi (2004)
10. Tang, Y., Zhang, Y.Q., Huang, Z.: FCM-SVM-RFE gene feature seclection algorithm for leukemia classification from microarray gene expression data. In: IEEE International Conference of Fuzzy Systems, pp. 97–101 (2005)

Tongueprint Feature Extraction and Application to Health Statistical Analysis

ZhaoHui Yang and Naimin Li

Department of Computer Science and Engineering, Harbin Institute of Technology (HIT),
Harbin 150001, China
Yangzhaohui7153@tom.com

Abstract. Tongueprint images of healthy populations can be differentiated from those of unhealthy populations by features of tongueprints (tongueprint is fissile texture on the tongue) according to observation by naked eyes, classification, and statistical analysis on tongueprints for large tongue images of healthy and unhealthy populations. Tongueprint binary image is gotten by an existed method, and then tongue images are classified as no-tongueprint and tongueprint images by our approaches. In terms of obtained statistical results on tongueprints, a series of computerized methods, for example computing length ratio of long to short axis for optimal fitting ellipse of tongueprint binary regions, getting location and amount of extremity and cross point of tongueprint skeletons by computing pixel connective numeral to determine pixel type, straight line segment approach, support vector machine (SVM) classifier and so on, are employed to recognize tongueprint images of healthy and unhealthy populations. Applying our method to the large database of tongue images, we achieve promising experimental results.

1 Introduction

Tongueprints are fissile texture on the tongue. Tongueprint diagnosis is a part of tongue diagnosis which is an important diagnostic method in Traditional Chinese Medicine (TCM) and has been applied to clinical practice for more than 2000 years, and has been used to differentiate syndromes and diagnose diseases for more than 600 years [1]. In recent several decades, some doctors have diagnosed early some diseases by inspecting shape, position, color of tongueprints and so on combined with observation of other information on tongue, for example tongue color etc [1], [2], [3]. In Chinese traditional medicine recordation, diagnostic theory of inspecting tongueprints thinks no-tongueprints are in healthy populations. However some scholars come to the conclusion that tongueprints can also appear on tongue of healthy adults by their observation [1], [4], [5]. But their observational samples amount is not so many (<1000 cases). Thus three problems emerge: 1. Can tongueprints appear in healthy populations and how about tongueprint quantity in healthy populations? 2. How to differentiate tongueprints between healthy and unhealthy populations by naked eyes? 3. Is it feasible to recognize tongueprints in healthy and unhealthy populations by computer? In order to answer these problems, we setup large sample tongue image database firstly. Then we analyze statistically these images on tongueprints and find many healthy persons also have tongueprints and tongueprint

D. Zhang (Ed.): ICMB 2008, LNCS 4901, pp. 9–16, 2007.

differences between healthy and unhealthy populations by naked eyes. At present, no articles about computerized recognition of tongueprints in healthy and unhealthy populations are reported. In this paper, Tongueprint binary image is gotten by an existed method, and then tongue images are classified as no-tongueprint and tongueprint images by our approaches. We use some computerized methods, e.g. computing length ratio of long to short axis for optimal fitting ellipse of tongueprint binary regions, getting location and amount of extremity and cross point of tongueprint skeletons by computing pixel connective numeral to determine pixel type, straight line segment approach and so on, to recognize tongueprint images regular or mixed. If a tongueprint image is a mixed tongueprint image, it is from an unhealthy person. A SVM classifier is used to recognize a regular tongueprint image belong to a healthy or unhealthy individual. Thousands of tongue images are used to test our methods effectiveness and the experimental results are encouraging.

2 Tongueprint Differences in Healthy and Unhealthy Populations by Naked Eyes

2.1 Large Sample Tongue Image Database

More than 3000 tongue images are captured by high-resolution cybershot under natural illuminating conditions at 9 and 10 o'clock in the morning. Let the person captured sit down and face upward. The person captured opens the mouth widely and sticks out the tongue naturally. Tongue images of healthy persons total 2044. Tongue images of unhealthy persons total 1253. Healthy and unhealthy persons have all credible and intact information, like age and sex etc. for healthy persons, and cases for unhealthy persons. In this paper, healthy person is the man who has no diseases or painful chief complaints, and who has not abnormal findings in regular physical examination. Based on those materials we setup large sample tongue image database.

2.2 Tongue Images Classification

By collective observation by naked eyes and discussion with some specialists on tongue diagnosis of Traditional Chinese Medicine, we classify all images in our database into no-tongueprint and tongueprint images, and find more than a tongueprint on some images, and recognize a tongueprint simple or complex according to shape complexity. If a tongueprint is a longitudinal, transverse or diagonal tongueprint then it is a simple tongueprint, otherwise a complex tongueprint. According to component proportion of tongueprint strength between all simple tongueprints and all complex tongueprints, tongueprint images are classified into regular and mixed tongueprints. Tongueprint strength is related to depth and area of tongueprints, namely tongueprints are bigger on area and deeper tongueprint strength is greater. Judging a tongueprint image regular or mixed is: a) if all tongueprints on an image are simple tongueprints the image is regular tongueprints. b) if all tongueprints on an image are complex tongueprints the image is mixed tongueprints. c) while there are not only simple tongueprints but also complex tongueprints on an image, if formed depth and area from all simple tongueprints are greater than that from all complex tongueprints the image is regular tongueprint image and otherwise mixed tongueprint image. d) or else the image is mixed tongueprint image. Thus all images can be classified into three classes: no-tongueprint, regular tongueprint and mixed tongueprint. Typical tongue images of no-tongueprint, regular tongueprint and mixed tongueprint are shown in Figure 1.

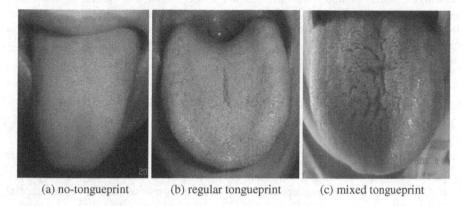

(a) no-tongueprint   (b) regular tongueprint   (c) mixed tongueprint

Fig. 1. Tongue images classification

2.3 Tongueprint Differences Between Healthy and Unhealthy Populations by Naked Eyes

Statistical results on no-tongueprint and tongueprint by age stage for tongue images of healthy populations in our database are shown in Table 1.

Table 1. No-tongueprint and tongueprint statistics by age stage in healthy populations

Age stage	Total	No-tongueprint (%)	Tongueprint (%)
0-6	112	74 (66.07)	38 (33.93)
7-30	781	507 (64.92)	274 (35.08)
31-50	680	438 (64.41)	242 (35.59)
51-	471	305 (64.76)	166 (35.24)
Total	2044	1324 (64.77)	720 (35.23)

From Table 1, we find tongueprints can appear and are not few in healthy populations.

Statistical results on regular and mixed tongueprint in healthy and unhealthy populations in our database are shown in Table 2.

Table 2. Statistical results on regular and mixed tongueprint in healthy and unhealthy populations

Populations	Total	Regular tongueprint	Mixed tongueprint
Healthy populations	720	720	0
Unhealthy populations	761	452	309
Total	1481	1172	309

From Table 2, we find mixed tongueprints are diagnostic tongueprints in unhealthy populations and if a man has mixed tongueprint he is unhealthy. From Table 2, we also find regular tongueprints may be on tongues of healthy persons and also on that of unhealthy persons. By collective observation by naked eyes and discussion with some specialists on tongue diagnosis of Traditional Chinese Medicine and reference for interrelated literature, we find regular tongueprints of healthy populations are on mid-tongue, light-red and their surfaces are tender, neat, not humid, and not dry. Regular tongueprints in unhealthy populations may be on any a position of tongue. They are light white, red, crimson, and purple and so on. Regular tongueprints in unhealthy populations are deep, large, coarse and dry compared with regular tongueprints in healthy populations.

3 Computerized Recognition of Tongueprints in Healthy and Unhealthy Populations

The binary image of tongueprint region BW_{syn} is gotten by [6]. If BW_{syn} of a tongue image has no foreground or its foreground only is tongue papillae or tongueprint points, the tongue image is a no-tongueprint image. We find a tongue papilla or tongueprint point on BW_{syn} is approximately circle shape and its area is little. Thus judging a tongue image to be a no-tongueprint or tongueprint image is described as follows:

Step 1: Compute foreground area of a tongue image and if area is zero the tongue image is a no-tongueprint image, otherwise goto Step 2.

Step 2: Compute circle degree [7] and area of every a connective region on BW_{syn}.

Set some thresholds, $CircleDegreeThresh_1$, $CircleDegreeThresh_2$ and $AreaThresh$. If circle degree and area of a connective region are respectively is between $CircleDegreeThresh_1$ and $CircleDegreeThresh_2$, and little than $AreaThresh$, the connective region is tongue papilla or tongueprint point and otherwise tongueprint. If all connective regions on BW_{syn} are tongue papillae or tongueprint points the tongue image is a no-tongueprint image, otherwise a tongueprint image.

In this paper, we set $CircleDegreeThresh_1 = 0.7$, $CircleDegreeThresh_2 = 1.3$ and $AreaThresh = 189$.

3.1 Computerized Recognition of Regular and Mixed Tongueprint Images

Because there is more than a tongueprint on some tongueprint images, we should recognize every a tongueprint on tongueprint images. Recognition of a tongueprint to be a simple or complex tongueprint is described as follows:

Step 1: Compute long and short axis length for optimal fitting ellipse of tongueprint binary regions [8], [9], a and b. Set two thresholds, LST_1 and LST_2 ($LST_1 > LST_2$). Let $LST = \dfrac{a}{b}$. Get location and amount of extremity and cross point of tongueprint skeleton by computing pixel connective numeral to determine pixel type [10].

Step 2: If $LST > LST_1$ the tongueprint is a simple tongueprint, otherwise goto Step 3.

Step 3: If $LST_2 \leq LST \leq LST_1$ and the tongueprint meets the following two conditions it is a complex tongueprint otherwise simple tongueprint. a) Hole or cross point numbers of its skeleton are greater than 0. b) Its skeleton has only two extremities and no cross point, and its skeleton has flexuous point(s) whose curvatures are comparatively greater.

Step 4: If $LST < LST_2$ and tongueprint skeleton has hole or cross point, the tongueprint is a complex tongueprint. Otherwise papilla or tongueprint point is recognized and ignored.

In this paper, get a bent line segment to fit a tongueprint skeleton with two extremities and no cross point by straight line segment approach [11]. If supplementary angle ($< 180°$) between two adjoining straight line segments on the bent line segment is greater than a threshold *AngleThresh*, cross point of two adjoining straight line segments is flexuous point. Here set $AngleThresh = 0.4363$ radian, $LST_1 = 2.5$ and $LST_2 = 1.5$.

After all tongueprints on a tongue image are recognized, compute tongueprint index of one or several tongueprint(s) *TPI* :

$$TPI = C \times \sum_{k=1}^{l}\left\{\sum_{i=1}^{m}\sum_{j=1}^{n}[TPG(i,j) \times BW_k(i,j)]^2\right\} \times \sum_{k=1}^{l}\left[\sum_{i=1}^{m}\sum_{j=1}^{n}BW_k(i,j)\right] \qquad (1)$$

Where *TPG* is tongueprint strength gotten by [6]. BW_k is the k th tongueprint binary image. m and n are respectively width and height of tongue image. l is tongueprint amount. C is a constant coefficient. By formula (1), compute tongueprint index of all simple tongueprints TPI_S and tongueprint index of all complex tongueprints TPI_C for a tongueprint image. If $\dfrac{TPI_S}{(TPI_S + TPI_C)} > RatioThresh$, then the image is regular tongueprint image, otherwise mixed tongueprint image. Here set $C = 0.0063$, $RatioThresh = 0.618$.

In terms of statistical results in section 2.3 once computer recognizes a tongue image is a mixed tongueprint image the tongue image is from an unhealthy person.

3.2 Computerized Recognition of a Healthy or Unhealthy Regular Tongueprint Image

Firstly, some features of regular tongueprint image are extracted as classified features of SVM classifier. They are *Rmean*, *Rstd* and *CRK*. *Rmean* and *Rstd* are respectively mean and standard deviation of component R in RGB color space on tongueprint regions. They describe quantitatively color and surface of tongueprints. *CRK* is crack index and gotten by [12].

We train a SVM classifier [13] *SVMC* by feature combination of *Rmean*, *Rstd* and *CRK* of some typical tongueprint images respectively from healthy and unhealthy population. Thus a regular tongueprint image made out by computerized methods remarked in above sections can sequentially be recognized to be from a healthy or an unhealthy person by *SVMC*.

4   Experimental Results and Analysis

In our large sample database, there are 1816 no-tongueprint images, 1172 regular tongueprint images and 309 mixed tongueprint images. These tongue images can be classified into three classes, namely no-tongueprint, regular tongueprint and mixed tongueprint. Classification results by our methods for all images in our database are shown in Table 3.

Table 3. Classification results by our methods for tongue images

Class	True ratio	False ratio
No-tongueprint	83.21%	16.79%
Regular tongueprint	82.79%	17.21%
Mixed tongueprint	81.51%	18.49%

In our large sample database, there are 1481 tongueprint images, thereinto 720 tongueprint images of healthy person, and 761 tongueprint images of unhealthy person. All tongueprint images can be classified into healthy person group and unhealthy person group. We choose 100 typical regular tongueprint images in healthy person group and 100 typical regular tongueprint images in unhealthy person group, then extract their feature combinations, *Rmean*, *Rstd* and *CRK*, to train a SVM classifiers.

Thus firstly recognize all tongue images in our database to be no-tongueprint or tongueprint images. If a tongue image is a tongueprint image, then recognize tongueprint(s) on it regular or mixed. If the tongueprint image is a mixed tongueprint image it is from an unhealthy person. If it is a regular tongueprint image recognized it to be from healthy or unhealthy populations by SVM classifier trained by *Rmean*, *Rstd* and *CRK* as mentioned above. Tongueprint image recognitions of healthy and unhealthy populations in our database by our methods are shown in Table 4.

Table 4. Tongueprint image recognitions of healthy and unhealthy populations in our database

Tongueprint image	True ratio	False ratio
In healthy	75.81%	24.19%
In unhealthy	74.61%	25.39%

5   Conclusions

According to observation by naked eyes, classification, and statistical analysis on tongueprints for large sample tongue images of healthy and unhealthy populations and reference for interrelated literature, and algorithmic design and implementation on recognitions of large sample healthy and unhealthy tongueprint images, we draw the following conclusions:

a) All tongue images can be classified into no-tongueprint or tongueprint images. There is more than one tongueprint on some tongueprint images. According to shape complexity, a tongueprint is recognized to be simple or complex by naked eyes. According to component proportion of tongueprint strength between all simple tongueprints and all complex tongueprints, tongueprint images are classified into regular and mixed tongueprint images by naked eyes. Tongueprint strength is related to depth and area of tongueprints, namely tongueprints are bigger on area and deeper tongueprint strength is greater.

b) Tongueprints can appear and are not few in healthy populations. Mixed tongueprints are diagnostic tongueprints in unhealthy populations.

c) According to observation of tongueprint position, tongueprint color, tongueprint depth, tongueprint surface and so on by naked eyes, regular tongueprint in healthy populations can be differentiated from those in unhealthy populations.

d) In this paper, it is the first time to recognize tongueprint images in healthy and unhealthy populations by computer and recognition results are encouraging. It is feasible to research tongueprints by computer.

Acknowledgement

This work is partially supported by the National Natural Science Foundation (NSFC) key overseas project under the contract no. 60620160097.

References

1. Li, N.M., et al.: Tongue Diagnostics. Academy Press (Xue Yuan), London (2006)
2. Wang, H., et al.: Tongueglyphics and Liver Disease. GanShu Science ansd Technology Press (1995)
3. Wang, H., et al.: Diagnose Disease by Tongueglyphics. Chinese Science and Technology Press On Medicine (2000)
4. Li, N.M., Wang, S.Y., Lin, X.D.: Principal Progress on Four Diagnostic Methods in Early 21 Century. The Seventh Selected Publication of Research on Four Diagnostic Methods, pp. 1–2 (2004)
5. Wang, S.Y., Li, N.M.: Research on Tongueglyphics. The Seventh Selected Publication of Research on Four Diagnostic Methods, 38–40 (2004)
6. Wu, X., Wang, K., Zhang, D.: Line Feature Extraction and Matching in Palmprint. In: The 2nd International Conference on Image and Graphics (ICIG 2002), Proceedings of SPIE, vol. 4875(1), pp. 583–590 (2002)
7. Jiang, Y.H.: Computerized Image Processing and Analyses, p. 151. Wu Han University Press (2002)
8. Wang, Y.M.: Moment Function of Image-Principle, Arithmetic and Application. Science and Engineering University in East of China Press, p. 8 (2002)
9. He, D.J., et al.: Digital Image Processing. Electronically Science and Technology University in Xi An Press, p. 210 (2004)

10. Jiang, Y.H.: Computerized Image Processing and Analyses, pp. 142–150. Wu Han University Press (2002)
11. Peng, Y.X.: Course of Digital Image Processing (2005), http://www.icst.pku.edu.cn/course/ ImageProcessing2005/12
12. Shen, L., Wei, B., Cai, Y., et al.: Image Analysis for Tongue Characterization. Chinese Journal of Electronic 12(3), 317–323 (2003)
13. Bian, Z.Q., Zhang, X.G., et al.: Pattern Recognition. 2nd edn., pp. 280–282. Press of Tsinghua University (2003)

RISC: A New Filter Approach for Feature Selection from Proteomic Data

Trung-Nghia Vu[1], Syng-Yup Ohn[1], and Chul-Woo Kim[2]

[1] Department of Computer Engineering,
Korea Aerospace University, Seoul, Korea
nghiavtr@gmail.com, syohn@kau.ac.kr
[2] Seoul National University School of Medicine
Seoul, Korea
cwkim@plaza.snu.ac.kr

Abstract. This paper proposes a novel feature selection technique for SELDI-TOF spectrum data. The new technique, called RISC (Relevance Index by Sample Counting) , measures the relevance of features based on each sample's discriminating power to partition the samples in the opposite class. We also proposes a heuristic searching method to obtain the optimal feature set, which makes use of the relevance parameters. Our technique is fast even for extremely high-dimensional datasets such as SELDI spectrum, since it has low computational complexity and consists of simple counting operations. The new technique also shows good performance comparable to the conventional feature selection techniques from the experiment on three clinical datasets from NCI/CCR and FDA/CBER Clinical Proteomics Program Databank: Ovarian 4-3-02, Ovarian 7-8-02, Prostate.

1 Introduction

The use of surface-enhanced laser desorption / ionization time-of-flight mass spectrometry technology (SELDI-TOF MS) has made promising achievements in disease diagnosis and biomarker identification. Petricoin *et al.* (2002) [1] reported finding patterns in SELDI-TOF proteomic spectra that can distinguish the serum samples from healthy women and those from women with ovarian cancer, even when the cancers are at early stages. These results are impressive and have received a good deal of attention. [2] SELDI-TOF MS technology produces a spectrum of the relative abundance of ionized peptides (y-axis) versus their mass-to charge (m/z) ratios (x-axis) from a sample. The m/z ratios are proportional to the peptide masses, but the technique is not able to identify individual peptides, because different peptides may have the same mass and the m/z resolution is limited [3]. Various statistical methods and machine learning techniques are used for feature selection problem of proteomic data like [3], [4], [5], [6], [7], [8].

A raw spectrum generally consists of hundreds of thousand m/z points and involves a high degree of noise. It is very challenging problem to develop a good feature selection technique which finds the optimal feature set for the classification of the

D. Zhang (Ed.): ICMB 2008, LNCS 4901, pp. 17–24, 2007.
© Springer-Verlag Berlin Heidelberg 2007

spectra from healthy and normal samples since the spectrum is a type of extremely high-dimensional datasets with relatively smaller number of samples.

Feature selection methods are divided into two categories depending on their approaches: Wrapper and embedded methods use an induction algorithm in learning process to find out the best feature subset maximizing the classification performance, and filter method is independent of machine learning algorithm. The wrapper approach uses a machine learning algorithm to measure the goodness of the set of selected features. It evaluates the goodness based on the performance measures of the learning algorithm such as accuracy, recall, and precision values. The disadvantage of the approach is high computational cost. Some researchers proposed methods that can speed up the evaluating process to decrease this cost. Embedded method incorporates feature subset generation and evaluation in training algorithm. Embedded methods are faster than wrapper approaches and have higher capacity than filter methods. The filter approach considers the feature selection process as a precursor stage of learning algorithms. One of the disadvantages of this approach is that there is no relationship between the feature selection process and the performance of learning algorithms.

In this paper, we propose a new feature selection method of filter approach for SELDI-TOF spectrum datasets. The new technique measures the relevance parameters of each feature based on the discriminating power of each sample to separate different classes and searches the optimal feature sets using the relevance parameters. The technique is very fast since it has low computational complexity and consists of the simple count operations. Our technique is applied to clinical proteome datasets from NCI/CCR and FDA/CBER Clinical Proteomics Program Databank, and shows good performance comparable to conventional feature selection techniques.

This paper consists as follows. In section 2, we survey the previous researches on filter methods. In section 3, a new ranking measure and a searching method making use of the properties of the ranking are presented. In section 4, the results from the experiments on three clinical datasets are shown, and section 5 is our conclusion.

2 Related Work

Filter method is term introduced by John, Kohavi and Pfleger (1994) because the method filters out irrelevant features before induction algorithm is used. Filter methods are independent of induction algorithm and usually have less expensive computation than wrapper and embedded methods.

The simplest one evaluates each feature individually based on its correlation with the class and then select k features with the highest value. The methods used to evaluate features usually are Pearson, T-test, and mutual information measure [7], [9].

RELIEF [10] algorithm follows this approach but incorporates a more complex feature evaluation function. It assigns a weight for each feature and estimates how well the value of a given feature helps to distinguish between instances that are near to each other. It samples instances randomly from the training set and updates the relevance value based on the difference between the selected instance and the two nearest instances of the same and the opposite class (the "near-hit" and "near-miss"). RELIEF does not deal with redundant features, many features having high correlation features with the label will not be removed by RELIEF.

In some approaches, features are ranked based on the distance between distributions. Kolmogorov-Smirnov [11] measures the difference between the joint and the product distributions. In other approaches, decision trees are used to select relevant features in top-down, hierarchical partition schemes. Cardie (1993) used a decision tree algorithm to select a subset of features for a nearest-neighbor algorithm.

In dealing with spectrum data, filter is often used as a preprocessing step to remove irrelevant features. In [12], [13], RELIEF was used in the first step to reduce the high dimension of feature space into a lower dimension. In [14], information gain, GINI, and F-test are used for feature ranking with 4-class classification problem for proteome datasets. They reported GINI and entropy seemed generally give better results than F-test.

3 RISC Method

RISC consists of two phases similarly to general filter methods. In the first phase, the relevance parameters of each feature are measured. In the second phase, the optimal feature set is sought using the relevance parameters obtained in the first phase. Each phase is presented in detail in the following.

3.1 Measuring Relevance

In the first phase, the relevance of each feature is measured based on the discriminating power of each sample for the feature. The discriminating power of a sample for a feature represents how well the sample separate the rest of samples into original classes based on the feature value the sample has. In the following, we present the details on how to measure the relevance of features.

Suppose we are given a dataset $D = (X, Y)$ with m samples each with d features and a class label, where X is the set of feature vectors consisting of m numeric vectors in d dimensions and Y is the set of m class labels each having a value from $\{-1, +1\}$ representing the class a sample belongs to. Furthermore, we suppose $x_i = (x_{i1}, x_{i2}, \ldots, x_{ij}, \ldots, x_{id})$ as a feature vector of a samples belonging to one class where x_{ij} represents jth feature value of x_i. Let $X^* = \{x^*_1, x^*_2, \ldots, x^*_k, \ldots, x^*_{m*}\}$ be the set of feature vectors of the samples belonging to the opposite class to the one x_i belongs to, where each $x^*_k = (x^*_{k1}, x^*_{k2}, \ldots, x^*_{kj}, \ldots, x^*_{kd})$ represents a feature vector of the samples in the class and m^* is the number of all samples in the class.

Relevance index of jth feature by ith sample, denoted as R_{ij}, which represents the capability of jth feature to discriminate ith sample from the opposite class, is defined as in (1).

$$R_{i,j} = \frac{\mid n(x^*_{kj} > x_{ij}) - n(x^*_{kj} < x_{ij}) \mid}{m^*} \tag{1}$$

where, $n(.)$ is the number of samples satisfying the (.) condition.

$R_{i,j}$ can have any value in the range of $[0,1]$. If it has the maximum value 1, the ith sample can be completely separated from the other class based on jth feature. If it has minimum value 0, it means that the sample does not give any relevant information on jth feature.

The relevance of a feature is defined by the sum of relevance of the feature on all samples in the data set. The relevance of jth feature, denoted as R_j, is defined as in (2)

$$R_j = \frac{\sum_{i=1}^{m} R_{i,j}}{m} \tag{2}$$

The relevance of R_j is considered as the degree of the importance of jth feature for classification. If we have an ideal classifier using jth feature only, its accuracy of classification on the dataset used for the calculation of the relevance should be equal to R_i.

The relevance of a feature calculated based on the comparison of values of the feature, and correlated features with a linear relationship usually give the same results.

One of important problems for a filter method is how to find out the best feature subset from the set of ranked features. The purpose in the next section is to find out the best feature subset with a small enough number of features and the smallest error rate.

3.2 Searching Strategy

The goal of wrapper or embedded methods is to find out the optimal feature subset maximizing accuracy for a certain classifier. Filter approach gives the optimal set of features which are generally gives good performance for most of the classifiers. In our case, we assume that a hidden classifier exists. For search strategy, we set a heuristic criterion in order to maximize the accuracy of the hidden classifier.

From the table of the relevance of feature on sample $R_{i,j}$, we can get the maximum relevance of a sample(MRS), denoted as MRS_i over all features:

$$MRS_i = \max_j (R_{i,j}) \tag{3}$$

The key idea of the searching strategy follows a conjecture that the best subset should include features containing MRS of all samples in the training set. We expect that if the hidden classifier is good enough, it is possible for the classifier using the feature subset to result in the best performance. In the ideal situation, the classifier can clearly separate all samples in the training set. Thus, all we have to do is to find out a subset in which features in that subset contain MRS of all samples in the training set. The heuristic strategy for selecting features is presented in the following:

```
RISC searching algorithm:
Input: R_{i,j}, R_j, MRS_i
Output: Optimal subset S
1. Sort features in decreased order of R_j.
2. S = {} # set of the best features
3. Set_MRS = {} # set of MRS_i found by the features in S
4. j = 1;
5. while (size of SET_MRS < m) do
6.     if  jth feature contains MRS_i  that does not belong
    to  SET_MRS then
```

```
7.                      S = S ∪ j
8.                      Update SET_MRS
9.         j = j + 1;
10. endwhile
```

The update procedure in step 8 finds out the new MRS_i retrieved from jth feature and then add them to the SET_MRS. The searching algorithm stops when SET_MRS contains MRSs of all the samples.

The number of the best feature subset is always less than or equal to the number of samples. The best subset doesn't include highly correlated features because the searching algorithm does not select the redundant features in the searching process.

3.3 Analysis of Computational Complexity

In feature ranking, only the formulas (1) and (2) need to be computed. It is not difficult to see that $O(m)$ is the complexity of the both formulas. However, in practice, we need to calculate dm times in cases of (1) and d times for (2). Therefore, computational costs of (1) and (2) are $O(dm^2)$ and $O(dm)$ respectively. We can complete the computation of $R_{i,j}$ for jth feature for all the samples in $O(dm\log m)$. The strategy for the computation is as follow: column j is sorted in decreased order before computing $R_{i,j}$, and then the procedure travels from top to bottom (or bottom to top) of the list to count the greater (or less) values of each sample for the formula (1). The complexity for this procedure is $O(m\log m)$ for sorting the column by using quicksort [15] and $O(m)$ for the counting. Finally, the complexity of computation for ranking features is $O(dm\log m)$. In the searching strategy, the computation of MRS_i of samples in formula (3) costs $O(md)$. After that, we need $O(d\log d)$ and $O(md)$ for sorting the R_j list and searching the best subset, respectively. In experiments, the time cost for searching them is reduced because the good features are usually on the top of the list. In summary, the computational complexity of RISC method for both ranking features and searching the best feature subset is $O(d \max(m\log m, \log d))$.

4 Experiments

We applied RISC method to 3 clinical proteome datasets Ovarian 4-3-02, Ovarian 7-8-02, Prostate of the NCI/CCR and FDA/CBER Clinical Proteomics Program Databank (http://home.ccr.cancer.gov/ncifdaproteomics/ppatterns.asp).

i) Ovarian 4-3-02
This ovarian dataset is produced by using WCX2 protein array. It consists of 216 samples, with 100 healthy, 16 benign and 100 cancer patterns. Samples were processed by hand and the baseline was subtracted, so creating negative intensities for some value. Each pattern consists of 15154 features (m/z values).

ii) Ovarian 8-7-02
The spectrum was collected from WCX2 chip. The dataset consists of 253 samples including 91 control and 162 ovarian cancer patterns. The preparing process is done by using robotic instrument. Each pattern consists of 15156 features (m/z values).

iii) Prostate

This dataset was collected using H4 protein chip consists of four classes representing a healthy control group, patients with benign conditions and elevated PSA value and two stages of prostate cancer. In experiment, we combined patterns of the two first groups in to healthy class (253 samples) and the rest of patterns (69 samples) formed the cancer class. Each sample consists of 15154 features (m/z values).

Table 1. Results for data sets using linear SVM

Dataset / Classifier	Ovarian 4-3-02		Ovarian 8-7-02		Prostate	
	Sensitivity	Specificity	Sensitivity	Specificity	Sensitivity	Specificity
RISC	0.943(0.074)	0.983(0.037)	1.000(0.000)	1.000(0.000)	0.762(0.137)	0.937(0.057)
T-test	0.943(0.074)	0.963(0.068)	0.984(0.036)	0.971(0.062)	0.827(0.117)	0.917(0.048)
Relief	0.945(0.084)	0.941(0.053)	1.000(0.000)	0.981(0.043)	0.810(0.118)	0.940(0.056)

Table 2. Results for data sets using radial SVM

Dataset / Classifier	Ovarian 4-3-02		Ovarian 8-7-02		Prostate	
	Sensitivity	Specificity	Sensitivity	Specificity	Sensitivity	Specificity
RISC	0.954(0.066)	0.934(0.091)	0.993(0.021)	1.000(0.000)	0.935(0.056)	0.901(0.121)
T-test	0.933(0.095)	0.982(0.038)	0.980(0.042)	0.971(0.062)	0.906(0.126)	0.892(0.055)
Relief	0.919(0.101)	0.976(0.052)	0.994(0.018)	0.993(0.021)	0.871(0.123)	0.965(0.040)

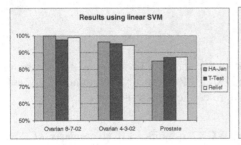 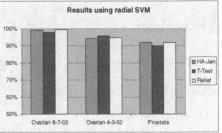

Fig. 1. Overall performances through balanced accuracy scores

We ran RISC on the datasets and got the number of features of the best feature subset in each time. After that we ran T-test, Relief and then cut off features from the top of ranking lists that the number of features is equal to the number of features in the best subsets. The complexities of computation of T-test and Relief are $O(dm)$ and $O(dm^2)$ respectively in which d is the number of features and m is the number of samples. Table 1 and 2 summarize the average results of 10-folds cross validation experiments with two classifiers: Support vector machine [16] with linear kernel and radial kernel, respectively. Using linear SVM, RISC works well on two ovarian datasets and archives the highest accuracies, but poorly implements on the prostate dataset. For case of radial SVM, RISC and Relief have the same balanced accuracy and better than T-test. Figure 1 presents a graph of balanced accuracies of the methods.

5 Conclusions and Future Work

We have proposed a novel filter method applied for proteomic data. RISC method includes a measure to calculate the rank of features and a heuristic searching algorithm making use of the characteristics of the ranking measure to find out the best feature subset. The feature selection method is fast and independent on learning algorithm. In experiments, we archived high performances and be comparable with other widely used filter methods like T-test and Relief.

Acknowledgements

The research on this paper was supported by Regional Innovation Center in Korea Aerospace University designated by Ministry of Commerce, Industry and Resources and Gyungi Province of the Republic of Korea.

References

1. Petricoin, E.F., Ardekani, A.M., Hitt, B.A., Levine, P.J., Fusaro, V.A., Steinberg, S.M., et al.: Use of proteomic patterns in serum to identify ovarian cancer. Lancet 359(9306), 572–577 (2002)
2. Baggerly, K.A., Morris, J.S., Coombes, K.R.: Reproducibility of SELDI-TOF protein patterns in serum: comparing datasets from different experiments. Bioinformatics 20(5), 777–785 (2004)
3. Jong, K., Marchiori, E., Sebag, M., van der Vaart, A.: Feature Selection in Proteomic Pattern Data with Support Vector Machines. In: CIBCB, pp. 41–48. IEEE, Los Alamitos (2004)
4. Levner, I.: Feature selection and nearest centroid classification for protein mass spectrometry. BMC Bioinformatics (2005)
5. Lilien, R.H., Farid, H., Donald, B.R.: Probabilistic disease classification of expression-dependent proteomic data from mass spectrometry of human serum. Computational Biology (2003)
6. Tibshirani, R., Hastiey, T., Narasimhanz, T., Soltys, S., Shi, G., Koong, A., Le, Q.: Sample classifcation from protein mass spectrometry by peak probability contrasts. BioInformatics (2004)
7. Wu, B., Abbott, T., Fishman, D., McMurray, W., Mor, G., Stone, K., Ward, D., Williams, K., Zhao, H.: Comparison of statistical methods for classifcation of ovarian cancer using mass spectrometry data. BioInformatics 19(13) (2003)

8. Qu, Y., Adam, B., Yasui, Y., Ward, M.D., Cazares, L.H., Schellhammer, P.F., Feng, Z., Semmes, O.J., Wright, G.L.: Boosted decision tree analysis of surface-enhanced laser desortion/ionization mass spectral serum profiles discriminates prostate cancer from noncancer patients. Clinical Chemistry 48(10), 1835–1843 (2002)
9. Guyon, I., Elissee, A.: An introduction to variable and feature selection. Machine Learning, Special Issue on variable and feature selection 3, 1157–1182 (2003)
10. Kononenko, I.: Estimating attributes: Analysis and extensions of relief. In: ECML, pp. 171–182 (1994)
11. Biesiada, J., Duch, W.: Feature Selection for High-Dimensional Data: A Kolmogorov-Smirnov Correlation-Based Filter Solution. Computer Recognition Systems. In: Kurzynski, M., Puchała, E., Wozniak, M., Zolnierek, A. (eds.) CORES 2005. Proc. of the 4th International Conference on Computer Recognition Systems. Advances in Soft Computing, pp. 95–104. Springer, Heidelberg (2005)
12. Plant, C., Osl, M., Tilg, B., Baumgartner, C.: Feature Selection on High Throughput SELDI-TOF Mass-Spectrometry Data for Identifying Biomarker Candidates in Ovarian and Prostate Cancer. In: Proceedings of the Sixth IEEE International Conference on Data Mining – Workshops, pp. 174–179 (2006)
13. Marchiori, E., Jimenez, C.R., West-Nielsen, M., Heegaard, N.H.H.: Robust SVM-Based Biomarker Selection with Noisy Mass Spectrometric Proteomic Data. In: EvoWorkshops, pp. 79–90 (2006)
14. Peterson, L.E., Hoogeveen, R.C., Pownall, H.J., Morrisett, J.D.: Classification Analysis of Surface-enhanced Laser Desorption/Ionization Mass Spectral Serum Profiles for Prostate Cancer. In: IJCNN 2006. International Joint Conference on Neural Networks, pp. 3828–3835 (2006)
15. Cormen, T.H., Leiserson, C.E., Rivest, R.L., Stein, C.: Introduction to Algorithms, Second Edition, Ch. 7, MIT Press and McGraw-Hill, Quicksort, pp. 145–164 (2001)
16. Cristianini, N., Shawe-Taylor, J.: Support Vector machines. Cambridge Press, Cambridge (2000)

An Effective Feature Set for ECG Pattern Classification

Rajesh Ghongade[1] and Ashok Ghatol[2]

[1] Vishwakarma Institute of Information Technology, Pune, India
rbghongade@gmail.com
[2] Dr. Babasaheb Ambedkar Technological University, Lonere, India
ashok.ghatol@gmail.com

Abstract. In this paper, QRS morphological features and the artificial neural network method was used for Electrocardiogram (ECG) pattern classification. Four types of ECG patterns were chosen from the MIT-BIH database to be recognized, including normal sinus rhythm, premature ventricular contraction, atrial premature beat and left bundle branch block beat. Authors propose a set of six ECG morphological features to reduce the feature vector size considerably and make the training process fast in addition to a simple but effective ECG heartbeat extraction scheme. Three types of artificial neural network models, MLP, RBF neural networks and SOFM were separately trained and tested for ECG pattern recognition and the experimental results of the different models have been compared. The MLP network exhibited the best performance and reached an overall test accuracy of 99.65%, and RBF and SOFM network both reached 99.1%. The performance of these classifiers was also evaluated in presence of additive Gaussian noise. MLP network was found to be more robust in this respect.

1 Introduction

Heart is one of the most important organs of the human body hence it is termed as a vital organ. There are numerous types of heart disorders, out of which only three critical problems like, premature ventricular contraction, atrial premature contraction and left branch bundle block are considered here. The ECG is one of the most effective diagnostic tools available to the medics[1]. Of the many thousand heartbeats available, it becomes tedious to locate the distorted heartbeat and then classify it.

The basic problem of automatic ECG analysis occurs from the non-linearity in ECG signals and the large variation in ECG morphologies of different patients. And in most cases, ECG signals are contaminated by background noises, such as electrode motion artifact and electro-myogram induced noise, which also adds to the difficulty of automatic ECG pattern recognition.

Various methods for pattern recognition exist; out of which artificial neural network models have been successfully applied to the problem of ECG classification [1, 2, 4, 5, 6, 7, 8, and 9]. Artificial neural network is attractive because of its non-linearity and robustness, which imparts good efficiency while dealing with non-linear problems in addition to good noise tolerance Compared with the traditional clustering

D. Zhang (Ed.): ICMB 2008, LNCS 4901, pp. 25–32, 2007.
© Springer-Verlag Berlin Heidelberg 2007

methods, the artificial neural network models have good adaptive ability to environmental changes and new patterns, and the recognition speed of neural network is fast, owing to its parallel processing capability. Therefore, we used artificial neural network models for ECG pattern recognition in our study.

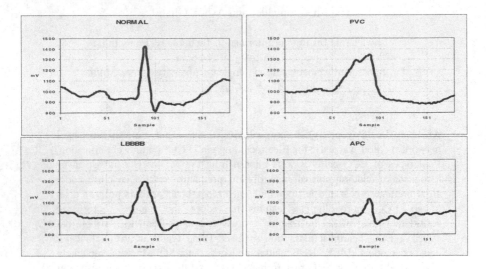

Fig. 1. The four types of heartbeats, Normal (N), Premature Ventricular Contraction (PVC), Atrial Premature Contraction (APC) and Left Branch Bundle Block Beat (LBBBB)

Figure 1 depicts the four types of heartbeats studied and analyzed in the present study. The heartbeats show a distinct morphological variation, which suggests the usage of artificial neural networks.

2 Methodology

Figure 2 depicts the overall methodology for the evaluation and search for the best network. The complete scheme includes various steps like the extraction of equal length ECG signals beat-wise; mean adjust, to remove the base line wander and dc shift, feature extraction and finally training of the ANN [2].

2.1 Data Source and Heartbeat Extraction

Since we are interested in only certain type of arrhythmias four records from MIT/BIH were used. Since each record is a continuous waveform it is necessary to extract only a single heartbeat. This is done by considering the R peak and extracting 90 samples on either side of this R peak. Since the MIT/BIH database comes with annotations for each heartbeat it is necessary to associate the categories with individual extracted beats. A total of 2400 beats were extracted with 600 beats belonging to each category viz. Normal, PVC, APC and LBBBB. Six different datasets were formed from the complete data. Thus each dataset consisted of 400

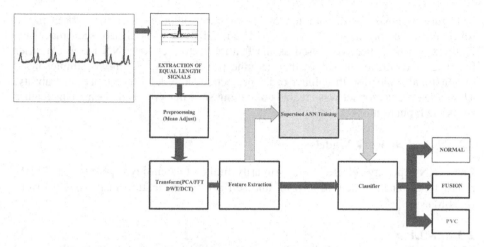

Fig. 2. Block diagram for the proposed scheme

samples with 100 samples per category. Three datasets were combined to form a group. Thus two groups A and B were used for training and testing. After the heartbeats were extracted in form of records each 180 sample long, a mean adjust was carried out to remove the base line shift.

2.2 Feature Extraction

Feature extraction is an important step so as to reduce the dimensionality of the input space. This ultimately reduces the required resources (number of neurons) and speeds up the learning. Feature extraction techniques are also numerous [1, 2, 7] but the real challenge is to have optimum performance with minimum resources. The authors propose six different features for characterizing the four classes of heartbeats; Mean R-peak value, mean power spectral density, Area under QRS complex, Energy of the signal, Q-S distance and autocorrelation value.

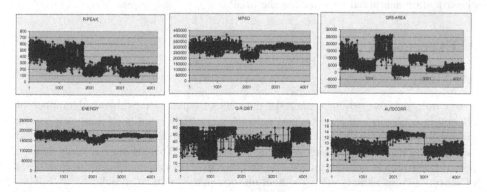

Fig. 3. Extracted features with class-wise distribution

Figure 3 shows the distribution of the extracted features over the dataset in the following order of classes; N, PVC, APC and LBBBB. It is clearly seen that these features can be collectively used as the feature vector set for ANN based classifier because of the different values they assume per class. This is only a simple one – dimensional projection the higher order projections may lead to a more separability. Thus a feature vector set was created containing six values per heart beat. This feature set is the input to the ANN.

2.3 Neural Network Models

The ANN topology selection was primarily limited to multilayer perceptron (MLP), radial basis function neural network and self-organizing feature map based network (SOFM).

2.3.1 MLP
Multilayer perceptrons (MLPs) are layered feedforward networks typically trained with static backpropagation. Their main advantage is that they are easy to use, and that they can approximate any input/output map [3].

2.3.2 RBF Neural Networks
Radial basis function (RBF) networks are nonlinear hybrid networks typically containing a single hidden layer of processing elements. This layer uses gaussian transfer functions, rather than the standard sigmoidal functions employed by MLPs. The centers and widths of the gaussians (clusters) are set by unsupervised learning rules, and supervised learning is applied to the output layer. These networks tend to learn much faster than MLPs.

2.3.3 SOFM
Self-organizing feature maps (SOFMs) transform the input of arbitrary dimension into a one or two dimensional discrete map subject to a topological (neighborhood preserving) constraint. [7] The feature maps are computed using Kohonen unsupervised learning. The output of the SOFM can be used as input to a supervised classification neural network such as the MLP.

3 Experiments

3.1 MLP

The whole data was divided into six datasets of equal size with equal number of classes in each set, and every neural network model is trained with three sets as one group A and tested with the remaining sets forming group B. This order is reversed and training and testing phases were carried out again. This strategy ensures that the network learning is not dataset specific and thus gives good generalization. Five types of learning rules namely step, momentum, conjugate gradient, quickprop and delta-bar-delta were evaluated. The training and cross-validation set consisted of 400 exemplars each while a separate test set consisted another 400 exemplars. Figure 4 depicts the performance of various learning rules. It is clearly noticed that the momentum and delta-bar-delta rules outperform the other types (Figures 4 (a) & (b)).

Additional test was carried out to evaluate the speed performance of each type of network. Time/epoch/exemplar was calculated and it was found out that momentum and quickprop required a minimum of 32.84 microseconds.

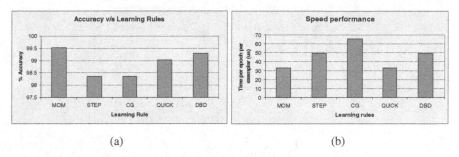

(a)   (b)

Fig. 4. (a) Performance of various learning rules in terms of accuracy (b) Speed performance of various learning rules

Based on these two tests the choice of MLP learning rule was momentum. This network was again subjected to extensive test for optimum parameters like the number of hidden layer neurons, learning rate and number of iterations. The training and testing was carried out for five times each per parameter so as to confirm the performance. Figure 5(a) & (b) clearly shows that the numbers of neurons affect the performance of the network. A network with 8 neurons in hidden layer was found to offer the best performance.

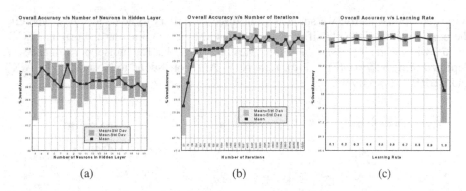

(a)   (b)   (c)

Fig. 5. (a) Average accuracy as a function of neurons in hidden layer (b) Optimum iterations for maximum accuracy

Figure 5(b) depicts the performance of the network as training iterations were varied form 75 to 45000. Clearly the accuracy is best at 2500 and 6000 iterations but in order to prevent memorization we choose 2500 iterations as the optimum value. Optimum learning rate was found to be best at 0.6 and 0.8 as shown by Figure 5 (c).

3.2 RBF Networks

Radial basis neural networks were evaluated for deriving the optimum network performance. A variation in the cluster sizes was carried out and the accuracy was found to be best for 40 clusters. Figure 6(a) depicts the same.

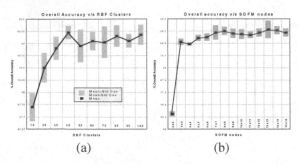

(a)   (b)

Fig. 6. (a) Average accuracy peaks at 40 clusters for RBF (b) Overall accuracy is best for 13x 13 SOFM architecture

3.3 SOFM Networks

SOFM network was tested with the same dataset and an optimum architecture was found. It was found that the best accuracy was obtained for 13x13 SOFM and momentum learning with learning rate 0.7. Increasing the SOFM size does not offer substantial enhancement in accuracy but on the other hand increases the training time.

3.4 Noise Analysis

As an additional metric we subjected the three classifiers to noise analysis, wherein the performance of the classifiers were evaluated by contaminating the original ECG signal with white Gaussian noise of varying strength. The noise performance is depicted in figure 7(a), (b) and (c). Here N, V, A, L correspond to Normal, PVC, APC and LBBBB respectively.

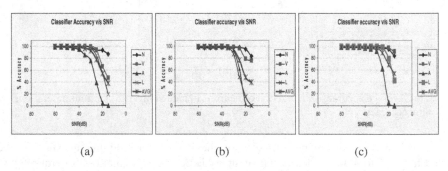

(a)   (b)   (c)

Fig. 7. Network performance in presence of additive white gaussian noise (a) MLP (b) RBF (c) SOFM

It can be concluded that performance of all three classifiers in presence of noise is fairly robust. This is an indication of the effectiveness of the selected features.

4 Results

Table 1 summarizes the complete comparative results for the experiment carried out. During all the experimentation the training (Trg), cross validation and the test (Tst) sets were same. The results correspond to the test set only.

Table 1. MLP, RBF and SOFM classifier performance

Classifier/		Accuracy (%)									
Group		Normal		PVC		APC		LBBBB		Average	
		Trg	Tst	Trg	Tst	Trg	Tst	Trg	Tst	Trg	Tst
MLP	A	99.65	99.8	99.65	99.9	99.85	100	99.5	100	99.78	99.8
	B	99.9	98.4	99.75	100	100	99.6	99.95	100	99.9	99.5
RBF	A	99.4	98.3	99.7	99.7	99.55	97.8	99.8	100	99.61	98.95
	B	99.45	98.4	99.7	99.9	98.6	99.7	100	99	99.43	99.25
SOFM	A	99.25	99	98.75	97	99.5	100	100	99.5	99.38	98.88
	B	99.75	98	99.75	100	99.75	99	100	100	99.81	99.25

5 Discussion

A definite improvement in the accuracy can be achieved by selecting the optimum network topology, learning rule, number of iterations for training and learning rate. Another important finding is that the feature extraction techniques play a crucial role in the performance of these classifiers. The features proposed in this paper namely mean R-peak value, mean power spectral density, area under QRS complex, energy of the signal, Q-S distance and autocorrelation value, are found to exhibit excellent performance for classification.

Since there are only six features per heartbeat the training phase is very fast and this scheme consumes very low computing resources. The noise analysis proves that classifiers making use of these features are fairly robust and noise tolerant. The three types of neural networks studied here exhibit excellent performance in conjunction with the six features. MLP gives the best performance as far as overall accuracy is considered, SOFM also exhibits good performance RBF neural network also performs very well, its main strength being, faster training, as compared to MLP. We can thus conclude that the six features proposed in this paper are truly sufficient for the four class classification irrespective of the ANN topology used.

References

1. Vargas, F., Lettin, D., de Castro, M.C.F., Macarthy, M.: Electrocardiogram Pattern Recognition by Means of MLP Network and PCA: A Case Study on Equal Amount of Input Signal Types. IEEE, Los Alamitos (2002)
2. Prasad, G., Krishna, Shambi, J.S.: Classification of ECG Arrhythmias using Multi-Resolution Analysis and Neural Networks. IEEE, Los Alamitos (2003)
3. Lau, C.G.Y.: Neural Networks: Theoretical Foundations and Analysis. IEEE 1, 18 (1992)
4. Maglaveras, N., Stampkopoulos, T., Diamantaras, K., Pappas, C., Strintzis, M.: ECG pattern recognition ans classification using non-linear transformations and neural networks: A review. International Journal of Medical Informatics 52, 191–208 (1998)
5. Ghongade, R., Ghatol, Dr. A.A.: Electrocardiogram Pattern Classification: An Approach Employing DWT and Artificial Neural Networks. In: Proceedings of INCON (2004)
6. Gholam Hosseini, H., Luo, D., Reynolds, K.J.: Reynolds, the comparison of different feed forward neural network architectures for ECG signal diagnosis. Medical Engineering & Physics 28, 372–378 (2005)
7. Bishop, C.: Neural Networks for Pattern Recognition. Oxford University Press, Oxford (1995)

Research on Gesture Definition
and Electrode Placement
in Pattern Recognition of Hand Gesture Action SEMG

Xu Zhang[1], Xiang Chen[1], Zhang-yan Zhao[1], You-qiang Tu[1], Ji-hai Yang[1],
Vuokko Lantz[2], and Kong-qiao Wang[3]

[1] Department of Electronics Science & Technology
University of Science & Technology of China, Hefei, China, 230027
zhx90@mail.ustc.edu.cn
[2] Nokia Research Center, Interaction CTC, Interacting in Smart Environments
P.O. Box 407, FI-00045 Nokia Group, Finland
vuokko.lantz@nokia.com
[3] Nokia Research Center, NOKIA (China) Investment CO., LTD., Beijing, 100013

Abstract. The goal of this study is to explore the effects of electrode placement on the hand gesture pattern recognition performance. We have conducted experiments with surface EMG sensors using two detecting electrode channels. In total 25 different hand gestures and 10 different electrode positions for measuring muscle activities have been evaluated. Based on the experimental results, dependencies between surface EMG signal detection positions and hand gesture recognition performance have been analyzed and summarized as suggestions how to define hand gestures and select suitable electrode positions for a myoelectric control system. This work provides useful insight for the development of a medical rehabilitation system based on EMG technique.

1 Introduction

In myoelectric control systems, surface electromyographic (sEMG) sensors are used for measuring the activities of the muscular system in a non-intrusive fashion. Detected muscle activities are identified as motion commands which can be used for controlling an externally powered device [1], especially including the artificial prosthesis for rehabilitation [2], [3]. So far, the control motions considered in EMG recognition research have been simple hand gestures with a large scale. Typically, the number of classifiable gestures has been limited between four and eight [3], [4].

In order to realize a highly accurate multi-gesture pattern recognition system, it is important to explore both the sEMG signal processing algorithms and the underlying myoelectric controlling mechanism [5]. Though much excellent work [3], [5] has been done on multi-gesture sEMG pattern recognition, the research effort has been focused mainly on the classification algorithm development. The relationship between the signal detection positions, muscles involved with the execution of the hand gestures, and the classification performance has been ignored. So far, there have not been systematic investigations on how to define usability-wise a good set of hand gestures

D. Zhang (Ed.): ICMB 2008, LNCS 4901, pp. 33–40, 2007.
© Springer-Verlag Berlin Heidelberg 2007

and select the appropriate EMG signal detecting positions for achieving a myoelectric control application with high recognition performance.

The main objective of this paper is to conduct a systematic study on the definition of gestures and the selection of signal measuring positions for a sEMG-based control system. On the basis of sEMG pattern recognition experiments with various kinds of hand gestures and various electrode positions, we have analyzed the dependencies between the electrode detecting positions and hand gesture recognition performance. These results are summarized in section 3. Suggestions about how to define proper hand gesture set and select sEMG signal measuring electrode positions for myoelectric control system are presented in the last section 4.

2 Surface EMG-Based Hand Gesture Recognition System

2.1 Hand Gesture Definition

In the design of hand gesture recognition system, the main principle is that the gestures should be different enough from each other in respect to the related muscle activities so that they can be classified accurately [6]. Furthermore, in addition to the ergonomic and technical requirements, there are also social limitations for the hand gesture definition. In order to be usable and easy to learn, gestures should be intuitive. And many frequently used hand gestures should also be studied to test their feasibility for sEMG-based classification.

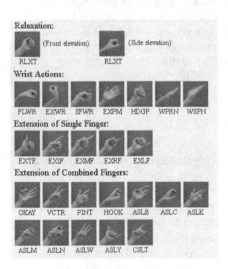

Fig. 1. Hand gestures defined in our work

Table 1. Hand gestures description and labeling

Sorts	Gesture Name	Brief Description
Relaxation	RLXT	Relaxation
	FLWR	Flexion of Wrist
	EXWR	Extension of Wrist
Wrist Actions	SFWR	Side Flexion of Wrist
	EXPM	Extension of Palm / Hand Extension
	HDGP	Fist /Hand Grasp
	WPRN	Wrist Pronation
	WSPN	Wrist Supination
	EXTF	Extension of Thumb (I)
Extension of Single Fingers	EXIF	Extension of Index Finger (II)
	EXMF	Extension of Middle Finger (III)
	EXRF	Extension of Ring Finger (IV)
	EXLF	Extension of Little Finger (V)
	OKAY	"OK" Gesture
	VCTR	"V" Gesture
	PINT	"POINT" Gesture
	HOOK	"HOOK" Gesture
Extension of Combined Fingers	ASLB	Letter 'B' in ASL and CSL
	ASLC	Letter 'C' in ASL and CSL
	ASLK	Letter 'K' in ASL and CSL
	ASLM	Letter 'M' in ASL and CSL
	ASLN	Letter 'N' in ASL and CSL
	ASLW	Letter 'W' in ASL and CSL
	ASLY	Letter 'Y' in ASL and CSL
	CSLT	Letter 'T' in CSL

We have defined and selected 25 different hand gestures (including relaxation), see Figure 1 and Table 1 for the illustrations and descriptions. These gestures include hand gestures used in former studies, some commonly used gestures in international or local cultures, and some proper sign language gestures. These gestures includes the relaxation of the hand, 7 kinds of wrist actions, 5 different extensions of a single finger, and 12 combined extensions of two or more fingers. All gestures are named by four-letter logograms of their English description, see Table 1.

2.2 Electrode Placement and EMG Acquisition

In total 10 electrode positions which cover all the main muscles of the forearm have been considered in this study as Figure 2 shows (marked with pairs of short lines). The electrode positions 1, 2, 3, 4, and 5 are on the posterior aspect of forearm and they are useful in the detection EMG activities of the extensors. These sensor positions are referred as "number electrode positions" from here on. The electrode positions A, B, C, D, and E are "letter electrode position" series which are defined on the anterior aspect of forearm and approximately parallel with number electrode position series.

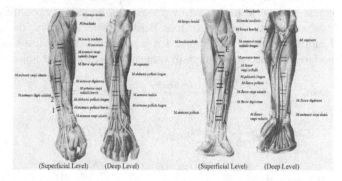

Fig. 2. The main muscles on the posterior (left) and anterior (right) aspect of human arm and the electrode position (anatomical pictures are adapted from [9])

We have explored various two electrode placement schemes in our experimental research work. Six electrode position pairs from the number electrode position series 23, 24, 25, 34, 35, and 45, are called "number + number" electrode position pairs as most of the gestures defined in the previous section are related to the extension of fingers. On the other hand, it is crucial to classify gestures that are composites of both the extensor and flexor muscles. At the same time, considering the convenience of sensor application, electrode position pairs 2B, 3C, 4D, and 5E, are chosen for further study. These pairs are called "number + letter" electrode position pairs. In these setups, such placement is practical for using a wrist or arm band to keep the electrodes in place. So, in total we have defined 10 electrode position pairs for our experiments with sEMG data acquisition and hand gesture recognition.

Two-channel Delsys Bangoli 2 sEMG system including electrodes with inbuilt band-pass filtering of 20 to 1000 Hz bandwidth and amplifiers with 60dB gain was used for data acquisition. The sEMG signals were digitized by an ADC card (NI DAQ PCI-6010). The bar-shaped electrodes were placed orthogonally to the arm and to the muscles to ensure the best detecting effect [7]. The sampling rate was 2048Hz.

While performing the sEMG acquisition experiments subjects sat comfortably on a chair and kept their arm and hand in relaxation between the gesture repetitions. They performed 25 different of hand gesture actions in a way they felt natural to them.

Each hand gesture action was repeated 20 times. One gesture action lasted about 1 second, and the interval between the gesture actions was about 1-2 seconds.

2.3 EMG Analysis Algorithm

The sEMG signals, recorded in the process of the hand gesture actions, are called active segments. Every sEMG active segment may represent a hand gesture action. The recognition procedure of hand gestures consists of signal segmentation, feature extraction from every active segment and classification.

At the segmentation step, the detection of active segments was based on the average signal of the two sEMG channels: first, compute the square of the average value of the two sEMG signal channels according to (1); then, apply the moving average algorithm with window size N=60 samples on the squared average sEMG signal according to (2); next, threshold the signal by preserving the values exceeding a certain threshold TH and setting the others to 0, as defined in (3). Finally, deter-mine the beginning and ending points of the gesture active segments. At the last step, abandon segments whose length is less than a certain value as a measurement noise.

$$SEMG_{averaged}(i) = \left[\frac{SEMG_{raw1}(i) + SEMG_{raw2}(i)}{2} \right]^2 \quad i \leq M \tag{1}$$

$$SEMG_{M\_A}(i) = \frac{1}{N}\sum_{j=i}^{i+N} SEMG_{averaged}(j) \quad i \leq M - N \tag{2}$$

$$SEMG_{rectified}(i) = \begin{cases} SEMG_{M\_A}(i); & if \quad SEMG_{M\_A}(i) \geq TH \\ 0 & ; \quad if \quad SEMG_{M\_A} \leq TH \end{cases} \tag{3}$$

Fig. 3 illustrates the extraction of the gesture active segments. The top two sub-figures correspond to the two channels of raw sEMG signals and the bottom one shows the rectified signal after the averaging and threshold steps. Every active segment is separated and the active segment intervals which represent the relaxation states are masked in Fig. 3. The names of every motions are also listed below the active segments. As we can see from Fig. 3, the described segmentation method can detect gesture action signals effectively from continuous sEMG measurements.

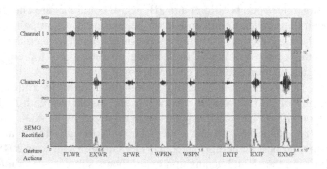

Fig. 3. Illustration of eight hand gesture actions sEMG signal segmentation

At the pattern recognition step, feature vectors were extracted from the segmented signal. Three main features were evaluated: the mean absolute value (MAV) of each channel, the MAV ratio of the two channels, and the autoregressive (AR) coefficients in 3-order of active segments [4]. Linear Discriminant Classifier (LDC) [8] was chosen as classifier algorithm. The first five repetitions of each gesture class were used for training the classifier and the rest of gesture samples were used for testing.

3 Experimental Results

Six healthy subjects (4 males and 2 females) with ages ranging from 20 to 24 years participated the hand gesture data collection in order to gain some insight into the individual differences in the sEMG measurements. The sEMG measurements were made from the left (2 subjects) or right (4 subjects) arm.

Classification experiments were carried out separately for each subject and for the different electrode position pairs. All the 24 gestures are classified together. Some of the gestures could not be distinguished from each other with a sufficient accuracy. We refined a well-classifiable gesture set by pruning out the most confusing gestures for each electrode setup on the basis of average recognition results of all the subjects.

3.1 Recognition Results and Gesture Set Recommendations

The gesture sets with the best recognition performance are listed in Table 2 for the 10 different electrode setups. The figures under the gesture names are the average classification rates for six subjects given as percentages of successfully recognized gesture samples. Several gesture classes can be distinguished from each other reliably with each of the experimented electrode position pair in Table 2.

In case of most of the electrode position pairs, about 7 hand motions could be well classified with the classification rate above 85% in average. Different electrode position

Table 2. The classification results under every electrode position pair

23	EXTF	EXRF	EXLF	VCTR	HOOK	ASLN	ASLY	CSLT	
AVG	97.76	95.55	88.23	93.85	93.33	94.07	97.77	100.0	
24	EXTF	EXIF	EXLF	OKAY	VCTR	PINT	ASLK	ASLM	CSLT
AVG	91.39	95.69	98.09	95.56	93.33	95.55	96.30	98.33	97.78
25	EXWR	SFWR	WPRN	WSPN	EXTF	EXIF	VCTR	ASLK	ASLY
AVG	85.90	100.0	90.47	89.02	93.85	98.04	97.91	95.92	94.07
34	FLWR	SFWR	WPRN	WSPN	EXLF	PINT	HOOK		
AVG	86.67	88.23	93.65	92.37	100.0	89.25	93.34		
35	FLWR	EXWR	SFWR	EXIF	OKAY	VCTR	HOOK	ASLY	
AVG	95.69	90.95	97.92	91.66	94.26	89.00	97.78	100.0	
45	FLWR	WSPN	EXMF	EXRF	EXLF	VCTR	HOOK		
AVG	97.22	100.0	100.0	98.24	100.0	100.0	97.92		
2B	FLWR	HDGP	WPRN	EXMF	ASLY				
AVG	95.56	93.05	96.25	97.78	94.07				
3C	FLWR	EXWR	SFWR	EXPM	HDGP	EXLF	ASLK	ASLN	ASLY
AVG	97.78	94.23	85.52	85.36	89.16	100.0	91.93	93.97	93.71
4D	FLWR	EXWR	EXPM	HDGP	PINT	ASLM	ASLN	CSLT	
AVG	100.0	100.0	88.89	89.17	94.44	90.5	96.19	92.89	
5E	FLWR	EXWR	SFWR	EXPM	HDGP	WSPN	WPRN	VCTR	
AVG	100.0	93.80	95.69	97.78	85.58	93.94	90.74	91.85	

pairs are applicable to classify different sets gesture classes. Among the "number + number" pairs, pair 24 provides the best performance with the highest number of distinguishable gesture classes and the best overall recognition rate, and among the "number + letter" pairs, 3C is the most promising one. EMG signals measured from these electrode positions can be classified accurately into 9 hand motions classes. Obviously 25, 4D, and 5E are also good electrode position pairs.

3.2 The Effects of Different Electrode Position Setups on Hand Gesture Pattern Recognition

In accordance with the experimental results, some regularities between the classifiable hand motions and electrode position setups can be summarized.

When a number electrode changes its position from 2 to 5, or moved from the wrist towards the elbow, it becomes less sensitive to the extension of I (thumb) and II (index) fingers, and more sensitive to the extension of III (middle) and IV (ring) fingers. Electrode positions 3 and 4 are more sensitive to the motions related to extension of V (little) finger. As can be seen in Fig. 4, high classification rates can be obtained for the gestures which involve the extension of I or II finger, such as EXTF, and EXIF, when one of the electrodes is in position 2. An electrode placed in position 3 or 4 will increase the classification rate of the V finger extension, the EXLF. Electrode in position 4 or 5 (for example, position pairs 35 and 45) improves the classification results of III and IV finger extensions, such as gestures VCTR, and EXRF. Almost all the gestures that can be classified reliably with electrodes placed at "number + number" positions are subtle finger extensions in Table 2. The electrode position pairs 24 and 25 yield higher average recognition rates than other "number + number" pairs because they have better coverage of the forearm muscles in the posterior aspect and can detect the activities of muscles in more detail.

As almost all the muscles below the letter electrode position are flexors, the gestures which involve the flexion of wrist, hand grasp, or combinations flexion and extension actions can be recognized easily with the "number + letter" electrode pairs. When moving on the forearm from wrist to elbow, the letter electrode positions become more

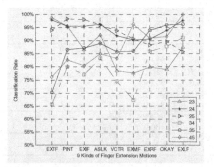
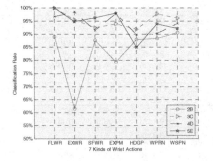

Fig. 4. Classification result for the 9 finger extension motions with the "number + number" electrode position pairs

Fig. 5. Classification result for the 7 wrist actions with the "number + letter" electrode position pairs

sensitive to the flexion of the wrist because stronger signals from *M.flexor carpi ulnaris* and *M.pronator teres* muscles can be detected near to the elbow. This phenomenon can be seen clearly in the classification results for the 7 different wrist actions. See the Fig. 5 for visualization. Electrode position pair 3C produces better results than the other "number + letter" pairs with the classification rate being above 90% for most of the gesture classes. The lowest classification rates are obtained with an electrode in the positions closest to the wrist. That is 2B. This is a demonstration of the fact that the anterior aspect of forearm near to the wrist consists mainly of tendons not muscles. This is also the reason why electrode positions A, and 1 were abandoned from our studies.

4 Discussion and Conclusions

To explore the effects of sEMG electrode placement on the hand gesture recognition, an extensive classification study on 25 different hand gestures and 10 electrode position pairs has been conducted and reported in this paper. The experimental results demonstrate some important relationships between the sEMG signal detection positions and hand gestures recognition rates. From these research results, we have concluded the following suggestions on how to define the hand gestures and select sEMG electrode measuring positions for a myoelectric control application:

Generally, the pairs of flexion and extension gestures of wrist and hand (FLWR and EXWR, EXPM and HDGP, WPRN and WSPN) can be classified accurately. Also finger gestures EXTF, EXIF, EXLF, OKAY, and VCTR can be easily distinguished from each other. As these gestures are easy to perform, socially acceptable in most of the cultures, and are convenient in respect to sEMG signal detection, they can be considered as good choices for myoelectrical control system.

Gestures EXMF, EXRF, ASLY, CSLT, and ASLN can be classified easily but they have negative connotations in many cultures. Thus these gestures should be used with caution. Gestures ASLB, ASLC, ASLY are similar with the gesture EXPM, and gesture ASLM is very similar with the ASLY, in sense of detected sEMG signals. Thus it is not recommendable to include more than two of these five gestures into the same gesture set.

If the gesture set contains many actions with subtle extension of fingers, the best choice of the electrode position pair is 24. If the gesture set consists of many wrist actions and extension of single or multiple fingers, the best choice is 25. If the gesture set contains many flexion and extension of wrist and fingers, the best choice is 3C. For the classification of various kinds of wrist motions, electrode position pairs 5E or 4D are recommendable choices.

The research work reported in this paper has focused on the definition of the hand gestures and on the selection of suitable sEMG electrode positions. The recognition results have served as a mean to compare the different electrode positions. In case rehabilitation even mobile HCI solutions a two-channel sEMG system is economical in regards to the manufacturing costs and computational complexity. Our work can set the groundwork for further study on myoelectric control. The future work will consider the more subjects and multiple use sessions in various environments. In addition, studies on fatigue and other physiological factors are still important, especially in respect repeatability and reusability of EMG measurement.

Acknowledgement

This work is supported by National Nature Science Foundation of China: 60703069. The authors would also like to thank all the volunteers for their help to do data collecting experiments.

References

1. Tarng, Y.-H., Chang, G.-C., Lai, J.-S., Kuo, T.-S.: Design of The Human/Computer Interface for Human with Disability- using Myoelectric Signal Controlled. In: Proceedings, 19th International Conference, IEEE/EMBS, vol. 5, pp. 1909–1910 (1997)
2. Francis, H.Y.C., Yang, Y.-S., Lam, F.K., Zhang, Y.-T., Parker, P.A.: Fuzzy EMG Classification for Prosthesis Control. IEEE Transactions on Rehabilitation Engineering 8(3), 305–311 (2000)
3. Chu, J.-U., Moon, I., Kim, S.-K., Mun, M.-S.: Control of Multifunction Myoelectric Hand using a Real-Time EMG Pattern Recognition. In: Intelligent Robots and Systems, pp. 3511–3516. IEEE, Los Alamitos (2005)
4. Knox, R., Brooks, D.H.: Classification of Multifunction Surface EMG using Advanced AR Model Representations. In: Bioengineering Conference, pp. 96–98. IEEE, Boston, MA (1994)
5. Nagata, K., Adno, K., Yamada, M., Magatani, K.: A Classification Method of Hand Movements Using Multi Channel Electrode, Engineering in Medicine and Biology Society. In: IEEE-EMBS, Shanghai, China, pp. 2375–2378 (2005)
6. Costanza, E., Inverso, S.A., Allen, R.: Toward Subtle Intimate Interfaces for Mobile Devices Using an EMG Controller. In: Proc CHI 2005, Portland or USA (2005)
7. Merletti, R., Lo Conte, L.R., Avignone, E., Guglielminotti, P.: Modeling of surface myoelectric signals. Part I: Model implementation. IEEE Transactions on Biomedical Engineering 46(7), 810–820 (1999)
8. Liu, C., Wechsler, H.: Robust coding schemes for indexing and retrieval from large face databases. IEEE Trans. Image Processing 9, 132–137 (2000)
9. Gao, S., Yu, Q.: Atlas of Human Anatomy (Revision), Shanghai scientific & Technical Publishers (1998)

Semantic Feature Extraction for Brain CT Image Clustering Using Nonnegative Matrix Factorization

Weixiang Liu[1], Fei Peng[1], Shu Feng[1], Jiangsheng You[2], Ziqiang Chen[2], Jian Wu[1], Kehong Yuan[1,*], and Datian Ye[1]

[1] Research Center of Biomedical Engineering, Graduate School at Shenzhen
Tsinghua University, Shenzhen, China 518055
yuankh@sz.tsinghua.edu.cn
[2] mTools Ltd., Suite 2418, No.102, Xian Lie Middle Rd.
Guangzhou, China 510070

Abstract. Brain computed tomography (CT) image based computer-aided diagnosis (CAD) system is helpful for clinical diagnosis and treatment. However it is challenging to extract significant features for analysis because CT images come from different people and CT operator. In this study, we apply nonnegative matrix factorization to extract both appearance and histogram based semantic features of images for clustering analysis as test. Our experimental results on normal and tumor CT images demonstrate that NMF can discover local features for both visual content and histogram based semantics, and the clustering results show that the semantic image features are superior to low level visual features.

1   Introduction

Brain computed tomography (CT) image based computer-aided diagnosis (CAD) system is helpful for clinical diagnosis and treatment. Many brain CT CAD systems depend on content based image retrieval (CBIR) system [1,2]. In CBIR system, images are always processed and analyzed with visual features, including original gray/color image, color space, texture, shape feature, regions, spatial relation features, even volume of interest, and their combination or fusion [3,4,5,6]. In recent years, semantic based image analysis has been proposed to close the gap between low level visual content and high level semantics of an image [4,7,8].

In representation of an image, the original and low level visual features always have large size. For example, for a 256×256 gray image, it contains 65536 pixel values. On the contrast, high level semantic features are more compact, and always less than such size. For example, histogram with several hundred scale levels (e.g. 256 scales or bins), is one approach for automatically extracting low level semantic features from visual features. For example, in [9] color histograms are adopted for image classification. And in [10], latent semantic indexing (LSI)

---

* Corresponding author.

D. Zhang (Ed.): ICMB 2008, LNCS 4901, pp. 41–48, 2007.
© Springer-Verlag Berlin Heidelberg 2007

is used for semantic feature extraction on color histogram based feature-image-matrix. However LSI is essentially based on single value decomposition (SVD) or principal component analysis (PCA), and it contains negativity values in decomposition, missing physical meanings.

Recently nonnegative matrix factorization (NMF) has been proven a powerful method for nonnegative data, such as images and documents [11]. NMF has parts based representation which can find local features with contrast to PCA. In addition, NMF is similar to K-means clustering method and essentially a soft clustering approach [11,12]. In a recent work [13], NMF is used for feature extraction on both visual content and histogram in image retrieval. However, how to find local semantic features from such color histogram is not shown.

In CT image based system, classification and retrieval can be used to predict the category of an incoming image. Here we consider CT image clustering and it is useful when image labels are not available. In some cases getting the image label is time consuming or sometimes wrong label by clinician is possible. And brain CT image clustering is also useful for comparison study of different diseases in the brain.

In this paper, we consider brain CT image feature extraction and clustering with NMF. We applied NMF on both brain CT gray images and their histogram based feature-image matrix . Our experimental results demonstrate that NMF can find significant local features from both visual content and histogram based semantic features, and results in clustering analysis show that histogram based semantic features are superior to visual appearance based features.

The rest of paper is organized as below. In section 2 we will discuss NMF for feature extraction, clustering and applications. In section 3 some experimental results on feature extraction and clustering are shown, and finally we conclude in section 4.

2   NMF for Feature Extraction and Clustering

NMF is a new method for nonnegative data analysis. The method considers nonnegative constraint on matrix factorization and has some advantages over traditional PCA [11], especially in face image analysis. Now it becomes a powerful technique for nonnegative data analysis; see [14,15,16] for recent literature review and more references therein.

Given a data matrix $\mathbf{X}$ with nonnegative values for all entries, NMF is to find an approximation decomposition $X \approx WH$, where W is $n \times k$ and H is $k \times m$, with nonnegative constraint on both W and H. There are two algorithms with multiplicative updates for NMF as [17]

$$W_{ik} \leftarrow W_{ik} \frac{(XH^T)_{ik}}{(WHH^T)_{ik}}, H_{kj} \leftarrow H_{kj} \frac{(W^T X)_{kj}}{(W^T WH)_{kj}} \tag{1}$$

and

$$W_{ik} \leftarrow W_{ik} \frac{\sum_j H_{kj} X_{ij}/(WH)_{ij}}{\sum_j H_{kj}}, H_{kj} \leftarrow H_{kj} \frac{\sum_i W_{ik} X_{ij}/(WH)_{ij}}{\sum_i W_{ik}}. \tag{2}$$

These learning rules can be derived, respectively, from minimizing different loss functions. One is Euclidean distance

$$f_{ED}(X; W, H) = \sum_{ij} [X_{ij} - (WH)_{ij}]^2,$$ (3)

and the other is generalized Kull-back Leibler divergence

$$f_{KL}(X; W, H) = \sum_{ij} \left[X_{ij} \log \frac{X_{ij}}{(WH)_{ij}} - X_{ij} + (WH)_{ij} \right].$$ (4)

These multiplication update rules can hold nonnegativity easily with nonnegative initialization.

Given a factorization as above, setting $k < n$ leads to dimension reduction. And in this sense, NMF is similar to PCA. As discussed in [11], NMF is also similar to K-means clustering method. Recently Brunet et al. applied NMF for clustering gene expression data [18]. In this case, each entry X_{ij} stands for the i-th gene expression level of sample j. Given an approximate factorization $V \approx WH$, in which each column of W stands for a 'metagene' while each column of H represents the metagene expression pattern of the corresponding sample. Given such a factorization, the clustering rule is defined as below according to the values of H: assign sample j to cluster k if the H_{kj} is the largest element in column j [18]. In [19] NMF is used to cluster genes.

However, we note that Brunet et al did not normalize each column of W. In our previous work, we have proposed a p-norm version of NMF for learning sparse features for classification [20]. We find that, during the update loop, normalizing the basis vector, each column of W leads to different sparse representation on H according to p-norm as

$$W_{ik} \leftarrow \frac{W_{ik}}{\left(\sum_i W_{ik}^p \right)^{1/p}}.$$ (5)

When $p = 1$, it reduces to the rule in paper [11]. Our theoretical analysis and experimental results show that large p value leads to more sparse representation for further classification; see [20] for more information. And we also applied this variant for improving gene expression data clustering [21]. In our following experiments, we adopt the basic rule as in paper [11].

In K-means method, each sample can only be assigned to one class. This is also called "hard" clustering in which the class membership of one sample is 1 or zero. By contrast, in "soft" clustering, the class membership of each sample belongs to a value in $[0, 1]$. Fuzzy clustering and probabilistic clustering are two popular "soft" clustering methods. In this sense, NMF is "soft" and K-means "hard". From the view point of matrix factorization, in K-means or vector quantization algorithm, each column of H is a unary vector with only one element being one and other elements being zeros [11]. For clustering, both NMF and K-means are stochastic, but NMF does not depends on the nearest neighbor criterion of K-means. More recently, the equivalence of nonnegative matrix factorization and spectral clustering is discussed in detail [12].

For real applications, Lee and Seung discussed two special cases: face gray images and semantic features of documents [11]. And this demonstrates that NMF can be used not only on nonnegative data directly, e.g. gray images, but also on transformed data with nonnegativity, e.g. frequency matrix of words in documents. In [14], NMF has been used for system call based intrusion detection, gray image watermarking, and EEG analysis. In [15,16] more references on applications of NMF are available.

3   Experimental Results

3.1   Dataset and Preprocessing

The used dataset contains brain CT images from 17 normal and 92 tumor related subjects (from mTools Ltd.). Currently the classes of tumor images are not clear. In this dataset, the minimum and maximum numbers of slices for each subject are 11 and 42, respectively.

The preprocessing included denoising, region of interest preserving, registration and normalization; see [22] for more information. The results of images before and after preprocessing from one normal subject are shown in Figure 1.

Original image of first slice from normal brain.   Image after preprocessing.

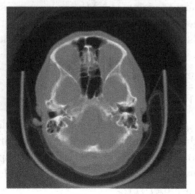 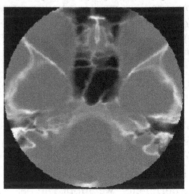

Fig. 1. Images before (left) and after (right) preprocessing from one normal subject

In order to take into account the spatial relation of multi-slice CT images, we used the average image of five slices close to normal or tumor tissue for each subject. In Figure 2, five images and their average image from one normal subject (top) and one tumor subject are shown respectively. Finally we got 109 average images for further analysis.

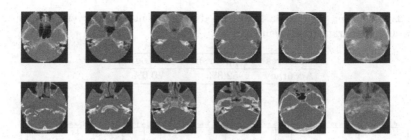

Fig. 2. Five images (from left to right) and their average image (right) from one normal subject (top) and one tumor subject (bottom)

3.2   Feature Extraction and Clustering Results

We first tested NMF on 109 average images. The learned two bases images are shown in Figure 3. We can see that these two basis images differ from each other based on their local features. From clustering viewpoint, such two basis images

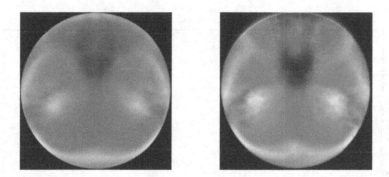

Fig. 3. Image bases (size 256 × 256) via NMF. Image on the left corresponds to tumor group and image on the right corresponds to normal group.

Next we calculated the histogram of average image with 256 scales to get the feature-image-matrix for learning semantic features via NMF. The histograms of images in Figure 2 are shown in Figure 4. And we used NMF on them again. The learned histogram bases are shown in Figure 5. We can see that two bases have a pulse at low scale. However the tumor basis is more flat than normal basis near the scale 100. This reflects the variation in tumor tissues. In this case, the clustering accuracy is about 70.6% which is higher than that on visual appearance features as shown in Table 1. And this demonstrates the advantage of histogram based semantic features over visual content features.

Table 1. Clustering results via NMF based on different features: visual appearance content and histogram based semantics

Features	Appearance	Histogram
Accuracy	52.3%	70.6%

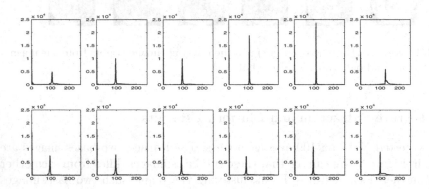

Fig. 4. Histograms of five images (from left to right) and their average image (right) from one normal subject (top) and one tumor subject (bottom) corresponding to those in Figure 2

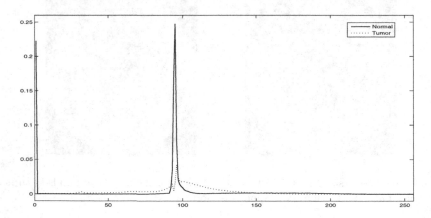

Fig. 5. Semantic image bases via NMF (normalized histogram with 256 levels), solid line for normal group and dotted line for tumor group

4   Conclusions and Future Work

Currently for a CBIR system, it is a challenging task to bridge the gap between the low level visual features and high level semantics of an image. Automatic extracting semantic features from an image is useful for image classification, retrieval and clustering.

We applied NMF for brain CT image feature extraction and clustering. Two kinds of features are discussed: visual content and histogram based semantic features. Our experimental results on normal and tumor CT images show that NMF can extract significant basis features which reflect the difference between normal and tumor images. Especially in clustering analysis by NMF, the histogram based semantic features are superior to the low level visual features.

Our primary work demonstrates the effectiveness of NMF on histogram based semantic features in feature extraction and clustering analysis. Currently the improvement of the method is considered. And we will investigate NMF and its new variants on brain CT images and apply them for retrieval in our CT based CBIR system as future work.

Acknowledgements

This paper is part of a project supported by Postdoctoral Fund of China (No. 20070410536). The authors would like to thanks all reviewers for their insightful comments on the improvement of the paper.

References

1. Müller, H., Michoux, N., Bandon, D., Geissbuhler, A.: A review of content-based image retrieval systems in medical applications-clinical benefits and future directions. International Journal of Medical Informatics 73(1), 1–23 (2004)
2. Greenspan, H., Pinhas, A.: Medical image categorization and retrieval for PACS using the GMM-KL framework. IEEE Transactions on Information Technology in Biomedicine 11(2), 190–202 (2007)
3. Gudivada, V., Raghavan, V.: Content based image retrieval systems. IEEE Computer 28(9), 18–22 (1995)
4. Smeulders, A., Worring, M., Santini, S., Gupta, A., Jain, R.: Content-based image retrieval at the end of the early years. IEEE Transactions on Pattern Analysis and Machine Intelligence 22(12), 1349–1380 (2000)
5. Veltkamp, R., Tanase, M.: Content-based image retrieval systems: A survey. Technical report, Department of Computing Science, Utrecht University (2002)
6. Kim, J., Weidong Cai, D.F., Wu, H.: A new way for multidimensional medical data management: Volume of interest (VOI)-based retrieval of medical images with visual and functional features. IEEE Transactions on Information Technology in Biomedicine 10(3), 598–606 (2006)
7. Zhao, R., Grosky, W.: Bridging the semantic gap in image retrieval.Distributed Multimedia Databases: Techniques and Applications, 14–36 (2001)
8. Datta, R., Li, J., Wang, J.: Content-based image retrieval: approaches and trends of the new age. In: Proceedings of the 7th ACM SIGMM international workshop on Multimedia information retrieval, pp. 253–262 (2005)
9. Chapelle, O., Haffner, P., Vapnik, V.: SVMs for histogram-based image classification. IEEE Transactions on Neural Networks 10(5), 1055–1065 (1999)
10. Zhao, R., Grosky, W.: Narrowing the semantic gap-improved text-based web document retrieval using visual features. IEEE Transactions on Multimedia 4(2), 189–200 (2002)

11. Lee, D.D., Seung, H.S.: Learning the parts of objects by non-negative matrix factorization. Nature 401, 788–791 (1999)
12. Ding, C., He, X.F., Simon, H.D.: On the equivalence of nonnegative matrix factorization and spectral clustering. In: Jonker, W., Petković, M. (eds.) SDM 2005. LNCS, vol. 3674, Springer, Heidelberg (2005)
13. Liang, D., Yang, J., Lu, J.J., Chang, Y.C.: The latent semantic image retrieval based on non-negative matrix factorization. Journal of Shanghai Jiaotong University (in Chinese) 40(5), 787–790 (2006)
14. Liu, W.X., Zheng, N.N., You, Q.B.: Nonnegative matrix factorization and its applications in pattern recognition. Chinese Science Bulletin (in English) 51(17-18), 7–18 (2006)
15. Berry, M.W., Browne, M., Langville, A.N., Pauca, V.P., Plemmons, R.J.: Algorithms and applications for approximate nonnegative matrix factorization. Computational Statistics & Data Analysis 52(1), 155–173 (2007)
16. Sra, S., Dhillon, I.S.: Nonnegative matrix approximation: Algorithms and applications. Technical report, Department of Computer Sciences, The University of Texas at Austin (2006)
17. Lee, D.D., Seung, H.S.: Algorithms for non-negative matrix factorization. Advances in Neural Information Processing Systems 13, 556–562 (2001)
18. Brunet, J.P., Tamayo, P., Golub, T.R., Mesirov, J.P.: Metagenes and molecular pattern discovery using matrix factorization. Proc. Natl. Acad. Sci. USA 101(12), 4164–4169 (2004)
19. Kim, P.M., Tidor, B.: Subsystem identification through dimensionality reduction of large-scale gene expression data. Genome Research 13, 1706–1718 (2003)
20. Liu, W.X., Zheng, N.N.: Learning sparse features for classification by mixture models. Pattern Recognition Letters 25(2), 155–161 (2004)
21. Liu, W.X., Yuan, K.H.: Sparse p-norm nonnegative matrix factorization for clustering gene expression data. International Journal of Data Mining and Bioinformatics (in press, 2007)
22. Peng, F., Yuan, K., Feng, S., Liu, W., Jia, S.: Combining region feature and Gabor texture feature for content-based brain CT image retrieval (submitted 2007)

Extracting Tongue Cracks Using the Wide Line Detector

Laura Li Liu and David Zhang

Biometrics Research Centre, Department of Computing,
The Hong Kong Polytechnic University, Kowloon, Hong Kong
{csliliu,csdzhang}@comp.polyu.edu.hk

Abstract. This paper attempts to extract tongue cracks, one of pathological features in tongue diagnosis. A detection scheme is proposed to extract tongue cracks. This scheme is based on the wide line detector which extracts the whole of the line by employing an isotropic nonlinear filter. The wide line detector is improved based on the properties of tongue cracks. The proposed scheme has been tested on a total of 286 cracked tongue images and our experimental results demonstrate its effectiveness.

1 Introduction

Tongue diagnosis [1] is one of the most important and valuable diagnostic methods in traditional Chinese medicine (TCM) and has been widely applied to clinical analyses and applications for thousands of years. In TCM theory [2], as the tongue is connected with a number of viscera via the meridians, the essential of the viscera can ascend to nourish the tongue and pathological processes are reflected on it. Whenever there is a complex disorder full of contradictions, examination of the tongue can instantly clarify the main pathological processes. Therefore, it is of great value in both clinic applications and self-diagnosis. Moreover, tongue diagnosis is a non-invasive technique that is in accord with the most promising direction in the 21st century: no pain and no injury.

Some researchers recently have paid attention to computerized tongue diagnosis [3-8] by developing a set of objective and quantitative features and measurements based on the theories of tongue diagnosis. So far, most investigation has been focused on extraction of chromatic features [4-7] and textural features [3,5-7]. Actually, according to the theories of tongue diagnosis, some features on tongue surfaces are pathological forms and thereby have clinical significance, for example, cracks on the tongue surface.

A cracked tongue, also called fissured tongue, is one kind of textural features and frequently seen in clinical practice. Tongue cracks refer to the surface of the tongue covered with all kinds of cracks or lines in deep or shallow shape, which are induced by the fusion or separation of the ligular papillae [9]. In [1], tongue cracks are divided into seven types according to the location and shape. Normally, the tongue's surface should be smooth and soft and show no cracks [1]. When obvious cracks appear on the tongue surface, it suggests the deficiency of *qi-blood* and the consumption of *yin* by excessive *heat* and, sometimes, the blood stasis. For instance, a deep crack in the center reaching to the tip reflects hyperactivity of Heart fire.

In spite of the clinical significance of the tongue crack, little work has been done on it. Li and Cai [10] constructed algorithms to calculate two features, which

D. Zhang (Ed.): ICMB 2008, LNCS 4901, pp. 49–56, 2007.
© Springer-Verlag Berlin Heidelberg 2007

indicated the roughness and the amount of cracks on the tongues, to analyze tongues of healthy condition and of different types of disease state with other four features. The roughness feature is measured by the differential-box-counting dimension which is an estimator of fractal dimension. The amount of cracks is obtained by computing the percentage of the areas containing cracks versus the total area of the tongue. The clinical significance of cracks, however, according to theories of tongue diagnosis, depends on the location of the cracks and their direction, length, width, and depth. That is the reason that Pham and Cai concluded that the roughness and amount of cracks do *not* reflect on the disease condition [11]. Therefore, in order to characterize these important pathological features of cracks, it is fundamental and essential to extract tongue cracks correctly and completely.

In this paper, we present a tongue crack detection scheme based on the wide line detector (WLD) [12]. The WLD algorithm detects the whole of the line by employing an isotropic nonlinear filter. Two parameters are used in the WLD algorithm, the brightness contrast threshold and the circular mask radius. The wide line detector is applied and improved based on the properties of tongue cracks.

The paper is organized as follows. Section 2 describes the tongue crack detection scheme. In Section 3, we describe the results of our experiments. Section 4 offers our conclusion.

2 Tongue Crack Detection Scheme

Given a segmented tongue image (see Fig. 1a), in the first step, we extracts the tongue body and, at the same time, creates the tongue body mask. In the second step, we employ the wide line detector to obtain the crack response image. Finally, the crack response image is post-processed to output the final results.

2.1 Preprocessing

The purpose of preprocessing is to segment the region of interest, i.e. the tongue body, from the captured tongue image which has a large background. We employ the segmentation method described in [8] to obtain the contour of the tongue body, as shown the white round in Fig. 1b. The tongue contour is then shrunk so that the influence of the uneven illumination caused by the deformation near the boundary can be eliminated. The shrunk distance should not be too large since some tongue cracks are very close to the boundary of the tongue body. Therefore, each pixel of the tongue contour is moved to the centroid of the tongue body with a distance (as shown the red round in Fig. 1b). The tongue body mask is created by binarizing the contour tongue image according to the shrunk contour and the tongue body image is consequently obtained, as shown in Fig. 1c and Fig. 1d, respectively.

2.2 Extracting Tongue Cracks

We improved the method proposed in [12] to detect the tongue crack based on their properties. This method, also called the *wide line detector*, extracts a line completely by using a nonlinear filter based on the isotropic response via a Gaussian weighting mask. Here, we replaced the Gaussian weighting mask G with an inverse-Gaussian profile

$$IG(x, y, x_0, y_0, r) = \frac{1 - e^{-\left((x-x_0)^2 + (y-y_0)^2\right)/2r^2}}{(2r+1)^2 - \sum_{\substack{x_0 - r \leq x \leq x_0 + r}}^{y_0 - r \leq y \leq y_0 + r} e^{-\left((x-x_0)^2 + (y-y_0)^2\right)/2r^2}}, \tag{1}$$

where (x_0, y_0) is the coordinate of the center, (x, y) is the coordinate of any other pixel within the mask, and r is the radius of the circular mask. The equation (1) gives a normalized version of the inverse-Gaussian profile.

The WLD first examines the intensity of the center of the mask and groups pixels having *similar* intensities to the center into the *weighted mask having similar brightness* (WMSB). In our method, this similarity is measured by:

$$c(x, y, x_0, y_0) = \begin{cases} IG \bullet \sec h\left(\left(I(x, y) - I(x_0, y_0)\right)/t\right)^5 & \text{if } I(x, y) \geq I(x_0, y_0) \\ IG & \text{otherwise} \end{cases}, \tag{2}$$

where $\sec h(x) = 2/(e^x + e^{-x})$, $I(x, y)$ is the brightness of the pixel (x, y) of the tongue body image, t is the brightness contrast threshold and c is the output of the weighting comparison. This function gives a smooth profile and does not have too large an effect on c as a pixel's brightness changes slightly, especially when it is near the threshold.

This comparison is done for each pixel within the mask. The WMSB mass of the center (x_0, y_0) is given by $m(x_0, y_0) = \sum_{x_0 - r \leq x \leq x_0 + r}^{y_0 - r \leq y \leq y_0 + r} c(x, y, x_0, y_0)$. The initial line strength L is the inverse WMSB mass obtained by using the following rule:

$$L(x_0, y_0) = \begin{cases} g - m(x_0, y_0) & \text{if } m(x_0, y_0) < g \\ 0 & \text{otherwise} \end{cases}, \tag{3}$$

Here g is the geometric threshold and $g = m_{max}/2$, where m_{max} is the maximum value which m can take. As a normalized circular mask is used, m_{max} is not larger than but very close to the unit and thereby the line strength ranges between zero and one. Fig. 1e shows the line strength image of Fig. 1d.

The WLD requires two parameters – the brightness contrast threshold, t, and the radius of the circular mask, r. In our method, the brightness contrast threshold is defined by

$$t = \left(\sum_{i=1}^N \left(I(x_i, y_i) - \overline{I(x_m, y_m)}\right)^2 / (N-1) \right)^{1/2}, \tag{4}$$

where $\overline{I(x_m, y_m)} = \sum_i I(x_i, y_i)/N$ and N is the number of non-zero pixels of the tongue body image. The brightness contrast threshold t is the standard deviation of the tongue body region.

In [12], the relationship between the width of lines detected and the size of Gaussian weighting masks is given via analysis. In the same way, if a line of width $2 \times w$ is fully detected by using an inverse-Gaussian weighting mask with radius r, it requires

$$\iint_L 1 - e^{-(x^2 + y^2)/2r^2} \, dxdy < \frac{1}{2} \iint_C 1 - e^{-(x^2 + y^2)/2r^2} \, dxdy = \pi r^2 \left(e^{-1/2} - 1/2\right), \tag{5}$$

where C denotes the region of the circular mask and L the region of the line which passes through the center of the circular mask. The relationship between the width of the detected line and the radius of a circular mask with inverse-Gaussian profile is consequently determined in terms of (7). Given the circular mask of radius r, the critical width of line detected, $2 \times w_c$, is obtained when the left and right arguments of (7) are equal. As the analytic form of the left function is not available, we only give the approximate results in Table 1. We also show in Table 1 the relationship between the width of line detected and the radius of a circular mask with Gaussian profile $e^{-(x^2+y^2)/2r^2}$. Comparing the two results, we find out that the detection capacity of the WLD using an inverse-Gaussian weighting mask is higher than that using a corresponding Gaussian weighting mask. It means that, with the same radius r, the circular mask of inverse-Gaussian profile can detect wider lines than that of Gaussian profile, while, in order to detect lines of same width, the size of an inverse-Gaussian weighting mask needed is smaller than that of a Gaussian weighting mask required. Therefore, the inverse-Gaussian weighting mask is more efficient than the Gaussian weighting mask.

2.3 Postprocessing

In the final stage, pixels of line strength below a threshold (=0.1) are removed firstly. Tongue cracks are extracted by applying the technique of hysteresis thresholding to the line-strength images, followed by some morphological operations. In the morphological operations, the crack will be discarded if (i) its length, l, is very short (< 20 pixels), (ii) its area, A, is too small (< 100 pixels), and (iii) its eccentricity, e, is less than 0.9. The eccentricity is the ratio of the distance between the foci of the ellipse and its major axis length. Fig. 1f shows the tongue crack detection result of Fig. 1d.

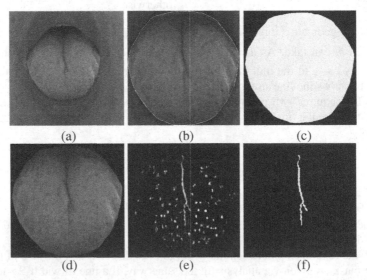

Fig. 1. The tongue crack detection scheme. (a) Captured tongue image, (b) contour tongue image with the centroid and corresponding contours, (c) tongue body mask, (d) segmented tongue body image, (e) the line-strength image using the wide line detector and (f) tongue crack image obtained by post-processing.

Table 1. Comparison of the relationship between radii of different profiles and approximately critical widths of detected lines (ACWL)

Radius of Circular mask (r)	Critical Width of Line Detected ($2 \times w_c$)			
	Gaussian weighting		Inverse-Gaussian weighting	
	ACWL	Digital ACWL	ACWL	Digital ACWL
3	2.6	2	4.0	4
4	3.5	3	5.3	5
5	4.4	4	6.6	6
6	5.3	5	7.9	8
7	6.2	6	9.2	9
8	7.1	7	10.6	10
9	7.9	8	11.9	12
10	8.8	9	13.2	13

3   Performance Evaluation

We have conducted a test of the proposed scheme on a total of 286 cracked tongue images. To establish the effectiveness of the wide line detector for the tongue crack detection, the performance of the described WLD algorithm is compared with the performance of two popular line detection methods, Steger's approach [13] and the line operator (LO) [14]. Steger's approach is a ridge-based line detector using two-dimensional Gaussian partial derivative kernels. This method uses a line model with an asymmetrical profile to remove the bias of the line position as well as to extract the line width. The line operator extracts linear features based on the difference between the average gray value of the pixels along the line direction and the average gray value of a square neighborhood with a similar orientation.

Performance evaluation of medical image segmentation is a challenging job due to the complexity and difficulty of medical image segmentation. Normally, a line detector performance is evaluated with specified ground truth [15]. Once the ground truth is given, quantitative evaluation can be readily carried out by comparing detected features with the ground truth features. For each sample of cracked tongue images used in our experiment, the ground truth was drawn by hand, which is a binary line map where tongue cracks are marked in white.

Let C_{GT} and C_{TD} denote the set of tongue crack pixels of the ground truth map and the tongue crack images detected by an approach, and B_{GT} and B_{TD} the set of background pixels, respectively. The set of correctly detected tongue crack pixels, called true positives, is $TP = C_{TD} \cap C_{GT}$ and the true positive rate is $R_{TP} = num(TP)/num(GT)$. False positives, i.e. spurious tongue crack pixels, are given by $FP = C_{TD} \cap B_{GT}$ and the false positive rate is $R_{FP} = num(FP)/num(GT)$, while false negatives, i.e. ground truth tongue crack pixels missed by the detected tongue crack images, are given by $FN = B_{TD} \cap C_{GT}$ and the false negative rate is $R_{FN} = num(FN)/num(GT)$. For true positives and false negatives, there always exists $R_{TP} + R_{FN} = 1$. Hence, we define the performance measure of a tongue crack detection approach as follows:

$$PM = R_{TP}/(1 + R_{FP}),$$ (6)

The performance measure PM ranges from 0 to 1. For perfect tongue cracks detection, $PM = 1$. For all other cases, the performance measure is smaller than one, being closer to zero with more tongue crack pixels falsely detected and/or missed by the tongue crack detection approach.

We compare the performance of the described WLD algorithm with the performance of Steger's approach and the line operator. Figure 2 shows comparative statistical box-and-whisker plots for the performance measures by using Steger's approach, the line operator (LO) and the WLD algorithm. Table 2 lists the mean values of the performance measures, true positive rates and false positive rate by the three approaches. The results reveal a much better performance of the WLD algorithm. False positive rates given by the WLD algorithm is more than 2 times lower than those of the two other methods. The reason is, compared to the two other methods, our WLD algorithm gives strong noise rejection due to no derivative used. In addition, the widths of cracks in a tongue image are different and even vary greatly, which is an important and special characteristic of tongue cracks. Our WLD algorithm keeps the width information of tongue cracks very well, while the Steger's approach and the line operator give detected tongue cracks

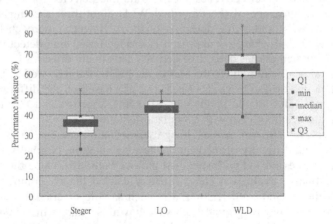

Fig. 2. Box-and-whisker plots for the performance measure of Steger's approach, the line operator (LO), and the wide line detector (WLD) for all test tongue images

Table 2. Performance evaluation results

Method Results	Steger	LO	WLD
PM (%)	35.83	42.60	63.15
R_{TP} (%)	68.34	72.08	82.18
R_{FP} (%)	83.41	70.52	28.78

almost same width. That is why the true positive rates given by the WLD algorithm are much higher than those of the two other methods.

4 Conclusions

This paper, for the first time, attempts to detect tongue cracks. A tongue crack detection scheme is proposed based on the wide line detector. The tongue crack detection scheme works well for all test tongue images. Because no derivative is used in the wide line detector, the tongue crack detection method gives strong noise rejection. The detection results obtained using our scheme keep line width information well due to no Gaussian smooth kernel applied.

Although the proposed tongue crack detection scheme gives a much better performance than Steger's approach and the line operator, the true positives generated by our method are relatively low while the false positives relatively high. This is mainly caused by the complexity and difficulty of tongue cracks. In the future, we will design a heuristic algorithm to overcome this problem and to improve the detection performance further.

Acknowledgement

This work is partially supported by the National Natural Science Foundation (NSFC) key overseas project under the contract no. 60620160097.

References

1. Kirschbaum, B.: Atlas of Chinese Tongue Diagnosis. Eastland, Seattle, WA (2000)
2. Yiu, H.: Fundamental of Traditional Chinese Medicine. Foreign language Press, Beijing (1992)
3. Chiu, C.C., Lin, H.S., Lin, S.L.: A Structural Texture Recognition Approach for Medical Diagnosis through Tongue. Biomedical Engineering, Application, Basis and Communication 7, 143–148 (1995)
4. Chiu, C.C.: A Novel Approach based on Computerized Image Analysis for Traditional Chinese Medical Diagnosis of the Tongue. Computer Methods and Programs in Biomedicine 61, 77–89 (2000)
5. Li, C.H., Yuen, P.C.: Regularized Color Clustering in Medical Image Database. IEEE Trans. Medical Imaging 19, 1150–1155 (2000)
6. Yang, C.: A Novel Imaging System for Tongue Inspection. In: 19th IEEE Proc. Instrumentation and Measurement Technology Conference, pp. 159–163 (2002)]
7. Pang, B., Zhang, D., Li, N., Wang, K.Q.: Computerized Tongue Diagnosis based on Bayesian Networks. IEEE Trans. Biomedical Engineering 51, 1803–1810 (2004)
8. Pang, B., Zhang, D., Wang, K.Q.: The Bi-Elliptical Deformable Contour and Its Application to Automated Tongue Segmentation in Chinese Medicine. IEEE Trans. Medical Imaging 24, 946–956 (2005)
9. Xin, Y., Guo, X.Z., Zhang, L.S.: Tongue Diagnosis (Chinese-English). Tianjin Science and Technology Translation Publisher (2001)

10. Li, G., Cai, Y.: Texture Analysis for Tongue Analysis. Technical Report BV-2003-2, Carnegie Mellon University (2003)
11. Pham, B., Cai, Y.: Visualization Techniques for Tongue Analysis in Traditional Chinese Medicine. In: Proc. SPIE, vol. 5367, pp. 171–180 (2004)
12. Liu, L., Zhang, D., You, J.: Detecting Wide Lines using Isotropic Nonlinear Filter. IEEE Trans. Imaging Processing 16, 1584–1595 (2007)
13. Steger, C.: An Unbiased Detector of Curvilinear Structures. IEEE Trans. Pattern Anal. Machine Intell 20, 113–125 (1998)
14. Zwiggelaar, R., Astley, S.M., Boggis, C.R.M., Taylor, C.J.: Linear Structures in Mammographic Images: Detection and Classification. IEEE Trans. Medical Imaging 23, 1077–1086 (2004)
15. Bowyer, K., Kranenburg, C., Dougherty, A.: Edge Detector Evaluation using Empirical ROC Curves. Comput. Vis. Image Understand 84, 77–103 (2001)

An Effective Recognition Method of Breast Cancer Based on PCA and SVM Algorithm

Jihong Liu and Weina Ma

College of Information Science and Engineering, Northeastern University,
Shenyang, 110004 China
liujihong@ise.neu.edu.cn

Abstract. Breast cancer is the leading cancer among females, the key technology of preventing breast cancers is early detection. Based on the advantage of support vector machine (SVM), finding global solution and possessing higher generalization capability on dealing with the small sample, a new method of diagnosing breast cancer by CAD is proposed in this paper. Firstly, a principal component analysis is used to represent the information of ROI image, which account for most of the variance of the original data set while significantly reducing the data dimension. After the extraction of principal components, only those data of which account for most part of variance were retained as the feature vector and input into a SVM classification and BP neural network classification to classify. Finally, the results of experiment show that the accuracy and specificity for the diagnosis of breast cancer using SVM classification is good.

1 Introduction

Breast cancer is the most common cancer among women. Generally, the features of breast cancer are divided into morphological features and texture features. The former focus on the shape of tumor, the smoothness of boundary and so on. It is good at detecting the benign tumor; The latter reflect the relativity between tumor region and its vicinity organization, and have a effective recognition on malignant tumor. For effected by the vicinity organization and itself shape greatly, the features parameter display a great difference. Breast cancer diagnosis has been dealt with using various machine algorithms, such as linear programming [1], decision tree [2], neural networks [3]. Considering that the texture features is disturbed by noise easily, and morphological features which are directly observable and on which noise effect is relatively small have a difficulty on recognising malignant tumor, the previous researcher [4] proposed that getting the features of tissue sample to classify malignant or benign in Breast biopsy used the principal component analysis method. Support vector machines, as a new generation of learning systems, was developed by Vapnik and co-workers in early'90s [5]. Due to its successful preventing overfitting and dimension disaster, SVM is applied widely in several fields, such as text categorization [6], hand written character recognition [7], face recognition, image classification [8], etc.

In this paper the PCA and SVM methods are applied on the computer assistant diagnosis of breast cancer field.

D. Zhang (Ed.): ICMB 2008, LNCS 4901, pp. 57–64, 2007.

2 Basic Principle

2.1 PCA Algorithm

Principal component analysis (PCA) [9] is an effective method for choosing the features from image in pattern recognition, which is a process to reduce the data dimension by removing correlations among the data and to describe the image by fewer feature vectors while retaining the necessary information of recognition. The primary principle of recognising breast cancer, a $h \times l$ ROI image is connected by column to a $M = h \times l$ column vector, where M is the vector dimension of the ROI image. Let N is the sample number of training set, x_j is the vector coming from the j th image. Thus, total scatter matrix of the training sample is shown in equation (1),

$$S_t = \sum_{i=1}^{N} (X_i - \mu)(X_i - \mu)^T \tag{1}$$

where μ is the average vector of training sample set and $\mu = \dfrac{1}{N} \sum_{i=1}^{N} X_i$. Assume $X = [X_1 - \mu, X_2 - \mu, \dots X_N - \mu]$, S_t can be rewritten as $S_t = XX^T$. For S_t is a symmetry matrix, it can be diagonalization,

$$S_t = W \bullet W^T \tag{2}$$

If making a linear transformation on X, the covariance matrix of Y, which transforms as equation (3),

$$\sum{}_X = YY^T = W^T XX^T W \tag{3}$$

is a triangular matrix. Thus, the redundance among data disappears after above linear transformation. Each volumn vector of W is dealt with orthogonal normalization, indexed as a vector $[W_1, W_2, \cdots, W_N]$. The vector of ROI image P_i projects to the subspace which is constituted by $W_1, W_2, \cdots W_N$. The projection is denoted as $Q = W^T P_i$. When reconstructing the image, P_i is written as the expression (4),

$$P_i = WQ = \sum_{i=1}^{K} W_i Q_i + \sum_{i=K+1}^{N} W_i Q_i \tag{4}$$

If only the top K projections are chosen to reconstruct, the reconstruction error is presented as equation (5),

$$e_{ms} = \sum_{i=K+1}^{N} \lambda_i \tag{5}$$

where λ_i is the eigenvalue of matrix S_t. Thus, the eigenvalues are ordered and chosen feature vectors of top K eigenvalue. Then project the vectors of ROI image to the subspace that is constituted by the feature vectors corresponding to these K eigenvalues. In this way, the dimension of ROI image can be reduced from original dimension M to K. The classification parameters are exactly the projection coefficient of K dimension in ROI image.

2.2 SVM Algorithm

SVM [10] based on the theory of uniform convergence in probability and structural risk minimization (SRM) principle, maps a set of input data to a high-dimensional feature space through a kernel function, avoids overfiting by choosing an optimal separating hyperplane (OSH) in the feature space that maximizes the width of the margin between classes. In general, the hyperplane corresponds to a non-linear decision boundary in the input space and depends only on a subset of the original input data called the support vectors. For the case of linearity separable classes, an optimal separating hyperplane can be directly constructed, and make all the vectors of sample set be satisfied with under conditions,

(1) Can be separated by one hyperplane.
(2) Maximize the width of the margin between OSH and vectors which are the closest ones to the hyperplane.

Where, condition (1) is to ensure the experience risk minimization, condition (2) is to make the VC confidence minimization, to minimize the expectation risk. Virtually, the question of OSH construction is an quadratic programming question under the restrict condition. The optimal separate function is denoted as expression (6),

$$f(x) = \text{sgn}\{\sum_{i=1}^{L} v_i \alpha_i k(x_i, x) + b\} \tag{6}$$

where $K(x, y)$ is a kernel function effectively defining on basis function for each data point in the training set, $\text{sgn}(x)$ is a sign function, and L is the number of training sample. The introduction of kernel functions in the SVM framework enables one to define the feature space implicitly and thus overcomes the problem of computational burden of explicitly mapping the input fata to the higher-dimensional feature space via non-linear mapping. However, in order to qualify as a legitimate kernel, the kernel function must have to satisfy Mercer's condition, that is, it must need to be a continuous symmetric kernel of a positive integral operator. In the kernel function, some α_i corresponding to x_i is zero while some α_i corresponding to x_i is nonzero, the vectors of the nonzero support the OSH, so called "support vector machine". Hereby, different support vectors will be gotten by choosing different kinds of kernel function $K(x, y)$.

3 Experimental Results

The system of breast cancer recognition mostly includes ROI orientation module, pre-processing module, feature extraction module, training module and classification module. The system flow is shown in Fig. 1.

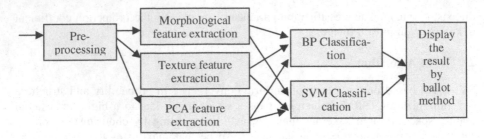

Fig. 1. The recognition system flow of breast cancer

According to the necessary of different pathological region, the methods of feature extraction or the different classifications can be chosen solely. But the case that is difficlut to classify the complex pathological image always happens. Thus, multi-features can be chosen respectively to classify firstly, and then make the final decision by voting the ballot. The SVM classification whose parameters are principal component feature gotten by PCA method is shown in this paper.

3.1 ROI Orientation Module

In order to reduce the disturbance from the vicinity organization of breast cancer, the ROI is segmented from the whole image by manual work. The detailed approach is that orienting the boundary points of the four directions of breast tumor by manual, which decide the rectangle region called as tumor region, then expanding the tumor region outwards to construct a standard rectangle contained the tumor, namely ROI.

3.2 Preprocessing Module

It is inevitably for the image to be disturbed by noisy in the process of transformation and transmission. So denoise processing to the ROI image is necessary firstly. The image is likely to thicken after dealed with traditional median filter, for the reason of bluring the boundary of object. An effective median filter which retains the boundary of image is used to preprocess in this paper. The basic idea of this method is below [11]:

(1) Construct a $m \times m$ function module whose central pixel is the next processing point.

(2) Choose k pixels whose gray values are closest to the central pixel in the module.

(3) Use the median value of these k pixels in the window to replace the central pixel. For example, a 3×3 module, where $k = 5$.

Then, the enganced ROI images are gained by histogram equalization to reduce the misdiagnosis of image recognition.

3.3 The Recognition Process

Principal component analysis (PCA) has a widely application in pattern recognition, especially facing recognition. Combining with the character that the pathological region is difficult to classify, the feature extraction method of PCA is chosen to apply on breast cancer recognition in this paper. The feature parameters gained by PCA method are added into training feature database, and then input the SVM classification to recognise.

Prior to choose the mapping kernel and calculate the kernel function $K(x,y)$, the feature data set must be trained in order to get the optimal parameter of separating hyperplane. Adjust the kernel function and penalty factor according the testing result and input the optimal result to learning module database to classify the predicted data.

The prime steps of training are below:

Step 1. Standardize and normalize the training sample to gain the standardized sample data X^*.

Step 2. Calculate the eigenvalue and eigenvector of X^* and order the eigenvalue to choose the principal components.

Step 3. Map each image to the subspace constituted by principal components and receive the feature parameter of image.

Step 4. Based on feature parameter to construct SVM classification, radial basis function is chosen as kernel function in this paper.

The prime steps of recognition module are below,

Step 1. Standardize and normalize the prediction sample.

Step 2. Map prediction sample to the principal components subspace to gain the feature parameter.

Step 3. Recognize by SVM classification.

4 Result Analysis

In this experiment, 120 pathological image are divided into two independent sets: training set and prediction set, containing 44 malignant and 76 benign. Alternating the testing data three times, the result is shown in Table 1.

Table 1. (a) The character parameters of BP and SVM classification. (b) The mean value of both classifications.

(a)

Sample	BP neural network classification			SVM classification		
	a	b	C	A	B	C
(malignant,benign)	(46,14)	(35,25)	(44,16)	(46,14)	(35,25)	(44,16)
False negative(FN)	3	3	2	1	2	2
False positive(FP)	2	1	1	1	1	0
Accuracy (%)	91.67	93.33	95.00	96.67	95.00	96.67
Sensitivity (%)	93.62	91.89	95.65	97.82	94.44	95.65
specificity (%)	84.62	95.83	93.33	92.86	95.83	100

(b)

Mean	False negative(FN)	False positive(FP)	Accuracy (%)	Sensitivity (%)	Specificity(%)
BP neural network	2.67	1.34	93.33	93.72	91.26
SVM classification	1.67	0.67	96.12	95.97	96.23

It is shown in the Table 1 that FN is false negative, FP is False Positive; accuracy = (TP + TN) / (TP + TN + FP + FN), where TP and TN denote the number of malignant and benign classified correctly respectively; sensitivity = TP / (TP + FN); specificity = TN / (TN + FP).

Compared with BP neural network classification (93.33%), seen from Table 1, the recognition rate Of SVM classification (96.12%) is higher and it also has an remarkable advantage in sensitivity and specificity. BP neural network is a multi-layer feedforward perceptron applied reverse error algorithm, while SVM based on structural risk minimization (SRM) principle.

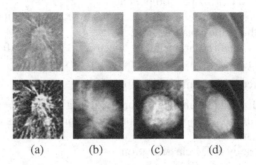

(a)   (b)   (c)   (d)

Fig. 2. The first row is 4 original ROI image, and the second row is 4 normalized ROI image. (a) is carcinoma simplex of long spicular signs. (b) is solid carcinoma of long spicular signs. (c) is fibroma. (d) is nerve fibroma.

The recognition of pathological region becomes more difficulty for the complexity of pathological classes and the difference from individual difference. The ROI images are shown in Fig. 2, where (a) (b) is the malignant tumor whose boundary is blurry and (c) (d) is benign which has a clear boundary of tumor.

Table 2. The parameter comparison of two classifications

BP neural network		SVM classification	
Sample number	10	Sample number	10
Nerve cell	8	SVM type	C_SVM
Transfer function	tansig, purelin	Kernel function	RBF
Training function	traingdm	Penalty factor	40
Iterative number	86	Total support vector	10
Error	1e-5	B	-0.508147
Learning rate	0.05	Malignant benign support vector	3, 7

The following part gives a detailed illumination of parameter setting by 10 sample (72×60) on BP neural network and SVM classification. In the training process of BP neural network classification, adjust each parameter to make the simulated value close to the object value. The result of simulation is shown in Fig. 3. Fig. 4 left is the histogram of input image, and Fig. 4 right is the weight of input image by PCA method. The training parameters are shown in Table 2. As increasing the amount of training sample, the advantage of SVM classification will be more visualization.

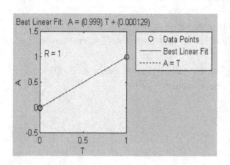

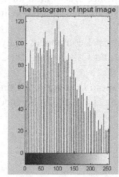

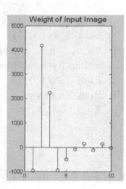

Fig. 3. The simulation of regressed value

Fig. 4. Left is the weight of input image, right is the weitht of input image

5 Conclusions

A computer assistant recognition system of breast cancer based on PCA and SVM method is proposed in this paper, which classifies the malignant and benign by SVM classification whose feature parameter extracts from ROI image by PCA method. The experiment result shows that this method presents an effective detectable rate. But there are various kinds of breast cancer, only one method can not apply to all cancer. Thus, the key point of future work should focus on collecting the complex pathological information, training classification and realizing other methods of feature extraction, extending the classification system to broad field.

References

1. Mangasarian, O.L., Nick Street, W., Wolberg, W.H.: Breast cancer diagnosis and prognosis via linear programming. Operations Research, 570–577 (1995)
2. Breiman, L., Friedman, J., Olshen, R.: Classification and Regression Trees. Wadsworth (1984)
3. Burke, H.B., Goodman, P.H., et al.: Artificial neural networks improve the accuracy of cancer survival prediction. Cancer, pp. 857–862 (1997)
4. Zhu, C., Palmer, G.M., Breslin, T.M., Harter, J., Ramanujam, N.: Diagnosis of Breast Cancer Using Diffuse Reflectance Spectroscopy: Comparison of a Monte Carlo Versus Partial Least Squares Analysis Based Feature Extraction Technique. Lasers in Surgery and Medicine, pp. 714–724 (2006)
5. Vapnik, V.: The Nature of Statistical Learning Theory. Springer, Heidelberg (1995)

6. Goertzel, B., Venuto, J.: Accurate SVM Text Classification for Highly Skewed Data Using Threshold Tuning and Query-Expansion-Based Feature Selection.Neural Networks. In: IJCNN 2006. International Joint Conference on, pp. 1220–1225 (2006)
7. LeCun, Y.: Comparison of learning algotithms for handwritten digit recognition. Image and Vision Computing, pp. 675–692 (2003)
8. Qin, J., He, Z.: A SVM face recognition method based on Gabor-featured key points. Machine Learning and Cybernetics. In: Proceedings of 2005 International Conference on, pp. 5144–5149 (2005)
9. Ye, Z., Auner, G.: Principal component analysis approach for biomedical sample identification. Systems, Man and Cybernetics. In: 2004 IEEE International Conference on, pp. 1348–1353 (2004)
10. Bian, Z., Zhang, X.: Pattern Recognition. Tsinghua University Press, Beijing (2000)
11. Xu, J.: Image processing and analysis. Science Press, Beijing (1994)

Predicting Protein Quaternary Structure with Multi-scale Energy of Amino Acid Factor Solution Scores and Their Combination

Shao-Wu Zhang, Wei Chen, Chun-Hui Zhao, Yong-Mei Cheng, and Quan Pan

College of Automation, Northwestern Polytechnical University, Xi'an, 710072, China
{zhangsw,zhaochunhui,chengym,quanpan}@nwpu.edu.cn

Abstract. In the protein universe, many proteins are composed of two or more polypeptide chains, generally referred to as subunits, which associate through noncovalent interactions and, occasionally, disulfide bonds to form protein quaternary structures. It has been known for long that the functions of proteins are closely related to their quaternary structure. With the number of protein sequences entering into data banks rapidly increasing, it is highly desirable to predict protein quaternary structures automatically from their primary sequences. Here, multi-scale energy of factor solution scores and feature combination were employed to form various input feature vectors, and the multi-class support vector machine (SVM) classifier modules were adopted for predicting protein quaternary structures. The rates of correct identification suggest that the individual primary sequence of an oligomeric protein do contain the information of its quaternary structure. The results of multi-scale energy of Factor 1 solution scores indirectly prove that biologically relevant complex formation is driven predominantly by the hydrophobic effect. The current approach is quite promising and may at least play a complimentary role to the existing methods.

1 Introduction

Proteins are at the center of the action in biologic processes. And their function can only be understood based on the structure of their constituent polypeptide chains. The structural hierarchy in proteins is traditionally described in terms of four levels: primary, secondary, tertiary, and quaternary. Quaternary structure refers to the number of polypeptide chains (subunits) involved in forming a protein and the spatial arrangement of its subunits. The concept of quaternary structure is derived from the fact that many proteins are composed of two or more subunits that associate through noncovalent interactions and, in some cases, disulfide bonds to form oligomers. In the protein universe, there are many different classes of subunit construction, such as monomer, dimmer, trimer, tetramer, and so forth. The oligomers may be homo-oligomers and hetero-oligomers; the former consist of identical polypeptide chains, whereas the latter are nonidentical. Such complexes are involved in various biological processes [1], including metabolism, signal transduction and chromosome replicating etc. The oligomeric proteins have more advantages than the monomers in the scope of functional evolutional points of view [2-4].

D. Zhang (Ed.): ICMB 2008, LNCS 4901, pp. 65–72, 2007.

With the number of protein sequences entering into data banking rapidly increasing, we are confronted with a challenge: how to develop an automated method to identify the quaternary attribute for a new polypeptide chain (i.e., whether it is formed just as a monomer, or as a dimer, trimer, or any other oligomer). This is important, because the functions of proteins are closely related to their quaternary attribute. For example, some critical ligands only bind to dimers but not to monomers; some marvelous allosteric transitions only occur in tetramers but not other oligomers; and some ion channels are formed by tetramers, whereas others are formed by pentamers. The association of subunits depends upon the existence of complementary 'patches' on their surfaces structure. This suggests that primary sequences contain quaternary structure information [5-8]. So, we can develop an automated method to predict protein quaternary structure from the protein primary sequences. To explore this problem, Garian [5] developed a method which used decision-tree models and a feature extraction approach (simple binning function) to successfully predict homodimer and non-homodimer. Chou and Cai [8] also researched this question with a pseudo-amino acid composition (PseAA) feature extraction method to predict monomer, homodimer, homotrimer, homotetramer, homopentamer, homohexamer and homooctamer. In our previous work, we had successfully predict homodimers and non-homodomers, homodimer, homotrimer, homotetramer, homohexamer with weighted auto-correlation functions feature extraction approach [6-7]. In this paper, we try to develop another approach, that is, multi-scale energy (MSE) pseudo-amino acid composition approach, to predict monomer (1EM), homodimer(2EM), homotrimer(3EM), homo-tetramer(4EM), homopentamer(5EM), homohexamer(6EM) and homooctamer(8EM).

2   Materials and Methods

2.1   Database

The training data used here was constructed by Chou and Cai [8], and it consists of 3174 protein sequences, of which 382 are with annotation of monomer, 817 of homodimer, 593 of homotrimer, 884 of homotetramer, 54 of homopentamer, 287 of homohexamer, and 157 of homooctamer. They each contain more than 50 sequences. The data set construction was governed by the following criterias: (1) Clearness, collected samples were only those protein sequences with a clear annotation of their quaternary attribute. (2) Non-redundancy, for those proteins with high sequence similarity to each other, to avoid redundancy, only one of them was kept. (3) Statistical significance, those subsets were dropped from further consideration if they contained too few entries to be of statistical significance.

2.2   Statistical Factors of Amino Acid Attribute

An amino acid index is a set of 20 numerical values representing different physico-chemical and biological properties. On-line AAindex database contains 494 such amino acid indices (www.genome.ad.jp/dbget/aaindex.html), which include general attributes, such as molecular volume or size, hydrophobicity, and charge, as well as more specific measures, such as the amount of nonbonded energy per atom or side chain orientation angle. Atchley et al. [9] used multivariate statistical analysis on these 494 amino acid attributes to produce a small set of five multidimensional numerical patterns, which describe the highly interpretable covariation among the original attributes. The resultant factors are linear functions of the original data that capture the underlying latent structure of the variables. These authors have further found that the transformed scores so obtained provide a general solution for a wide variety of sequence analysis problems. The five statistical factor solution scores for each amino acid proposed by Atchley et al. [9] are listed on Table 1.

Table 1. Five factor solution scores for each nature amino acid computed by Atchley et al. [9]

Amino Acid	Factor1	Factor2	Factor3	Factor4	Factor5
A	-0.591	-1.302	-0.733	1.570	-0.146
C	-1.343	0.465	-0.862	-1.020	-0.255
D	1.050	0.302	-3.656	-0.259	-3.242
E	1.357	-1.453	1.477	0.113	-0.837
F	-1.006	-0.590	1.891	-0.397	0.412
G	-0.384	1.652	1.330	1.045	2.064
H	0.336	-0.417	-1.673	-1.474	-0.078
I	-1.239	-0.547	2.131	0.393	0.816
K	1.831	-0.561	0.533	-0.277	1.648
L	-1.019	-0.987	-1.505	1.266	-0.912
M	-0.663	-1.524	2.219	-1.005	1.212
N	0.945	0.828	1.299	-0.169	0.933
P	0.189	2.081	-1.628	0.421	-1.392
Q	0.931	-0.179	-3.005	-0.503	-1.853
R	1.538	-0.055	1.502	0.440	2.897
S	-0.228	1.399	-4.760	0.670	-2.647
T	-0.032	0.326	2.213	0.908	1.313
V	-1.337	-0.279	-0.544	1.242	-1.262
W	-0.595	0.009	0.672	-2.128	-0.184
Y	0.260	0.830	3.097	-0.838	1.512

Factor 1 is bipolar (large positive and negative factor coefficients) and reflects the simultaneous covariation in portion of exposed residues versus buried residues, polarity versus no polarity, hydrophobicity versus hydrophilicity, nonbonded energy versus free energy. Factor 2 is a secondary structure factor, which represents the relationship of relative propensity for various amino acids in secondary structure configurations like helix, turn or coil. Factor 3 relates to molecular size or volume. Factor 4 reflects the relative amino acid composition in various proteins. Factor 5 refers to electrostatic charge with high coefficient on isoelectric point and net charge.

2.3 Multi-scale Energy Feature

Using amino acid factor solution scores shown in Table 1, the protein sequence of English letters can be translated into a numerical sequence, for example, with Factor 1 solution scores, the sequence 'ACEAE' can be expressed as ' -0.591, -1.343, 1.357, - 0.591, 1.357'. The numerical sequence can be considered as digital signal. Projecting the signal onto a set of wavelet basis functions with various scales, the fine-scale and large-scale physicochemical information of a protein can be simultaneously investigated. Here, the wavelet basis function used is symlet wavelet [10]. Consequently, the protein can be characterized as the following multi-scale energy (MSE) feature vector [11].

$$MSE = [d_1, \cdots, d_j, \cdots d_m, a_m]$$ (1)

Here, m is the coarsest scale of decomposition, d_j is the root mean square energy of the wavelet detail coefficients in the corresponding j-th scale, and a_m is the root mean square energy of the wavelet approximation coefficients in the scale m. The energy factors d_j and a_m are defined as:

$$d_j = \sqrt{\frac{1}{N_j} \sum_{n=0}^{N_j-1} [u_j(n)]^2} \quad , \quad a_m = \sqrt{\frac{1}{N_m} \sum_{n=0}^{N_m-1} [v_m(n)]^2} \quad , \quad j = 1, 2, \cdots, m$$ (2)

Here, N_j is the number of the wavelet detail coefficients, N_m is the number of the wavelet approximation coefficients, $u_j(n)$ is the n-th detail coefficient in the corresponding j-th scale, and $v_m(n)$ is the n-th approximation coefficient in the scale m. In general, for the protein sequence with length L, m equals $INT(\log_2 L)$. But, the diverse lengths of protein sequences make that m value must be optimized to select. Here, we select $m=12$.

According to the above description, we can extract five attribute parameter sets based on the five statistical factors of amino acid attribute from protein primary sequences, which are represented as F1, F2, F3, F4 and F5 respectively.

2.4 Multi-attributes Combination

According to the concept of Chou's pseudo-amino acid composition [12], we combine the MSE feature vector with amino acid composition (AAC) which is consisted the 20-D components of the amino acid frequencies. The protein can be represented by the following $(20+m+1)$-D vector.

$$X = \left[f_1, f_2, \cdots, f_\alpha, \cdots, f_{20}, d_1, d_2, \cdots, d_j, \cdots, d_m, a_m \right]^T$$ (3)

Here f_α ($\alpha = 1, 2, \cdots, 20$) is the occurrence frequencies of 20 amino acid in the protein concerned, arranged alphabetically according to their signal letter codes.

The protein can also be represented by multi-attribute combination, that is,

$$X = \left[f_1, f_2, \cdots, f_\alpha, \cdots, f_{20}, d_1^{F1}, d_2^{F1}, \cdots, d_j^{F1}, \cdots, d_m^{F1}, a_m^{F1}, \cdots, d_1^{F5}, d_2^{F5} \cdots d_j^{F5}, \cdots d_m^{F5}, a_m^{F5} \right]^T$$ (4)

Obviously, there are various combinational manners for the six feature vector sets (AAC, F1, F2, F3, F4, F5). The combination of two feature vector sets (AAC, F1) constitutes another feature vector set, which is represented by AACF1; The combination of four feature vector sets (AAC, F1, F2 and F4) constitutes another feature vector set, which is represented by AACF1F2F4; and so forth.

2.5 Multi-class Support Vector Machine

Support vector machine (SVM) is a learning machine based on statistical learning theory [13]. Due to its powerful discrimination, it was successfully applied to medicine, bioinformatics, computational biology, etc. SVM was originally designed for binary classification, while predicting protein quaternary structures is a multi-class prediction problem. We can decompose the multi-class into a series of binary class, constructing multi-binary class SVM classifiers to solve such problem. Normally, "one-versus-one" or "one-versus-all" approach is employed for multi-class SVM classifier [14]. In present study, "One-versus-one" approach was used. This method involves construction of individual binary SVM classifier corresponding to each pair of the classes. Hence, if there are k classes, a total of k(k-1)/2 classifiers will be constructed. Unseen test instances prediction follows the voting strategy. Predictions are made with each binary classifiers and label is assigned to a class with maximum number of votes. In case when tie arise, i.e. two classes have identical votes, label assignment to the class is made on the basis of smallest index.

All the computations were performed using LIBSVM standard package, and can be freely downloaded from http://www.csie.ntu.edu.tw/~cjlin/libsvm/ for academic research [14]. The various user-defined parameters e.g., Radial basis kernel function (RBF) parameter γ and regularization parameter C were optimized on the training dataset.

2.6 Assessment of Prediction System

The prediction quality can be examined using the jackknife test. The cross-validation by jackknifing is thought the most objective and rigorous way in comparison with sub-sampling test or independent dataset test [15-16]. During the process of jackknife analysis, the datasets are actually open, and a protein will in turn move from each to the other. The total prediction accuracy (Q) and the prediction accuracy (Q_k) for each class of protein quaternary structure calculated for assessment of the prediction system are given by:

$$Q = \sum_{k=1}^{7} p(k) \bigg/ N, \qquad Q_k = p(k) \big/ obs(k) \tag{5}$$

Here, N is the total number of sequences, $obs(k)$ is the number of sequences observed in k class protein quaternary structure, $p(k)$ is the number of correctly predicted sequences of k class protein quaternary structure.

3 Results and Discussion

Different feature vector sets and their combination were employed as input feature vector for RBF SVM. The performance of each trained module was evaluated with jackknife cross validation test. The classification performance of different SVM modules with "one-versus-one (OVO)" approach is summarized in Table 2 and 3. From table 2, we can see that the results of F1 and F4 are the best in all the statistical factors (e.g. F1, F2, F3, F4 and F5), and their total accuracies are 66.3% and 67.5% respectively; AAC based module performed better with 84.4% total accuracy.

Subsequently, to improve the prediction accuracy, various combinations of different feature vector sets were employed. Out of various combinations tried, combination of AAC, F1, F2 and F4 feature vector predicted the protein quaternary structures better than others with 86.7% total accuracy.

From table 3, we can also find that the results of AACF1 and AACF4 are better than AACF2, AACF3 and AACF5. Their total accuracies are 1% and 1.9% higher than that of AAC. As discussed by Atchley et al. [9], Factor 1 represents the physical properties like hydrophobicity, hydrophilicity and polarity. Factor 4 signifies importance of relative amino acid composition. These results suggest that biologically relevant complex formation is driven predominantly by the hydrophobic effect [17].

The feature vector extracted based on AAC approach includes more statistical information of protein quaternary structures within the primary sequence, while the feature vector extracted based on multi-scale energy of factor solution scores include sequence orders and amino acid physicochemical and biological property information. Generally, combination of these feature vectors can improve the prediction performance. But from table 3, we can see that some combination schemes do not increase the prediction accuracy, in contrast, they decrease the accuracy. For example, the total accuracy for AAC and F3 combination is 82.8%, but the total accuracy for AAC is 84.4%; another example is that the total accuracy for AAC, F1, F2, F3, F4 and F5 combination is 85.8%, while the total accuracy for AAC and F4 combination is 86.3%. The reason is that there may be some redundancy and conflict information between these feature sets.

Table 2. The results (in percentage) of six feature vector sets with RBF SVM and OVO approach in Jackknife test

	AAC	F1	F2	F3	F4	F5
1EM	89.0	71.2	61.3	49.7	68.1	50.5
2EM	89.6	73.1	56.8	61.0	71.5	61.4
3EM	81.3	64.9	59.4	53.6	67.8	58.2
4EM	89.1	73.9	66.4	60.5	76.4	64.7
5EM	75.9	22.2	27.8	22.2	35.2	20.4
6EM	62.4	39.0	39.4	24.7	44.9	31.0
8EM	74.5	46.5	42.7	26.8	46.5	24.8
Q %	84.4	66.3	57.7	52.5	67.5	55.2

Table 3. The results (in percentage) of different feature vector combination with RBF SVM and OVO approach in Jackknife test

	AACF1	AACF2	AACF3	AACF4	AACF5	AACF1F2F4	AACF1F2F3F4F5
1EM	88.0	82.2	86.9	88.2	87.4	86.6	87.4
2EM	91.1	93.4	89.0	90.5	90.7	91.6	89.5
3EM	82.8	79.4	79.8	83.1	78.2	84.5	84.7
4EM	89.5	90.8	87.8	90.8	88.1	90.7	90.7
5EM	75.9	66.7	68.5	75.9	72.2	85.2	79.6
6EM	66.2	63.8	59.6	71.4	61.0	70.4	68.6
8EM	75.2	72.0	70.7	77.7	68.8	77.7	72.6
Q %	85.4	84.5	82.8	86.3	83.2	86.7	85.8

Table 4. Comparison with Chou's method [8]

	1EM	2EM	3EM	4EM	5EM	6EM	8EM	Q %
Chou's method	80.9	85.7	77.9	85.4	1.9	62.7	54.1	78.5
Our method (AACF1F2F4)	86.6	91.6	84.5	90.7	85.2	70.4	77.7	86.7

The corresponding comparison with Chou's method [8] is shown in Table 4. Our prediction performance is superior to Chou's method. The results show that the multi-scale energy of factor solution scores and feature combination can successfully predict protein quaternary structures. It may be very relevant for similar prediction tasks.

4 Conclusions

In present study, multi-scale energy of factor solution scores and feature combination were employed for predicting protein quaternary structures. The rates of correct identification suggest that the individual primary sequences of an oligomeric protein do contain the information of its quaternary structure. The feature vectors composed of amino acid composition and multi-scale energy of factor solution scores appear to capture essential information about the composition and hydrophobicity of residues in the surface patches that buried in the interfaces of associated subunits. The results also indicate that current approach is quite promising and may at least play a complimentary role to the existing methods.

Acknowledgements

This paper was supported in part by the National Natural Science Foundation of China (No. 60775012 and 60634030) and the Technological Innovation Foundation of Northwestern Polytechnical University (No. KC02), and the Science Technology Research and Development Program of Shaanxi (2006k04-G14).

References

1. Terry, B.F., Richard, M.C.: Determination of protein–protein interactions by matrix-assisted laser desorption/ionization mass spectrometry. J. Mass Spectrom. 33, 697–704 (1998)
2. Klotz, I.M., Darnell, D.W., Langerman, N.R.: Quaternary structure of proteins. In: Neurath, H., Hill, R.L. (eds.) The proteins, 3rd edn., vol. 1, pp. 226–241. Academic Press, New York (1975)
3. Einstein, E., Schachman, H.K.: Determing the roles of subunits in protein function. In: Creighton, T.E. (ed.) Protein function: A practical approach, pp. 135–176. IRL Press, London (1989)
4. Price, N.C.: Assembly of multi-subunit structure. In: Pain, R.H. (ed.) Mechanisms of Protein Folding, pp. 160–193. Oxford University Press, New York (1994)
5. Garian, R.: Prediction of quaternary structure from primary structure. Bioinformatics 17, 551–556 (2001)

6. Zhang, S.W., Pan, Q., Zhang, H.C., Zhang, Y.L., Wang, H.Y.: Classification of protein quaternary structure with support vector machine. Bioinformatics 19, 2390–2396 (2003)
7. Zhang, S.W., Pan, Q., Zhang, H.C., Shao, Z.C., Shi, J.Y.: Prediction protein homo-oligomer types by pesudo amino acid composition: approached with an improved feature extraction and Naive Bayes feature fusion. Amino Acids 30, 461–468 (2006)
8. Chou, K.C., Cai, Y.D.: Predicting protein quaternary structure by pseudo amino acid composition. Protein: structure, function, and genetics 53, 282–289 (2003)
9. Atchley, W.R., Zhao, J.P., Fernandes, A.D., Druke, T.: Solving the protein sequence metric problem. PNAS 102, 6395–6400 (2005)
10. Pittner, S., Kamarthi, S.V.: Feature extraction from wavelet coeffi-cients for pattern recognition tasks. IEEE Trans Pattern Anal Mach Intell. 21, 83–88 (1999)
11. Shi, J.Y., Zhang, S.W., Pan, Q., Cheng, Y.M., Xie, J.: SVM-based Method for Subcellular Localization of Protein Using Multi-Scale Energy and Pseudo Amino Acid Composition. Amino Acids 33, 69–74 (2007)
12. Chou, K.C.: Prediction of protein cellular attributes using pseudo-amino acid composition. Proteins: Structure, Function, and Genetics 43, 246–255 (2001)
13. Vapnik, V.: Statistical Learning Theory. Wiley, New York (1998)
14. Hsu, C., Lin, C.J.: A comparison of methods for multi-class support vector machines. IEEE Transactions on Neural Networks 13, 415–425 (2002)
15. Chou, K.C., Zhang, C.T.: Review: Prediction of protein structural classes. Crit Rev Biochem Mol. Biol. 30, 275–349 (1995)
16. Zhou, G.P., Assa-Munt, N.: Some insights into protein structural class prediction. Protein: structure, function, and genetics 44, 57–59 (2001)
17. Glase, F., Steinberg, D.M., Vakser, I.A., Ben-Tal, N.: Residue frequencies and pairing preferences at protein–protein interfaces. Protein: structure, function, and genetics 43, 89–102 (2001)

A Knowledge Discovery Approach to Diagnosing Intracranial Hematomas on Brain CT: Recognition, Measurement and Classification

Chun-Chih Liao[1,2], Furen Xiao[1], Jau-Min Wong[1], and I-Jen Chiang[1,3]

[1] Graduate Institute of Biomedical Engineering, National Taiwan University,
1, Sec.1, Jen-Ai Road, Taipei, Taiwan
[2] Department of Neurosurgery, Taipei Hospital, Department of Health, Taipei, Taiwan
[3] Graduate Institute of Medical Informatics, Taipei Medical University
250 Wu-Xin Street, Taipei, Taiwan
ijchiang@tmu.edu.tw

Abstract. Computed tomography (CT) of the brain is preferred study on neurological emergencies. Physicians use CT to diagnose various types of intracranial hematomas, including epidural, subdural and intracerebral hematomas according to their locations and shapes. We propose a novel method that can automatically diagnose intracranial hematomas by combining machine vision and knowledge discovery techniques. The skull on the CT slice is located and the depth of each intracranial pixel is labeled. After normalization of the pixel intensities by their depth, the hyperdense area of intracranial hematoma is segmented with multi-resolution thresholding and region-growing. We then apply C4.5 algorithm to construct a decision tree using the features of the segmented hematoma and the diagnoses made by physicians. The algorithm was evaluated on 48 pathological images treated in a single institute. The two discovered rules closely resemble those used by human experts, and are able to make correct diagnoses in all cases.

1 Introduction

Computed tomography (CT) is the imaging modality of choice for unconscious patients in the emergency room, many of them suffered from various type of intracranial hematomas, such as hypertensive intracerebral hemorrhage (ICH), subdural hematomas (SDH) or epidural hematomas (EDH) caused by trauma. These hematomas appear as hyperdense (whiter than the gray level of the brain) areas on CT slices. Compared to magnetic resonance imaging (MRI), CT is faster and can be safely applied to patients with unstable vital signs. Physicians make diagnosis by interpreting the result of CT scan. Although being digital in nature, quantitative evaluation of CT findings has not been standardized until recent 10 years, when it has been incorporated into clinical practice guidelines [1-4].

On the other hand, current textbook descriptions on diagnosis of intracranial hematomas remain qualitative. For example, EDH is described as "a hyperdense biconvex or planoconvex collection along the calvarium" [5]. This kind of expression is not

D. Zhang (Ed.): ICMB 2008, LNCS 4901, pp. 73–82, 2007.
© Springer-Verlag Berlin Heidelberg 2007

only far from quantification and standardization, but also difficult to be implemented in decision support systems. Moreover, the extrinsic hematomas (those outside the brain itself), namely EDH and SDH, located just between the isodense brain and the hyperdense skull, have CT numbers just between the brain and the skull. This makes segmentation of these two types of hematomas very difficult by applying thresholding alone. As a result, there has not been any published work focusing on automated segmentation of EDH or SDH, according to our knowledge. Evaluation of the interface between the brain and the skull, or the epidural/subdural space, has also been excluded in earlier rule-based labeling of brain CT images [6].

The goal of this paper is to develop an algorithm that can successfully recognize all types of hyperdense hematomas (ICH, SDH, and EDH). In addition to localization, we also hope to label the long and short axes of these hematomas and to discover rules that can distinguish one type of hematoma from another. Since the spatial resolution within each slice of a routine non-volumetric brain CT is far better than that between slices, we only consider planimetry on the slice containing the largest area of hematoma rather than volumetry to minimize errors caused by partial volume effect [5].

2 Materials and Methods

2.1 Materials

From July 2003 to June 2004, 86 consecutive patients were admitted to the intensive care unit (ICU) of Taipei Hospital, Department of Health. Forty-eight of them have significant hyperdense intracranial hematoma, including 26 ICHs, 16 SDHs and 6 EDHs. We define significant hematomas as ICH larger than $0.6cm^2$ in size and EDH/SDH thicker than 0.4cm. These criteria are far smaller than the indications for surgical treatment [1-4]. Therefore, no hematoma requiring surgical removal would be missed. Hypodense (blacker than the gray level of the brain) or isodense hematomas are excluded because they cannot be separated from the brain by gray level criteria alone. All brain CT scans were done with a standard protocol. The field of view (FOV) was 25×25cm. Each image was 512×512 pixels in size, resulting in a resolution of 0.49mm per pixel. The original CT number was transformed with brain window (center 40, width 150) into 256 gray levels. The CT slice containing the largest area of hematoma is picked out by one of the human experts (CCL) and downloaded to a personal computer in JPEG format. We are currently developing algorithms that can automatically select the most pertinent pathological slice from the whole set of CT slices.

2.2 Preprocessing

The flowchart of our algorithm is shown in Fig. 1. The gray level of pixel (x,y) in the original CT slice is denoted as $G_O(x,y)$ in the range between 0 and 255. The coordinates satisfy $0 \leq x \leq 511$, $0 \leq y \leq 511$. We strip the extracranial part of $G_O(x,y)$ to produce $G_S(x,y)$, containing only the skull and the intracranial pixels. We then perform a depth-dependent gray level normalization for $G_S(x,y)$ to produce $G_1(x,y)$, the image on which hematoma recognition, measurement, and classification will be done.

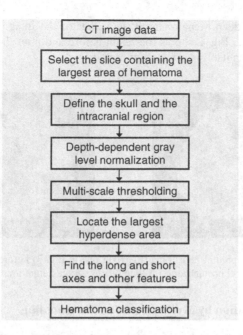

Fig. 1. Flowchart of our algorithm

Segmentation of the brain region is a very important preprocessing step for brain CT recognition [7]. By defining the region of interest (ROI), the noise is reduced and the efficiency is improved. We define the skull as the largest region after applying region-growing algorithm on all pixels with bony density. Applying region-growing again for pixels with brain density at the center of the skull image can define the intracranial region, or pixels within the skull. Pixels outside the skull, or those in the extra-cranial region, are discarded. The details are described elsewhere [8].

After recognizing the skull region, we can calculate the depth of each intracranial pixel, $D(x,y)$, defined as the city block distance between the pixel and the skull. Because of the irregularity and the complexity of skull base anatomy, images of skull base and/or cerebellar hematomas are not included in this study. Defining the depth enables us to measure the depth of hematoma from the brain/skull interface, which has become an important criterion in determining the necessity of surgery [9]. Furthermore, for some images with prominent hyperdensity at the brain/skull interface, applying region-growing algorithm directly will delineate the complete 'circle' in addition to the hematoma itself even with proper thresholding (Fig. 2). To reduce the artefact, we perform a depth-dependent normalization to alleviate the hyperdense artefact beneath the skull:

$$G_I(x, y) = G_S (x, y) + (A^* - A(D(x, y))) (1 - D(x, y) / D_{MAX}), \qquad (1)$$

where $A(D)$ is the average gray level of all pixels with depth D, A^* is the average of A, and D_{MAX} is the maximal depth. The result is rounded to integer values with the last term preventing deep hematomas at the center of the image, such as a thalamic ICH, to be 'wiped out'. Fig. 2 shows the result before and after the normalization procedure. The hematoma itself is affected minimally.

Fig. 2. An image with epidural hematoma (the right one in Fig. 3) before (*left*) and after (*right*) depth-dependent gray level normalization. White blocks denote hematoma areas by thresholding.

2.3   Lesion Localization by Multi-resolution Thresholding

White matter, gray matter and intracranial hematoma have CT numbers of 25-35, 35-50, and 50-70 Hounsfield units (HU), respectively. A mean difference of about 5 HU between an object and its environment is adequate for its recognition manually [5]. Theoretically, setting the threshold at 50 HU, or about the 154th gray level with our windowing, is enough to recognize all intracranial hematomas. However, segmentation of intracerebral hematoma is difficult with earlier algorithms based on clustering if the hematoma is too heterogeneous to form a 'cluster' on the histogram [6]. Furthermore, the optimal threshold chosen by human experts for hematoma segmentation differs from case to case. Therefore, we develop a multi-resolution thresholding procedure to decrease the instability of the segmentation result and to obviate the need for clustering.

Let G_1, G_2, G_4 and G_8 denote the gray level image at the original, 2×2, 4×4, and 8×8 resolution (roughly 0.5×0.5, 1×1, 2×2, and 4×4mm^2 per pixel), with a size of 512×512, 256×256, 128×128, and 64×64 pixels, respectively. The gray levels of pixels at given resolution is computed by averaging those of the four corresponding pixels at previous level of resolution, and then rounded to integer values. We only consider points that are completely within the intracranial area. The gray level is set to 0 otherwise.

$$G_i(x, y) = (G_{i-1}(2x-1, 2y-1)+G_{i-1}(2x, 2y-1)+G_{i-1}(2x-1, 2y)+G_{i-1}(2x, 2y)) / 4. \qquad (2)$$

The histograms of the intracranial pixels at different resolutions are obtained. From the histograms, the maximal and the average gray levels at any given resolution can be calculated. We set the threshold for hematoma detection at the midway between these values.

$$t_i = (Average(G_i (x,y)) + Max(G_i (x,y))) / 2 \qquad (3)$$

Applying this scheme into a brain CT slice without any hematoma would segment the white matter from the gray matter because the threshold is likely to fall between the gray levels of these two groups. Therefore, we set the minimal threshold at a gray level of 145, corresponding to 45 HU in CT number, to ensure that only hyperdense pixels are picked out. To maximize the stability of our results, only the data of the coarsest resolution (G_4 and t_4) is processed. Any areas smaller than 4 blocks (about 0.6 cm2) are discarded.

2.4 Recognition of the Long and Short Axes and Other Features

After identifying the largest area of intracranial hematoma in the coarsest resolution on the given CT slice, the long and short axes of the hematoma can be approximated by following the steps: (1) Measure the largest diameter, or the long axis; (2) Measure the largest diameter 90 degrees to the long axis [10]. We denote the end points of the long and short axes as SA1 and SA2, LA1 and LA2, respectively. To simplify the recognition process, only the largest connected hyperdense region is taken into consideration and other smaller hyperdense regions are omitted in the axis recognition step.

At the 4-mm resolution, the long axis is readily found by exhaustively testing the distance between any two hematoma blocks and choosing the point pair with the largest distance. By moving along each block on the long axis, the short axis can be found as the point pair with the largest distance in the perpendicular direction. The Euclidean distances between LA1/LA2 and SA1/SA2, denoted as |LA| and |SA|, are calculated. Because some hematomas (especially SDHs) assume a concave shape, points SA1 and SA2 lying at the same side of the long axis are permitted as long as they formed the largest distance perpendicular to the long axis (Fig. 3, middle).

After defining the long axis, the hematoma area can be divided into two parts lying on each side. Depending on the shape of hematoma, the number of blocks at each side may vary. To decrease aliasing, only blocks having a distance one unit (4mm) away from the long axis are taken into account.

2.5 Constructing the Decision Tree for Diagnosing the Type of Hematoma

Index Miner (Index Software, Saratoga, CA) is an integrated data mining tool that includes several state-of-the-art data mining utilities in Java programming language that is widely available for all major computer platforms. It provides a uniform interface to many different learning algorithms, along with methods for pre- and post-processing and for evaluating the result of learning schemes on any given dataset. The purpose of Index Miner aims to help users who need to use the learning algorithms to analyze the dataset and researchers who wish to experiment with new self-designed algorithms.

We constructed a spreadsheet in CSV format for the information obtained from the 48 images and fed it to Index Miner. There are ten attribute for each image in addition to the serial numbers. The dependent attribute is the diagnosis, assigned by human experts. The other 9 attributes can be divided into two groups: those related to the axes and those related to the 'halves'. The former group contains the lengths of the long and short axes, the depth of points LA1 and LA2, D(LA1), D(LA2), and their sum. In other trials we also tested the ratio between the lengths of long and short axes. The latter group of attributes contains the number of blocks in the larger and smaller halves on each side of the long axis, and the percentage of the smaller half. All data is used as the training set to generate the decision tree using C4.5 algorithm [11].

3 Results

3.1 Automatic Hematoma Recognition

The results of automatic hematoma recognition are summarized in Table 1. Our algorithm automatically measures the lengths of the long and short axes, the depth of the long axis expressed as the sum of the depth of its end points (D(LA1) + D(LA2)), and counts the block numbers of the larger and smaller halves (LH and SH) as well as their ratios. Each type of hematoma has its distinctive features. The extrinsic hematomas (EDH and SDH) have shallow long axes just beneath the skull. Subdural hematomas assume a much 'slender' shape as their smaller axes are much smaller than the long axes. Almost all hematoma blocks of SDH lie on one side of the long axis, resulting in a very small SH. On the other hand, ICH and EDH are ellipsoid in shape and the size of the two halves between the long axes, SH and LH, differs less.

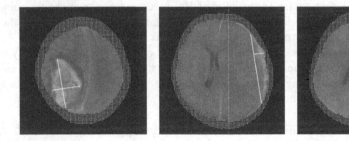

Fig. 3. Examples of automatic recognition of ICH (*left*), SDH (*middle*) and EDH (*right*) with measurement of the long and short axes. The skulls are shown as stippled areas.

In order to quantitatively evaluate the recognition results, a board-certified neurosurgeon (FRX) independently reviewed all 48 images and manually labeled the hematoma blocks. The overlap metric is computed according to the formula described for measuring the accuracy of cerebral ventricle recognition [12]:

$$\%overlap = (2\times TP)/(2\times TP+FP+FN), \tag{4}$$

where TP, FP and FN denote the numbers of true positive, false positive and false negative blocks. We arbitrarily define 'incomplete recognition' as having an overlap metric of less than 60%. All ICHs are completely recognized. Four (25%) SDHs and one (17%) EDH are incompletely recognized. However, the data from these five images are still fed into the data mining process.

Table 1. Results of automatic hematoma recognition counted in 4×4mm2 blocks. Data are expressed as mean±standard deviation.

Type(no)	|LA|	|SA|	D(LA1)+D(LA2)	SH	LH	%overlap
ICH(26)	10.3±4.9	6.0±3.4	18.9±6.4	13.7±15.6	24.3±20.2	92.2±5.9
SDH(16)	15.8±9.1	2.1±1.9	2.5±0.9	1.1±1.9	21.8±21.0	68.9±21.3
EDH(6)	21.5±6.6	6.7±2.4	2.5±0.5	25.5±17.7	39.0±23.7	81.2±19.2
Total(48)	13.8±7.9	4.8±3.4	11.1±9,4	10.8±15.3	26.2±23.0	83.3±17.6

3.2 The Discovered Knowledge

Fig. 4 shows the resulting decision tree with the confusion matrix in Table 2. All hematomas are correctly classified despite incomplete recognition in 5 of them. The decision tree is composed of two rules, one for separating ICH from SDH and EDH and the other for separating SDH from EDH. Our first rule classifies hematomas with D(LA1)+D(LA2) (depth of the long axes) larger than 5 as ICHs (Fig. 3, left). Hematomas with smaller sums of depths are classified as SDHs or EDHs, or extrinsic hematoma collectively. In the words of human experts, this rule equals to dividing hematomas into extrinsic (juxtacalvarial, lying just beneath the skull) and intrinsic (intracerebral) ones, listed as chapter headings in the text-book, under the form of "The intracerebral foci have no apparent relationship to the calvarium although they can expand to the cerebral cortex" [5]. In fact, our rule is the quantitative form of textbook description, transforming the term "relationship to calvarium" into "depth of the end points of the long axis", D(LA1)+D(LA2).

Our second rule deals with extrinsic hematomas. Hematomas with the smaller halves smaller than or equal to 6 blocks are classified as SDHs (Fig. 3, middle). Otherwise, hematomas are classified as EDHs (Fig.3, right). The ratio between SH and (SH+LH) is another feature that can successfully differentiate SDH from EDH, generated after excluding the column of SH at the input data (Fig. 4, right). Both versions of this rule corresponds to textbook descriptions of SDH as "a subcalvarial crescentic hyperdensity" and EDH as "a hyperdense biconvex collection along the calvarium" [5]. A crescent is a shape enclosed by two circular arcs of different diameters which intersect at two points. Since the long axis of SDH is located juxtacalvarially, the two intersection points correspond to these two intersection points. Geometrically, SDH is concave and EDH is convex. As a result, part of the long axis of the former lies outside the hematoma itself and most hematoma blocks are placed on one side of it. On the other hand, the long axis of the biconvex EDH usually bisects the hematoma. However, since the density of an EDH is not always uniform, exact bisection is not common. Despite the variation in CT number, we derive a rule that can correctly classify all SDHs and EDHs.

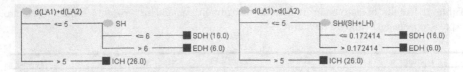

Fig. 4. The decision tree with (*left*) and without (*right*) column "SH". See text for details.

Table 2. Confusion matrix of our decision tree

Case number	Classified as		
True Diagnosis	ICH	SDH	EDH
ICH	26	0	0
SDH	0	16	0
EDH	0	0	6

4 Discussion and Conclusions

Medical diagnosis involves distinguish one disease from another. Visual assessment on diagnostic images depends on the experience and expertise of a physician. Although there are clinical guidelines [1-4,9], the standardization process is not so intuitive because of inter-observer variations. We applied several techniques to achieve totally computerized evaluation of "computerized" tomography. First, we applied several image processing techniques to generate several features of the hematoma within the image. Secondly, the features are put into a data mining software to generate rules that can distinguish one type of hematoma from another. Our method translates millions of bits of pixel intensities into nuggets of knowledge.

The first part of this study presents an algorithm that can recognize any type of intracranial hematoma on brain CT. This is the first report of successful recognition of epidural and subdural hematomas. Intracranial hematomas have a notoriously complex intensity profile that varies with time and location. However, recognition of intracranial hematomas on brain CT images is fairly easy since most of them have CT numbers within certain range. The problem in recognizing extrinsic hematomas is their locations and frequent heterogeneity in some cases [5]. By extensive averaging in a multi-resolution scheme, the histograms of the brain area and the hematoma area are stabilized. The heterogeneity and irregularity at the brain-hematoma interface is greatly reduced. Another advantage of multi-resolution processing is simplicity. By reducing the number of data from millions to thousands we speed up the later stages of processing.

Depth-dependent normalization is the key pre-processing step in reducing the artifact around the extrinsic hematomas. The interface between the skull and the brain, where all EDHs and SDHs occur, is subject to many types of artifacts such as partial volume effect and beam-hardening [5]. The artifacts cannot be totally corrected by calibration because of the anatomical variations. The human head is not the same as the phantom for calibration. Some modifications after image generation still play an important role despite improvements in controlling the physical conditions and imaging parameters during the scanning process. By focusing the normalization process on the superficial part, we minimize the adverse effect of normalization to recognition of deep hematoma. However, superficial hematomas, including EDHs, SDHs, and sub-cortical ICHs are still affected. After applying a procedure to increase the specificity, one must pay the price of reducing sensitivity, manifested as the lower overlap metric for SDHs.

The discovered knowledge in our study closely resembles the textbook descriptions. However, the discovered rules are expressed quantitatively and can be easily integrated into any decision support systems. In contrast, direct application of the qualitative textbook rules by choosing thresholds empirically is only time-consuming, and sometimes can get redundant or confused. For example, we have failed differentiating SDH from EDH by evaluating the length of the short axis alone. In this study, only two attributes are "distilled" from the ten given to the data miner system. We can save much time in manually testing the combination of attributes to assimilate the text book rules and in reducing the redundancy of information. Since the global shape descriptors such as "crescent-shaped" or "biconvex" cannot be formulated into a simple mathematical formula, our system derives simple rules that only depend on existing features. Moreover, these rules are consistent with expert knowledge are not "black boxes". This rather abstract form can be realized across different resolutions, different platforms, even with different imaging modalities such as MRI. This kind of insight is particular useful in dealing with unfamiliar conditions or unexplored fields. Moreover, the two rules are so robust that can classify the five partially-recognized images correctly. In other words, our rules can tolerate inaccurate recognition or irregular hematoma shape/intensity by selecting more stable features.

This study also illustrates an important difference between knowledge discovery approaches and traditional statistical methods. In order to derive the decision tree, information gain rather than statistical significance is used as the quantitative measure for feature selection. Features having higher 'statistical significance' do not always having higher efficiency in discriminating one class of examples from another. For example, when comparing the group of SDH with EDH using t-test, the feature SH has a probability of 0.01 while SH/(SH+LH) has a probability of 0.00026. However, these two features generate rules with the same efficiency as shown in Fig. 4. Length of the shorter axis, |SA|, has a lower probability of 0.002 compared to SH. However, it fails to discriminate EDH from SDH because four cases of EDH have the same values of |SA| as SDH.

References

1. Broderick, J.P., Adams, H.P., Barsan, W., Feinberg, W., Feldmann, E., Grotta, J., Kase, C., Krieger, D., Mayberg, M., Tilley, B., Zabramski, J.M., Zuccarello, M.: Guidelines for the management of spontaneous intracerebral hemorrhage. Stroke 30, 905–915 (1999)
2. Bullock, M.R., Chesnut, R., Ghajar, J., Gordon, D., Hartl, R., Newell, D.W., Servadei, F., Walters, B.C., Wilberger, J.E.: Surgical management of acute epidural hematomas. Neurosurgery 58, S7–15 (2006)
3. Bullock, M.R., Chesnut, R., Ghajar, J., Gordon, D., Hartl, R., Newell, D.W., Servadei, F., Walters, B.C., Wilberger, J.E.: Surgical management of acute subdural hematomas. Neurosurgery 58, S16–24 (2006)

4. Bullock, M.R., Chesnut, R., Ghajar, J., Gordon, D., Hartl, R., Newell, D.W., Servadei, F., Walters, B.C., Wilberger, J.E.: Surgical management of traumatic parenchymal lesions. Neurosurgery 58, S25–46 (2006)
5. Kluge, W., Kretzschmar, K., Roesler, A., Grumme, T.H.: Cerebral and Spinal Computed Tomography, 3rd edn. Blackwell Publishers, Berlin (1998)
6. Cosic, D., Loncaric, S.: A Rule-based Labeling of CT Head Image. In: Proceedings of the 6th Conference on Artificial Intelligence in Medicine Europe, Grenoble, France. LNCS (LNAI), pp. 453–456. Springer, Heidelberg (1997)
7. Hu, Q., Qian, G., Aziz, A., Nowinski, W.L.: Segmentation of brain from computed tomography head images. In: 27th Annual International Conference of the Engineering in Medicine and Biology Society, pp. 3375–3378. IEEE Press, New York (2005)
8. Liao, C.C., Xiao, F., Wong, J.M., Chiang, I.J.: A simple genetic algorithm for tracing the deformed midline on a single slice of brain CT using quadratic Bézier curves. In: 6th IEEE International Conference on Data Mining Workshops, pp. 463–467. IEEE Press, New York (2006)
9. Broderick, J., Connolly, S., Feldmann, E., Hanley, D., Kase, C., Krieger, D., Mayberg, M., Morgenstern, L., Ogilvy, C.S., Vespa, P., Zuccarello, M.: Guidelines for the management of spontaneous intracerebral hemorrhage in adults: 2007 update. Stroke 38, 2001–2023 (2007)
10. Bullock, M.R., Chesnut, R., Ghajar, J., Gordon, D., Hartl, R., Newell, D.W., Servadei, F., Walters, B.C., Wilberger, J.E.: Post-traumatic mass volume measurement in traumatic brain injury patients. Neurosurgery 58, S61 (2006)
11. Quinlan, J.R.: C4.5: Programs for Machine Learning. Morgan Kaufmann, San Mateo, CA (1993)
12. Xia, Y., Hu, Q., Aziz, A., Nowinski, W.L.: A knowledge-driven algorithm for a rapid and automatic extraction of the human cerebral ventricular system from MR neuroimages. Neuroimage 21, 269–282 (2004)

An Adaptive Feature Extractor for Gesture SEMG Recognition

Xu Zhang[1], Xiang Chen[1], Zhang-yan Zhao[1], Qiang Li[1], Ji-hai Yang[1],
Vuokko Lantz[2], and Kong-qiao Wang[3]

[1] Department of Electronics Science & Technology
University of Science & Technology of China, Hefei, China, 230027
zhx90@mail.ustc.edu.cn
[2] Nokia Research Center, Interaction CTC, Interacting in Smart Environments
P.O. Box 407, FI-00045 Nokia Group, Finland
vuokko.lantz@nokia.com
[3] Nokia Research Center, NOKIA (China) Investment CO., LTD., Beijing, 100013

Abstract. This paper proposes an adaptive feature extraction method for pattern recognition of hand gesture action sEMG to enhance the reusability of myoelectric control. The feature extractor is based on wavelet packet transform and Local Discriminant Basis (LDB) algorithms to select several optimized decomposition subspaces of origin SEMG waveforms caused by hand gesture motions. Then the square roots of mean energy of signal in those subspaces are calculated to form the feature vector. In data acquisition experiments, five healthy subjects implement six kinds of hand motions every day for a week. The recognition results of hand gesture on the basis of the measured SEMG signals from different use sessions demonstrate that the feature extractor is effective. Our work is valuable for the realization of myoelectric control system in rehabilitation and other medical applications.

Keywords: Feature Extraction, Surface Electromyogram, Gesture Recognition.

1 Introduction

Myoelectric control has attracted more and more attention for its application in the artificial prosthesis for rehabilitation [1, 2] and virtual input devices [3] for human-computer interfaces. In myoelectric control systems, surface electromyographic (sEMG) sensors are widely used for measuring the activities of the muscular system in a non-intrusive fashion. Detected muscle activities are identified as motion commands which can be used for controlling externally powered devices, for example, the prosthesis for the individuals with amputations.

Accurate recognition of the user's intent based on the measured sEMG signals is the key problem in the realization of myoelectric control. From early 1970', researchers have studied the classification of hand motions such as wrist flexion-extension and supination-pronation by measuring the activities of forearm muscles [2, 4]. However, although the recognition rates have reached above 90 percent in the recent research work, there are still many problems that need to be solved for realizing practical applications of myoelectric control.

D. Zhang (Ed.): ICMB 2008, LNCS 4901, pp. 83–90, 2007.
© Springer-Verlag Berlin Heidelberg 2007

One of the problems is the reusability. Most of the current proposed sEMG pattern identification methods only work on signals from the same use sessions. However, even on the same subjects, the sEMG measured in one day is relatively different from that in another day. The differences of sEMG between different use sessions are mainly caused by slight misplacement of the reinstalled sensors and individual changes of subjects. It is essential to find robust feature extraction methods to extract efficient features independent of both of the above factors.

Recently, the features extracted by time-frequency analysis such as the wavelet packet transform can provide more information about the properties of hand gesture sEMG. Discriminable features for classification of hand motions can often be extracted from some narrow frequency bands of SEMG signal. These features represent the basic properties of each hand motion pattern and are not overly sensitive to sensor misplacement or other typical noises in different use sessions.

This paper proposed an adaptive feature extractor based on the wavelet packet transform and local discriminant basis (LDB) algorithms for pattern recognition of hand gesture sEMG signals in section 2. We recognize six kinds of hand motions on the basis of four channel sEMG signals collected from different days in section 4. The experiment results demonstrate that our method can enhance reusability of myoelectric control.

2 Feature Extractor Based on Wavelet Packet Transform and LDB

In the purpose of forming a feature vector from the hand gesture SEMG signals, Wavelet Packet Transform (WPT) was used as a powerful multi-resolution analysis method [4, 6]. A finite signal x with N points whose scaling space is assumed as $S_{0,0}$ is decomposed into a set of subspaces with different time-frequency localization characteristics. A subspace $S_{j,k}$ is decomposed into two orthogonal subspace $S_{j+1,2k}$ and $S_{j+1,2k+1}$.

$$S_{j,k} = S_{j+1,2k} \oplus S_{j+1,2k+1} \tag{1}$$

where j denotes scale and k indicates the subband index within the scale. Each subspace $S_{j,k}$ is spanned by orthogonal basis vectors $\{w_{j,k,n}\}$, $n = 0, ..., 2^{n_0 - j} - 1$, here $n_0 = \log_2 N$ and the wavelet packet coefficients $D_{j,k}(n)$ at this subspace is calculated by:

$$D_{j,k}(n) = \mathbf{w}_{j,k,n}^T \mathbf{x}_i^{(c)} \tag{2}$$

WPT first expends the origin signal into a redundant set of orthogonal basis with a binary tree structure. To choose the best basis, we use the local discriminant basis algorithm (LDB) proposed by Satio and Coifman [7]. The discriminant measure in LDB is chosen as the symmetric relative entropy:

$$D(\mathbf{p}, \mathbf{q}) = \sum_{i=1}^{n} p_i \log \frac{p_i}{q_i} + \sum_{i=1}^{n} q_i \log \frac{q_i}{p_i} \tag{3}$$

where $\mathbf{p}=\{p_i\}$, $\mathbf{q}=\{q_i\}$, $i=1,2,\ldots,n$ are measures which represent some characteristics of two different classes. Since the total energy of signal is constant during the wavelet package transform, the time-frequency energy map of each class is used for the input parameters to the symmetric relative entropy because it is additive and can make LDB algorithm fast [10]:

$$\Gamma_c(j,k,n) = \sum_{i=1}^{N_c}\left(\mathbf{w}_{j,k,n}^T \mathbf{x}_i^{(c)}\right) \Big/ \sum_{i=1}^{N_c}\left\|\mathbf{x}_i^{(c)}\right\|^2 \qquad (4)$$

where $j=0,1,\ldots J$, $k=0,1,\ldots,2^j\text{-}1$, and $n = 0,\ldots,2^{n_0-j}-1$. $\left\{x_i^{(c)}\right\}_{i=1}^{N_c}$ is a set of training signals belonging to class c. Then the symmetric relative entropy of the subspace $S_{j,k}$ for C classes can be written from the (2) and (3):

$$D\left(\left\{\Gamma_c(j,k,\bullet)\right\}_{c=1}^C\right) = \sum_{n=1}^{2^{n_0-j}-1} D\left(\Gamma_1(j,k,n),\ldots,\Gamma_C(j,k,n)\right) \qquad (5)$$

The LDB maximizes the discriminant measure on the time-frequency energy distributions of classes. It uses the bottom-to-top search method to compare the children nodes $S_{j+1,2k}$ and $S_{j+1,2k+1}$ with the parent node $S_{j,k}$. If the discriminant measure in the parent node is smaller than the sum of that in two children nodes, we keep the children nodes, otherwise prune the children nodes and keep the parent node. We also order the output of LDB according to the discriminant measures in every subspace and select several subspaces with maximum discriminant measures.

Instead of the relative wavelet packet energy in some predetermined subspaces in [6], the square roots of the mean energy in every subspaces selected by LDB are used to form the feature vector of original signal. The square root of the mean energy in subspace $S_{j,k}$ is:

$$F = \sqrt{E\left[\left\|D_{j,k}(n)\right\|^2\right]} \qquad (6)$$

According to the sets of LDB, the feature vector may be formed to represent the origin signal and then sent to the classifier in pattern recognition procedure. We call this feature extraction method is Optimized Wavelet Packet Energy Distribution (OWPED), since the features can be extracted by the energy distribution in optimized subspaces selected by discriminant measures.

3   SEMG Signal Processing Method

3.1   Active Segmentation

The SEMG signals, recorded in the process of the hand gesture actions, are called active segments. Every active segment may represent a hand gesture action. The detection of active segments was based on the average signal of the four sEMG channels: first, compute the square of the average value of the four sEMG signal channels according to (7); then, apply the moving average algorithm with window size $N=60$ samples on the squared average sEMG signal according to (8); next, threshold the signal by preserving the values exceeding a certain threshold value TH and setting the others to 0, as defined in (9). Finally, determine the beginning and ending points of the gesture action sEMG segments. At the last step, abandon segments whose length is less than a certain value as a measurement noise.

$$SEMG_{averaged}(i) = \left[\frac{1}{L} \sum_{l=1}^{L} SEMG_l(i) \right]^2 \qquad i \le M \tag{7}$$

where L is the number of channels.

$$SEMG_{M\_A}(i) = \frac{1}{N} \sum_{j=i}^{i+N} SEMG_{averaged}(j) \qquad i \le M - N \tag{8}$$

$$SEMG_{rectified}(i) = \begin{cases} SEMG_{M\_A}(i); & if \quad SEMG_{M\_A}(i) \ge TH \\ 0 & ; \quad if \quad SEMG_{M\_A} \le TH \end{cases} \tag{9}$$

Figure 1 illustrates the extraction of the gesture active segments. The top four sub-figures correspond to the four channels of raw sEMG signals and the bottom one shows the rectified signal after the averaging and threshold steps. Every active segment is separated and the active segment intervals are masked. The names of every hand motions are also listed below the active segments. As we can see from Figure 3, the described segmentation method can detect gesture action signals effectively from continuous sEMG measurements.

3.2 Feature Extraction and Classification

In the pattern recognition procedure, feature vectors were extracted from the active segments. As the section 2 shown, the OWPED was proposed as feature extractor. Discreet wavelet packet transform was used to decompose signals in every active segment. The depth of decomposing level was specified as five and the Daubechies 2 was used as mother wavelet. Then, LDB algorithm was implemented to determine the best basis. The LDB was constructed independently for each channel to increase the class separability [4]. We specified the number of selected subspaces of the output from the LDB of each channel as ten and extracted the square root of the mean energy as features, so that there were 40-dimension features from every active segment.

Principal Component Analysis (PCA) was also proposed to compress the features. In the PCA learning procedure, the covariance matrix from the feature vectors of active segments was calculated. We selected twenty eigenvectors corresponding to the twenty largest eigenvalues from the covariance matrix as the PCA projection matrix used for the dimensionality compression. As the result of PCA procedure, the feature vectors can be compressed into twenty dimensions, which can approximate the class distribution of origin features [4].

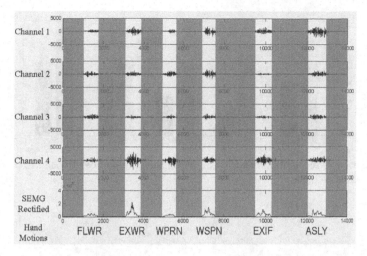

Fig. 1. Illustration of segmentation for hand gesture action sEMG signal

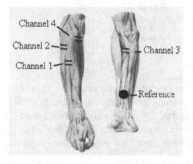

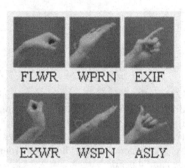

Fig. 2. The four channels sensor placement. The background anatomical picture is adapted from [9].

Fig. 3. Six classes of hand gesture used for recognition

Table 1. The results of recognition of six classes of hand motions SEMG from five days on subject 1

		Hand Gesture Motion Recognized:						Correct
		FLWR	EXWR	WPRN	WSPN	EXIF	ASLY	Rate
Gesture Class	FLWR	71	0	0	8	1	0	88.7%
	EXWR	0	77	1	0	0	2	96.2%
	WPRN	1	0	76	1	2	0	95.0%
	WSPN	1	0	0	73	6	0	91.2%
	EXIF	0	0	0	2	78	0	97.5%
	ASLY	0	1	0	0	0	79	98.7%
						Average Classification Rate:		94.6%

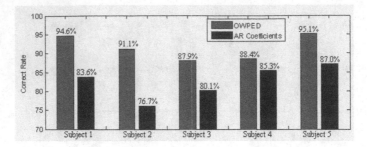

Fig. 4. The average recognition results comparison between the OWPED and AR coefficients feature extraction method

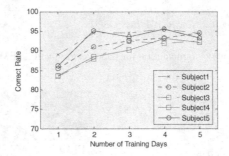

Fig. 5. The effect of training time on average recognition rate of five subjects with training data from different days. The number "1" in horizontal axis means the 20 active segments of SEMG used for training came from the only one day; the number "2" means the training data came from two days and 10 active segments per day; "3" means training data from three days and 7 per day; "4" means training data from four days and 5 per day; "5" means training data from five days and 4 per day.

The classifier used in this paper is the Linear Discriminant Classifier (LDC) [8]. Since AR model coefficients are thought to be sufficient features for sEMG classification [5], The AR model were also employed to be compared with OWPED as the feature extractor in pattern recognition procedure.

4   Experimental Results

4.1   SEMG Acquisition

Delsys Myomonitor IV multiple channel sensor system with inbuilt band-pass filters (20-1000 Hz) and amplifier (60 dB) was used for the sEMG signal record. In each channel, there are two silver bar-shaped electrodes with 10mm x 1mm contact dimension and 10mm electrode-to-electrode spacing. The four channel sensors are placed on *M.extensor digitorum communis*, *M.extensor carpi ulnaris*, *M.palmaris longus* and *M.supinator*, as the Figure 2 shown. The sample rate is 2048Hz.

Five healthy right-handed subjects with ages ranging from 20 to 26 years implemented six classes of hand motion in five different days. The hand motions used were

FLWR (flexion of wrist), EXWR (extension of wrist), WPRN (wrist pronation), WSPN (wrist supination), EXIF (extension of index finger), and ASLY (extension of thumb and little finger), which are shown in Figure 3. In every day's experiments, subjects performed six different hand motions in a sequence and in a way they felt natural to them. Each hand motion was repeated more than 20 times. One gesture action lasted about 1 second, and the interval between the gesture actions was about 1-2 seconds.

4.2 The Recognition Results

The 10 beginning active segments in each class from the first two days, 20 active segments in total, were used for OWPED learning and classifier training, and the other 80 active segments from five different days were used for testing. A typical recognition result from one subject is listed in Table 1. Most of the hand motions in six classes even from five different days were recognized with above 90% average correct rate using the OWPED feature extractor.

For the comparison between OWPED and AR coefficients features, both of the two kinds of feature extractor were used to form feature vectors from the same SEMG datasets. The averaged recognition results in five subjects were listed in the histogram shown in Figure 4. The OWPED features perform better than the AR coefficient features with higher average recognition rate in all of the five subjects. This results show that the method proposed in this paper achieves good performance in pattern recognition of hand gesture motion SEMG signals from different days.

In addition, the relationship between recognition accuracy and the number of days used to form training data sets was also explored in this paper. 20 active segments from different number of days were chosen for training. The effect of training days on the average recognition rates of six kinds of hand motions for each subject is shown in Figure 5. The data used for training from more days, the performance of hand gestures recognition may be improved consequently with higher pattern recognition rate. It accords with the statistic perspective that training dataset from more days contains more details about every hand motion pattern. From Figure 5, it is also suggested that the relatively effective choice of number of days for training is three, because the recognition results improve obviously when the number added into three for most of subjects in our experiments and the recognition performance change slightly when the number is specified as 3, 4, or more.

5 Conclusions

An adaptive feature extractor called OWPED based on the WPT and LDB algorithms is proposed for the pattern recognition of surface EMG caused by hand gesture motions in this paper. In the OWPED learning procedure, discriminable features were extracted from several narrow frequency bands with the ability of time-frequency analysis. Hand gesture sEMG signals were collected during various days. The experimental results of six kinds of hand gesture SEMG recognition demonstrate that our method is effective and can enhance the reusability of myoelectric control. Despite of the changes of SEMG from different days, the OWPED can be regarded to automatically extract something unchanged that can represent the class characteristics. We also suggest that three is the sufficient number of days to form the training datasets for stable performance in practical application. This work is valuable for the realization of myoelectric control system in rehabilitation for multi-functional prosthesis design and other medical applications using human-computer interface.

Acknowledgement

This work is supported by National Nature Science Foundation of China: 60703069. The authors would also like to thank all the volunteers for their help to do data collecting experiments.

References

1. Francis, H.Y.C., Yang, Y.-S., Lam, F.K., Zhang, Y.-T., Parker, P.A.: Fuzzy EMG Classification for Prosthesis Control. IEEE Transactions on Rehabilitation Engineering 8(3), 305–311 (2000)
2. Ajiboye, A.B., Weir, R.F.ff.: A Heuristic Fuzzy Logic Approach to EMG Pattern Recognition for Multifunctional Prosthesis Control. IEEE Transactions on Neural Systems & Rehabilitation Engineering 13(3), 280–291 (2005)
3. Wheeler, K.R., Jorgensen, C.C.: Gestures as Input: Neuroelectric Joysticks and Keyboards, Pervasive computing, 1536–1268 (2003)
4. Chu, J.-U., Moon, I., Kim, S.-K., Mun, M.-S.: Control of Multifunction Myoelectric Hand using a Real-Time EMG Pattern Recognition. In: Intelligent Robots and Systems, pp. 3511–3516. IEEE, Los Alamitos (2005)
5. Knox, R., Brooks, D.H.: Classification of Multifunction Surface EMG using Advanced AR Model Representations. In: Bioengineering Conference, pp. 96–98. IEEE, Boston, MA (1994)
6. Hu, X., Wang, Z., Ren, X.: Classification of surface EMG signal using relative wavelet packet energy. Computer Methods and Programs in Biomedicine 79, 189–195 (2005)
7. Saito, N., Coifman, R.R.: Local discriminant bases and their applications. Journal of Mathematical Imaging and Vision 5(4), 337–358 (1995)
8. Liu, C., Wechsler, H.: Robust coding schemes for indexing and retrieval from large face databases. IEEE Trans. Image Processing 9, 132–137 (2000)
9. Gao, S., Yu, Q.: Atlas of Human Anatomy (Revision), Shanghai scientific & Technical Publishers (1998)

Approach to Health Supporting System Using Traditional Chinese Medicine

Tadashi Watsuji[1], Shoji Shinohara[1], and Seizaburo Arita[2]

[1] Department of Traditional Acupuncture and Moxibustion,
Meiji University of Oriental Medicine, Honoda Hinotani 6-1, Hiyoshi-cho,
629-0392 Nantan City Kyoto, Japan
{t_watsuji,s_shinohara}@meiji-u.ac.jp
[2] Department of Mathematics, Kansai Medical University,
573-1136 Uyamahigashimachi 18-89, Hirakata City, Osaka, Japan

Abstract. The primary prevention of disease related to the lifestyle is an essential theme in medical research. Preventing before it arises is the important concept in traditional Chinese medicine (TCM). Since TCM, which emphasizes individual physical condition in medical treatment, has recently attracted considerable attention globally, objective diagnostic methods in TCM have been investigated in this work. Firstly, the fuzzy theory was applied to develop a tongue diagnosis supporting system based on the tongue diagnosis in TCM. Secondly, the usefulness of TCM health questionnaire was examined to identify individual physical condition. Our results suggest that the TCM health questionnaire is useful in the construction of a health supporting system based on TCM.

1 Development and Verification of the Tongue Diagnosis Supporting System in Traditional Chinese Medicine Using the Fuzzy Theory

1.1 Introduction

In traditional Chinese medicine, various mental and physical conditions are examined using the 5 senses, and syndromes are diagnosed. It has been indicated that diagnosis based on physician's experience may be subjective and lacking objectivity. Therefore, it is desirable to present traditional Chinese medicine as an objective and theoretical diagnostic system. Among diagnostic methods by traditional Chinese medicine, tongue diagnosis is one of the strongest diagnostic methods of objectivity. Firstly, the authors developed a tongue diagnosis supporting system based on the tongue diagnosis in traditional Chinese medicine using the fuzzy theory. And the system was evaluated using clinical data. Secondly, in order to enhance an accuracy of the diagnostic system, the author examined the relationship between observation of the tongue and syndrome diagnosis, and performed development of a tongue diagnosis supporting system based on the physician's diagnostic process using the fuzzy theory and verification using clinical data.

The doctor diagnosed the patient's syndrome and indicated tongue findings based on traditional tongue diagnosis. Then the doctor input the findings (of the tongue diagnosis) into the diagnostic system using fuzzy logic. System Ver.1 was used to evaluate clinical data from 80 patients (mean age; 62.9 yo, 24 males and 56 females).

D. Zhang (Ed.): ICMB 2008, LNCS 4901, pp. 91–98, 2007.
© Springer-Verlag Berlin Heidelberg 2007

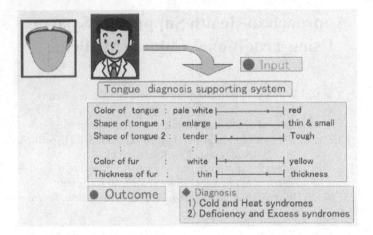

Fig. 1. Structure of Tongue diagnosis supporting system

1.2 Methodology

The system was evaluated using clinical data in 73 patients. The observation of tongue and diagnosis of syndromes performed by 37 physicians in traditional Chinese medicine were examined using images of the tongue. The physicians' logic of diagnosis of tongue syndromes was also evaluated. Based on these evaluations, we improved the tongue supporting system, and examined the accuracy of diagnosis with the system using clinical data in 80 patients and their syndromes diagnosed by the physicians.

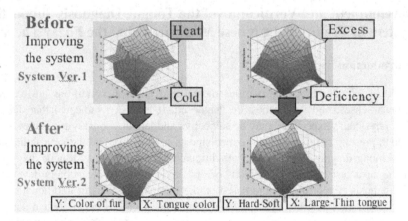

Fig. 2. Comparison of the system's If-then rule (fuzzy logic). This Figure 2 shows two If-then rules (rules involving Cold-Heat syndromes, Deficiency-Excess syndromes) of the system by three dimensions. Both rules were changed to improving the system as shown in figure. As for the rule, one result is output from two input variables. For example, Result of the Cold-Heat syndromes is output by two input variables (Color of fur value and Tongue color value). Fuzzy logic (MATLAB, MathWorks, Inc.) was used.

Table 1. Accuracy of the tongue diagnosis supporting system. The accuracy of diagnosis using the tongue diagnosis supporting system was above 70% for both cold and heat syndromes, and deficiency and excess syndromes by evaluation of the results obtained by the system and physicians in traditional Chinese medicine.

Accuracy	Cold-Heat syndromes	Deficiency-Excess syndromes
Before Improving	53.8 %	53.8 %
After Improving	70.0 %	71.3 %

1.3 Results

1) Diagnosis of cold and heat syndromes in the tongue was closely related to its color.
2) Diagnosis of deficiency and excess syndromes was performed based on the tongue's roughness - tenderness, and teeth prints on the tongue. It was found from the research that the evaluation of observation of the tongue and syndrome diagnosis differ with physician's clinical experience.
3) The accuracy of diagnosis using the tongue diagnosis supporting system was higher than 70% in both cold and heat syndromes, and deficiency and excess syndromes by evaluation of the results obtained by the system and the physicians in traditional Chinese medicine (Figure 2, Table 1).

1.4 Conclusions

It was suggested that diagnosis of syndromes in the tongue from its observation could be objectively presented by constructing a tongue diagnosis supporting system developed using the fuzzy theory.

2 Study of Health Supporting System Using Traditional Chinese Medicine

2.1 Introduction

In recent years, with the increase in lifestyle disease, and the change in disease structure, individually fitted medical treatments have come to be sought after. For this reason, traditional Chinese medicine (TCM) is being reassessed globally. In Japan, the aging of society coupled with the health trend has resulted in an increased social need for oriental medicine compared to several years ago.

Our task should prove the usefulness of TCM so that it may be utilized in modern medicine. This consists of making clear whether or not abnormalities of physical condition are accurately diagnosed with the medical examination observations of TCM. Accordingly, to construct a health supporting system based on TCM, a questionnaire for identifying individual physical condition with TCM was used in our investigation. The results of questionnaire were compared with the results of examination, and the usefulness of the oriental medicine health questionnaire was investigated. In addition, it is expected that this health questionnaire will be incorporated in the health supporting system.

2.2 Methodology

The subjects of the study were eight adult volunteers (Average, 22.3±2.7 years), to observe change with time; every other day in the afternoon for a total of six times, a medical examination and inspection were carried out under standardized conditions after rest.

2.2.1 Diagnostic Methods of TCM
During the medical examination observations of TCM were made of the complexion, tongue, auscultation, and pulse. An interview was also conducted.

2.2.2 Tongue Diagnosis Supporting System
A tongue diagnosis supporting system was used; cold - heat, deficiency - excess were diagnosed. Additionally, the tongue diagnosis supporting system was a system of applied fuzzy set theory (Figure 1). The system is composed of 10 rules with one rule including the if-then rules of 47. Fuzzy logic (MATLAB, MathWorks, Inc.) was used.

2.2.3 TCM Health Questionnaire and SF-8
The TCM health questionnaire and SF-8™ Health Surveys (SF-8) [1] were carried out. The TCM health questionnaire was created at Meiji University of TCM in 2005. The TCM health questionnaire diagnoses the 17 syndromes of Oriental medicine. The Severity of each symptom was classified in 4 stages, serious (3), moderate (2), slight (1), none (0), and the score of each syndrome is calculated, a maximum score is 15 points. Moreover the grade of each syndrome judged by the totaled points (Table 2). To examine the usefulness of the TCM health questionnaire, it was compared with the SF-8 health QOL scale.

Table 2. Grade of each syndrome judged by the totaled points on the TCM health questionnaire

	Grade	Total Score
1	Health	0 ~ 4
2	Pre-symptom	5 ~ 9
3	Disease	10 ~ 15

2.2.4 Objective Examination
Objective examination was made and measurements such as skin temperature of the face, electro-cardiogram, and respiration were made. The voice was recorded and an aspect such as the vocal spectrum was analyzed. We used the Spearman's correlation coefficient by rank, Simple regression, a P value of < 0.05 was considered to indicate

statistical significance. All statistical analyses were performed on a personal computer with the statistical package StatView5.0 for Macintosh.

2.3 Results

2.3.1 Relationship Between the TCM Health Questionnaire and Tongue Diagnosis Supporting System

No connection was observed between the score on the TCM health questionnaire and the output value of the tongue diagnosis support system. Furthermore, the change in the cold syndrome - heat syndrome or deficiency syndrome - excess syndrome score of the TCM health questionnaire for each case often differed from the output value for change given by the tongue diagnosis supporting system.

2.3.2 Relationship Between the TCM Health Questionnaire and Heart Rate

A correlation was observed between heart(R=0.59, p<0.0001) and lung (R=0.42, p=0.019) items of the TCM health questionnaire and heart rate in all cases. However the score on each item of the personal TCM health questionnaire had no connection with heart rate.

2.3.3 Relationship Between the TCM Health Questionnaire and the Voice Information

A correlation between the deficiency of qi score on the personal TCM health questionnaire and the fundamental frequency of the voice was observed in four cases. Additionally, a correlation was observed between the deficiency of qi (R=0.59, p<0.0001) or deficiency of constitution on the TCM health questionnaire and the fundamental frequency in all cases (Fig 3).

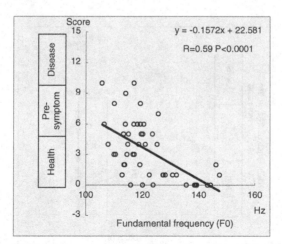

Fig. 3. Relationship between the deficiency scores on the TCM health questionnaire and the fundamental frequency of the voice

2.3.4 Relationship Between the TCM Health Questionnaire and SF-8

A connection between the TCM health questionnaire deficiency of qi or deficiency of constitution score and the PCM of SF-8 was observed for only two cases. In all cases the results of the TCM health questionnaire showed a trend primarily related to the PCS of SF-8 (Physical component summary). Additionally, a correlation was observed between a deficiency of qi or deficiency(R=0.53, p=0.0009) of constitution on the TCM health questionnaire and the fundamental frequency in all cases (Fig 4). However a deficiency on the TCM health questionnaire had no correlation with the MCS of SF-8 (Fig 5).

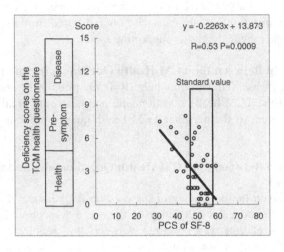

Fig. 4. Relationship between the deficiency scores on the TCM health questionnaire and the PCS of SF-8

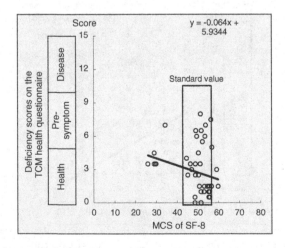

Fig. 5. Relationship between the deficiency scores on the TCM health questionnaire and the MCS of SF-8

2.4 Discussion

2.4.1 Relationship Between the TCM Health Questionnaire and Tongue Diagnosis Supporting System

Hitherto, a few diagnosis supporting systems that apply TCM have been created[2,3]. These TCM diagnosis supporting systems were primarily for determining deficient constitution and it was difficult to use them for identifying sequential changes in physical condition. Accordingly, we are engaged with the development of a health supporting system that perceives individual physical condition over time. The diagnosis supporting system utilizing observation of the tongue has been already constructed[4,5]. If there is some specific evidence of disease, it is possible to track its chronological change with this system. Essentially, TCM integrates complexion and tongue diagnosis, voice information, heart and body status, and pulse rate to judge various changes in physical condition. From this information, and joined together with information from the medical examination, judgments of physical condition are necessary. Accordingly, in this investigation we simply examined the usefulness of the TCM health questionnaire that makes it possible to perceive the status of the heart and the body. As a result, the change in score on the TCM health questionnaire did not correlate with the change in the output value of the tongue diagnosis supporting system, and showed a different change of pattern. From the observed connection between the TCM health questionnaire deficiency of qi score and the fundamental frequency of the voice, it is suggested that changes in physical condition such as fatigue can be perceived with this health questionnaire. Furthermore, the results of the TCM health questionnaire primarily show a trend connecting with the PCS (physical component summary) of SF-8. According to another investigation, the results of the TCM health questionnaire relate to MCS more than PCS. This suggests that utilizing the results of the TCM health questionnaire is useful to construct the TCM health supporting system. By integrating the information from each medical examination, it is possible to create a health supporting system that applies TCM.

Hereafter, we would like to increase the number of cases in the study, and develop a health supporting system that can individually track chronological physical condition.

Acknowledgement

This study was supported in part by a scientific research grant from the Ministry of Education, Culture, Sports, Science and Technology in Japan.

References

1. Fukuhara, S., Suzukamo, Y.: Manual of the SF-8 Japanese version. Institute for Health Outcomes & Process Evaluation Research. Kyoto Japan (2004)
2. Kitmura, S., Tsuji, S., Mori, E., et al.: An Expert System for Classification Base on Symptoms in Oriental Medicine. J of Systems and Control 30(1), 37–38 (1986)

3. Shinohara, S., Yano, T., Kitade, T., et al.: Development of Acupuncture Clinical Educational Support (ACSE) system (2nd Report) J. of the Japan Society of Acupuncture 37(1), 125 (1987)
4. Watsuji, T.: Development and Verification of the Tongue Diagnosis Supporting System in Traditional Chinese medicine using the Fuzzy Theory (Japan). The Bulletin of Meiji University of Oriental Medicine 33, 11–33 (2003)
5. Watsuji, T., Shinohara, S., Arita, S.: Construction of Supporting System in traditional Chinese medicine using fuzzy theory. J of Biomedical Fuzzy Systems Association, Japan, 23–29 (2003)

A Multimodal Database for a Home Remote Medical Care Application

Hamid Medjahed[1,2], Dan Istrate[1], Jerome Boudy[2], François Steenkeste[3], Jean-Louis Baldinger[2], and Bernadette Dorizzi[2]

[1] RMSE/ESIGETEL, 1 rue du Port de Valvins,
77215 Avon-Fontainebleau cedex, France
{hamid.medjahed,dan.istrate}@esigetel.fr
[2] EPH/INT, 9 rue Charles Fourier,
91011 Evry, France
{hamid.medjahed,jerome.boudy,jean-louis.baldinger,
bernadette.dorizzi}@int-edu.eu
[3] U558/INSERM,37 allées Jules Guesde,
31073 Toulouse Cedex, France
{steenkeste.f}@chu-toulouse.fr

Abstract. The home remote monitoring systems aim to make a protective contribution to the well being of individuals (patients, elderly persons) requiring moderate amounts of support for independent living spaces, and improving their everyday life. Existing researches of these systems suffer from lack of experimental data and a standard medical database intended for their validation and improvement. This paper presents a multi-sensors environment for acquiring and recording a multimodal medical database, which includes physiological data (cardiac frequency, activity or agitation, posture, fall), environment sounds and localization data. It provides graphical interface functions to manage, process and index these data. The paper focuses on the system implementation, its usage and it points out possibilities for future work.

1 Introduction

Today, the elderly is becoming an increasing part of the whole population, and the capacities of admission in the hospitals are limited. Consequently, several medical remote systems have been developed but there are few commercial solutions and business models. These specific research projects are scattered and they vary in their purposes and concepts. These systems focus either on implementing a generic architecture for the integrated medical information system, on improving the daily life of patients using various automatic devices, specific equipment, and basic alarm, or on providing healthcare services to patients suffering from specific diseases like asthma diabetes, cardiac, pulmonary, or Alzheimer.

Among existing systems, there is the TelePat project [1]: agitation, posture and cardiac rate data extracted from different sensors by a microcontroller based computing unit, are sent through radio connection to a remote central server

D. Zhang (Ed.): ICMB 2008, LNCS 4901, pp. 99–106, 2007.

application for exploitation and alarm decision. Currently, in the frame of the Tandem project(national project founded by the French RNTS program), additional accelerometer sensors,initially designed in previous TelePat project are implemented this system for the detection of falls. D. Istrate et al. have presented in [2] an overview of projects related to home health telecare [3] where a system of multi-channel sound acquisition charged to analyse in real time the home sound environment to detect abnormal noises (i.e., call for helps or screams) is integrated to the Health Integrated Smart Home Information System for data fusion. The most crucial issue for all these devices is the lack of experimental data and information representing many situations and many people's profiles.

In order to develop and evaluate telemonitoring systems, it is very important to have a multimodal medical database. We have developed an environment for acquiring and recording a multimodal database where a user can interpret a patients activity by following a scenario which summarizes the everyday life of a patient. Our software implementation gathers three subsystems which have been technically validated from end to end, through their hardware and software. This specific platform is multimodal since it allows us to record physiological data via RFpat [4] subsystem, audio information via Anason [5] subsystem and patient's localization through infra-red sensors via Gardien [6] subsystem. Taking into account the multimodaldata character of the data, a multidimensional-indexing process is used in order to obtain a full description of data sets. Additional process of simulation is currently under finalization and will be integrated in our platform as a way to overcome the lack of experimental data and the difficulty of recording some medical data such as the cardiac frequency during distress situations. For these reasons building a platform of acquiring, recording, simulating and indexing a multimodal medical database seems to us of a great benefit for evaluating and improving medical remote systems. The main goals of this database recording platform are twofold:

- First to design and develop data fusion-based decision algorithms exploiting the measurements obtained from this platform in order to propose new processes to reinforce the secure detection of patient's distress events, in particular the fall situations: indeed one or more televigilance modalities might be out of order, or a particular environmental situation (ambiant noise, bad wireless conditions, sensors disabilities) can hide one particular modality or more. This is a very challenging issue for hospital emergency units such as for instance SAMU in France or Telecare services providers in general.
- Secondly to allow a better description and investigation on Telecare situations for the patient at home: indeed the lack of real emergency situations data has strongly motivated our idea to develop simulation routines that would be easily adapted to the platform, for instance to simulate cardiac profiles or fall situations, or even correlated ones. This work developped for some years in GET [1] and for more time in TIMC and CLIPS [2] has for target to create a more diverse and close to real patients situations.

2   System Architecture

We define an intelligent environment as one that is able to acquire and apply knowledge about its inhabitants and their surroundings in order to adapt to the inhabitant and to improve its comfort and efficiency. To record the multimodal medical database our first aim is focused on providing such an environment. We consider our environment as an intelligent agent, which perceives the state of the environment using sensors and acts upon the environment using device controllers.

The first part of this intelligent environment was realised within the framework of TelePat project, in order to study the secure detection of patient's fall event. This database is developed in the frame of project Tandem (RNTS 2005).

2.1   Hardware Architecture

Our platform is installed in our laboratory and it consists in a simulated flat of 20 m^2 surface which is arranged in two rooms with a technical area in order to evaluate and to supervise the experiments. It integrate smart sensors(infra-red, audio, physiologic) linked to a PC. The two microphones for audio surveillance are linked to the PC through an external sound card, and can be interpreted as a single smart audio sensor for the Anason software. Eight infra-red sensors are fixed on specific places of the house (walls and ceiling), they are linked to an acquisition card (ADAM)[7], which is linked to the serial port of the PC. The card output is RS485 which is converted in RS232 in order to allow Gardien software to acquire the patient position at any time. The RFpat subsystem is composed of two main components: (1) a wearable terminal worn by the patient, continuously recording his physiological data and urgency call, (2) an in-door reception base station linked to the PC via RS232 serial link providing informations every 30 seconds. The layout of our environment house is shown in Figure 1.

2.2   Software Architecture

The multimodal system has three main subsystems like in Figure 2 and provides a general user interface which encapsulates the Anason subsystem. It is

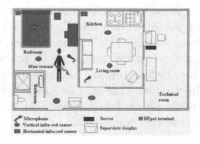

Fig. 1. Layout of the environment house

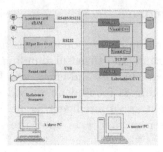

Fig. 2. Software architecture of the system

implemented under LabWindows/CVI software and communicates with RFpat subsystem and Gardien subsystem by client-server model using TCP/IP and appropriate application protocols. Gardien is implemented under C++ and recovers data every 500 ms. RFpat is also implemented under C++ and receives data from receiver every 30 s. The use of the inter-module communication through TCP/IP socket allows each module (subsystem) to be run on a different computer, and to synchronize each televigilance modality channel. The user can interact with the system via internet navigator and supervises the different applications. For instance, we use this web server to communicate with the person, who interprets a patients activity by displaying a reference scenario on the monitoring screen. This feedback provides a significant help to the system manipulation and the system flexibility obtained through TCP/IP socket communication allows to add other potential sensors such as a heart monitoring sensor (ECG).

3   Technical Performance of the System and Usage

Several tests have been elaborated to validate the hardware and the software implementations. Firstly, different measurements were realized with all the sensors inside the environment in order to test their operation one by one. Secondly we have validated each subsystem through predefined standard scenarios, defined and specified for each one. These standard scenarios are performed before each recording in order to calibrate the system. Figure 3 shows the front panel of the software system. The user must firstly select the modality to record and to configure its relative parametrisation as shown in Figure 4. RFpat and Gardien need only to select the IP address and the TC/IP port number, while Anason requires the selection of the sound card (if two are present), the sampling rate and the location of the backup file. Before running the recording, a reference scenario must be selected from the Scenarios menu. This graphical interface can globally show the whole data of our multimodal database and enables us to visualize in a graph the real time evolution of some data.

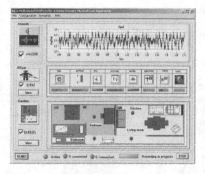

Fig. 3. General interface during the acquisition step

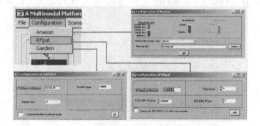

Fig. 4. Graphical interface configuration for each subsystem

4   The Reference Scenario

In order to support the person simulating a type of a patient and a given situation, recordings performed by using pre-defined scenario leading him during the recording process. The software system allows to write or to modify different scenarios via graphical interface, and save them in an XML annotation file (Figure 5).

This graphical interface is composed of two parts: the first one concerned with personal information relative to the person to be recorded (see Figure 5), the second one is dedicated to the scenario edition (cf. Figure 6) using a table composed of columns corresponding to each sensor to be activated and a summary on the actions to be carried out. The scenario is described by the expected output from each modality like the room for infrared sensors or the recorded sound for sound modality. These reference scenarios are based on real situations and they aim to reflect the everyday life of a patient. The scenarios are divided into two categories: either a critical scenario with one or more distress events, or a normal one. These scenarios are automatically displayed on the monitoring screen during the recording step as show in Figure 6.

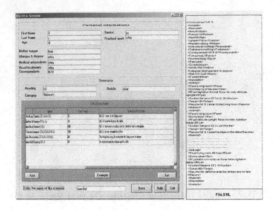

Fig. 5. Graphical interface for writing scenario and the XML file corresponding

Fig. 6. Graphical interface for displaying scenario

5   The Multimodal Medical Database

Data acquired from the patient are stored on the Master PC in a folder named with a code number corresponding to the patient. Each recording is composed from five files corresponding to the different subsystems.

The first one, named personnel.xml, contains the patient's identifier and some personal information like age, native language, usual drugs treatment...etc. The second, named scenario.xml, describes the reference scenario. All these data relative to the actor are protected for his privacy and let to his agreement.

The sound data is saved in real time, in a wav file with 16 bit of resolution and a sampling rate of 16 KHz, a frequency usually used for speech applications.

The clinical data acquired from RFpat are saved in a separate file which contains information about patient's attitude (lied down or upright/seated), his agitation (between 0% and 100%), his cardiac frequency, fall events and urgency call in a binary type. The acquisition sample rate is 0.03 Hz.

The data acquired every 500 ms by Gardien subsystem are saved in a separate text adapted file format. Each line of this file contains the infra-red sensors which are excited (they are represented by hexadecimal numbers from 1 to D) plus the corresponding date and hour.

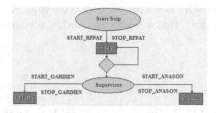

Fig. 7. Schematic of the synchronization between the three subsystems

To tackle the problem of the variety of each data sampling rates, a synchronization prototype between the three subsystems is obtained through TCP/IP protocol. The RFpat modality is started in first position, because of his low acquisition rate. After RFpat has been started a supervisor software launches Gardien and Anason applications with TCP/IP commands (Figure 7).

Thus, our multimodal database acquisition software provides a very helpful and well-targeted application to elaborate and assess the data fusion-based decision methods. The low level data recorded by our system will be useful for the development of each modality processing algorithms and their combination strategies.

In order to index our multimodal database, we have retained the SAM standard indexing file [8] generally used for Speech Databases descriptions. The SAM labelling of a sound file indicates information about the file and describes it by delimiting the useful part for analyzing and processing. For each modality of the database a corresponding indexing file is created, we have adapted this type of files to the specificities of each modality, and we have added another indexing file for the entire database. This conceptual indexation model is guided by a priori knowledge and the reference scenarios. This aims to obtain the reference information for our Multimodal Database, and therefore to generate a novel type of database to validate different modality signal processing techniques and approaches of multimodal data fusion algorithms.

6   Conclusions and Perspectives

In this study, we have developed a new multi sensors environment for recording a multimodal medical database including patients clinical data, usual environment sounds and patient localization. The originality of this system is the synchronized combination of three different televigilance modalities for recording a multimodal database and automatically generating its indexation. In relation to experimentation, integrating a simulation process to our platform enables us to have a full and tightly controlled universe of data sets and to evaluate the decision part of remote monitoring systems. Telemedicine systems can significantly benefit from this multimodal database, since a large sets of data representative of several situations and many people's profiles can easily be generated. A better a posteriori knowledge of parameters observed at home and the trends of their joint variations will be provided by the simulation process. This database fully responds to the crucial need for an objective and systematic evaluation of promising multimodal data fusion methods that are currently investigated and developed.

References

1. Boudy, J., Baldinger, J.L., Delavault, F., Irosita, Dr., Andreao, R., Torres-Muller, S., Serra, A., Rocaries, F., Dietrich, C., Lacombe, A., Steenkeste, F., Bear, Dr., M., Ozguler, Dr., Gaiti, D.: Telemedecine for elderly patients at home,The telepat project. In: ICOST conference. Belfast (2006)
2. Virone, G., Istrate, D., Vacher, M., Serignat, J.F., Noury, N., Demongeot, J.: First Steps in Data Fusion between a Multichannel Audio Acquisition and an Information System for Home Healthcare. In: Engineering In Medicine And Biology Society Conference, pp. 1364–1367. IEEE, Cancun Mexique (2003)
3. Bellego, G.L., Noury, N., Virone, G., Mousseau, M., Domongeot, J.: Measurement and model of the activity of a patient in his hospital suite. In: TITB, vol. 10, pp. 92–99. IEEE, Los Alamitos (2006)
4. Baldinger, J.L., Boudy, J., Dorizzi, B., Levrey, J.P., Andreo, R., Perpere, C., Devault, F., Rocaries, F., Deitrich, C., Lacombe, A.: Tele-surveillance System for Patient at Home,The MEDEVILLE system. In: ICCHP, Paris (2004)
5. Istrate, D., Castelli, E., Vacher, M., Besacier, L., Serignat, J.F.: Information extraction from sound for medical telemonitoring. Transactions on Information Technology in Biomedicine 10(2), 264–274 (2006)
6. Banerjee, S., Steenkeste, F., Couturier, P., Debray, M., Franco, A.: Telesurveillance of elderly patients by use of passive infra-red sensors in a smart room. J. Telemed. Telecare, 23–29 (2003)
7. Steenkeste, F., Bocquet, H., Chan, M., Vellas, B.: Remote monitoring system for elders in a geriatric hospital. In: Promoting Independence and quality of life for older persons: An international conference on aging, Arlington (1999)
8. Well, D., Barry, J., Grice, W., Fourcin, M., Gibbon, A.: SAM ESPRIT PROJECT 2589-multilingual speech input/output assessment, methodology and standardization. Final report. Technical Report SAM-UCLG004, University College London (1992)

Adaptive Segmentation and Feature Quantization of Sublingual Veins of Healthy Humans

Zifei Yan and Naimin Li

School of Computer Science and Technology
Harbin Institute of Technology (HIT), Harbin, 150001 China
yanzifei@hit.edu.cn

Abstract. The Sublingual Vein Diagnosis, one part of Tongue Diagnosis, plays an important role in deciding the healthy condition of humans. This paper focuses on establishing a feature quantization framework for the inspection of sublingual veins of healthy humans, composed of two parts: the segmentation of sublingual veins of healthy humans and the feature quantization of them. Firstly, a novel technique of sublingual vein segmentation is proposed here. Sublingual Vein Color Model, which combines the Bayesian Decision with CIEYxy color space, is established based on a large number of labeled sublingual images. Experiments prove that the proposed method performs well on the segmentation of images from healthy humans with weak color contrast between sublingual vein and tongue proper. And then, a chromatic system in conformity with diagnostic standard of Traditional Chinese Medicine doctors is established to describe the chromatic feature of sublingual veins. Experimental results show that the geometrical and chromatic features quantized by the proposed framework are properly consistent with the diagnostic standard summarized by TCM doctors for healthy humans.

1 Introduction

Tongue diagnosis, which inspects tongue to examine the physiological function and pathological changes of human body, is one of the most important diagnostic methods in the Traditional Chinese Medicine (TCM). The advantage of tongue diagnosis is its simplicity and immediacy in that the examination of tongue can instantly clarify the main pathological process [1, 2]. In recent years, research on the feature extraction of tongue surface has achieved considerable progress [3]. But the sublingual vein diagnosis (SVD), which is part of tongue diagnosis, is rarely referred. Inspection of sublingual veins can provide valuable insights in the healthy condition of humans. However, SVD is usually based on detailed visual discrimination, which mainly depends on the subjective analysis of the examiners. Therefore, it is necessary to establish a quantitative and objective inspection system for SVD.

In early researches [4-6], only the color information from the sublingual veins was considered in evaluating the severity of the blood stasis. Moreover, only a few spots on the sublingual veins of each subject were examined, which might cause bias in the data analysis. Chiu et al. [7] tried to develop a computerized inspection system in order to quantitatively extract the chromatic and geometrical properties of sublingual veins. Quantitative features of twenty four subjects, which were grouped into three categories

D. Zhang (Ed.): ICMB 2008, LNCS 4901, pp. 107–114, 2007.
© Springer-Verlag Berlin Heidelberg 2007

based on the severity of blood stasis, were recomposed to serve as the parameters for classifying them into each category. In their research, the segmentation algorithm of sublingual vein was under the hypothesis that the contrast between the sublingual veins and tongue proper was differentiable enough. However, under normal conditions, the appearances of sublingual veins of healthy humans, which are traveling naturally without meandering or exhibiting any varicosity, and covered by lingual mucosa, usually show little difference beyond the tongue proper.

In this paper, we present a feature quantization framework for the inspection of sublingual veins of healthy humans. In section 2, a novel technique for sublingual vein segmentation is proposed. A Sublingual Vein Color Model (SVCM) is used to differentiate sublingual-vein color and non-sublingual-vein color. The chromatic and geometrical features of sublingual veins of healthy humans are quantized in section 3. In section 4, experiments are carried out on 150 samples, which are selected from a tongue-image database that contains 20,000 samples. Section 5 concludes this paper.

2   Adaptive Segmentation of Sublingual Vein

2.1   Sublingual Vein Color Model

A sublingual vein color model (SVCM) is used to decide if a pixel is in sublingual-vein color or non-sublingual-vein color. Generally, a SVCM is characterized by a classification algorithm and a color space that is used to represent color of pixels. The SVCM used in our work is based on the Bayesian decision for minimum cost. Let z represent the feature vector of a pixel. Let ω_1 represent the sublingual-vein color class and ω_2 represent the non-sublingual-vein color class. Let $p(z \mid \omega_1)$ and $p(z \mid \omega_2)$ represent the class-conditional probability density of class ω_1 and ω_2 respectively. For each pixel z, a sublingual color score (also know as likelihood ratio) is defined as follows:

$$S(z) = \frac{p(z \mid \omega_1)}{p(z \mid \omega_2)} \tag{1}$$

The higher the score $S(z)$, the more likely z can be considered as a sublingual-vein color. Classification decision usually involves a fixed threshold τ :

$$If \ S(z) \geq \tau \ then \ z \in \omega_1, \ Else \ z \in \omega_2 \tag{2}$$

There exists an optimum threshold τ in a sense that it minimizes the overall classification cost. Let $C_{ij} \geq 0$, $(i, j) = \{1,2\}$, denotes the cost of deciding $z \in \omega_i$ when $z \in \omega_j$ it represent the cost of correct classification when $i = j$ and false classification when $i \neq j$. Let $P(\omega_i \mid z)$ represents a posteriori probability of class ω_i; that is $P(\omega_i \mid z)$ is the probability of a given sample z belonging to class ω_i. Let $P(\omega_i)$ represents a priori probability of class ω_i; that is $P(\omega_i)$ is the probability of observing a sample from class ω_i. Let $R_i(z)$ denotes the conditional cost of deciding $z \in \omega_i$ given z. For the above two classes, $R_i(z)$ is computed as:

$$R_1(z) = C_{11}P(\omega_1 \mid z) + C_{12}P(\omega_2 \mid z)$$
$$R_2(z) = C_{21}P(\omega_1 \mid z) + C_{22}P(\omega_2 \mid z) \tag{3}$$

The classification problem becomes finding the class which gives the minimal cost, considering different cost weighting on classification decisions. The decision rule is:

$$R_1(z) < R_2(z) \Rightarrow z \in \omega_1$$
$$R_1(z) > R_2(z) \Rightarrow z \in \omega_2 \tag{4}$$

Substituting (3) into (4) and rearranging terms gives:

$$If \ \frac{P(\omega_1 \mid z)}{P(\omega_2 \mid z)} \geq \frac{C_{12} - C_{22}}{C_{21} - C_{11}} \ then \ z \in \omega_1, \ Else \ z \in \omega_2 \tag{5}$$

From (5), we obtain, by applying the Bayesian formula, the following relation:

$$If \ S(z) = \frac{p(z \mid \omega_1)}{p(z \mid \omega_2)} \geq \frac{C_{12} - C_{22}}{C_{21} - C_{11}} \cdot \frac{P(\omega_2)}{P(\omega_1)} \ then \ z \in \omega_1, \ Else \ z \in \omega_2 \tag{6}$$

Therefore, the optimum threshold τ in (2) is:

$$\tau_1 = \frac{C_{12} - C_{22}}{C_{21} - C_{11}} \cdot \frac{P(\omega_2)}{P(\omega_1)} \tag{7}$$

Because the priori probabilities $P(\omega_i)$ are usually unknown, it is difficult to estimate the above theoretical threshold. In practice, the threshold τ is often chosen experimentally to achieve a trade-off between false detections and false rejections. A false detection occurs when the classifier considers a non-sublingual-vein color as sublingual-vein color; a false rejection occurs when the classifier considers a sublingual-vein color as non-sublingual-vein color. According to (2), a larger value of τ leads to more false rejections while a smaller value of τ leads to more false detections.

To utilize the decision rule summarized in (1) and (2), we need an accurate estimate of the class-conditional probability density $p(z \mid \omega_i)$ $i = \{1,2\}$. Here we use color histogram to achieve this goal. The existence of large image datasets makes it possible to build powerful generic models for low-level image attributes like color using simple histogram learning techniques [8]. In this SVCM we utilize the CIEYxy coordinate space. The plane formed by the x and y coordinates is the Chromaticity Diagram, which describes the pure color information without influence of intensity. The size of the histogram depends on the number of significant digit with which the x or y coordinate is expressed. When this number is 4, the model has a size of 10000 bins per coordinate channel, which corresponds to $(10000)^2$ bins, each mapped to a specific coordinate. From a set of labeled sublingual-vein colors and non-sublingual-vein colors, we obtain two histograms $H_{sv}(z)$ and $H_{nsv}(z)$. $H_{sv}(z)$ is the count of sublingual-vein color pixels that have feature vector z, and $H_{nsv}(z)$ is the count of non-sublingual-vein color pixels that have feature vector z. The class-conditional density is simply normalized histograms:

$$p(z \mid \omega_i) = \frac{H_i(z)}{\sum_z H_i(z)} \qquad (8)$$

2.2 Adaptive Sublingual Vein Segmentation Algorithm

Let ω_{sv} and ω_{nsv} denote the sublingual-vein class and non-sublingual-vein class segmented by some threshold, respectively. Let n_{sv} denote the sample amount of ω_{sv} ,and n_{nsv} denote the sample amount of ω_{nsv} , P_{sv} and P_{nsv} denote the priori probabilities of the two classes respectively. Let z_k^{sv} and z_l^{nsv} denote the 2-D feature vector of ω_{sv} and ω_{nsv} , which is composed of x and y coordinates of the *CIEYxy* coordinate space. The mean vector of these two classes is denoted by m_{sv} and m_{nsv} :

$$m_{sv} = \frac{1}{n_{sv}} \sum_{k=1}^{n_{sv}} z_k^{sv}, \quad m_{nsv} = \frac{1}{n_{nsv}} \sum_{l=1}^{n_{nsv}} z_l^{nsv} \qquad (9)$$

The total mean vector of these two classes is denoted by m :

$$m = P_{sv} \cdot m_{sv} + P_{nsv} \cdot m_{nsv} \qquad (10)$$

Thus, the estimate of within-class scatter matrix S_w and between-class scatter matrix S_b is:

$$\tilde{S}_w = P_{sv} \cdot \frac{1}{n_{sv}} \sum_{k=1}^{n_{sv}} (z_k^{sv} - m_{sv})(z_k^{sv} - m_{sv})^T + P_{nsv} \cdot \frac{1}{n_{nsv}} \sum_{l=1}^{n_{nsv}} (z_l^{nsv} - m_{nsv})(z_l^{nsv} - m_{nsv})^T \quad (11)$$

$$\tilde{S}_b = P_{sv} (m_{sv} - m)(m_{sv} - m)^T + P_{nsv} (m_{nsv} - m)(m_{nsv} - m)^T \qquad (12)$$

To attain better classification result, the between-class scatter should be as large as possible, simultaneously; the within-class scatter should be as small as possible. Here we utilize criterion in (13) as the similarity measurement to set the score threshold τ . The larger the between-class scatters of sublingual-vein class and non-sublingual-vein class, the smaller the within-class scatter of them, and then the larger J_d is:

$$J_d = \mathbf{tr}(\tilde{S}_w^{-1} \tilde{S}_b) \cdot \qquad (13)$$

3   Feature Extraction of Sublingual Veins of Healthy Humans

3.1   Width Measurement of Sublingual Veins

A simple approach to measure the width of sublingual veins is to apply a horizontal projection process, and the number of pixels can be calculated for each position in ordinate n-axis, which works under the assumption that the sublingual veins parallel each other. Take the individual difference in distribution of each sublingual vein into consideration, the morphological skeletonization is applied, according to the growing direction of sublingual veins, to obtain the morphological skeleton of each sublingual vein, and then twice the distance between the skeleton points and the edge of sublingual vein is considered to be the width of sublingual vein in that direction. Recall that the resolution of the digitized image is $0.1 \times 0.1 mm^2$ per pixel. Therefore, the exact scale for the width can be easily obtained. Finally, the largest width obtained under these two considerations is taken to be the width of the specific subject the sublingual veins belonging to, as shown in Fig.1.

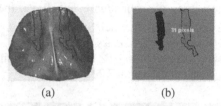

(a)   (b)

Fig. 1. The width measurement estimated by the proposed procedure. a) The sublingual veins region is contoured; b) the largest width under two considerations. According to the resolution the width of this sublingual image is 3.1mm.

3.2 Chromatic Features of Sublingual Veins

The 'color' described in Tongue Diagnosis is quite different from that used in general definition of color. The colors used as diagnostic measurements in Tongue Diagnosis are usually compounds of several colors due to complex disorder caused by some pathological processes. The existing tongue color analysis mainly utilize the RGB triple values or Hue values of single pixel or the mean of tongue texture block [9], which makes no sense to depict the chromatic characteristic of the whole region of interest, not mention to assist diagnosing. Therefore, to establish a new chromatic system in line with the diagnostic measurement standards of TCM doctor will greatly clarify the relationship between the diseases and the appearances of tongue. In our work, the chromatic system is composed of several significant Sublingual Vein Color Blocks (SVCB) summarized by clustering the color information of sublingual vein regions from a large amount of manually labeled sublingual images. 550 manually extracted sublingual vein sample images, from 150 healthy humans and 400 in patients, constitute the input of the sublingual-vein-color clustering. The clustered results are represented as color blocks shown in Fig. 2. These 9 SVCBs are named Tinge (TE), Light Red (LR), Light Blue (LB), Light Purple (LP), Dark Red (DR), Purple (PE), Crimson (CN), Blue (BE) and Dark Purple (DP), respectively. They are of significance in Sublingual vein Diagnosis and defined by professional TCM doctors.

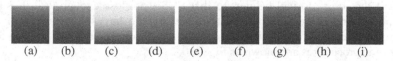

(a)   (b)   (c)   (d)   (e)   (f)   (g)   (h)   (i)

Fig. 2. Sublingual Vein Color Blocks. a) Tinge (TE); b) Light Red (LR); c) Light Blue (LB); d) Light Purple (LP); e) Dark Red (DR); f) Purple (PE); g) Crimson (CN); h) Blue (BE); i) Dark Purple (DP).

4 Experimental Results and Analysis

4.1 Sublingual Vein Segmentation

650 sublingual images of healthy humans, including 500 images labeled under the supervising of professional TCM doctors, are selected from our tongue database with over 20,000 clinical images of the tongue. These images are gathered using automatic tongue image acquisition device invented by our research center [10]. The 500 labeled sublingual images constitute the training set to construct the SVSM look-up table. Here x and y coordinates preserve four significant digits, the corresponding SVSM possesses 10000 bins per coordinate channel. Stepwise implementation of the proposed sublingual vein segmentation approach on a sublingual image of healthy human and the final segmentation result is shown in Fig. 3. 150 sublingual images of healthy humans are segmented and the result is shown in Table1.

Fig. 3. Segmentation procedures with incremental threshold and the final segmentation results. From left to right, the initial sublingual image, thresholds τ are 0.1, 0.5, 1.8, and 2.1, and the final segmentation result, respectively.

Table 1. Comparison of segmentation results using Four-significant-digit SVSM

Type of SVSM	The number of testing images	The number of images being correct segmented	Correct segmentation ratio
Four-significant-digit SVSM	150	121	80.7%

4.2 Feature Quantization of Sublingual Veins of Healthy Humans

In this section, the 121 sublingual images with exact sublingual vein contours acquired by utilizing the four-significant-digit-based SVSM are considered. Each sublingual image is firstly segmented using the adaptive segmentation algorithm, and then width measurement will be implemented to the extracted sublingual vein regions. To characterize the chromatic features based on the SVCB, the color of each pixel belonged to sublingual vein region is compared with each SVCB, and characterized by the one if the color of pixel belongs to that SVSB or close enough to it. Lastly, the dominant sublingual vein color is determined by the largest percentage of pixels mapping to given SVCB over the whole sublingual vein regions. The whole feature quantization procedures are shown as Fig. 4.

The width of sublingual veins of the 121 sublingual images is shown in Fig. 5 and the overall average width is 2.37mm. Table 2 illustrates the confusion matrix. The row denotes the chromatic features distinguished by professional TCM doctor, and the column denotes the quantization result. As Table 2 shows, the chromatic features of 22 sublingual images are miss classified, namely, the quantization results did not conform to the diagnostic conclusion the professional TCM doctor made. Thus, the correct color classification rate is 81.8%.

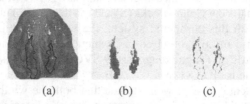

(a)   (b)   (c)

Fig. 4. Example of feature quantization of sublingual veins of healthy human. (a) The result after adaptive segmentation; (b) 77.37% extracted sublingual vein region is characterized as DR; (c) 21.77% extracted sublingual vein region is characterized as CN. The sublingual vein color of this subject is DR; its width is 2.3mm.

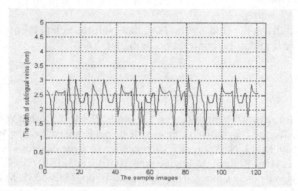

Fig. 5. The width of sublingual vein of 121 sublingual images

Table 2. The miss classifying matrix of chromatic features of sublingual veins

	TE	LR	LB	LP	DR	PE	CN	BE	DP	Total
TE	-	0	0	0	0	0	0	0	0	0
LR	0	-0	0	0	0	0	0	0	0	0
LB	0	0	-	5	0	0	0	2	0	7
LP	4	0	0	-	3	0	0	0	1	8
DR	0	1	0	6	-	0	0	0	0	7
PE	0	0	0	0	0	-	0	0	0	0
CN	0	0	0	0	0	0	-	0	0	0
BE	0	0	0	0	0	0	0	-	0	0
DP	0	0	0	0	0	0	0	0	-	0
Total	4	1	0	11	3	0	0	2	1	22

5   Conclusions

In this paper, we propose a feature quantization framework for the inspection of sublingual veins of healthy humans. The adaptive sublingual vein segmentation algorithm based on Bayesian decision is proposed, and the correct segmentation rate is up to 80.7% by using the four-significant-digit-based SVSM. The geometrical and chromatic features of 121 sublingual images are quantized. The overall average width of sublingual veins is 2.37mm, below the critical width 2.7mm [11]. A new chromatic system in line with the diagnostic measurement standards of TCM doctor is established by defining Sublingual Vein Color Blocks (SVCB) as the basis of chromatic features of sublingual veins. With this chromatic system, the color of sublingual veins can be described in the sense of compound colors, which closely accord to the diagnostic measurement standards of Tongue diagnosis. 9 SVCB are established and the correct color differentiate rate is up to 81.8%.

From the experimental results, we conclude that both the width and the chromatic features quantized in this paper properly reflect the physiological characteristics of sublingual veins of healthy humans summarized in Tongue Diagnosis.

Acknowledgement

This work is partially supported by the National Natural Science Foundation (NSFC) key overseas project under the contract no. 60620160097.

References

1. Kirschbaum, B.: Atlas of Chinese Tongue Diagnosis. Eastland, Seattle,WA (2000)
2. Maciocia, G.: Tongue Diagnosis in Chinese Medicine. Eastland, Seattle, WA (1995)
3. Pang, B., Zhang, D., Li, N., Wang, K.: Computerized tongue diagnosis based on Bayesian Network. IEEE Trans Biomedical Engineering 51(10), 1803–1810 (2004)
4. Li, N., et al.: Handbook of Chinese Tongue Diagnosis, pp. 1333–1335. Xueyuan Publishing Company, Peking (1994)
5. Takeichi, M., Sato, T.: Computerized color analysis of 'Xue Yu' (Blood Stasis) in the sublingual vein using a new technology. Am. J. Chinese Med. 25, 213–219 (1997)
6. Takeichi, M., Sato, T.: Studies on the psychosomatic functioning of ill-health according to Eastern and Western medicine. Am. J. Chinese Med. 27, 213–219 (1999)
7. Chiu, C.C., et al.: Objective assessment of blood stasis using computerized inspection of sublingual veins. Computer Methods and Programs in Biomedicine 69, 1–12 (2002)
8. Jones, M.J., Rehg, M.J.: Statistical color models with application to skin detection. In: Proc. IEEE-CVPR, pp. 274–280 (1999)
9. Li, C.H., Yuen, P.C.: Regularized color clustering in medical image database. IEEE Trans. Med. Imaging 19(11), 1150–1155 (2000)
10. Zhang, D., Li, N., et al.: Tongue images acquisition device, Invent Patent of The People's Republic of China, No. ZL 02132458.1
11. Li, N., Zhang, D., Wang, K.: Tongue Diagnostics, pp. 118–126. Xueyuan Publishing Company, Peking (2006)

Using Formal Concept Analysis to Leverage Ontology-Based Acu-Point Knowledge System

Kwoting Fang[1], Chingwei Chang[2], and Yenping Chi[2]

[1] National Yunlin University of Science & Technology, Yunlin, 123 University Road,
Section 3, Touliou, Yunlin, Taiwan
fangkt@yuntech.edu.tw
[2] National Chengchi University, NO. 64, Sec.2, ZhiNan Rd., Wenshan District,
Taipei City 11605, Taiwan
{channing,ypchi}@mis.nccu.edu.tw

Abstract. In the past decade, perhaps, the most dramatic evolution, a new agenda, in organization is the dawn of the new economy associated with the value of intellectual assets. The main goal of this paper is to integrate Formal Concept Analysis (FCA) with Protégé to build up ontology-based Traditional Chinese Medicine, with Acu-point serving both as an example, and a knowledge-sharing platform. This may make the experts' knowledge visualization and understand with the general public, provide that a patient has the opportunity to participate in, and be totally aware of, the complete symptoms of his/her illness. Moreover, the platform could contribute towards eliminating the phenomenon of information disparity between patients and physicians.

1 Introduction

There is much evidence pointing to a problem: although patients accept medical treatment, the majority of them will not exhaust all avenues in fully informing themselves of all aspects of medically-related information, such as: the curative effects, side effects of medication, the treatment process, the inference of diagnosis, and the principles of treatment for pain relief, etc. All of the above can lead to an information disparity between physician and patient. Previously, a certain lack of information was due to insufficient time, manpower, or because information-sharing through education or further explanation, might prove too costly and time consuming. Due to a lack of resources and expert knowledge, patients are therefore usually ill-informed regarding their particular situation.

Thus, the call to bridge the understanding gap between physicians and patients become loud. Given the lightning fast progress of web service technology associated with the continued rapid growth in data management [7], it is imperative that we reduce this information gap between patient and physician. Using a medical knowledge sharing platform and reviewing their own symptoms or medical history, the patients themselves obtain medical knowledge spontaneously, which may improve interactivity while their questions are being processed.

How information retrieval (IR) should be set to better echo with the user's mindset, and make the retrieval of information easier in executing the functions included in the system. The main objective of this study is to integrate Formal Concept Analysis (FCA) with Protégé to shed the light of the main structure of knowledge in terms of ontology, for

D. Zhang (Ed.): ICMB 2008, LNCS 4901, pp. 115–121, 2007.
© Springer-Verlag Berlin Heidelberg 2007

effectively break down the restrictions of IR, and also to exploit the intention of the document by automatically building a support structure and inter-document relationship.

2 Ontology

Ontology is a formal model of a shared understanding within a certain domain [8]. Based on this concept, ontology is considered a key technique for information management, largely due to its promise of bringing a consensus to the way in which a particular area of expertise is described. The fundamental sharing concept is not only limited in its terminology, but also in the way concepts and objects may be organized and constructed within the domain [7].

2.1 Using Ontology in Knowledge Retrieval

Ontology as applied in data retrieval, markedly changes the strategy from the pull to push style [1]. Previously, the retriever inserted a certain keyword for looking up information in the system, which is a type of pull style data retrieval. However, at present, construction via ontology concepts provides the vocabulary for expressing personal interest profiles for information, while the push service automatically delivers the data and information for categories in which a user is interested.

This study uses Formal Concept Analysis, which is a mathematical principle to apply the main spirit of ontology, allowing the knowledge to be constructed more reasonable and more logically.

2.2 Formal Concept Analysis

In essence, formal concept analysis was originally developed as a field of applied mathematics based on a mathematical concept and concept hierarchy. From a philosophical point of view, a concept is a unit of thoughts; an idea for reinforcing connections with our general culture by interpreting the theory as concretely as possible.

Sciences have to examine their disciplines, which means uncovering their hidden purposes, to declare their real purpose, to select and adjust their means according to those purposes, to explain possible consequences comprehensively and publicly, and to make their methods of scientific findings and results accessible via everyday language [6][9].

The advantage of the FCA is that the main ideas are quickly understood by means of formal lattices, and the knowledge model obeys FCA concepts which explain the extraction schema from the documents or experts opinions we have. Hence, the reason this study adopts FCA as an automatic technique to elicit the attributes of dependency schemas extracted from the documents and Acu-point references. Therefore, building up ontology, is coding the knowledge as concept lattice.

2.3 FCA Application for Information Retrieval

Putting FCA into practice for IR usually involves the three steps listed below [2]:

Step1: Extracting indexes from documents
The principle is brought up by IR scholars for extracting a set of index terms from the documents. Those terms describe the documents appropriately. Researchers can use

selective criterion to restrict the index set, or, by means of weights in the documents, sift a needed index from the inordinate one, in order to maximize the performance of a certain domain IR task [5].

Step2: Lattice Construction
In a Formal Concept Analysis study, concept eliciting is always a key factor in the success of the study. However, the more objects/documents we get, the more concepts that it will contain. It is always debated how best to control the number of concepts extracted from documents by several field experts and the different backgrounds of applied researchers. However, the Claudio and Giovanni [2] study referred to keyword limitations to manipulate the increasing number of extracted concepts, typically, it consists of a focus concept technique, i.e, to select a focused-concept/centered-concept, then views its neighboring concepts and choose which thought is closest to the centered-concept with which to merge [2], hence ,the contribution generated by all of the nearest neighbors of a given concept, has been addressed, both for building a full lattice, and to find just the portion of lattice around which that concept is centered.

Step3: Effective Lattice Visualization
In some cases the outcome concept lattices of a real application are usually too large to show on the screen or graph. The common approach or solution is to show or hide parts of the lattice via an interactive specification of a focus concept and/or subsets of terms. Nested line diagrams, similar to the tree structure, make the focus concepts the roots and associate each sequence of concepts below the focus with a path like the trunk of a tree.

The FCA nested line diagrams are based on combining multiple partial views of the data represented in the context. The building steps of an FCA nested line diagram are as follows three steps [4]: (1) Two or more subsets of attributes are chosen by the user. (2) The concept lattices of the sub-context are identified by the attribute subsets of the previous steps chosen by the users. (3) The full concept lattice is embedded in the direct product of the lattices of sub-context as a joint-semi-lattice.

The overall effect of building nested line diagrams is mapping concepts into a clear identifiable picture of reality. That means having several complete lattices of a partial context nested into one another rather than a partial lattice of a context.

3 Implementation of AKMS

In this section, we will introduce the Acu-point Knowledge Management System (AKMS), in more detail, by following the three step principle mentioned earlier; for instance, how to organize queries about domain knowledge related articles or the principles introducing system retrieval which were constructed by the integrated software tool – Protégé, with Protégé building Acu-point ontology for AKMS.

This design provides system with the capability of handling ambiguous questions from different users. AKMS provides two kinds of retrieval methods for acquiring certain information for the users. First, an intelligent query gives the user additional choices between the expert and the beginner. If a beginner looks up the Acu-point domain data from AKMS, we presume that a beginner would not be as concerned as an expert, multiple combo-boxes supply the user with a flexible combination for their understanding and purpose, however, for the most part, experts' queries require more accuracy and efficiency. The purpose of the other retrieval mechanism is to provide a keyword method for retrieving information. It is mentioned that there is an ancillary function that is searching for specific news and Acu-point knowledge, users insert the keyword that are specifically interest in, and then function will return the relevant Acu-point news report and articles as feedback. In the following section, we will introduce the three main steps for building the searching function, as well as the process for constructing the ontology by Protégé.

3.1 Extracting a Set of Index Terms

In this step, by using the Protégé application which was developed for creating the ontology-based systems, we focus on creating the slots for each information item, such as documents, clinical diagnoses etc. These slots are also known as 'roles' in the description logic and relations in FCA construction and other object-oriented notions. They are also called attributes in some other formats, we define this system as an Acu-point consulting platform, hence, the study limits the scope of the data applied in the medical Acu-point treatment domain. The system will then try to figure out the relationship of the Acu-point terminology mentioned in the references and documents, this study employs the Acu-point related domain data from literature, documents, CD's etc. and creates Acu-point ontology via the Protégé integrated software. The process of setup interfaces is shown in the diagram below.

For example, Traditional Chinese Medicine argues that the human body can be divided into four main parts: the head, neck, limbs and the trunk/main body. Then we treat these four parts as a kind of super-class and place the special regions which will be treated as a sub-class, into the appropriate super-class. Hands and feet should be classified in the limb class.

Therefore, using the same logic, the shoulder, wrist, elbow, arm and palm should belong to the hand class. As we reach the lowest level, where the scope narrows and becomes more specific, we find the class where the slots for Acu-point are set. Slots are roles in description logics, and relations in FCA construction. Some FCA research label attributes as slots, which is the characteristic part of an object. For example, the Hegu Acu-point is described in terms of 8 slots. Different Acu-points may reveal different attributes, and are provided with different characteristics, such as how to treat remedial massage with certain Acu-points, and what degree of pressure should be applied. Those different places are specified by different allotted-values of slots, as displayed in Fig.1.

The slot curative effect, indicates results caused by massaging Hegu Acu-points and determines how certain illnesses should be improved or eased. The slot degree of power represents how much strength should be applied to the patient when massaging the Hegu Acu-point. The slot direction of massage specifies the direction for applying pressure. The slot of effective positions, is the style of massage specifying the manner in which a massage therapist treats a patient, such as pressing down, pushing aside, or tapping, etc,. Every Acu-point is a setup slot in Protégé for modeling ontology structure. Acu-point is described by different slots in every aspect. Furthermore, building the relationship and constructing concept lattices must be based on these slots which belong to each Acu-point, as in the following steps.

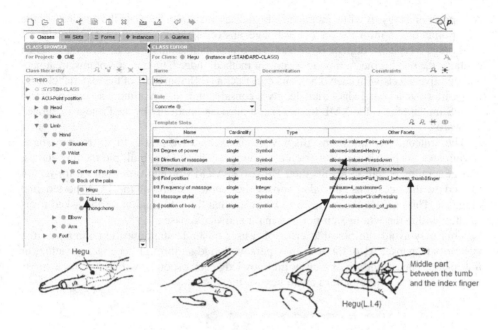

Fig. 1. Interface of constructing Protégé classes

3.2   Concept Lattice Construction

Ontology describes the concepts in certain domains, and the relationship that exists between those concepts. In this section we will map the concepts into the appropriate classes. Classes are interpreted as sets that contain instances, with the construction of links between the concepts by the related degree of attributes which ranks each different concept, in order to find the common parts of two classes and determine their relationship. Furthermore, several similar objects are merged as a new concept in representing them.

In this process, five concepts gradually emerge and become the main essence of the Acu-point ontology: "Prescription class", "Prescription references", "Medicinal materials", "Prescription types", and "Treatments for illness".

Although the diagram below is difficult to read, its purpose is to show the result which was built via formal concept analysis. By setting the attributes and concepts through the use of mathematics, and making the facts more objective and reasonable, it is not difficult to reassure people or for a beginner to understand. Furthermore, it makes the constructed data-base cheaper and diminishes the need for experts.

3.3   Queries Outcome Visualization

By using the relationship between the concepts constructed in step two, users are allowed to view certain Acu-point domain information in which they are most interested. After constructing the ontology of certain domain data set up by the experts and builders, ontology is described by an accredited standard text format, the Extensible Markup Language, XML [3], which is generated by Protégé, while we finish the construction of

Acu-point ontology. It will simultaneously and automatically translate the ontology of the Acu-point domain information to a webpage, answering users' questions effortlessly.

Protégé compiled a domain information rule and relationship by the XML syntax, which contains the rule for the Acu-point treatment method. Indeed, linking symptoms, treatment and curative effects with each other, and constructing different parts of the experts' clinical know-how into a knowledge- triangle, gives consideration to two or more aspects of health care. Simultaneously, the XML format is compiled automatically by the Protégé integrated software.

The outcome of questions displayed via website response to users may have advantages, such as being user-friendly, giving feedback from multiple media sources, and generating dynamic results etc., However, AKMS provides not only information related to the questions, but also shows the whole picture of the FCA nested line diagram. This enables the retriever to be aware that the information he/she asked for is located within the whole Acu-point domain knowledgebase.

This may avoid the possible error of a user misunderstanding the contents of the system's response. Also, the user may personally judge, through feedback, whether or not his/her understanding of Acu-point knowledge corresponds with that of the experts according to the whole picture awareness of the domain.

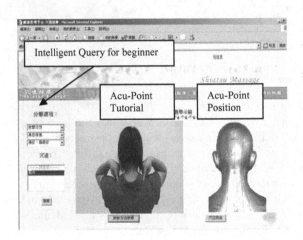

Fig. 2. Interface of Acu-point knowledge System   **Fig. 3.** Presentation Construction

4   Conclusions

To bridge the understanding gap between the physicians and patients, we have worked on improving the knowledge management as applied to the Traditional Chinese medicine (TCM) domain. Acu-point medicine served as an example, with the technique of FCA used to build an automatic ontology-based system menu that replaces the pull style, with a push style of IR service.

The goal for developing our FCA-constructed retrieval mechanism was to improve the traditional ways of managing both information items, as well as minimizing the additional effort required in information retrieval and content management. The content also required us to emphasize an intelligent query interface when building the hierarchy menu on the ontology concept. The concept differs greatly from previous ones, as it formulates user queries accordingly; ambiguity can be avoided when interpreting both the question and answers. Such normalization and retrieval promise a precise search beyond what is possible with the current keyword-based methods.

Furthermore, the long-term object of this study is to create a platform for sharing the Chinese Medical data with the user and also to eliminate the phenomenon of the information disparity between the patient and physician. This study's perspective creates "images" for eliminating the disparity, and offers the potential for generating new insights into the field as it advances.

References

1. Andreas, A., van Elst, L.: Ontologies for knowledge management. In: Hand book of Ontology, vol. 4, Springer, Heidelberg (2003)
2. Claudio, C., Giovanni, R.: Using Concepts Lattices for Text Retrieval and Mining. Formal Concept Analysis Foundations and Applications. Springer, Heidelberg (2005)
3. David, H., Andrew, W., et al.: Beginning XML, 3rd edn. Wiley Publishing, Chichester (2004)
4. Vogt, F., Wachter, C., Wille, R.: TOSCANA – A graphical tool for analyzing and exploring data. In: Vogt, F., Wachter, C., Wille, R. (eds.) Graph Drawing 1994, pp. 226–233. Springer, Heidelberg (1995)
5. Meng, J., Zhou, C.: Traditional Chinese medical Introduction. Zhi-Yin publisher (1994)
6. Botting, R.M.: A formal and structured approach to the use of task analysis in accident modeling, vol. 49, pp. 223–244. Academic Press, London (1998)
7. Kishore, R., Ramesh, R., Sharman, R.: Computational Ontologies: foundations, representations, and methods. In: Ninth Americas Conferences on Information Systems (2003)
8. Gruber, T.R.: Towards Principles for the design of Ontologies Used for Knowledge Sharing. Formal Ontology in Conceptual Analysis and Knowledge Representation. Kluwer Academic, The Netherlands (1993)
9. Priss, U.: Linguistic Applications of Formal Concept Analysis. Formal Concept Analysis Foundations and Applications. Springer, Heidelberg (2005)

Implementation of a Portable Personal EKG Signal Monitoring System

Tan-Hsu Tan[1], Ching-Su Chang[1], Yung-Fu Chen[2], and Cheng Lee[1]

[1] Department of Electrical Engineering, National Taipei University of Technology,
Taipei, Taiwan
{thtan,s2319004}@ntut.edu.tw, magic.lee@tainet.net
[2] Department of Health Services Administration, China Medical University
yungfu@mail.cmu.edu.tw

Abstract. This research develops a portable personal EKG signal monitoring system to help patients monitor their EKG signals instantly to avoid the occurrence of tragedies. This system is built with two main units: signal processing unit and monitoring and evaluation unit. The first unit consists of EKG signal sensor, signal amplifier, digitalization circuit, and related control circuits. The second unit is a software tool developed on an embedded Linux platform (called CSA). Experimental result indicates that the proposed system has the practical potential for users in health monitoring. It is demonstrated to be more convenient and with greater portability than the conventional PC-based EKG signal monitoring systems. Furthermore, all the application units embedded in the system are built with open source codes, no licensed fee is required for operating systems and authorized applications. Thus, the building cost is much lower than the traditional systems.

1 Introduction

There are numerous systems designed to monitor heart diseases in the market, but most of them are not affordable to the general public and only used in medical institutions. Patients are unable to monitor their physiological status at all times. As a result, some studies have developed PC-based personal EKG (electrocardiogram) signal monitoring systems [1]. However, PC-based systems are not portable; they cannot instantly monitor physical conditions. To overcome this difficulty, this study aims to design a portable personal EKG signal monitoring system to help patients monitor their EKG signals instantly so as to avoid the occurrence of tragedies.

Since the procedures of measuring heart rate (HR) and heart rate variability (HRV) have been standardized [2-3], using EKG to identity cardiovascular diseases have received much attention [4-9]. For instance, a PC-based system [10] has employed LabVIEW to perform time-domain, frequency-domain, and time—frequency domain HRV analyses. It also simplifies the process of data transfer between different PCs. In [11], a novel EKG signal display system was proposed to demonstrate EKG signals with 3D graphs. Recently, several studies that transmit EKG signals using Internet and/or GPRS have been proposed [12-13]. However, most of the aforementioned studies need the assistance of PC for signal analyses; mobility was not fully provided. For users, this is undoubtedly an inconvenient thing.

D. Zhang (Ed.): ICMB 2008, LNCS 4901, pp. 122–128, 2007.
© Springer-Verlag Berlin Heidelberg 2007

2 System Design

The proposed system is composed of two main units: the signal processing unit and the monitoring and evaluation unit. The signal processing unit, namely EKG Front End, consists of EKG signal sensor, signal amplifier, digitalization circuit, and related control circuits. The monitoring and evaluation unit is built on an embedded Linux platform (called CSA). A software tool is designed to capture EKG signals, to analyze 12-lead EKG signals by calculating time-domain and frequency-domain responses, and to save EKG signals. In addition, QT application software is used to draw and display graphs, and Qtopia is applied to construct a human-machine interface [14].

High-Portability, low-cost, high-reliability, and ease of use are the design purposes of this study. The CSA platform is a commercial product developed by Autologic Technology [15], which is convenient for system integrations. The 12-lead EKG signals are presented on CSA color LCD, allowing users to execute related functions such as enlarging or down-sizing single-lead or multiple-lead signals, by using the touch screen. To pursuit higher system reliability, we use 12-Lead EKG signal simulator from Fluke Corporation for signal simulation [16].

2.1 Hardware Structure

Figure 1 shows the hardware structure of the system, which has 4 units: 12-lead EKG signal collection, storage, calculation, and display. The function of each unit is described as follows:

(1) Signal collection: Signals detected by the EKG sensor are delivered to the CSA platform.
(2) Signal storage: EKG signals (measured values and computed values) are stored in the RAM Disk and SD (Secure Disk) Card of the CSA platform.
(3) 12-Lead EKG signals calculation: Including the mathematic equations required by the US Patent US6, 638,232 [17] and DFT (defibrillation threshold) to generate time / frequency domain responses of 12-lead EKG signals.
(4) Graphic display: Including the measured values and graphs of time / frequency domain responses of each EKG sensor on the CSA platform.

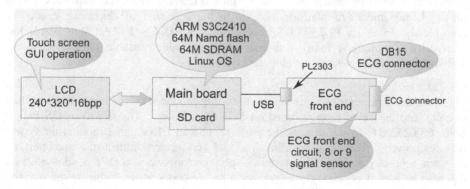

Fig. 1. Hardware structure

2.2 Software Structure

Basically, an ideal portable 12-lead EKG signal monitoring system should have six functions; they are Signal Collection, Signal Reading and Saving, Calculation, Display, Analysis and Alarm, and Remote Medical. The focus of this study will be placed on the first four of the aforementioned six parts since the remaining two parts require the support from related medical, telecommunication, and governmental institutions. The remaining two parts will be improved in the future. Figure 2 shows the data flow of an ideal portable 12-lead EKG signal monitoring system. The software structure of the first four parts will be described later.

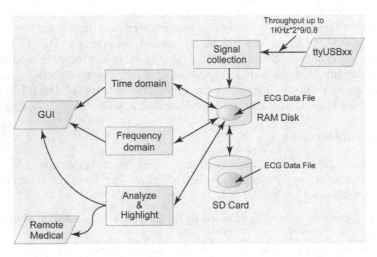

Fig. 2. Data flow of the proposed 12-lead EKG signal monitoring system

(1) Signal collection
When we designed the signal amplification and digitalization functions of the EKG Front End, we referred to the circuit suggested in US Patent US6, 638,232 and related literature [18]. There was a gap between the suggested circuit and the design objective, because the cost would be too high and the size was larger than the capacity of the Linux-embedded platform (CSA). In the selection of chips, we needed to compile the driver for PL2303 USB controller and ADuC841 MPU 4bits blank data (zero-fill). Fortunately, many reference programs are available on the supplier's website for us to shorten the development time.

(2) Calculation
The potential difference of input signals is mainly produced by the hardware (amplifier circuit), and the calculation is based on FFT (Fast Fourier Transform) of US Patient US6, 638,232 B1. In our design, the portable 12-lead EKG signal monitoring system features powerful reading, saving functions and a convenient human-machine interface. It is not necessary to stress the graphic display performance, so DFT is adopted (FFT can also be used if necessary). Related open source codes are available on the website, so our development time will not be increased. In this section, our focus is still placed on the integration of Qtopia human-machine interface.

Table 1. 12 lead time domain signals and EKG signals correlation equations

LEAD		EKG SIGNALS:
I	=	LA-RA
II	=	LF-RA
III	=	LF-LA
aVR	=	RA-(RA + LA + LF)/3
aVL	=	LA-(RA + LA + LF)/3
aVF	=	LF-(RA + LA + LF)/3
V1	=	C1-(RA + LA + LF)/3
V2	=	C2-(RA + LA + LF)/3
V3	=	C3-(RA + LA + LF)/3
V4	=	C4-(RA + LA + LF)/3
V5	=	C5-(RA + LA + LF)/3
V6	=	C6-(RA + LA + LF)/3

Through FFT, the standard 12-lead time-domain signals will derive 12 corresponding power spectrum signals, denoted as $S[i]$, where i is used to indicate the power spectrum signal of each lead. Its conjugate representation is $S*[i]$. The 12-lead power spectrum signals required in US Patent US6, 638, 232 are derived through Equ. (1)

$$P[i] = S[i]S*[i].\tag{1}$$

where $P[i]$ is the ith power spectrum signal, and the standard 12 leads will correspond to 12 power spectrum signals.

(3) Display

Qt was designed and developed by Trolltech Corp. It was officially commercialized in early 1996. Qt is a cross-platform C++ application development system, allowing developers to design GUI (graphic user interface) at will. Developers need to be proficient with only an API when compiling programs and the programs can be operated on any kind of platform. In addition, Qt is an object-oriented development tool, which ensures convenient expansion in cross-platform operations or when the original program is not well designed.

2.3 Issues to be Resolved in Practical Design

When designing the EKG signal monitoring system, no matter PC Labview or microelectronic circuits are adopted, it is not necessary to deal with the human-machine interface. In the proposed 12-lead EKG signal monitoring system, embedded Linux is used, so the display of graphics and applications on the human-machine interface should be integrated on Linux-supported tools. This is the most difficult part in practical design. We select Qt and Qtopia not only for the reason that the software can be converted into commercial versions instantly but also for the reason that supports provided by Qt and Qtopia users on the Internet have proven the advantage of Linux open source codes.

3 Experimental Results

Qtopia V1.7 was used to compile the human-machine interface. The GUI graphics of each function on the 12-lead EKG signal monitoring system are described as follows:

Figure 3 shows the human-machine interface of the designed system: (a) initialization of the 12-lead EKG signal monitoring system, (b) display of EKG signals, (c) display of EKG spectrums for medical diagnosis and a reference of this study, and (d) Control bar, which provides the functions of enlarging, down-sizing, and window adjustment.

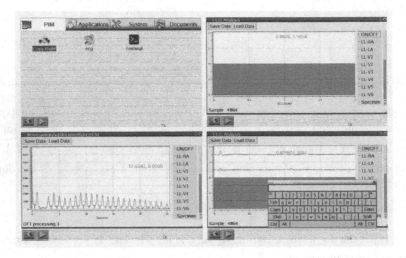

Fig. 3. Human-machine interface. (a) initialization of the 12-lead EKG signal monitoring system, (b) display of EKG signals, (c) display of EKG spectrums for medical diagnosis and study, and (d) Control bar.

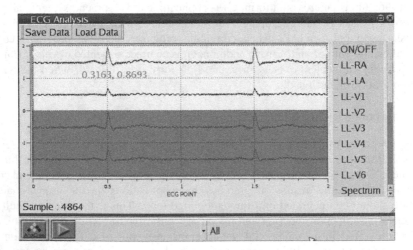

Fig. 4. Display of four-lead EKG signals (LL-RA, LL-LA, LL-V1, LL-V2) on CSA

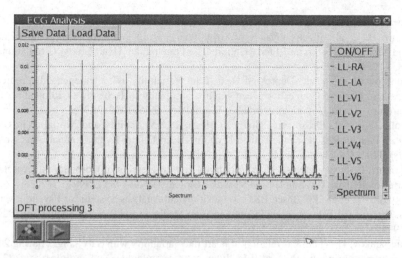

Fig. 5. Frequency responses of four-lead EKG signals (LL-RA, LL-LA, LL-V1, LL-V2) on CSA

The signal simulator from Fluke Corporation was used, to generate standard 12-lead EKG signals. The 12-lead EKG signal sensor from BioTechNet Corp. was connected to our system. When the 12-lead EKG signal simulator was turned on, we could see the EKG signals generated by the simulator displayed on the CSA screen. By using the designed human-machine interface, the display could be switched between single-lead and multiple-lead signal display.

When users used the EKG Front End, the captured data were delivered through DB9 interface to the 12-lead EKG signal monitoring system. Users could see their EKG related information. Figure 4 presents the four-lead (LL-RA, LL-LA, LL-V1, LL-V2) EKG signals on CSA. Figure 5 displays the frequency responses of four-lead (LL-RA, LL-LA, LL-V1, LL-V2) EKG signals on CSA.

4 Conclusions

In this study, the implementation of a portable 12-lead EKG signal monitoring system is described. The result demonstrates that our proposed system is more convenient than the conventional PC-based EKG signal monitoring systems with greater portability. In addition, all the application units embedded in the system are built with open source codes; no licensed fee is required for operating systems and authorized applications. Thus, the building cost is much lower than the traditional systems. In this study, we emphasized on the graphic display and integration of the human-machine interface to make it popular. Moreover, the adopted CSA platform also supports Ethernet interface, which could provide more diverse interactive models between medical institutions and users.

References

1. Bojanic, D., et al.: Dyadic Wavelets for Real-time Heart Rate Monitoring. In: Proc. of IEEE International Conference on Neural Network Applications, pp. 133–136 (2006)
2. http://www.escardio.org/

3. http://www.naspe.org/
4. Tsuji, H., et al.: Electrophysiology/Arrhythmias/Pacing Reduced Heart Rate Variability and Mortality Risk in an Elderly Cohort. The Framingham Heart Study, Circulation, 878–883 (1994)
5. Ponikowski, P., et al.: Depressed Heart Rate Variability as an Independent Predictor of Death in Chronic Congestive Heart Failure Secondary to Ischemic or Idiopathic Dilated Cardiomyopathy. American Journal of Cardiology, 1645–1650 (1997)
6. Nolan, J., et al.: Prospective Study of Heart Rate Variability and Mortality in Chronic Heart Failure: Results of the United Kingdom Heart Failure Evaluation and Assessment of Risk Trial (UK-Heart), pp. 1510–1516 (1998)
7. Huikuri, H.V., et al.: Heart Rate Variability and Progression of Coronary Atherosclerosis. Arteriosclerosis, Thrombosis and Vascular Biology, 1979–1985 (1999)
8. Gavidia, L., et al.: PC Based EKG Acquisition and Analysis System for Psychophysiology. In: Proc. of IEEE International Conference on Medicine and Biology Society, pp. 825–826 (1991)
9. Sapoznikov, D., et al.: Correlation of heart rate variability with ST changes during 24 hour Holter monitoring. In: Proc. of IEEE International Conference on Cardiology, pp. 327–329 (1989)
10. O'Brien, E.M., Rogge, R.D.: LabVIEW usage as part of the biomedical engineering senior design experience. In: Proc. of IEEE International Conference on Medicine and Biology, pp. 23–26 (2002)
11. Kuo, C.D., Chiang, H.K.: Three-dimensional electrocardiogram display method. United States Patent 5, 773–782 (1997)
12. Dong, J., Zhu, H.: Mobile EKG detector through GPRS/Internet. In: Proceedings of the 17th IEEE Symposium on Computer-Based Medical Systems (CBMS 2004), pp. 1063–7125 (2004)
13. Rasid, M.F.A., Woodward, B.: Bluetooth Telemedicine Processor for Multichannel Biomedical Signal Transmission via Mobile Cellular Networks. IEEE Trans. on Information Technology in Biomedicine, 35–43 (2005)
14. Trolltech Corp., http://www.trolltech.com/
15. Biologic Technology Inc., http://www.autologictek.com.tw/
16. Fluke Corporation, http://www.fluke.com/
17. Fang, et al.: US 6, 638, 232 B1. United States Patent (2003)
18. Segura-Juarez, J., et al.: A Microcontroller-Based Portable Electrocardiograph Recorder. IEEE Trans. Biomed. Eng. 51, 1686–1690 (2004)

Examining the Influence of Occupational Therapy and Its Effectiveness in Long-Term Care on Dementia Patients Through Ontology-Based Clustering

Kwoting Fang[1], Chingwei Change[2], Miao Yuliao[3], and Yenping Chi[2]

[1] National Yunlin University of Science & Technology, Yunlin,
123 University Rd, Section 3, Touliou, Yunlin, Taiwan
fangkt@yuntech.edu.tw
[2] National Chengchi University, NO. 64, Sec. 2, ZhiNan Rd.,
Wenshan District, Taipei City 11605, Taiwan
{channing,ypchi}@mis.nccu.edu.tw
3 Department of Family Medicine, Taichung Hospital, No. 199, Sec. 1,
San-min Rd., West District, Taichung City 403, Taiwan
liaomiaoyu@gmail.com

Abstract. Over the past decade, the number of long-term care (LTC) residents has increased, and many have accepted treatments such as medication, rehabilitation and occupational therapy. This study discusses the effectiveness of occupational therapy when given to dementia patients of different contexts. The results of this study showed that patients of a good condition in the first stage present a more positive attitude towards participation in the occupational therapy designed by the institution; therefore, they have a greater chance of their condition improving or remaining the same. However, patients of an average condition have a more passive attitude towards taking part in any therapy; therefore, they have a greater chance of their condition deteriorating. In conclusion, occupational therapy has an effect on all kinds of patients.

1 Introduction

In the epidemiological studies of Fratiglioni [6] it was reported that Alzheimer's disease (AD) is the most common form of dementia in the elderly. The prevalence of dementia is reported in these studies to be between 0.3 and 1.0 per 100 people in individuals aged 60 to 64 years, increasing to a range from 42.3 to 68.3 per 100 people in individuals aged 95 years and older. There is a rise in the elderly population of 3.08% per year, and geriatrics aged over 65 years constituted 9.74% of the population last year in Taiwan. Therefore, due to the rapidly increasing population of elderly people, the number of dementia cases, which are prevalent in the elderly, is also increasing rapidly. Therefore, senile dementia (SD) is becoming a more and more important issue in the Taiwanese geriatric population.

1.1 The Impact of Senile Dementia

Determining the proportion of a population who have dementia or are cognitively impaired is not as straightforward as it might sound, because the populations of most

D. Zhang (Ed.): ICMB 2008, LNCS 4901, pp. 129–136, 2007.
© Springer-Verlag Berlin Heidelberg 2007

industrialized countries are showing a marked increase in life expectancy. In most of these countries, the older population is growing substantially more quickly than the younger. However, the rates of increase are not uniform all over the world – a study by Ferri [2] mentioned that the number of cases in developed countries are predicted to increase by 100% between 2001 and 2040, but by more than 300% in India, China and their south Asian and western Pacific neighbors.

Based on the above facts, this study integrates several quantitative techniques in order to explore and interpret the effects of therapies on SD patients in long-term care institutions, and aims to find out the relationship between patient context and patient outcome. The study also attempts to draw some knowledge from patients who have already accepted care services.

2 Samples and Procedure of Analysis

The data to be analyzed by formal concept analysis (FCA) were supplied by Taichung Hospital Long-term Care Institution. Thirty-three patients were included, and each could be clustered by their own attributes under three phases: first phase, the initial status of the patients; second phase, details of the therapy; and third phase, the outcome status.

The constructs are referenced from the Gunilla Nordberg study [5] and are used to evaluate the patient's attributes in the initial phase. The socio-demographic construct, as the characteristics of the patients, is a comprehensive construct that includes age, education level, number of languages spoken by the patient, level of social contact, ability to express themselves, etc., The functional capacity construct is evaluated by the Barthel Index, which is a method of rating the activities of daily living designed by Mahoney and Barthel [7]. The items relate to feeding, transfer, grooming, toilet use, bathing, mobility, climbing stairs, dressing, bladder control and bowel control. In the analysis, the Barthel Index was used as a dichotomic variable (<60/100 and >= 60/100), considering a score of 60 to be a pivotal score at which patients move from assisted independence to dependence in the basic activities of daily living [4]. In the second phase, there are two constructs of input data. The first construct is pharmaceutical, in which we only consider the medicines that relate to the dementia disease; therefore the items included are facilitating brain blood circulation medicine, circulation medicine, and antidepressant medicine. The occupational therapy construct included a range of other non-pharmaceutical treatments, such as playing little games to stimulate the patients, painting, photographic recall; most of these activities had the same purpose, i.e., to stimulate the patient's memory in a gentle way.

3 Methodology

In the beginning, a concept lattice was built by patient attributes; and then, following the principle of formal concept analysis, according to the concept lattice diagram, patients are drawn as nodes with a hierarchical structure. Each node distance and information content is then used to compare and calculate the similarity between all patients. In the next step, the patients are clustered into several groups using the fuzzy clustering approach. Finally, from the results of observing the changing path of patients in different groups by the scenario analysis method, it may be possible to identify the appropriate therapy for patients in different situations.

3.1 Formal Concept Analysis

Formal concept analysis was originally developed in the field of applied mathematics, based on the mathematization of concepts and concept hierarchy. The philosophical point of view of a concept is that of a unit of thoughts, and it is hoped that connections in our general culture will be re-identified by interpreting the theory as accurately as possible. The aim and meaning of FCA, as a mathematical theory of concepts and concept hierarchies, is to support the rational communication of humans by mathematically developing appropriate conceptual structures that can be logically activated, and it can help in the restructuring of science disciplines; this is the main concept of FCA. The sciences have to examine their disciplinary structure, which means they have to uncover their unconscious purposes, declare their conscious purposes, select and adjust their means according to those purposes, explain possible consequences comprehensibly and publicly.

According to the main philosophical tradition, that the FCA concepts relationship is a hierarchical network, concepts can exist in relationships with many other concepts, where the sub-concept and super-concept relation plays a prominent role – in other words, being a sub-concept of a super-concept means that the extension of the sub-concept is contained in the extension of the super-concept.

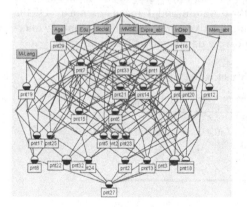
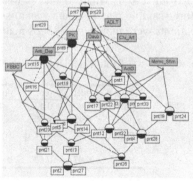

Fig. 1. First phase concept lattice   **Fig. 2.** The second phase concept lattice

Results of Formal Concept Analysis. Most of the values in the database we used were not on an interval or ratio scale: for example, if patient A has a medical history of 'congestive heart failure,' we cannot mark the field as any value other than yes or no. This is the main reason for choosing formal concept analysis as our analysis tool in order to investigate the relationship between patients and concepts in long-term care institutionalization. The figures one and two show the concept lattices representing the initial phase and the therapy phase.

3.2 Concepts Similarity

As a FCA lattice is often represented as a hierarchical structure, which can be seen as a special case of network structure, evaluation of the concept similarity between objects in the concept lattice makes use of the distance between patients themselves; moreover, this evaluation can detect the structural information embedded in the network. In other words, the calculation of the association of A and B can be transformed into the estimation of the conceptual similarity between nodes in the conceptual space generated by the FCA. Ideally, this kind of knowledge base should be of reasonably broad coverage, well-structured and easily manipulated in order to derive the desired associative or similarity information. Leacock and Chodorow [1] also rely on the length, len(pnt1; pnt2), of the shortest path between two objects for their measure of similarity. However, this approach is limited to IS-A links and scales the path length by the overall depth D of the taxonomy. The FCA concept lattice is drawn using the principle that the object is an IS-A sample of the attribute; therefore, this study adopted the Leacock and Chodorow distance approach to generate the dementia patient similarity matrix. Equation (1) was used to calculate the similarity of all patients to each other, the result generated in this step being the similarity matrices of the initial and therapy phases.

$$Sim\left(pnt\,1,\,pnt\,2\right) = -\log\frac{len\left(pnt\,1,\,pnt\,2\right)}{2\,D} \tag{1}$$

Results of Concept Similarity Counting. The similarity value between patients is of a range from 0 to 1, where 0 means totally different and 1 means identical. Of the thirty-three sample patients, data was missing for five patients; therefore, only twenty-eight patients were included. 28×28 matrix were developed as following table.

Table 1. Patients' similarity matrix in Phase I (partial)

Object	pnt1	pnt2	pnt3	pnt4	...	Pnt33
pnt1	1.00	0.43	0.43	0.43		0.47
pnt2	0.43	1.00	0.59	0.43		0.43
pnt3	0.43	0.59	1.00	0.53		0.47
:	:	:	:	:		:
Pnt33	0.47	0.43	0.47	0.68		1.00

3.3 Fuzzy Clustering

This study uses the formal concept lattice network diagram as the analysis subject to compute the similarity between patients, combined with the concepts of distance and content, as discussed in the previous section. In the previous process, the similarity matrix was generated, but the patients are not yet classified into groups. In order to process the similarity matrix, the study uses the fuzzy clustering technique to class patients into several different groups.

Results of Fuzzy Clustering. Fuzzy clustering set the twenty-eight patients into three groups in the first phase: the adequate group, the critical dementia group and the hopeful group. The hopeful group is of a good condition at the beginning of hospitalization; all patients in this group have the ability to communicate, with just slight dependency and slight dementia. The patients of the critical dementia group are of the worst initial condition, being of high dependency, with critical dementia, a negative social contact ability, and a weak ability to express themselves. The adequate group is the middle group, which consists of patients whose condition is not as good as the patients in the hopeful group, but better than those in the critical dementia group. The details are listed in Table 2 below.

Table 2. The three groups in Phase one

GroupName	Common features	Amount
Adequate Group 1	All of the patients suffer from heart disease, high blood pressure and diabetes. Most are Mandarin speakers. Most are well-educated (>10 years). Most are able to express themselves.	6
Critical Dementia Group 2	Most patients in this group are of high dependency in activities of daily living (Barthel Index score <40). Most have dementia (MMSE<9). Social contact is offensive (patients are nervous, attacking, self-contained). Most can only speak one language. Their ability to express themselves is poor.	11
Hopeful Group 3	Social contact is positive (patients are enthusiastic, cooperative, obedient). Most patients are slightly dependent in activities of daily living (Barthel Index score >60). Most have only slight dementia (MMSE>12). Their ability to express themselves is good.	11

In the second phase, fuzzy clustering again set the twenty-eight patients into three groups: the no therapy group, the accepted therapy group, and the passively accepted therapy group. In the no therapy group, some of the patients are unwilling to take part in any activities designed by the long-term care institution; however, some bedridden patients have lost the ability of take part in any activities. The patients in the passively accepted therapy group are not interested in taking part in any activities: a nurse may force them to join in some training activities, but most of the patients in this group try

Table 3. The three groups in Phase two

Group Name	Common features	Amount
No Therapy Group 1	Patients took no part in therapy activities.	9
Accepted Therapy Group 2	Most patients completely accepted therapy activities. Most had positive attitude towards taking part in activities	10
Passively Accepted Therapy Group 3	Patients did not completely accept therapy activities. Most only passively took part in activities.	9

to resist or are passive in performing any task. Table 3 gives the details of each of the classes in phase two resulting from fuzzy clustering.

In the third phase, fuzzy clustering is not used to cluster the patients into several groups; instead, we set the patients' outcomes into three situations after living in the long-term care institution: progress, maintenance and degeneration. The outcome of each patient was estimated by nurses and by using the MMSE and IADL scores.

3.4   Scenario Analysis

Scenario analysis is a decision tool that has been applied in management, economics and environmental decision-making. The principle of scenario analysis is that, based on a reliable scenario analysis, the reality can be re-perceived, and individual engagement, commitment and mental flexibility can be enhanced, so that the most effective response strategies can be developed [8]. According to the study by Gotze [3], researchers adopting scenario analysis should take into account consistent scenarios, because inconsistent scenarios draw no realistic image of the future; therefore, our study draws the main change path of the patients in different phases.

Results of Scenario Analysis. In order to find the consistent scenarios, we counted the rates of each group moving from the pre-phase groups: adequate condition patients are more likely move into the passively accepted therapy group, and there was a high number of critical dementia patients moving into the no therapy status group, perhaps because most of these patients are not in a well enough condition to be able to take part in any training or game activities, and some have a tendency to attack, some have no movement ability, etc. In addition, half of the patients in the hopeful condition group completely accepted therapy. In the change from phase two to phase three, if the patient did not accept any therapy, they have a 50:50 chance of their condition degenerating; however, if they

Table 4. The change rates in the three phases

Phase I	Phase II Group	Rate%	Phase II	Phase III Group	Rate %
Adequate	No Therapy	0%	**No Therapy**	Progress	12.5%
	Accepted Therapy	33%		Maintenance	37.5%
	Passively Accepted Therapy	_66%_		Degeneration	_50%_
Critical Dementia	No Therapy	_64%_	**Accepted Therapy**	Progress	40%
	Accepted Therapy	18%		Maintenance	_50%_
	Passively Accepted Therapy	18%		Degeneration	10%
Hopeful	No Therapy	18%	**Passively Accepted Therapy**	Progress	33%
	Accepted Therapy	_55%_		Maintenance	33%
	Passively Accepted Therapy	27%		Degeneration	33%

accepted partial therapy, this chance will be reduced to 33%. The best outcome is achieved when patients receive whole therapy, and with a high willingness and coordination, they have only a 10% of their condition becoming worse, and a 90% chance of at least being able to control their dementia. A list of the outcome rates are shown in Table 4, and the highest rate in each group is highlighted in underline typeface.

4 Limitations

Although the results only show the main change path of the patients in different phases, the number of sample patients is insufficient, and therefore the effects of each therapy are not disclosed very obviously. However, we still expect to have developed a new clustering approach that will help institutions to elicit tacit rules from the original data of dementia patients.

5 Conclusions

The study presents a novel clustering approach by patients' relationships in a concept lattice diagram drawn using an ontology-based method. We counted the similarity and used this as the input matrix for fuzzy analysis in order to set patients into several different groups. In the final stage, the main change paths of the patients in each of the three phases were calculated, and the result show that occupational therapy has a positive effect on the condition of dementia patients in long-term care. This study inferred, from series clustering and analysis, that therapy for patients who live in long-term care institutions is effective in improving their condition, and patients of a hopeful condition do understand that occupational therapy activities designed by the institution are helpful in their treatment and can also be enjoyable; therefore, the rate of positive joint therapy is quite high. In contrast, patients with low social contact ability are quick to mistrust, attack, evade or refuse any opportunity to interact with others; hence, their willingness to participate in therapy activities is lower, and it is therefore difficult to make any progress in their condition.

It is vitally important that improvements are made to the current state of occupational therapy, and it seems necessary to force patients to participate in occupational therapy if it will be of benefit to the patient and improve their condition. Even though some critical dementia patients show no reaction to or willingness to accept treatment, the nurses or care workers should ensure that there are opportunities for them to interact. No matter how critical the condition of a patient, nobody should be given up on: saving and caring for patients is always the duty of LTC institutions and hospitals.

The number of people with dementia is expected to increase by 12% every 5 years [9]. As we look to the future of long-term care for those with dementia, the prospect of high-quality care lies ahead, and this study aims to stress the importance of therapy in long-term care institutions, and the fact that providing more encouragement may change the willingness of patients to participate in therapy activities.

References

1. Claudia, L., Martin, C.: Combining local context and WordNet similarity for word sense identification. Fellbaum, 265–283 (1998)
2. Ferri, C., Prince, M., Brayne, C., et al.: Global prevalence of dementia: a Delphi consensus study. Lancet, 211–217 (2005)
3. Gotze, U.: Scenario technique for strategic business planning. second edn. Deutscher University-Verlag Wiesbaden (1993)
4. Granger, C.V., Devis, L.S., Peters, M.C., et al.: Stroke rehabilitation: Analysis of repeated Barthel Index measures. Arch. Phys. Med. Rehabil. 60, 14–17 (1979)
5. Gunilla, N., Anders, W., et al.: Time use and costs of institutionalised elderly persons with or without dementia: results from the Nordanstig cohort in the Kungsholmen Project—a population based study in Sweden. International Journal of Geriatric Psychiatry, Wiley InterScience, Chichester (2006)
6. Fratiglioni, L., De Ronchi, D., Aguero-Torres, H.: Worldwide prevalence and incidence of dementia. Drugs Aging 15, 365–375 (1999)
7. Mahoney, F., Barthel, D.: Functional evaluation: the Barthel index. MD State Med. J. 14, 61–65 (1965)
8. Scholz, R.W., Tietje, O.: Embedded Case Study Methods: Integrating Quantitative and Qualitative Knowledge. Thousand Oaks (2002)
9. Steinhardt, B.: Report to the Secretary of Health and Human Services: Alzheimer's disease, estimates of prevalence in the United States. US General Accounting Office, 1–45 (1998)

Automatic Classification of Tongueprints in Healthy and Unhealthy Individuals

ZhaoHui Yang and Naimin Li

Department of Computer Science and Engineering, Harbin Institute of Technology (HIT),
Harbin 150001, China
Yangzhaohui7153@tom.com

Abstract. Tongueprints are fissile texture on tongue and one of observational contents of tongue diagnosis, which is an important diagnostic method in Traditional Chinese Medicine (TCM). With deep researches on tongueprints, three basic problems emerge: (1) TCM has always held that healthy individuals do not exhibit tongueprints, but in the recent years some medical researchers have found some healthy individuals in their small sample (<1000 cases) tongue image database do exhibit tongueprints. How about do tongueprints in a large amount of healthy individuals (>2000 cases)? (2) If about a third of a large amount of healthy individuals have tongueprints, mainstream diagnosis by inspecting tongueprints should lead to an over-diagnosis problem and some healthy individuals are diagnosed mistakenly as unhealthy individuals because it holds tongueprints themselves declare publicly diseases. Thus it is necessary to diagnose definitely a tongueprint image belong to an unhealthy individual based on tongueprint features. This is a basic problem and is of theoretical and practical importance for diagnosis by inspecting tongueprints. And which features of tongueprints can be used to diagnose definitely a tongueprint image belong to an unhealthy individual? (3) Actually, the second problem is recognition and classification of tongueprints in healthy and unhealthy individuals. To further promote the modernization process of the traditional tongue diagnosis, how are the researches done on automatic classification of tongueprints in healthy and unhealthy individuals? After further making sure there appear tongueprints in healthy individuals and finding which features of tongueprints can be used to diagnose definitely a tongueprint image belong to an unhealthy individual by statistic analysis on a large database of tongue images (more than 3000 cases), this paper do the researches about automatic classification of tongueprints in healthy and unhealthy individuals based on the large database. Firstly tongeprint regions are extracted by multi-direction synthetic tongueprint extraction. Then a SVM classifier is used to recognize a tongueprint image belong to a healthy or unhealthy individual based on tongueprint features. Recognition accurate rate of tongueprints in healthy and unhealthy individuals respectively are 75.81% and 74.61% based on the large database.

1 Introduction

Tongue diagnosis is an important diagnostic method in Traditional Chinese Medicine (TCM) and its observational contents are very rich. Tongueprints are fissile texture on

D. Zhang (Ed.): ICMB 2008, LNCS 4901, pp. 137–144, 2007.

tongue and one of observational contents of tongue diagnosis. By inspecting the condition of tongueprints, some diseases, for example liver disease, are diagnosed easily, with no pain and no injury and early [1, 2, 3].

TCM has always held that healthy individuals do not exhibit tongueprints and if a human being has tongueprints, he is ill. However, with deep researches on tongueprints, some medical researchers found some healthy individuals of their small sample (< 1000 cases) tongue image database do exhibit tongueprints [1, 4, 5]. The divarication on tongueprints in healthy individuals is a basic problem for diagnosis by inspecting tongueprints. Mainstream clinical practices on tongueprints distinguished tongues in healthy individuals from those of unhealthy individuals by examining color and texture features of tongue and so on, but yet without regard to tongueprint itself features. After diagnosing a tongue healthy or unhealthy, the unhealthy tongue is diagnosed a disease or a group of diseases by inspecting the condition of tongueprints. This diagnostic flow roots from the knowledge of no tongueprints in the healthy individuals. If the view of having tongueprints in the healthy individuals is true, mainstream diagnosis by inspecting tongueprints should lead to an over-diagnosis problem, namely some healthy individuals are diagnosed mistakenly as unhealthy individuals. Therefore, the divarication is of theoretical and practical importance for diagnosis by inspecting tongueprints. To address the divarication, it is necessary to setup a large database of tongue images, and then analyze statistically them, and finally confirm having tongueprints in the healthy individuals or not and establish rules of diagnosing a tongueprint image belongs to an unhealthy individuals based on tongueprint features if tongueprints do exist in healthy individuals. Our front works of statistical analysis on tongueprints in this paper just are related to the divarication.

Traditional tongue diagnosis has been researched objectively for more than ten years to settle its qualitative, subjective and experience-based nature. The objective researches mainly circumvent color and texture features of tongue [6], and rarely regard to tongueprint. In recent years, applied computation researchers have become increasingly interested in objective researches on tongueprints. Previous works on computerized methods used in researching objectively tongueprints can be divided into two classes: based on texture feature of full tongue and based on tongueprints own feature. The latter need determine position of tongueprint regions and is implemented difficultly in computer (articles about it are few), but it can extract tongueprints own feature exactly compared with the former. And at present, in the literature on researching objectively tongueprints, no articles are related to the topic associated with tongueprints in healthy individuals. To do across-the-board the objective researches on traditional tongue diagnosis and research objectively the subject correlative with tongueprints in healthy individuals, in this paper, some computerized methods based on tongueprint itself features are employed to classify automatically tongueprints in healthy and unhealthy individuals on the base of statistical analysis obtained by forenamed statistic works on tongueprints based on the tongueprint image collection in our large database of tongue images.

In this paper, we begin to establish a large database of tongue image (>3000 images). Under statistical analysis we show that healthy individuals do exhibit tongueprints and that tongueprints are in fact not few in healthy individuals. In consultation with TCM professionals, we recognize tongueprints in our large database to be part of healthy or unhealthy individuals by the feathers of tongueprints, such as color, depth, area and so on. To classify automatically tongueprints in healthy and unhealthy individuals based on our large database of tongue images, digital image processing techniques are applied to this subject. By multi-direction synthetic tongueprint extraction, we extract binary regions of tongueprints. Then based on tongueprint itself features, a SVM classifier is then applied to recognizing tongueprint images belong to healthy or unhealthy individuals. Finally, 75.81% and 74.61% recognition accurate rate of tongueprints are respectively found for healthy and unhealthy individuals in our large database of tongue images.

The remainder of this paper is organized as follows. Differences of tongueprint in healthy and unhealthy individuals are obtained in Section 2. Section 3 classifies automatically tongueprint images as belonging to healthy or unhealthy individuals. Section 4 contains the experimental results, and Section 5 offers our conclusion.

2 Differences of Tongueprint in Healthy and Unhealthy Individuals

The tongue image large database used in this work consists of 3297 tongue images captured with a high-resolution cybershot camera under in natural light between 9 and 10 o'clock in the morning in various locations. The large database contains 2044 tongue images of healthy persons and 1253 images from unhealthy persons. In this paper, a healthy person is one who has no current diseases or painful complaints and whom a physical examination revealed to have no health problems. The tongue images came from healthy subjects of a wide demographic background, male and female, old and young and residing in Harbin City. The tongue images of the unhealthy subjects were also collected in Harbin City and came from hospitals associated with both Western medicine and TCM and a variety of departments concerned with general surgery, digestive conditions, leukaemia and endocrinopathy, nephropathy, and chest conditions. Details of the large database can be found in Appendix.

In consultation with specialists in TCM, 35.23% of tongue images of healthy individuals in the large database are tongueprints. Furthermore, in consultation with specialists in TCM, we obtain the differences of tongueprint in healthy and unhealthy individuals. Comparison of tongueprints in healthy and unhealthy individuals is shown in Table 1.

Table 1. Comparison of tongueprints in healthy and unhealthy individuals

Feature items	Tongueprints in healthy	Tongueprints in unhealthy
Color	Light-red	Light-white, red and so on
Coarse degree of surface	Tender and neat	Coarse
Lenitive degree of surface	Not humid and not dry	Dry
Depth	Shallow correspondingly	Deep correspondingly
Area	Small correspondingly	Big correspondingly

3 Automatic Classification of Tongueprints in Healthy and Unhealthy Individuals

In this section we describe our approach to the computerized recognition and classification of tongueprint patterns. The discussion is in two parts. In subsection 3.1

we describe our tongueprint extraction approach. In subsection 3.2 we describe our approach to classify automatically tongueprint images as belonging to healthy or unhealthy individuals.

3.1 Multi-direction Synthetic Tongueprint Extraction

According to statistical results in section 2, the tongueprints in healthy individuals are differentiated from those in unhealthy individuals by tongueprint own features. Thus in this subsection we extract tongueprint regions by multi-direction synthetic tongueprint extraction. This approach includes four main processes, namely smoothing along eight directions, enhancements along eight directions, binary image extraction after fusing eight directional enhanced results, and synthetic strong and weak smoothing extraction.

Let I be the G component of true color tongue image in RGB color space. Thus in smoothing process, we respectively get eight directional smoothed results by convolving I with smoothing templates of eight directions. The smoothing template in horizontal direction $G_{\alpha s}{}^0$ is defined as follows:

$$G_{\alpha s}{}^0(x, y, \alpha_s) = \frac{1}{2\sqrt{\pi\alpha_s}} exp\left(-\frac{x^2 + y^2}{4\alpha_s}\right), \alpha_s > 0 \qquad (1)$$

And the smoothing template in direction θ, $G_{\alpha s}{}^\theta$ is obtained by rotating $G_{\alpha s}{}^0$ with angle degrees θ in a counterclockwise direction.

In enhancement process, we get eight directional enhanced results by respectively convolving eight directional smoothed results mentioned above with enhancement templates of eight directions. The enhancement template in horizontal direction g''^0 is defined as follows:

$$g''^0(x) = \frac{1}{\sqrt{2\pi}} exp(-\frac{x^2}{2})(x^2 - 1) \qquad (2)$$

And the enhancement template in direction θ, g''^θ is obtained by rotating g''^0 with angle degrees θ in a counterclockwise direction.

Then in binary image extraction process we fuse eight directional enhanced results by maximum operation to get the enhancement of I. Let I_{ss} be the enhancement of I. We use some thresholds to convert I_{ss} into tongueprint binary regions BW.

We find α_s is greater and smoothing effectiveness is better, but some tongueprints are lost, while α_s is smaller and more tongueprints are held, but noises are also more. Thus in synthetic strong and weak smoothing extraction process, we set α_s two values, namely α_{s1} and α_{s2} ($\alpha_{s1} < \alpha_{s2}$). Let $BW_{\alpha s1}$ represents the obtained BW if $\alpha_s = \alpha_{s1}$ and $BW_{\alpha s2}$ represents the obtained BW if $\alpha_s = \alpha_{s2}$. Look for the tongueprint points in 8-connectivity with each tongueprint pixel of $BW_{\alpha s2}$ on $BW_{\alpha s1}$ and then fuse them with $BW_{\alpha s2}$ to produce synthetic tongueprint binary regions BW_{syn} by logical "OR" operation.

3.2 Classifying Automatically Tongueprint Images as Belonging to Healthy or Unhealthy Individuals

From section 2, we know tongueprint images may be recognized by features of color, depth, and area and so on to be part of the healthy or unhealthy individuals. Thus, in this subsection we classify tongueprint images as belonging to the healthy or unhealthy individuals using a SVM (support vector machine) classifier trained by the following features of tongueprints, $Rmean$, $Rstd$, $TPGE$ and TPA, in that SVM classifier has been found to be effective in small sample learning problems and outperform other methods on two-class classification [7].

$Rmean$ and $Rstd$ are respectively mean and standard deviation of component R in RGB color space on tongueprint regions. They describe quantitatively color and surface of tongueprints. $TPGE$ represents tongueprint grads energy and describes quantitatively tongueprint depth. $TPGE$ is defined as follows:

$$TPGE = \sum_{i=1}^{m}\sum_{j=1}^{n}[TPG(i, j) \times BW_{syn}(i, j)]^2 \tag{3}$$

TPA represents tongueprint area and is gotten by the following formula:

$$TPA = \sum_{i=1}^{m}\sum_{j=1}^{n} BW_{syn}(i, j) \tag{4}$$

Where TPG is I_{ss} obtained while $\alpha_s = \alpha_{s1}$ (in subsection 3.1). BW_{syn} is explained in subsection 3.1.

We train and obtain a SVM classifier, $SVMC_{RTP}$, by feature combination of $Rmean$, $Rstd$, $TPGE$ and TPA of some typical tongueprint images respectively from healthy and unhealthy individuals in our large database.

After obtaining $SVMC_{RTP}$, we can classify a tongueprint image as belonging to the healthy or unhealthy individuals.

4   Experimental Results and Analysis

The tongueprint database used in this section contains 720 tongueprint images of healthy person and 761 tongueprint images of unhealthy person. In subsection 3.1, tongueprint regions are extracted along eight directions (0°, 22.5°, 45°, 67.5°, 90°, 112.5°, 145°, 167.5°). The thresholds are gotten by [8]. In addition, let $\alpha_{s1} = 0.85$, $\alpha_{s2} = 1.2$. In smoothing templates, if $\alpha_s = \alpha_{s1}$ let $x, y \in [-3,3]$ and if $\alpha_s = \alpha_{s2}$ let $x, y \in [-5,5]$. Here $x, y \in Z$. Let $x \in [-7,7]$ in enhancement templates and $x \in Z$. Z is integer set symbol.

We choose 150 typical tongueprint images of healthy person and 150 typical tongueprint images of unhealthy person, then extract their feature combinations, $Rmean$, $Rstd$, $TPGE$ and TPA, to train a SVM classifier, $SVMC_{LAB}$.

Thus a tongueprint image is recognized to be from healthy or unhealthy individuals by the $SVMC_{LAB}$ mentioned above. Tongueprint recognitions of healthy and unhealthy individuals in our large database by our methods are shown in Table 2.

Table 2. Tongueprint recognitions of healthy and unhealthy individuals in our large database

Tongueprints	Recognition true ratio	Recognition false ratio
In healthy	75.81%	24.19%
In unhealthy	74.61%	25.39%

5 Conclusions

Tongueprints are fissile texture on tongue and one of observational contents of tongue diagnosis. In this paper, to diagnose a tongueprint image in our tongue image large database to belong to health or unhealthy individuals by computerized methods, we proposed an automatic classification of tongueprints in healthy and unhealthy individuals belong to our tongue image large database according to statistical results on the large database. Experiments are implemented on a tongueprint image collection in our tongue image large database, and the results are promising.

The main contribution of this research is that, this is the first time, to the best knowledge of the authors, that the topic which is of theoretical and practical importance for diagnosis by inspecting tongueprints and associated with tongueprints in healthy individuals is researched by computerized means, namely by digital image processing techniques tongueprint images in our tongue image large database are classified automatically as being part of healthy or unhealthy individuals.

Even though this paper has explored for the first time automatic classification of tongueprints in healthy and unhealthy individuals in our tongue image large database, it just diagnoses tongueprints images in our tongue image large database belong to healthy or unhealthy individuals. Definitely discussing and automatically researching the subject on diagnosing a disease or a group of diseases by inspecting tongueprint might overcome this limitation, but this is a subject for future study.

Acknowledgement

This work is partially supported by the National Natural Science Foundation (NSFC) key overseas project under the contract no. 60620160097.

References

1. Li, N.M., et al.: Tongue Diagnostics. Academy Press (Xue Yuan), London (2006)
2. Wang, H., et al.: Tongueglyphics and Liver Disease. GanShu Science and Technology Press (1995)
3. Wang, H., et al.: Diagnose Disease by Tongueglyphics. Chinese Science and Technology Press On Medicine (2000)
4. Li, N.M., Wang, S.Y., Lin, X.D.: Principal Progress on Four Diagnostic Methods in Early 21 Century. The Seventh Selected Publication of Research on Four Diagnostic Methods, pp. 1–2 (2004)
5. Wang, S.Y., Li, N.M.: Research on Tongueglyphics. The Seventh Selected Publication of Research on Four Diagnostic Methods, 38–40 (2004)
6. Pang, B., Zhang, D., Wang, K.: Computerized Tongue Diagnosis Based on Bayesian Networks. IEEE Transactions on Biomedical Engineering 51(10), 1803–1810 (2004)
7. Bian, Z.Q., Zhang, X.G., et al.: Pattern Recognition, 2nd edn., pp. 280–282. Press of Tsinghua University (2003)
8. Wu, X., Wang, K., Zhang, D.: Line Feature Extraction and Matching in Palmprint. In: The 2nd International Conference on Image and Graphics (ICIG 2002), Proceedings of SPIE, vol. 4875(1), pp. 583–590 (2002)

Appendix: Large Database of Tongue Images

Source list of our large database of tongue images are narrated as follows and the instance of tongue images of healthy persons firstly is reported:

a) 1063 tongue images are from Physical Examination Station in Centre of Controlling Disease in Harbin City. Those healthy persons are from 18 to 45 years old and men and women approximately are half-and-half.

b) 136 and 34 tongue images of healthy undergraduates are respectively gotten from Hei Long Jiang University of Chinese Medicine and Harbin Institute of Technology.

c) 46 tongue images are from healthy old folks in Place of Prevention and Cure to tuberculosis in Harbin.

d) 247 healthy old folks in community offer their tongue images.

e) 518 tongue images are obtained from healthy children in kindergarten, elementary school and high school.

Tongue images of healthy persons total 2044.
Now we report source of tongue images of unhealthy persons:

a) We capture 333 tongue images from general surgery, digestive medical department, aspiratory medical department, circular medical department, leukaemia and endocrinopathy medical department, nephropathy medical department and so on in the 211 Hospital of the Chinese People's Liberation Army.

b) 27 tongue images are shot from general surgery in Central Hospital of Red Cross in Harbin.

c) 6 tongue images are shot from circular medical department in Harbin Hospital of Traditional Chinese Medicine.

d) 61 tongue images are from Chest Hospital in Harbin.

e) 817 tongue images are shot from digestive medical department in the Second Affiliated Hospital of Harbin Medical University.

f) 9 tongue images are shot from circular medical department in the First Affiliated Hospital of Hei Long Jiang University of Chinese Medicine.

Tongue images of unhealthy persons total 1253.

VWPS: A Ventilator Weaning Prediction System with Artificial Intelligence

Austin H. Chen[1] and Guan-Ting Chen[2]

[1] Department of Medical Informatics, Tzu-Chi University, No. 701, Sec. 3,
Jhongyang Rd. Hualien City, Hualien County 97004, Taiwan
achen@mail.tcu.edu.tw
[1, 2] Graduate Institute of Medical Informatics, Tzu-chi University, No. 701, Sec. 3,
Jhongyang Rd. Hualien City, Hualien County 97004, Taiwan
achen@mail.tcu.edu.tw, 96325101@stmail.tcu.edu.tw

Abstract. How to wean patients efficiently off mechanical ventilation continues to be a challenge for medical professionals. In this paper we have described a novel approach to the study of a ventilator weaning prediction system (VWPS). Firstly, we have developed and written three Artificial Neural Network (ANN) algorithms to predict a weaning successful rate based on the clinical data. Secondly, we have implemented two user-friendly weaning success rate prediction systems; the VWPS system and the BWAP system. Both systems could be used to help doctors objectively and effectively predict whether weaning is appropriate for patients based on the patients' clinical data. Our system utilizes the powerful processing abilities of MatLab. Thirdly, we have calculated the performance through measures such as sensitivity and accuracy for these three algorithms. The results show a very high sensitivity (around 80%) and accuracy (around 70%). To our knowledge, this is the first design approach of its kind to be used in the study of ventilator weaning success rate prediction.

1 Introduction

We present a Ventilator Weaning Prediction System (VWPS) using Artificial Neural Network (ANN) algorithms in this paper. VWPS is a user friendly system based on the patients' clinical data. It helps doctors predict objectively and effectively whether weaning is appropriate for patient.

Using a ventilator has many disadvantages such as the risk of ventilator pneumonia, patient discomfort, and the economic burden to the family [1, 2]. The number of patients requiring mechanical ventilation is increasing as the average age of the population increases. Since there is no standard for doctors to decide when to begin a weaning process, weaning too late not only wastes limited medical resources but also increases the infected rate. Development of a reliable system using computer techniques provides a possible solution for these questions.

Artificial Neural Network is one of the most promising candidates among all the possible computer techniques. ANN is a bionic analysis technique for Artificial Intelligence. It has been widely used in health care studies; examples include the diagnosis of myocardial infarction [3], the analysis of transplants [4], the monitoring of lung embolism [5], the prediction of trauma death rate [6], the probability of child meningococcus [7], and the operation decision support for brain surgery [8].

D. Zhang (Ed.): ICMB 2008, LNCS 4901, pp. 145–152, 2007.
© Springer-Verlag Berlin Heidelberg 2007

The goal of this study was to develop a prediction system with ANN techniques which can serve as an intelligent tool for doctors to predict the ventilator weaning success rate based on a patient's direct test data.

2   Materials and Methods

2.1   Selection of Features

Burns et al. first developed a ventilator weaning estimation form - BWAP (Burns Wean Assessment Program) [9, 10]. BWAP is composed of 26 factors (12 general

Table 1. Features and characteristics

	Features	Characteristics
1	Age	Age is one of the most danger factors causing weaning fail for people more than 70 years old [11]
2	Days of Intubation	Not only the rate of infecting in the hospital will increase but also decrease the thaw and endurance of breathe. The ventilator weaning success rate is going to decrease with more days of intubation [12].
3	Days of Estimating	During days of intubation, medical officers should make a precise plan to estimate days of weaning.
4	Heartbeat	It should be 60 and 120 per minute. Medical officers should observe the condition of angina pectoris and arrhythmia with people.
5	Systolic Pressure	It should be between 90 and 150 mmHg without using methoxamine or low dose (dopamine 5μg/kg/min or dobutamin 5μg /kg/min).
6	Body Temperature	It should be between 35.5 ℃ and 37.5℃ with no infecting.
7	Specific Volume of Blood	Observe that the specific volume of blood is more than 30% or not.
8	Sodium (Na)	It should be between 137 to 153 mEq / L.
9	Potassium (K)	It should be between 3.5 to 5.3 mEq / L.
10	Max Pressure of Inhaling	It uses to be the significant referring that estimating patient could spontaneity breathe.
11	Max Pressure of Expiration	It should be more than 30 cmH2O.
12	Index Number of Shallowly Quick Breath	It should less than 105 per minute.
13	Air Exchanging Capacity per Minute	It should be smaller than 10 1/min.
14	Cough	Appraise the ability of patients to exclude secretions of the breathing passage.
15	X-ray	It will be an important evidence whether weaning is successful
16	Capacity of Urine	BUN takes a high estimation with heart failure or kidney function destroyed. Patients would be dysuria which would effect weaning.

classifications and 14 breathing-related classifications). Among these 26 features, it is considered that weaning will be successful if more than 17 features are satisfied within the requirements. In this study, we selected and screened 16 features after thorough discussion with experts and doctors. Our results demonstrated that the selection of these features produced a very high accuracy in the prediction of ventilator weaning success. Table 1 summarizes the features and their characteristics.

In this paper, we collected 121 sets of data from a medical center in the middle region of Taiwan. These records contain data on patients who are on a ventilator and form the basis of our feature set. After weaning, if the patient can breathe by himself/herself, we define it as a successful weaning.

2.2 Artificial Neural Network

We use two-thirds of the 121 datasets, or 81 sets of data, for training, and one-third, or 40 sets of data, for testing. ANN codes were written in MatLab using Back Propagation Network (BPN). The network contains 3 layers of forward neural networks: the input layer, the hidden layer, and the output layer. There are 16 neurons in the input layer, 7 neurons in the hidden layer, and 1 neuron in the output layer. Three kinds of BPN training algorithms were used to obtain optimal results: conjugate gradient algorithm [13], Levenberg-Marquarft algorithm [14], and the One-Step-Secant algorithm [15]. The training framework of the model is shown in Fig. 1.

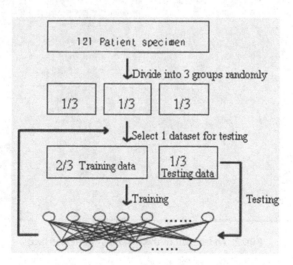

Fig. 1. Training framework of the model

3   System Implementation

In this study, we have developed a ventilator weaning success rate prediction system (VWPS) that can help medical professionals predict weaning success rate based on clinical test data. The system generates its predictions based on ANN techniques. VWPS utilizes MATLAB codes and interfaces together to display the prediction results on a user-friendly interface.

VWPS is a human-based system that provides two main functions to the users. The first function of the system generates two types of databases. One database records the basic information and clinical test data of the patients, and the other database records the codes of the doctor who is on duty and the conditions of the hospitalized patients. The second function of VWPS is the core of the system. After users input the test data, the system will analyze the data and display the results on the interface. VWPS converts codes written in MATLAB and integrates the results onto the MATLAB GUIDE interface.

3.1 The VWPS System Interface (Fig. 2)

There are three panels in the VWPS interface: Patient Data, Input Data, and ANN Prediction. Users enter basic patient data (Patient ID, Endo ID and Date) in the Patient Data panel. This data can serve as foreign keys in the database. The Input Data Panel contains 16 patient features used in this study. The "DataInput submit" bottom can save the patient data into the database.

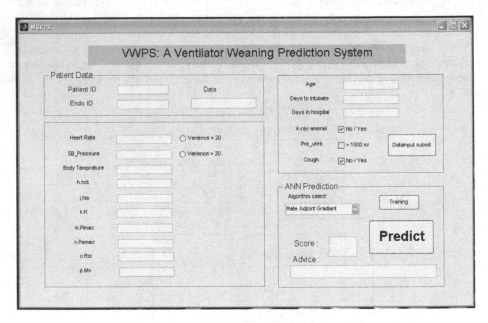

Fig. 2. The screen of the VWPS system interface

In the ANN Prediction panel, three algorithms (Rate Adjoint Gradiant, Levenberg-Marquaft, and One-Step-Secant) in Artificial Neural Network were available. After selecting the algorithm and clicking the "Predict" bottom, a score and advice will be displayed.

3.2 The BWAP System Interface (Fig. 3)

Except for the VWPS system, we also provide the BWAP prediction interface. By using the 20 features from the input data of a patient, a results (score and advice) can be displayed after the users clicking the "Predict" button.

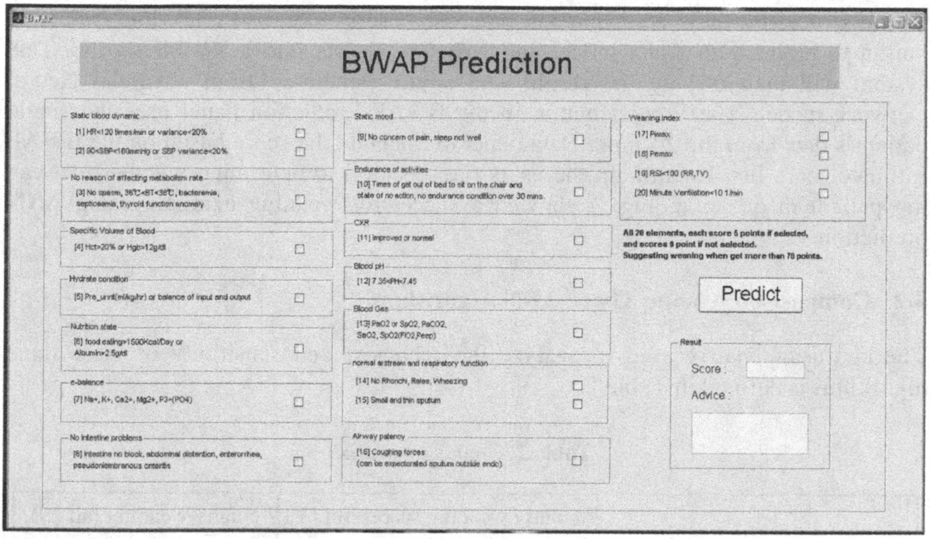

Fig. 3. The screen of the BWAP system interface

4 Results and Discussion

4.1 Outputs from the System

Users may select either the BWAP or ANN Prediction method for analysis. In the ANN Prediction panel, users first select the algorithm and then click the Training

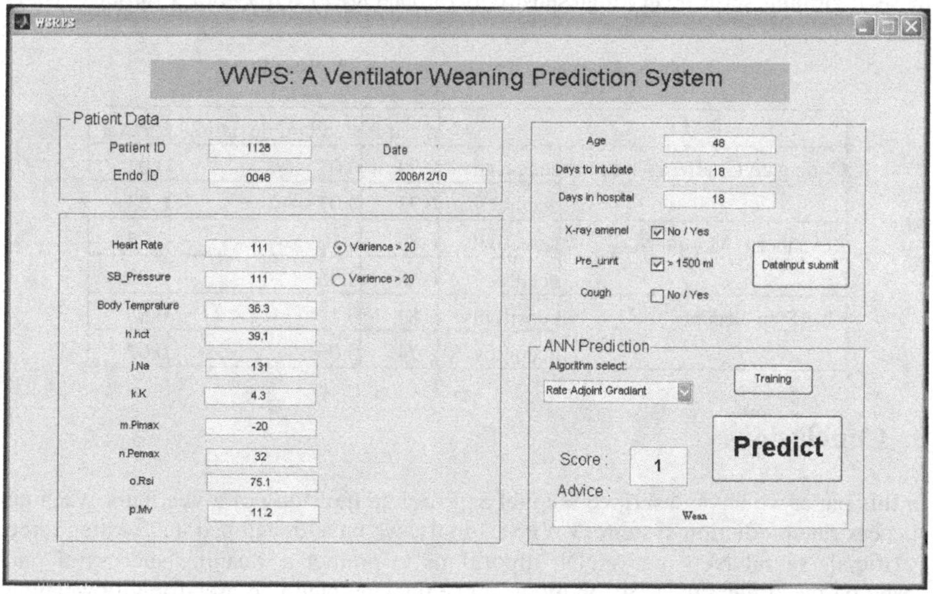

Fig. 4. A successful example of the VWPS prediction system

button to add the new data into the database. Users may also click the Predictive button to produce an ANN model and write the results into a VWPS.xls file. This system will then display the results and advice generated from Artificial Neural Network model. The Predict button in the BWAP Prediction panel uses the single patient's data from the 20 Input Data panel to calculate the score based on the BWAP estimate score list. It can help the users (i.e. doctors) to determine whether to wean the patient in question. Fig. 4 showed a successful weaning example using ANN prediction.

4.2 Comparison Among Three ANN Algorithms

The confusion matrix used to analyze the accuracy, and sensitivity of these three algorithms is defined in Table 2.

Table 2. Confusion matrix

	Actually weaning successful (Y)	Actually weaning fail (N)
predict weaning successful (Y)	A	B
predict weaning fail (Y)	C	D

Where Accuracy, Sensitivity, and Specificity are defined by

Accuracy = (A+D)/ (A+B+C+D)
Sensitivity = A/ (A+C).

Table 3 summarizes the results from these three algorithms. The results from all these algorithms show a very high sensitivity (around 80%) and accuracy (around 70%).

Table 3. Analyzing results from 3 ANN algorithms

		mean	standard deviation	95%CI
Conjugate Gradient Method	sensitivity	0.79	0.07	0.03
	accuracy	0.73	0.07	0.03
Levenberg- Marquarft	sensitivity	0.80	0.10	0.05
	accuracy	0.68	0.06	0.03
One-Step-Secant	sensitivity	0.83	0.11	0.05
	accuracy	0.74	0.05	0.02

5 Conclusions

In this paper we have described a novel approach to the study of a ventilator weaning success rate prediction system (VWPS). Firstly, we have developed and written three Artificial Neural Network (ANN) algorithms to predict a weaning successful rate based on the clinical data. Secondly, we have implemented two user-friendly weaning success rate prediction systems; the VWPS system and the BWAP system. Both systems could be used to help doctors objectively and effectively predict whether weaning is appropriate for patients based on the patients' clinical data. Our system utilizes the powerful processing abilities of MatLab. Thirdly, we have calculated the performance through measures such as sensitivity and accuracy for these three algorithms. The results show a very high sensitivity (around 80%) and accuracy (around 70%).

Acknowledgements

The authors thank the National Science Council of the Republic of China for their financial support of project NSC 95-2221-E-320-001.

References

1. Kurek, C.J., Dewar, D., Lambrinos, J., McLeBooth, F.V., Cohen, I.L.: Clinical and economic outcomes of mechanically ventilated patients in New York State during 1993. Chest. 114, 214–222 (1998)
2. Rosen, R.L., Bone, R.C.: Financial implications of ventilator care. Crit. Care. Clin. 6, 797–805 (1990)
3. Baxt, W.G.: Use of an artificial neural network for the diagnosis of myocardial infarction. Ann. Intern. Med. 115(11), 843–848 (1991)
4. Dorsey, S.G., Waltz, C.F., Brosch, L., Connerney, I., Schweitzer, E.J., Barlett, S.T.: A neural network model for predicting pancreas transplant graft outcome. Diabetes Care 20(7), 1128–1133 (1997)
5. Kemeny, V., Droste, D.W., Hermes, S., Nabavi, D.G., Schulte-Altedo-rneburg, G., Siebler, M., Ringelstein, E.B.: Automatic embolus detection by a neural network. Stroke 30, 807–810 (1999)
6. DiRusso, S.M., Sullivan, T., Holly, C., Cuff, S.N., Savino, J.: An Artificial Neural Network as a Model for Prediction of Survival in Trauma Patients: Validation for a Regional Trauma Area. J. Trauma 49, 212–223 (2000)
7. Nguyen, T., Malley, R., Inkelis, S., Kuppermann, N.: Comparison of prediction models for adverse outcome in pediatric meningococcal disease using artificial neural network and logistic regression analyses. Journal of Clinical Epidemiolog 55, 687–695 (2002)
8. Li, Y.C., Liu, L., Chiu, W.T., Jian, W.S.: Neural network modeling for surgical decisions on traumatic brain injury patients. Int. J. Med. Inf. 57(1), 1–9 (2000)
9. Burns, S.M., Earven, S., Fisher, C., Lewis, R., Schubart, J.R., Truwit, J.D., Bleck, T.P.: University of Virginia Long Term Mechanical Ventilation Team: Implementation of an institutional program to improve clinical and financial outcomes of mechanically ventilated patients: One-year outcomes and lessons learned. Critical Care Med., 2752–2763 (2003)
10. Burns, S.M., Ryan, B., Burns, J.E.: The weaning continuum use of Acute Physiology and Chronic Health Evaluation III, Burns Wean Assessment Program, Therapeutic Intervention Scoring System, and Wean Index scores to establish stages of weaning. Critical Care Med., 2259–2267 (2000)
11. Kaohsiung Veterans General Hospital: Shallow talking about ventilator, http://www.vghks.gov.tw/cm/html/health/symptom/EduMV.htm

12. Esteban, A., Anzueto, A., Frutos, F., Alía, I., Brochard, L., Stewart, T.E., Benito, S., Epstein, S.K., Apezteguía, C., Nightingale, P., Arroliga, A.C., Tobin, M.J., et al.: Characteristics and Outcomes in Adult Patients Receiving Mechanical Ventilation. JAMA 287(3), 345–355 (2002)
13. Moller,s M.F.: A Scaled Conjugate Gradient Algorithm for Fast Supervised Learning. Neural networks, 525–533 (1993)
14. Marquez, G., Wang, L.V., Wang, C., Hu, Z.: Development of tissue-simulating optical phantoms: poly-N-isopropylacrylamide solution entrapped inside a hydrogel. Phys. Med. Biol., 309–318 (1999)
15. Battiti, R.: First and second order methods for learning: Between steepest descent and Newton's method. Neural Computation, 141–166 (1992)

A Method of Classifying Tongue Colors for Traditional Chinese Medicine Diagnosis Based on the CIELAB Color Space

Bocong Li[1], Qingmei Huang[1], Yan Lu[1], Songhe Chen[2],
Rong Liang[2], and Zhaoping Wang[3]

[1] National Laboratory of Color Science and Engineering
Beijing Institute of Technology
Beijing 100081, China
huangqm@bit.edu.cn
[2] School of Preclinical Medicine
Beijing University of Chinese Medicine
Beijing 100029, China
shchenathena@126.com
[3] Medical Examination Center of Beijing TongRen Hospital
Beijing 100730, China

Abstract. Objective tongue color analysis is an important research point for tongue diagnosis in Traditional Chinese Medicine. In this paper a research based on the clinical process of diagnosing tongue color is reported. The color data in RGB color space were first transformed into the data in CIELAB color space, and the color gamut of the displayed tongue was obtained. Then a numerical method of tongue color classification based on the Traditional Chinese Medicine (for example: light white tongue, light red tongue, red tongue) was developed. The conclusion is that this research can give the description and classification of the tongue color close to those given by human vision and may be carried out in clinical diagnosis.

1 Introduction

The analysis of tongue color is one of the important research points. The objective of it is to describe and classify the color of the tongue with some objective data system or method, and to provide a new way to do the research. In the last 10 years, the development of the technology has provided some new methods for the objective research. In the current researches, the RGB color space is always utilized in the collecting devices (e.g. digital cameras) and displaying devices (e.g. monitors)[1-5].

When RGB color space is used, there is a problem that the color data we got or displayed are closely related to the devices we used. Therefore, the same tongue color data from different digital cameras may be represented with different color. In order to display the tongue color uniquely and truly, we need to characterize the display devices.

Even though, we can only analyze tongue color data in definite display device to make sure of the correctness of the research. Once the data are transmitted to other

D. Zhang (Ed.): ICMB 2008, LNCS 4901, pp. 153–159, 2007.
© Springer-Verlag Berlin Heidelberg 2007

devices, the problem of color distortion will also appear. According to this, the conclusion of analysis based on the RGB color space can't truly describe the tongue color.

In order to conquer this problem, we brought forward a method based on the CIELAB color space. According to it, we studied the distribution of the tongue color in the color gamut to find a more suitable method to classify the tongue color of Traditional Chinese Medicine (i.e. red tongue, light red tongue, light white tongue). Then we analyzed and described tongue colors based on the vision characters, and got the typical color of every kind of tongue colors. All of these are used to work out an exact and simple method which can be widely applied to classifying the tongue color for the clinical tongue diagnosis of Traditional Chinese Medicine.

2   Tongue Color and CIELAB Uniform Color Space

The diagnosis of tongue color is to get the relationship between the visual color stimulations and clinical syndrome-complexes. What is important is to describe the visual stimulation quantificationally (to describe visual stimulation with some data). Then how to choose an appropriate method of tongue description quantificationally is the crux of solution.

For the purpose of quantificational description of the visual stimulations and measurement, CIE (The International Commission on Illumination) set up the CIEXYZ and CIE1931RGB system according to the experiments of matching three primitive colors. Later, they also did a great deal of quantity research to make the CIEXYZ system uniform and set up the CIELAB uniform color system. In CIELAB color space, the description of chromatic difference (or the calculation of the chromatic difference) was closer to the difference of human visual perception. So it has become the basis of color criterions in many countries. [6]

When we studied the tongue color diagnosis based on the CIELAB color system, we can get more impersonal and actual tongue color data because the description of color is independent of the color devices. And the distribution and classification of the tongue color in CIELAB color space are more suitable to clinical description and judgment of tongue color in TCM. Accordingly, the CIELAB color system is adopted in this research.

3   Typical Colors of Tongue and Classification

3.1   Three Typical Colors of Tongue

The data of tongue color samples were collected by a tongue analysis instrument in Beijing University of Chinese Medicine and Beijing TongRen Hospital. The tongue analysis instrument had its color performance characterized, i.e. it can transform the data in RGB color space to those in XYZ color space. Then we transformed the data to the CIELAB uniform color space to get the values of L^*, a^*, b^* at all interested points on the tongue. The classification of tongue colors (i.e. red tongue, light red tongue, light white tongue) is accomplished by experienced doctors.

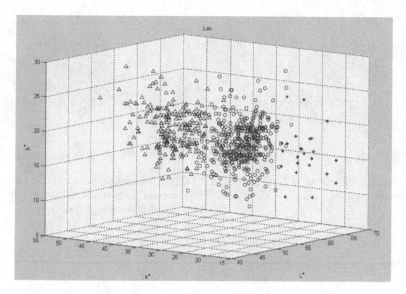

Fig. 1. Three kinds of tongue points in $L^*a^*b^*$ space triangle: red tongue; circle: light red tongue; star: light white tongue

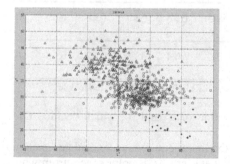

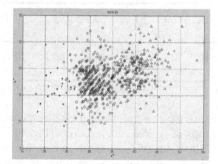

Fig. 2. The sample points in L^*-a^* plane   **Fig. 3.** The sample points in a^*-b^* plane

Fig. 1 shows different kinds of samples of tongue color, from which we can find out that the distribution of different kinds of tongue samples in the color space has some rules and the L^*-a^* plane and the a^*-b^* plane can describe the distribution of color data best (Fig. 2 and Fig. 3).

One of the objectives of the analysis of tongue color is to get the typical color of each kind of tongue, which can be utilized in the clinical diagnosis. We found that conic curves can be used to simulate the distribution in the L^*-a^* plane (Fig.4) and both linear equations and conic equations can be used to simulate the distribution in the a^*-b^* plane (Fig.5). Of course, those lines only show the average positions of respective data group, so they are here called as central lines.

According to these curves, we divided the values of L^* into ten parts uniformly, then we can get the values of eleven typical points of each color (Table 1). From these

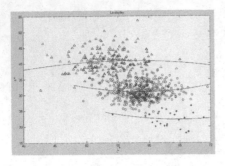

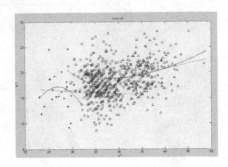

Fig. 4. The sample points in L*-a* plane and the three central lines

Fig. 5. The sample points in a*-b* plane and the central lines (the solid curves are conic, the dot ones are straight lines)

Table 1. The values of L^* of all kinds of tongue color

T-P	1	2	3	4	5	6	7	8	9	10	11
LW	54	55.5	57	58.5	60	61.5	63	64.5	66	67.5	69
LR	49	51.1	53.2	55.3	57.4	59.5	61.6	63.7	65.8	67.9	70
R	42	44.4	46.8	49.2	51.6	54	56.4	58.8	61.2	63.6	66

T-P: typical points; LW: light white tongue; LR: light red tongue; R: red tongue

values we can calculate the corresponding value of a* and b*, which decided three groups of typical tongue colors (Fig. 6).

The value of L*, a* and b* which we used the linear equations to calculate made up of the sample data. Then, we transformed the data into RGB color space, from which we can make typical color blocks of tongue color for reference. (Fig. 7, Fig. 8, Fig. 9).

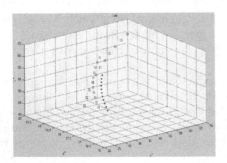

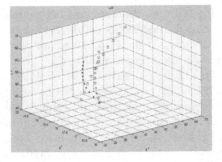

Fig. 6. 11 typical color points for each straight line

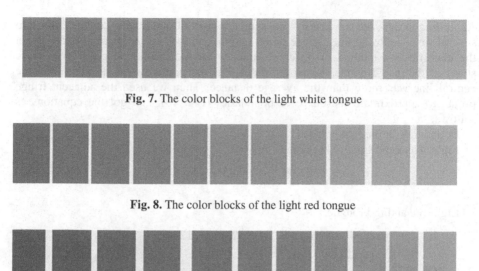

Fig. 7. The color blocks of the light white tongue

Fig. 8. The color blocks of the light red tongue

Fig. 9. The color blocks of the red tongue

3.2 Classification of Tongue Color

The aim of description curves and typical color blocks of tongue color was to classify the tongue color. Therefore, how to get the boundaries of different tongue colors was the key of the problem. We got not only the planar and 3 dimensional distribution of tongue colors but also the distance from each sample point to the central line.

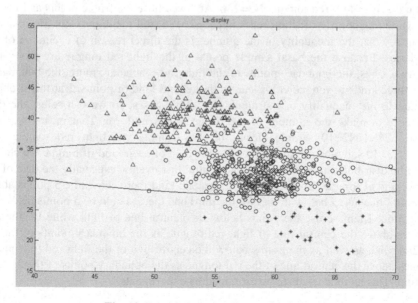

Fig. 10. Boundaries according to simulation

According to that, we can classify the sample points of one kind of tongue color into several sorts: central points, fringe points and the points between them. In order to get the classification method of different kinds of tongue colors, we need to do more study of the fringe points, which are defined as the points whose distance from the central line was more than the average distance. Then we used the adjacent fringe points to approximate the curve of boundaries (Fig. 10), and got the equations as follows:

Boundaries in the L^*-a^* plane:

Light white and light red tongue:

$$a^*=0.0065277*L^{*2}-0.77895*L^*+50.873 \qquad (1)$$

Light red and red tongue:

$$a^*=-0.0096454*L^{*2}+0.95232*L^*+12.463 \qquad (2)$$

3.3 Verification

We used the equations of classification above to deal with other data of tongue color and got the results as follows:

The 1st kind of sample points (the light white tongue), the correctness degree is 96%; The 2nd kind of sample points (the light red tongue), the correctness degree is 81.98%; The 3rd kind of sample points (the red tongue), the correctness degree is 97.88%.

From the results above, we can find that the correctness degree of the first and third kinds were higher. However, the correctness degree of the second one was lower than others, which might be related to the selection of sample points.

In the experiment, the number of samples were: light white tongue, $N1=25$; light red tongue, $N2=444$; red tongue, $N3=236$. And we chose the fringe points as follows: light white tongue, $n1=11$; light red tongue, $n2=186$; red tongue, $n3=98$. From above we can see that the inequality of the number is the direct reason of excursion of the boundaries. Because the basal sample points of the light red tongue are more than other two kinds, the boundary points of the light red tongue are more, the boundaries of the three kinds of tongue color lean to the second kind of points. But this problem was due to the inequality of the number of clinic cases, so we can select the data repeatedly to make the number of the fringe points uniform. That means we may choose $n2*N1/N2=10$ samples from the 444 samples of light red tongue, and $n3*N1/N3=10$ samples of red tongue. But the data of each kind of tongue we choose should be distributed in both sides of the central line evenly, especially the data of the second kind of tongue. Therefore, for the second kind there should be 5 points above the central line and 5 below it; and for the third one there should be 5 points below the central line. Then we use the points below the central line of light white tongue and the ones above the central line of light red tongue as the boundary points of the 1st and 2nd kind, as well as the points below the central line of the light red tongue and the ones above the central line of the red tongue as the boundary points of the 2nd and 3rd kind. This method needs to be examined by experiments.

4   Conclusions and Prospect

This paper made use of the CIELAB color space to describe, analyze and classify the tongue color according to the process of the tongue diagnosis of Traditional Chinese Medicine. First, we transformed large amount of RGB data of color samples to the data in the CIELAB color space. And then, we made use of the numeric simulation method to classify the sorts of tongue color in Traditional Chinese Medicine based on the distribution of the sample points. Considering the difficulty of describing the boundaries in three-dimensional space, we chose the L^*-a^* and the a^*-b^* plane to simplify the process. We simulated the boundaries from the adjacent sample points of tongue color. At last, we brought forward the typical colors of three kinds of tongue color. From the result of the experiment, we can analyze and classify the different tongue color in TCM and find out the typical colors as well.

This research involves a combination of the theories of color science and the tongue diagnosis, which need more clinical experiments to verify.

References

1. Zhang, Z., Wang, Z., Zhou, C., et al.: The Design And Implement of the WXZ analysis system of traditional Chinese medicine. Medical Information 18(6), 550–553 (2005)
2. Zhang, Z., Zhou, C., Xu, J.: Application of Visual Measurement Method of Tongue Color to Evaluate Therapeutic Effects of Ready-Made Chinese Medications. Acta Uniiversitatis Traditionis Medicalis Sinensis Pharmacologiaeque ShangHai 19(3), 45–48 (2005)
3. Xu, J., Zhou, C., Zhang, Z., et al.: Computerized Analysis and Recognition of Tongue and Its Coating Color in Tongue Diagnosis. Acta Uniiversitatis Traditionis Medicalis Sinensis Pharmacologiaeque ShangHai. 18(3), 43–47 (2004)
4. Zhang, H., Li, B., Yao, P., et al.: Research on the Tongue Color Classification with Automatic Tongue Analysis in Traditional Chinese Medicine. Beijing Biomedical Engineering 25(1), 47–50 (2006)
5. Wong, W., Huang, S.: Studies on Externalization of Application of Tongue Inspection of TCM. Engineering Science. 3(1), 78–82 (2001)
6. Tang, S., Chromatics, M.: Beijing Institute of Technology Press, pp. 25–27 (1990)

Hepatitis Diagnosis Using Facial Color Image

Mingjia Liu and Zhenhua Guo

Bio-computing Research Center, Shenzhen Graduate School of
Harbin Institute of Technology, China
63025648@163.com, denis@hit.edu.cn

Abstract. Facial color diagnosis is an important diagnostic method in traditional Chinese medicine (TCM). However, due to its qualitative, subjective and experience-based nature, traditional facial color diagnosis has a very limited application in clinical medicine. To circumvent the subjective and qualitative problems of facial color diagnosis of Traditional Chinese Medicine, in this paper, we present a novel computer aided facial color diagnosis method (CAFCDM). The method has three parts: face Image Database, Image Preprocessing Module and Diagnosis Engine. Face Image Database is carried out on a group of 116 patients affected by 2 kinds of liver diseases and 29 healthy volunteers. The quantitative color feature is extracted from facial images by using popular digital image processing techniques. Then, KNN classifier is employed to model the relationship between the quantitative color feature and diseases. The results show that the method can properly identify three groups: healthy, severe hepatitis with jaundice and severe hepatitis without jaundice with accuracy higher than 73%.

1 Introduction

Traditional Chinese Medicine diagnosis (TCM) includes four parts: inspection, listening and smelling, inquiry and pulse-taking and palpation [3]. Inspecting facial color is one important aspect of "inspection". And facial color diagnosis is one of the most valuable and widely used diagnostic methods in TCM by observing any abnormal change on the face. The biggest advantage of facial color diagnosis lies in its simplicity immediacy and no pain. Whenever organs inside body occur lesions, it will be reflected on the face. This theory is very valuable for clinical diagnosis.

As facial color diagnosis play so important role in the diagnosis and treatment of disease, it is attracting more and more attention both in clinical medicine and in biomedicine. However, due to historical limitation, facial color diagnosis of TCM has been based on human eyes to judge and human language to describe, which has many shortcomings. For example, it is so subjective and limited by the medical experience and language capacity of doctors [4]. Therefore, different doctors may use different standards to diagnose disease, which, obviously, will impact the efficiency of diagnosis. At the same time, facial color diagnosis is not understood by Western medicine and modern biomedicine very well. Therefore, it is necessary to build an objective and quantitative diagnostic standard for facial color diagnosis.

D. Zhang (Ed.): ICMB 2008, LNCS 4901, pp. 160–167, 2007.
© Springer-Verlag Berlin Heidelberg 2007

Currently, the color measurement methods include using colorimeter, vascular volume instrument, infrared thermograph instrument, digital camera, spectro-photometer, and so on. In China, Cai [5-8] has used portable colorimeter to do some research about pathological color, facial color of hepatitis and tuberculosis and blood disease of patients. And Chen [9] has used infrared thermography to detect facial temperature. The results of these researchers prove that the basic theories of color diagnosis of TCM are right and the lesions inside body does change facial color.

All of above provides the foundation for our facial color diagnosis. In medicine, liver disease, especially severe hepatitis, could obviously cause liver dysfunction and facial telangiectasia; at last, the facial color will change gradually. Therefore, in this paper, we focus on severe hepatitis diagnosis only. Severe hepatitis could be classified into severe hepatitis with jaundice and without jaundice. Modern medicine thinks the content of bold red pigment in the blood over 2mg% will cause sclera, mucosal, skin and humeral yellow. Therefore, the characteristics of severe hepatitis with jaundice are facial yellowing. However, severe hepatitis without jaundice will cause face dark, because of liver dysfunction [4].

In this paper, we present a computerized facial color inspection approach, which is called a facial color-computing model based on quantitative features and KNN classifier, for the diagnosis of disease. In the following section, we introduce a framework to segment the face region and extract the skin blocks. We provide experiment results in section 3 and draw some conclusions in section 4.

2 Detect and Segment Face Region and Extract Skin Blocks

If we use the all part of facial image, there would be so many noises; the calculation and cost of time are too big. Therefore, we extract some skin blocks as the feature from a face image uniformly. Therefore, we locate the position of eyebrow, eyes, nostril and mouth firstly, and then we get the center points of skin blocks. Fig 1 shows the process in this section.

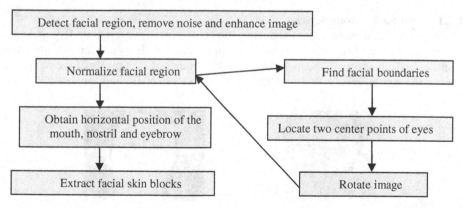

Fig. 1. Flowchart of detecting and segmenting face region and extracting skin blocks

2.1 Detect Facial Region

Until now, there are many methods to detect the facial region from an image. In this paper, we use the method proposed by Rein-Lien Hsu [10]. They proposed a skin color model which is used to segment the facial region from background. After skin color clustering model, the skin pixels are white and other pixels are black. Fig. 2 shows some segmentation results.

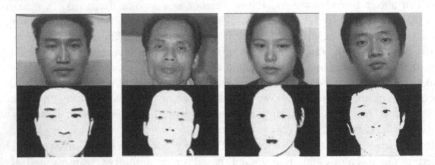

Fig. 2. The images after skin color clustering model (The four images of the first row are original images and the four images of the second row are processed images)

There are noises in the image after skin color clustering model. Here we use 7*7 median filter to remove noises. Because some people's eyes may be small and median filter weakens the eye region as well, we use dilation for black pixels method to enhance the eye region [11] for the future need.

2.2 Normalize Facial Region

After we have detected the facial region and removed noises, for the further work, we locate the two center points of the eyes, rotate the image and locate the horizontal position of the nostril, mouth and eyebrow to normalize facial region.

2.2.1 Find Facial Boundaries

After removing the noises and enhancing image, to obtain the top boundary of facial region, we find a horizontal line including most skin pixels as a reference line, and then we find a horizontal line including the half number of skin pixels of the reference line as the top boundary of facial region. The method of finding the left and right

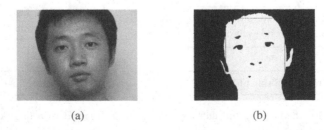

(a)   (b)

Fig. 3. The blue lines in the right image are the facial boundaries found

boundaries is similar. Due to the implication of neck skin region, as is shown in Fig. 3 (b), we can't locate the bottom boundary of the facial region here temporarily.

2.2.2 Locate Two Center Points of Eyes and Rotate Image

Because some persons' posture is not standard, here we use two center points of eyes to rotate the image.

We can see from Fig. 3 (b), because the color of eye is white and black, which is the same as background color, the eye region after skin color clustering model is black. For eyebrow, some people's are strong, but some people's are weak. Therefore, in the image after skin color clustering model, we can't always see the eyebrow region. Nostril and mouth are similar. The size of nostril changes with face posture. But eye is different. Eye region will always exist as long as the eye is not closed completely and the black region of eye is always surrounded in a white region of skin. Based on this characteristic, we could find the center points of eyes directly.

Main method: After locating three facial boundaries, we obtain a candidate facial region. In the region, firstly we take a proper proportion of height as the bottom boundary because we could not locate the bottom boundary of facial region and the location of eyes in the images from our database is relatively fixed; and then according to relative location relations of eye, eyebrow and nostrils, we could find the accurate boundaries of eyes through scanning line and column, as is shown in Fig. 4 (a). Then, we could obtain the center points according to the following formula.

$$x_{center} = \frac{1}{\Omega} \sum_{x_i \in \Re} x_i \qquad y_{center} = \frac{1}{\Omega} \sum_{x_i \in \Re} y_i \qquad (1)$$

$\Re$ stands the eye region and Ω stands the number of pixels in $\Re$. The result is shown in Fig. 4 (b).

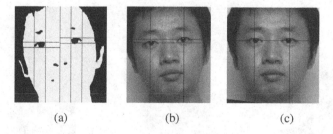

| (a) | (b) | (c) |

Fig. 4. (a) The accurate boundaries of eyes. (b) The center points of eyes. (c) Rotated image.

According to the two center points of eyes, we could obtain the angle to rotate:

$$a = \arctan(\frac{right\_eye\_column - left\_eye\_column}{right\_eye\_line - left\_eye\_line}) \qquad (2)$$

Then, we do coordinate transformation to rotate the image, as is shown in Fig 4 (c)

$$x' = x \cdot \cos a - y \cdot \sin a$$
$$y' = y \cdot \cos a + x \cdot \sin a \qquad (3)$$

2.3 Obtain Horizontal Position of the Mouth, Nostril and Eyebrow

To obtain horizontal position of the mouth nostril, and eyebrow, we use horizontal integral projection method [12].

$$V(x) = \frac{1}{y_2 - y_1} \sum_{y=y_1}^{y_2} I(x, y) \tag{4}$$

Here y_1 and y_2 is the minimal and maximal column values of the integral projection region and $I(x, y)$ is gray value of (x, y) point.

After we have located the eye center points and rotated the image, we could obtain a candidate integral projection region for mouth, the left and right boundaries of the candidate region are the column values of the two eye center points and the top boundary is a line, moving the line value of the two eye center points downward some a distance according to size of image, as shown in Fig. 5 first row image of (a). We can see in Fig. 5 second row image of (a) that the minimum of horizontal integral projection is the horizontal position of mouth respectively. For nostril the method is similar. For eyebrow, around the middle position, there is a valley, which is the horizontal position of eyebrow, as is shown in Fig. 5 (c).

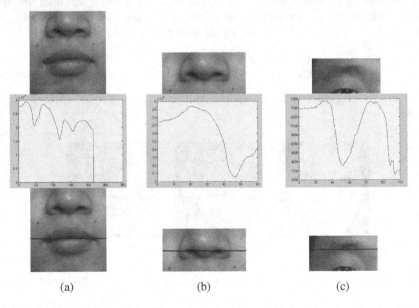

(a)   (b)   (c)

Fig. 5. The three images of the first row are the scopes of integral projection, the three images of the second row are the curve of integral projection and the three images of the third row are the horizontal position we find according to the curve

2.4 Extract Facial Skin Blocks

If we use the all part of facial image, there would be so many noises, the calculation and cost of time are too big. TCM thinks when organs inside body occur lesion; the

Fig. 6. Five parts extracted

lesion could be reflected on the face. Therefore, according to the facial structure and TCM theory, we exact five 32*32 blocks from a facial image, which is 777*583, as is shown in Fig. 6.

Not all of the images in the database are segmented and extracted correctly because of the impact of hair such as color. For example in Fig. 7. The color of hair is so close to the color of skin, which will be considered as facial region after skin color clustering model so that we can not find the facial boundaries and center points of eyes properly. For these images, we extract skin blocks manually.

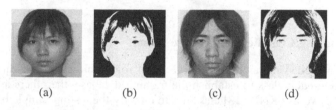

(a)   (b)   (c)   (d)

Fig. 7. The images that can't be segmented and extracted correctly. (a) and (c) are original images; (b) and (d) are the images after skin color clustering model.

3 Experimental Results

We have established a small facial images database which includes 29 healthy volunteers from Harbin Institute of Technology in China, 29 patients of severe hepatitis with jaundice and 87 patients of severe hepatitis without jaundice from the Third Affiliated Hospital of Zhongshan University in China. We take one picture from one person through Olympus digital camera; and the sampling environmental is indoor without sunlight and the illumination condition is normal fluorescent light.

We extract five blocks from a facial picture. In this chapter, we will quantize these skin blocks and construct classifier for the test and analysis.

3.1 Quantizing the Skin Blocks

After obtaining five blocks, we compute their mean value of three color channel R, G and B respectively. Then, we take the mean value $\overline{R}$, $\overline{G}$ and $\overline{B}$ in the following experiment as feature. As Fig. 7 shows, the color difference among the healthy people and severe hepatitis patients with and without jaundice is obviously.

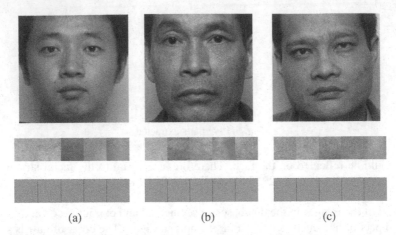

(a)   (b)   (c)

Fig. 8. (a) A health sample (b) A severe hepatitis with jaundice sample (c) A severe hepatitis without jaundice sample. The three images of the first row are original images; the three images of the second row are the five blocks extracted from the images of the first row. And the three images of the third row are the mean value of R, G and B image from the images of the second row.

3.2 Constructing Classifier and Analyze Result

We divide each class of samples into five equal folds uniformly. We randomly take four folds from each class to establish the training database, the others as the testing samples. Then we use KNN [13] classifier to classify the testing sample by Euclidean distance. Iteratively run the above procedure 125 times, the average result is shown in the Table 1.

Table 1. The result of classification K=5

	Health	With Jaundice	Without Jaundice	Average
Health	49.2%	0	50.8%	
With Jaundice	0.4%	66.67%	32.93%	
Without Jaundice	8.85%	7.03%	84.12%	
				73.6%

From Table 1, we could see that the health class and with Jaundice class are mainly classified as Without Jaundice kind wrongly, the Without Jaundice class is classified best, and the Health and With Jaundice classes, specially the Health kind, are not classified well. The possible reason is that everybody's facial color is different, and somebody's facial color is yellow or dark when he is born. In this situation, he looks ill, but in fact he is healthy. And because of condition restriction, we did not take the pictures of patients when they are healthy as the health samples. We may need to take it into consideration in the future research.

4 Conclusions and Future Work

In this paper, we proposed a novel computerized facial color diagnosis approach based on the TCM theory, which is called a facial color-computing model and aims at eliminating the subjective and qualitative characteristics of traditional facial color diagnosis and establishing the relationship between facial color appearance and diseases. We use skin block-extracting framework to extract five skin blocks from a facial image through locating the positions of facial organs. KNN classifier based on quantitative feature, namely color feature, is employed as the decision models for diagnosis. The results are promising with accuracy higher than 73%.

In the future work, we will build new, dedicated and closed sampling equipment with a better illumination condition and more advanced camera that could reflect the color information better. We will set up a bigger facial image database and test on the more complex and effective classifiers.

References

1. Pang, B., Zhang, D., Li, N.M., Wang, K.: Computer Aided Tongue Transactions on biomedical engineering. 10(51), 1803 (2004)
2. Pang, B., Zhang, D., Li, N.M., Wang, K.: Computerized Tongue Diagnosis Based on Bayesian Networks. IEEE Transactions on biomedical engineering 51(10), 1803 (2004)
3. Wang, L.: Diagnostics of Traditional Chinese Medicine. Shanghai University of Traditional Chinese Medicine (2006)
4. Ying, A.: Quantitative Study of Facial Color of Patient with Jaundice. Journal of TCM Univ. of Human (Chinese) 13(5), 71 (1998)
5. Cai, G.: Quantitative Measurement of 508 Cases Pathological Color. China Journal of Traditional Chinese Medicine and Pharmacy (Chinese) 11(1), 20–21 (1996)
6. Cai, G.: Quantitative Research of Facial Color of Different Kinds of Deficiency Syndrome Patients. Traditional Chinese Medicine of Shanxi (Chinese) 4, 10–11 (1988)
7. Cai, G., Ai, Y.: Quantitative Experimental Study of Facial Color of Patients with Chronic Hepatitis. China Academic Journal Electronic Publishing House (Chinese) 2(2), 36–37 (1996)
8. Cai, G.: Quantitative Preliminary Study on Facial Color of Patients with Blood Disease. Journal of TCM Univ. of Human (Chinese) 1(3) (1985)
9. Zhenxiang Chen, Y., Yang: Cold Infrared Map. Academic periodical Beijing College of Traditional Chinese Medicine (Chinese) 3(3), 38 (1980)
10. Hsu, R., Abdel-Mottaleb, M., Jain, A.k.: Face Detection in Color Images. IEEE transactions on Patten Analysis and Machine Intelligence 24(5), 696–706 (2002)
11. Gonzalez, R., Woods R.E.: Digitial Image Processing. Publishing House of Electronics Industry (2004)
12. Kim, J.S., Park, R.H.: A Fast Feature-Based Block Matching Algorithm Using Integral Projections. IEEE Journal on selected areas in communications 10(5) (1992)
13. Duba, R.O., Hart, P., David, G.S.: Pattern Classification. China Machine Press (2005)

Texture Feature Extraction and Classification for Iris Diagnosis

Lin Ma and Naimin Li

School of Computer Science and Technology, Harbin Institute of Technology,
Harbin, Heilongjiang 150001, China
malin_li@hit.edu.cn

Abstract. Appling computer aided techniques in iris image processing, and combining occidental iridology with the traditional Chinese medicine is a challenging research area in digital image processing and artificial intelligence. This paper proposes an iridology model that consists the iris image pre-processing, texture feature analysis and disease classification. To the pre-processing, a 2-step iris localization approach is proposed; a 2-D Gabor filter based texture analysis and a texture fractal dimension estimation method are proposed for pathological feature extraction; and at last support vector machines are constructed to recognize 2 typical diseases such as the alimentary canal disease and the nerve system disease. Experimental results show that the proposed iridology diagnosis model is quite effective and promising for medical diagnosis and health surveillance for both hospital and public use.

1 Introduction

In the eye, iris is the annulation part of some color that locates around the pupil. Usually, iris is regarded as an inner organ of human body. However, it may be easily observed from exterior. Iris has a very fine structure that contains five layers of fibre-like tissues. These tissues are very complex and reveal in various forms such as thread-like, linen-like, burlap-like, reticulation, *etc.* The surface of iris contains also very complex texture structures such as crystals, thin threads, spots, concaves, radials, furrows, stripes, *etc.* Nowadays, there exists two kinds of opinions considering the formation of the physical structure of iris.

The iris recognition point of view believes that the iris characteristics are formed randomly with the birth of the person and will never change during his life. The iris recognition technology then bases on this life-long invariability and individual otherness to realize the identification. In 1993, Daugman[1] proposed the first schema of an iris recognition system and the iris feature extraction and matching methods based on phrase analysis. Thereafter, Wildes[2] proposed an iris texture analysis method, Boles[3] proposed an iris recognition method based on the detection of zero-cross points. These are three most recognized iris recognition methods and the Daugman's is the most applied one[4].

The opposite iridology point of view believes that the iris has very close relationship with every organ in the body. Since the iris contains large amount of blood

D. Zhang (Ed.): ICMB 2008, LNCS 4901, pp. 168–175, 2007.
© Springer-Verlag Berlin Heidelberg 2007

vessels and nerves, changes in the body organs will cause corresponding variance in the interior blood and pheromone environment. As the result, tissue fibres in the iris will be influenced and visible iris features will appear on the iris[5]. In western countries, the iridology has a history of more than 100 years, profit from such advantages of iridology as un-touchiness and un-damage. Recently, it's reported that iridology technology has been applied in health surveillance for athletes in several countries like Germany, US, Canada and France[5,6]. Similarly in the traditional Chinese medicine (TCM), iridology methods have been recorded about 2000 years ago and many diagnosis theories believe that the eye (especially iris) plays a dominant role in human healthy system and accumulate the information and changes of all other body organs. Nowadays, the iridology attracts the attention of more and more researchers in the world and is regarded as an important development direction of medicine and prevent medicine in the future [5,6].

Under the support of techniques for iris recognition, we study in this paper the methods for pathological feature extraction and disease recognition for several typical illness, explore the relation and the difference between normal iris and un-healthy iris. Our aim is to verify the correspondence of the healthy problem with the iris changes, to demonstrate the correctness of the famous iris charts and to contribute to both the occidental iridology and the TCM iridology.

The following parts of the paper are organized into 5 section: Section 2 introduces the data collection and preprocessing issues for irido-diagnosis; Section 3 proposes 2 kinds of methods for pathological texture feature extraction; Section 4 gives a simple SVM based disease classifier; Section 5 presents our experiments and results; and latterly Section 6 concludes this paper.

2 Iris Acquisition and Image Pre-processing

The task of iris image acquisition is very hard, because the iris is very small, usually only about 10 mms in diameter, the eyeball moves very frequently, the pupil is very sensitive to light changes and it's very difficult to light up the iris. In order to reduce the influence of these factors, we use snapshot pictures from iris acquisition video to assure the high quality of iris image for later iridological analysis. Each image contains 640×480 pixels in 256 gray levels.

Precisely localize the iris in the image is the basis for further feature extraction and iridology analysis. Firstly, since the applied CCD data collection instrument uses double light sources that always create 2 highlight spots on the iris. An auto-adaptive neighboring insertion method is thus introduced to fulfill them.

Secondly, we apply a simple algorithm which bases on the special characteristics of the gray level distribution: the pupil has the lowest gray level and occupies the largest circle area in the middle of the eye image; the iris is a circular zone around the pupil and the both centers locate at nearly the same position. This algorithm includes 2 steps: a rough localization step and a precise localization step. The rough localization bases on the gray level projection on the horizontal and vertical direction; finding out the minimums of projections as candidate center and applying a gray level difference conducted search, both the pupil diameter R_P and the iris diameter R_I may be obtained. The precise localization uses a standard circle detector to improve the global accuracy[7]; the search area is limited by a center variation of 5 pixels, and diameter variations of 5 pixels; a Gassian function is used for gray level convolution calculation. In such a way, the inner and outer boundaries of the iris may be detected precisely and rapidly. The results of highlight spot fulfill and iris localization are shown in Fig. 1.

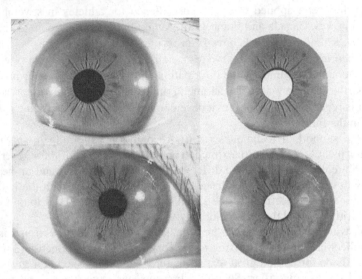

Fig. 1. Examples of highlight spot fulfill and iris localization. On the left, 2 samples of the original iris images are given, and on the right the corresponding processing results are shown.

3   Texture Feature Extraction and Description

Iris image contains abundant types of textures, most of them are visible with naked eyes and their structure features are quite obvious. In this section, we present how to efficiently represent the iris textures and measure the features of different kinds of textures. This is very critical for iridology diagnosis.

From the iris anatomy figure[8], it is noticed that the iris transverse section includes several tissue layers and the iris envisage reveals very abundant texture types, as the result the iris tissues may form cupped recesses, radiate stripes, crypts, contractile furrows, freckles, *etc*.

Depending on the comparison of iris of healthy people and that of people with health problem, it's noticed that the texture of ordinary iris looks uniform and stable, while the pathology iris texture presents some kinds of changes, among which the hyper pigmentations, radii solaris, and nerve rings are the most frequently observed disease focuses. The specific location of these focuses implies illness appears in the specific organ, depending on the famous iris chart of Jansen[9]. In our research, we studied 2 kinds of diseases such as the alimentary canal disease and the nerve system disease, observed the appearance of illness focuses and analyzed the texture energy of iris comparing with ordinary iris. Thereafter, the iris pathology features are defined and extracted for disease diagnosis.

3.1 2-D Gabor Iris Texture Energy Feature

As a comparison benchmark, we firstly use the 2-D Gabor filter to measure the global texture energy feature in various directions and dimensions[10]. The 2-D Gabor filter was wildly applied in Daugman's iris recognition technology, because it can offer good distinguish ability in both frequency domain and space domain with very high speed.

The 2-D Gabor filters may be expressed as:

$$\begin{cases} g(x, y) = g'(x, y)\exp(j2\pi\omega\xi) \\ g'(x, y) = \dfrac{1}{2\pi\sigma^2}\exp(-\dfrac{x^2 + y^2}{2\sigma^2}) \\ \xi = x\cos\theta + y\sin\theta \end{cases} \quad (1)$$

Where, the (x, y) is the coordinate in the space domain, σ is the standard deviation of the Gaussian function, ω is the frequency component and θ is the direction parameter of the filter. Usually, ω and θ take some discrete values to form several filter channels.

The texture energy feature is extracted by the following steps: firstly, for each pre-defined filter channel ω_i ($i=1,2, \ldots,M$) vs. θ_j ($j=1,2, \ldots,N$), the original image $I(x, y)$ is convolved by the Gabor filter $g(x, y)$ to form the output frequency domain figure $s(x, y)$:

$$s(x, y) = I(x, y) * g(x, y) \quad (2)$$

The response energy $e(\omega_i, \theta_j)$ for this channel (ω_i, θ_j) is then calculated by:

$$e(\omega_i, \theta_j) = \sqrt{s_R^2(x, y) + s_I^2(x, y)} \quad (3)$$

Here, $s_R(x, y)$ is the real part of the Gabor filter's output, and $s_I(x, y)$ is the imaginary part.

In our experiments, we selected 4 directions like the horizontal, vertical and 2 diagonal directions for the θ_j parameter, and 3 frequencies for ω_i. Thus, each original image is then measured by 12 (4×3) texture energy features like the following:

$$E(x, y) = [e(\omega_1, \theta_1), e(\omega_1, \theta_2), \cdots, e(\omega_i, \theta_j), \cdots e(\omega_M, \theta_N)] \quad (4)$$

Pathology iris texture has different features to ordinary iris. In our experiments, we used in total 30 iris images in the test, 16 iris with radii solaris, and 10 iris with hyper pigmentation, and 4 normal iris. It may be easily noticed that this 2-D Gabor texture feature have very good distinguish ability among these 3 kinds of textures, while the deviation within each class is very small.

3.2 Fractal Iris Texture Feature

Fractal means that the portion resembles the total in certain sense[11]. From mathematical point of view, fractal describes the extent to which a set may fulfill a space, and it is also the measure of the scrambling. On images, fractal means one kind of texture possess some stable feature which is invariant to sizes. Thus the fractal parameter serves very well to the description of the roughness of various textures[12].

There exists a number of methods to define and calculate the fractal dimension of a given subspace, but the box dimension is one of the simplest and most applied ones. Given a set A in the Euclidean space, use boxes of a as the border length to tightly contain A, if $N(a)$ is the minimum amount of boxes needed, then the box dimension D is calculated by:

$$D = -\lim_{a \to 0}\left(\log \frac{N(a)}{\log a} \right) \tag{5}$$

For images, N.Sarkar[13] proposed a simple, fast and accurate method which is based on the idea that an image forms a subspace in which pixel coordinate for the X-Y plane, and the gray level locates on the Z direction.

Imagine there's a 3-D box that just contains the image space, a scale ratio r is defined on the X, Y, Z directions to divide the box into many sub-boxes. Each sub-box can then be located by 3 numbers (m_x, m_y, m_z). Consider the 1st sub-box (1, 1, 1), the gray level of pixels locate within this area can be limited into $n=max-min+1$ sub-boxes, where (1, 1, max) contains the maximum gray level and (1, 1, min) contains the minimum gray level. The total number of sub-boxes N is the sum of all n.

Given different scale ratio r_i ($i=1,2,...M$), the total sub-box number $N(r_i)$ can be obtained accordingly. Since $\log(r)$ is linear to $\log N(r)$, the slope of this line can by easily estimated through a MSE algorithm that the negative slope is exactly the box dimension D of this image.

Table 1. Average of fractal dimensions of 3 kinds of texture. To the 30 example irises in the former experiment, it is find that the fractal dimensions are quite different among the 3 kinds of pathology irises.

Areas	Average Fractal Dimension
Collarette with rough texture (Damaged stomach ring)	2.514
Radii Solaris	2.321
Normal Area	2.107

4   Disease Recognition by Support Vector Machine

Because of the difficulty of data collection for pathological iris images, large amount of data has not yet been accumulated in our experiments. Lack of training data makes the iridology diagnosis task very hard, especially the construction of a reliable disease classifier.

The support vector machine (SVM) is firstly proposed by Cortes and Vapnik in 1995. It bases on the idea of minimizing the classification risk, it's very simple, needs few data for training and may produce great generalized classification. What's more, SVM may obtain an optimal solution on current information rather than the optimal solution when training data quantity augments to infinity. Nowadays, SVM is wildly applied in many fields such as text classification, image recognition, DNA sequence analysis *etc.*, and achieved very satisfactory performances[14]. So in our iridology problem, SVM is used to recognize typical diseases. And radial basis functions are used as kernel functions.

SVM is usual a 2-class classifier. In order to recognize more than H classes pattern, there are usually 2 approaches: in the first approach, H SVMs are constructed and each of them separate one class from all the H-1 other classes; in the second approach, each SVM is designed to distinguish only 2 classes, then $n(n-1)/2$ SVMs are needed in total. In both approaches, a posterior probability should be calculated to each class and the pattern is assigned to the class with the largest probability. In our system, the second approach is followed.

In our experiments, we designed a system to diagnosis nerve system disease and alimentary canal disease. Through observing the collected pathological iris, it's noticed that: for nerve system diseases, the typical illness focuses are radii solaris appears in the sector between 11 o'clock location and 13 o'clock location; for alimentary canal diseases, the collarette texture becomes more rough and the stomach circle is often damaged.

Thus we calculate the 2 types of the formerly proposed texture features in these 2 areas, and form a feature vector for each iris. For each area, the 2-D Gabor filters produces 12 parameters, and the fractal analysis creates 1 parameter, so far a 26 dimension feature vector is formed for each iris. After the values are aligned within scale of [0, 1] considering the maximum and minimum values, the feature vector can be used for SVM training.

5 Experimental Results

We use the proposed texture feature extraction method and standard SVM to train and test the iridology diagnosis model. Here 3 SVM are used to identify 3 kinds of iris. A total of 429 subjects, including 123 patients of alimentary canal disease, 104 patients of nerve system disease and 202 healthy volunteers, are involved in the following experiments. The pathologic iris were collected at the No.211 Military Hospital and all the diseases were definitely diagnoses through doctors' investigation and approved

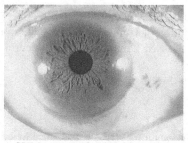
SVM outputs: 0.15, 0.29, 0.55
(a) Alimentary disease sample

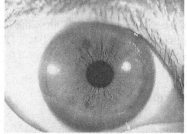
SVM outputs: 0.09, 0.76, 0.15
(b) Nerve disease sample

Fig. 2. Classification results of some testing images

by other classical medical examination methods. The healthy volunteers were freshman students at Harbin Institute Technology.

We randomly pick up examples from these 3 classes and form a training set of 252 samples and a testing set of 177 samples. Since the quantity of data is relatively small, so we implement 5 cross validation for each experiment and report the average recognition rate. The following figure gives some recognition examples in our experiments. Fig. (2-a) shows an example of alimentary canal disease, and the 3rd SVM gives the largest probability estimation of 0.55, Fig. (2-b) shows the case for a nerve system disease, and 2nd SVM gives definitely the largest probability of 0.76.

Table 2. Experimental results of iris diagnosis for 2 kinds of diseases from healthy conditions

Disease or Healthy	Example Number Used	Accuracy (%)
Nerve Disease	44	86.4
Alimentary Disease	53	84.9
Healthy	80	85.0
Average Recognition Rate		85.4

6 Conclusions

In this paper, we propose a computerized iris diagnosis method aimed at eliminating the subjective and qualitative characteristics of the traditional iridology and establishing the relationship between iris texture appearance and diseases. 2-D Gabor filter based texture energy calculation method and texture fractal dimension estimation method are employed for pathologic texture feature extraction. SVM classifiers are used as the decision models for diagnosis. Experiments are carried out on a total of 429 iris including 227 patients affected by 2 common diseases and 202 healthy volunteers. The iridology diagnosis accuracy is up to 85.4%. The experimental results reasonably demonstrate the effectiveness of the method described in this paper, thus establishing the potential usefulness of computerized iris diagnosis in clinical medicine.

Acknowledgements

The work in this paper is partially supported by the Specialty Leader Support Foundation of Harbin (2003AFLXJ006), the Foundation of Heilongjiang Province for Scholars Returned from Abroad (LC04C17) and the NSFC Key Oversea Project under the contract (60620160097).

References

1. Daugman, J.G.: High Confidential Visual Recognition by Test of Statistical Independence. IEEE Transactions on Pattern Analysis and Machine Intelligence 15, 1148–1161 (1993)
2. Wildes, R.P., Asmuth, J.C., Green, G.L.: A Machine-vision System For Iris Recognition. Machine Vision and Applications 9(2), 1–8 (1996)

3. Boles, W.W.: A Wavelet Transform Based Technique for the Recognition of The Human Iris. In: International Symposium of Signal Processing and Its Applications, Australia, pp. 601–604 (1996)
4. Wang, Y.h., Zhu, Y., Tan, T.: Iris based personality identification. Journal of Automation 28(1), 1–10 (2002)
5. Ma, B.y.: Human is part of the world. Chinese Basic TCM Journal 10(2), 8–10 (2005)
6. Fang, H., Tingli, L.: Research on an iris recognition system. Computer Engineering and Application 17, 82–84 (2002)
7. Wildes, R.P., Asmuth, J.C., Green, G.L.: A Machine-vision System For Iris Recognition. Machine Vision and Applications 9(2), 1–8 (1996)
8. Daugman, J.G.: Statistical Richness of Visual Phase Information: Update on Recognizing Persons by Iris Patterns. International Journal of Computer Vision. 45(1), 25–38 (2001)
9. Colton, J., Colton, S.: Iridology, 10–25 (1991)
10. Ma, L., Wang, Y.h., Tan, T.: Iris Recognition Based on Multi-channel Gabor Filtering. In: The 5th Asian Conf. Computer Vision, Melbourne, pp. 279–283 (2002)
11. Chang, H.T., Kao, C.J.: Fractal Block Coding Using Simplified Finite-state Algorithm. In: Proceeding of SPIE, pp. 536–544 (1995)
12. Gambini, M.M., Jacobo, D.: SAR Image Segmentation through Bspline Deformable Contours and Fractal Dimension. International Society for Photogrammetry and Remote Sensing 15(23), 101–106 (2004)
13. Chaudhuri, B.B., Sarkar, N.: Texture Segmentation using Fractal Dimension. IEEE Trans on Pattern Analysis and Machine Intelligence 17(1), 72–77 (1995)
14. Liu, H., Li, J.T., Cui, G.: Writer Identification using Support Vector Machine and Texture Feature. Journal of Computer-Aided Design and Computer Graphics 15(12), 1479–1484 (2003)

Screening Diabetic Retinopathy Through Color Retinal Images

Qin Li[1], Xue-Min Jin[3], Quan-xue Gao[1], Jane You[1], and Prabir Bhattacharya[2]

[1] Department of Computing, The Hong Kong Polytechnic University, KLN, Hong Kong
{csqinli,csyjia,csqxgao}@comp.polyu.edu.hk
[2] Institute for Information Systems Engineering, Concordia University, Quebec, Canada
prabir@ciise.concordia.ca
[3] The First Affiliated Hospital of Zhengzhou University, Zhengzhou, China
xmjin@zzu.edu.cn

Abstract. Diabetic Retinopathy (DR) is a common complication of diabetes that damages the eye's retina. Recognition DR as early as possible is very important to protect patients' vision. We propose a method for screening DR and distinguishing Prolifetive Diabetic Retinopathy (PDR) from Non-Prolifetive Retinopathy (NPDR) automatatically through color retinal images. This method evaluates the severity of DR by analyzing the appearnce of bright lesions and retinal vessel patterns. The bright lesions are extracted through morphlogical reconsturction. After that, the retinal vessels are automatically extracted using multiscale matched filters. Then the vessel patterns are analyzed by extracting the vessel net density. The experimental results domonstrate that it is a effective solution to screen DR and distinguish PDR from NPDR by only using color retinal images.

1 Introduction

Diabetic retinopathy (DR) is a common complication of diabetes that damages the eye's retina. It is a major cause of adult blindness. Recognition DR as early as possible is very important to protect patients' vision. DR can be classified by four stages: mild Non-Prolifetive Diabetic Retinopathy (NPDR), moderate NPDR, severe NPDR, and Prolifetive Diabetic Retinopathy (PDR). If the DR is recognized at early stages, some medicine or surgery based intervention can be used to prevent major vision loss [1]. Even in the early stage of PDR, patients' vision still can be saved in some extent through laser treatment. But in the late stage of PDR, there will be no effective treatment. Therefore, regular screening of diabetic patients' retina is very important. And, automated or computer-assisted analysis of diabetic patients' retina can help eye care specialist to screen larger populations of patients. In [2], DR was evaluated through Fluorescien Angiograms (FA). FA is a common medical estimation tool for screening DR. It produces very clear gray-scale retinal images and is good at describing hemorrhages and Neovascularization. But FA is not well-accepted by patients because it is an intrusive method and costs lots of time. In [3], a method of staging DR using Transient Visual Evoked Potential (TVEP) was introduced. However, the procedure of generating TVEP signal is complicate and costs lots of

D. Zhang (Ed.): ICMB 2008, LNCS 4901, pp. 176–183, 2007.
© Springer-Verlag Berlin Heidelberg 2007

time. Diabetic patients wish a safe, easy, and comfortable method for screening their retina. Color retinal images obtained through ocular fundus camera should be a good solution because obtaining of this kind of image is non-intrusive, very fast and easy. In [4], color retinal images are used to distinguish mild NPDR from severe NPDR. In this paper, we propose a method for screening DR and distinguish PDR from NPDR by analyzing color retinal images.

The appearance of bright lesions such as cotton wool spots and waxy exudates is sign for DR. We propose a bright lesion detection method based on morphological reconstruction and edge detection. The appearance of Neovascularization (new vessels growth) stands for PDR [5]. Neovasculars are small, circuity, and easy to be tufty. To analysis the vessel patterns, vessels have to be extracted first. We extract the vessels by matched filters [6] [7] and thresholding multiscale products [8] [9] [10]. After that, the vessel patterns can be analyzed to determine that it is PDR or NPDR.

2 Bright Lesion Extraction

Because the size and brightness of bright lesions can vary a lot in a retinal image with DR, edge detection is the most robust strategy among the literatures [11-15]. Our bright lesion detection scheme is as follows:

Step 1): Eliminating vessels. Because vessels also produce strong edges, they have to be eliminated before edge detection. In [11], a morphological closing was applied before the edge detection. But the closing operation will generate many "disk" like structures, which means the image will be not as smooth as before. These "disk" like structures may bring false detection of bright lesions. The morphological "erode followed by reconstruction" operation generally will produce smoother results than closing. But its effect of eliminating local minimum regions is not as good as closing. We propose a controlled reconstruction here. First, the vessels will be eliminated by erode $I_1 = \overline{I_g} \Theta B_{S1}$, where I_g is the complement of the green channel of the original image, Θ is erode, B_{S1} is a disk structure with radius S1 pixels. S1 should be large enough to eliminate all vessels. After that, with initializing $I_2 = I_1$, the eroded image will be reconstructed by

$$R = \min\left(I_2 \oplus B_1, \overline{I_g}\right); \quad I_2 = R \tag{1}$$

where $\oplus$ is dilate, B_1 is a disk structure with radius 1 pixel. The minimum of dilated I_2 image and I_g is assigned to R. Equation (2) will be repeated N times where N is larger than S1. Fig. 1 shows I_1 and I_2.

Step 2): Detecting edges. Once the vessels are eliminated, all edges remained on the image should be caused by bright lesions. We apply canny edge detector and double thresholding [16] on I_2. The double thresholding is good at avoiding broken edges. Fig. 2 shows this step.

Step 3): finding contour of the bright lesions. This step is similar with [11]. With filling of the holes in I_3, the filled objects will be regarded as bright lesion candidates. The exact contour of the bright lesions will be extracted by morphological reconstruction. The marker image I_4 is generated by setting all the candidates to 0 in the green channel of the original image I_g. The mask image is I_g. The difference between the reconstructed image I_5 and I_g is doubling thresholded to generate the bright lesions I_6. Further, the optic disk will be detected through PCA based method [12] and be deleted from bright lesions. Fig. 3 illustrated this step.

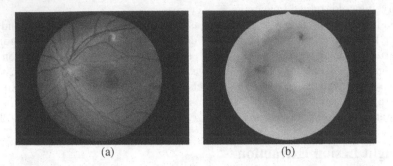

(a)   (b)

Fig. 1. Eliminating vessels. (a) The green channel of original image I_g, (b) I_2: erase vessel by reconstruction.

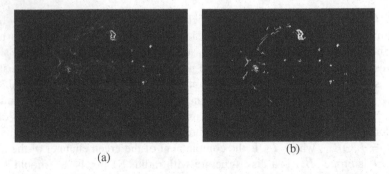

(a)   (b)

Fig. 2. Detecting edges. (a) Canny edge detecting; (b) I_3: Double thresholding (a).

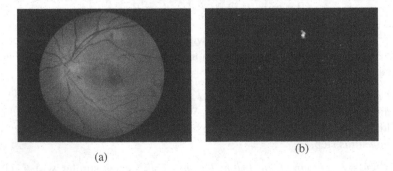

(a)   (b)

Fig. 3. Finding contour of bright lesions. (a) Reconstructed image I_5, (b) Difference between I_5 and I_g.

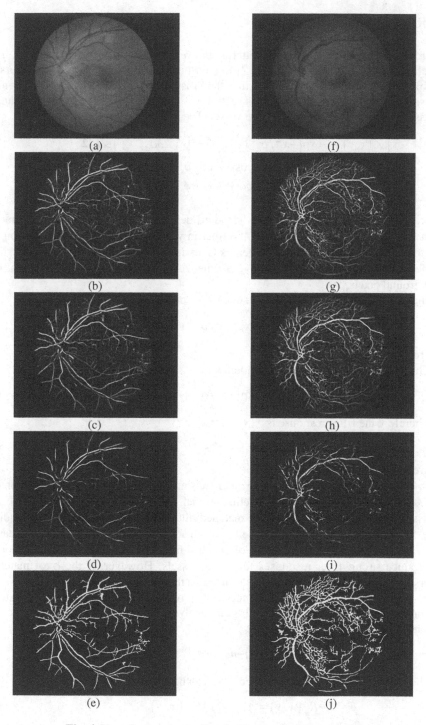

Fig. 4. Vessel extraction by thresholding multiscale products

3 Retinal Vessel Extraction

In order to analysis retinal vessel patterns, the vessels have to be extracted first. The matched filters were proposed in [6, 7] to detect retinal vessels. This kind of filters is established on the prior-knowledge that the cross-section of a vessel is similar to a Gaussian is used. Because the cross-section of a vessel is similar to a Gaussian, a Gaussian-shaped filter to "match" the vessel. The matched filters were defined as

$$\begin{cases} g_\phi(x,y) = -\exp\left(-x'^2/\sigma_x^2\right) - m, & \text{for } |x'| \le 3\sigma_x, \ |y'| \le L/2 \\ x' = x\cos\phi + y\sin\phi \\ y' = y\cos\phi - x\sin\phi \end{cases} \tag{2}$$

where ϕ is the filter direction, σ is standard deviation of Gaussian, m is the mean value of the filter, L is the length of the filter in y direction which is set according to experience. This filter can be regarded as Gaussian filter in x direction. A Gaussian-shaped filter can help to denoise and the zero-sum can help to suppress the background pixels.

The cross-section of vessel (1-D line) can be denoted as

$$G(x) = -\exp\left(-x^2/\sigma_1^2\right) + e \tag{3}$$

where e is the error from Gaussian.

The 1-D matched filter can be denoted as

$$g(x) = -\exp\left(-x^2/\sigma_2^2\right) - m \tag{4}$$

Therefore the filter response is

$$R(x) = G(x) * g(x) \tag{5}$$

where $*$ denotes convolution.

In order to achieve strong $R(x)$, σ_1 must be similar to σ_2. In [7], σ_x of Equation (1) was set as 2 because most of the retinal vessel cross-sections in their database are Gaussian with σ around 2. And, the matched filter with larger σ is better at denoise. But, for PDR detection, most of useful information is in the small vessels because Neovasculars are very small. The σ of matched filters have to be set as small enough to produce strong filter responses for small vessels. However, if the σ of matched filters is very small, there will be lots of noise in the filter responses.

To enhance vessels and suppress noise, we propose a multiscale scheme to extract retinal vessels [8] [9] [10]. For Multiscale analysis, a scale parameter s is added to Equation (1) to control the filter size:

$$g_{\phi,s}(x,y) = -\exp\left(-x'^2/s\sigma_x^2\right) - m, \quad \text{for } |x'| \le 3s\sigma_x, \ |y'| \le sL/2 \tag{6}$$

The response of multiscale matched filter can be expressed by

$$R_g(x,y) = g_{\phi,s}(x,y) * f(x,y) \tag{7}$$

where $f(x,y)$ is the original image and $*$ denotes convolution.

The scale production is defined as the product of filter responses at two adjacent scales

$$P^{s_j}(x, y) = R_g^{s_j}(x, y) \cdot R_g^{s_{j+1}}(x, y) \tag{8}$$

Because the bright lesions can cause false detection of vessels, we apply vessel detection on the reconstructed image I_5 (Fig. 3(a)).

Fig. 4 shows the procedure of our multiscale vessel extraction scheme. The left column shows the vessel extraction for a NPDR image; the right column shows the vessel extraction for a PDR image. Fig. 4(a) is a reconstructed (bright lesion erased) NPDR image; Fig. 4 (b) and (c) are matched filter responses at different scales (lots of noise in these two images); Fig. 4(d) is the scale product of (b) and (c) (noise is suppressed); Fig. 4(e) is the binarized image of (d). Fig. 4(f)~(j) are the corresponding images of a PDR image.

4   Analysis of Retinal Vessel Patterns

Once the vessels have been extracted, the retinal vessel patterns can be analyzed through these binarized images (Fig. 4(e) and (j)). Neovasculars are small, circuity, and easy to be tufty (Fig. 4(f) and (j)). The tufty means there are more vessels in the retinal region with Neovasculars. We use a term vessel density to denote this feature. The circuity means a single vessel changes its direction frequently. Therefore, in the 2-D images, there are more cross points of vessels in the retinal region with Neovasculars. That means Neovasculars look like a net. We use a term vessel net density to denote this feature. To analysis vessel density and vessel net density, the vessels (Fig. 4(e) and (j)) have to be thinned to be single pixel width. Actually, Fig. 4(j) is the case of very serious PDR. Normally, Neovasculars is a very small region in a retina. Therefore the vessel density and vessel net density have to be calculated locally. If the size of local window used to calculate the densities is close to the size of the Neovasculars net, the densities should reach their maximum. Based on this observation, we propose a multiscale scheme to calculate the vessel density and vessel net density. For each point of the thinned image, the vessel points and vessel cross points are counted in its 10*10, 20*20, 50*50 neighborhoods. The maximum of all scales of neighborhoods of all points is regarded as the number of local vessel points and vessel cross points of one image. The vessel density and vessel net density are calculated by dividing this number by the size of the neighborhoods.

5   Experimental Results

The database we used is obtained from the patients in Ophthalmological Department of the First Affiliated Hospital of Zehngzhou University. We observed 50 patients including 30 NPDR patients and 20 PDR patients. One image of each patient is used for our experiments. The color retinal images were captured from Kowa VK-3 fundus camera at 45° FOV. These images were stored in digital forms of 800*608 pixels and 8 bits per color channel.

Fig. 5(a) evaluates the bright lesion extraction ability of our system by plotting sensitivity against predictive value [11]. The proposed "erode by reconstruction" is compared with the detection based on "open". Our system achieves sensitivity 80.5% at predictive value 90.8%.

Fig. 5(b) evaluates the performance of distinguishing PDR from NPDR using ROC curve. The True Positive Rate (TPR) is plotted against the False Positive Rate (FPR). TPR means the rate of PDR images being recognized as PDR images. FPR means the rate of NPDR images being recognized as PDR images. The discriminating ability of vessel net density is better than vessel density. And the fusion of them gives a better discriminating ability than each of them (Because the value range of both vessel density and vessel net density is in 0~1, the fusion is simply done by calculate their product.). And our system reaches TPR 95.8% at FPR 16.7%. This result is not ideal. But it still shows that screening DR patients and distinguishing PDR from DR through vessel pattern analysis is possible.

Most of the false results come from mild PDR. In this case, the vessel density and vessel net density of PDR are very similar to NPDR. That means more features are required to distinguish mild PDR from NPDR. Another problem is the lesions in retina. Some of the lesions may be detected as vessels. That means the vessel extraction algorithm needs to be improved.

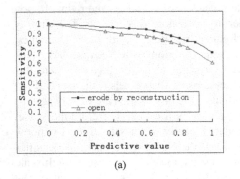
(a)

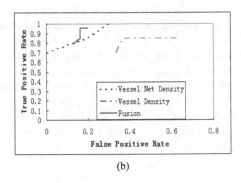
(b)

Fig. 5. Performance evaluation

6   Conclusions and Future Works

Diabetic Retinopathy (DR) is a common complication of diabetes that damages the eye's retina. Recognition DR as early as possible is very important to protect patients' vision. We propose a scheme for screening DR and distinguishing Prolifetive Diabetic Retinopathy (PDR) from Non-Prolifetive Retinopathy (NPDR) automatically through color retinal images. This scheme evaluates the severity of DR by extracting bright lesions and analyzing the retinal vessel patterns through the features defined as vessel density and vessel net density. The experimental results demonstrate that it is a possible solution to screen DR and distinguish PDR from NPDR by only using color retinal images. The current result is not ideal for applying our scheme in clinic. First, there are bright lesions that don not belong to DR. Further classification of bright lesions is required. Second, there are false negatives of PDR come from mild PDR whose vessel density and vessel net density are very similar to NPDR. More features are required to generate better result.

References

1. Taylor, H.R., Keeffe, J.E.: World blindness: A 21st century perspective. Brit. J. Ophthalmol. 85, 261–266 (2001)
2. Domingo, Ayala, J., Sim, G., de Ves, A.E., Martlnez-Costa, L., Marco, p.: Irregular motion recovery in fluorescein angiograms. Pattern Recognition Letters 18, 805–821 (1997)
3. Sivakumar, R.: Staging of Diabetic Retinopathy using TVEP Phase Spectral Periodicity Analysis. In: IEEE International Conference on Engineering of Intelligent Systems, pp. 1–5 (2006)
4. Sinthanayothin, C., Kongbunkiat, Phoojaruenchanachai, V.S., Singalavanija, A.: Automated screening system for diabetic retinopathy. IEEE ISPA 2, 915–920 (2003)
5. Sussman, E.J., Tsiaras, W.G., Soper, K.A.: Diagnosis of diabetic eye disease. J. Am. Med. Assoc. 247, 3231–3234 (1982)
6. Chaudhuri, S., Chatterjee, K.S.N., Nelson, M., Goldbaum, M.: Detection of blood vessels in retinal images using two-dimensional matched filters. IEEE Trans. Med. Imag. 8, 263–269 (1989)
7. Hoover, A., Kouznetsova, V., Goldbaum, M.: Locating blood vessels in retinal images by piecewise threshold probing of a matched filter response. IEEE Trans. on Medical Imaging 19(3), 203–210 (2000)
8. Bao, P., Zhang, L.: Noise Reduction for Magnetic Resonance Image via Adaptive Multiscale Products Thresholding. IEEE Trans. on Medical Imaging 22, 1089–1099 (2003)
9. Bao, P., Zhang, L., Wu, X.L.: Canny Edge Detection Enhancement by Scale Multiplication. IEEE Trans. Pattern Analysis and Machine Intelligence 27(9) (2005)
10. Li, Q., You, J.L., Zhang, D., Bhattacharya, P.: New Approah to Automated Retinal Vessel Segmentation Using Multiscale Analysis. In: IEEE ICPR (2006)
11. Walter, T., Klein, J.C., Massin, P., Erginay, A.: contribution of image processing to the diagnosis of diabetic retinopathy detection of exudates in color fundus images of the human retina. IEEE Trans. Med. Imag. 21(10) (2002)
12. Li, H., Chutatape, O.: Automated Feature Extraction in Color Retinal Images by a Model Based Approach. IEEE Trans. on BME 51(2), 246–254 (2004)
13. Sagar, A.V., Balasubramaniam, S., Chandrasekaran, V.: A Novel Integrated Approach Using Dynamic Thresholding and Edge Detection (IDTED) for Automatic Detection of Exudates in Digital Fundus Retinal Images. In: IEEE Conference on Computing: Theory and Applications (2007)
14. Zhang, X.H., Chutatape, A.: Detection and classification of bright lesions in color fundus images. IEEE International Conference on Image Processing 1, 139–142 (2004)
15. Sinthanayothin, C., Boyce, Williamson, J.T., Cook, H., Mensah, E., Lal, S., Usher, D.: Automated detection of diabetic retinopathy on digital fundus images. Diabetic Med. 19, 105–112 (2002)
16. Canny, J.: A computational approach to edge detection. IEEE Transactions on Pattern Recognition and Machine Intelligence PAMI 8, 679–698 (1986)

Real-Time RFID-Based Intelligent Healthcare Diagnosis System

Rajiv Khosla and Belal Chowdhury

School of Business, La Trobe University
Melbourne, Victoria 3086, Australia
r.khosla@latrobe.edu.au,
mbchowdhury@students.latrobe.edu.au

Abstract. In a health care context, the use of RFID (Radio Frequency Identi-fication) technology can be employed for not only bringing down health care costs but also to facilitate automatic streamlining patient identification processes in health centers and assist medical practitioners in quick and accurate diagnosis and treatments. In this paper, we outline a describe design and application of RFID-based Real-time Intelligent Clinical Diagnosis and Treatment Support System (ICDTS) in health care.

1 Introduction

In recent years, in almost every country in the world substantial financial resources have been allocated to the health care sector. Technological development and modern medicine practices are amongst the outstanding factors triggering this shift. Develo-ped countries like Australia are currently facing a middle and older-aged health care marketplace. This trend is resulting in a greater demand for health care-related services and greater competition among health care providers [1].

There is growing concern about maintaining one's health as population ages, mobile/ sensor technology are expected to provide real-time information about vital signs and other physiological indicators of one's health and fitness. Such monitoring systems are expected to find greater use in such applications as hospitals, home health monitoring, physician's offices, elderly care facilities, fitness centers, and health research studies [2].

The application of these principles can be facilitated by the use of the mobile technology such as Radio Frequency Identification (RFID) [3]. In this paper, we integrate RFID technology with a multi-layer multi-agent architecture for intelligent health care systems. The paper is structured as follows: Section 2 outlines the RFID model used for developing an intelligent health care system. Section 3 outlines the seven layers of the health care systems architecture. Section 4 illustrates the application of in-telligent health care systems architecture using a RFID-based ICDTS. Section 5 illus-trates the implementation of ICDTS application. Section 6 concludes the paper.

2 RFID Model for Intelligent Healthcare Diagnosis Systems

The main components of RFID-based ICDTS system is shown in Figure 1. It mainly consists of a patient tag (i.e., wristband), a reader and health centre IT systems (i.e.,

D. Zhang (Ed.): ICMB 2008, LNCS 4901, pp. 184–191, 2007.
© Springer-Verlag Berlin Heidelberg 2007

ICDTS). Each unique patient tag can be passive, semi-passive or active [2]. Passive patient tags can be used for both reading/writing capabilities by the reader and do not need internal power (i.e., battery). They get energized by the reader through radio waves and have a read range from 10mm to almost 10 meters.

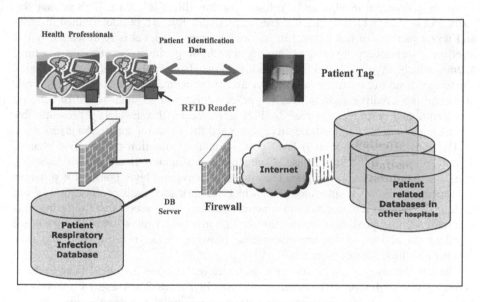

Fig. 1. Main components of RFID-based Clinical and Diagnosis System

The passive patient tag (used in ICDTS with a frequency of 13.56MHz) antenna picks up radio-waves or electromagnetic energy beamed at it from an RFID reader device and enables the chip to transmit patient's unique ID and other information to the reader device, allowing the patient to be remotely identified. The reader converts the radio waves reflected back from the patient tag (i.e., wristband) into digital information [5] then pass onto ICDTS system for processing.

Patient's basic information is stored in the back-end server for processing data. Patient database can also be linked through Internet into other health centers databases [4] for retrieving patients past history.

3 Context-Aware Multilayer Multi-agent Architecture for Intelligent Health Care Systems (CAHCS)

CAHCS used for the design of RFID-based ICDTS is shown in Figure 2. The various layers of the CAHCS architecture are outlined in the context of the three behaviour levels, namely, perception, procedural and construction [7]. At the perception-action level, skills direct inference. There are hard-coded inference mechanisms that provide immediate responses to appropriate sensed information. They correspond to the need for urgency of action. In terms of the multi-agent architecture, this level is represented by the reactive layer. The reactive layer consists of agents which represent stimulus-response phenomenon in a user defined environment. The agents in this layer may include data aggregation agents, data transformation agents, data visualization agents which may not need learning.

At the procedural level, a set of rules or patterns direct inference. This set may be large, but is always closed, i.e., it corresponds to pre-formed, pre-determined insights and learnt patterns of behaviour. In our architecture this level is represented by the intelligent technology layer. The intelligent technology layer contains data mining agents which involve learning to find patterns from data. This layer includes clustering, fusion (e.g., fuzzy-neuro), GA and other agents. At the construction level, inference is a creative and constructive process based on an open world of actions, constraints and resources. In the CAHCS architecture, this level is represented by layers, namely, sensemaking (cognitive) layer and the situation-adaptation layer.

The sensemaking (cognitive) layer consists of four situation construction phases, namely, Context Elicitation Phase, Context-based Situation Interpretation Labeling Phase, and Situation-action phase. The situation-adaptation layer consists of situation monitoring, situation adaptation agents which monitor the result of the action of the system on the user /environment in a given situation (e.g., acceptance/ rejection of a recommendation, prediction by the user/environment) and incorporate this feedback to adapt the actions of the situation-action phase agents. An example in the next section will illustrate this aspect.

Overall, there are seven layers in the architecture, five of which have been outlined above. The distribution and coordination layer in Figure 2 consists of agents who process data on behalf of agents in other layers in a parallel and distributed manner to meet the real-time and speed up needs of the data mining process [8]. The coordination layer agents are used to coordinate communication between the user and the agents in sensemaking (cognitive), and optimization layers of the architecture. The coordination layer agents are also used to coordinate communication between agents in the six layers [8] and maintaining a blackboard type global system state representation. The object layer is used to represent ontology of the domain objects which are manipulated by the sensemaking (cognitive) layer agents defined by a user in a particular situation.

Finally, RFID Middleware is the interface between the RFID reader and health centers back end database and ICDTS system. The middleware layer is an important element of RFID-based systems, which enables health professionals/consultants a quick connectivity with RFID readers. This layer lowers the volume of information that healthcare system applications need to process by grouping and filtering raw RFID observations from readers. This layer also provides an application-level interface for managing RFID readers, to process large volumes of patient data for their applications. In addition, the middleware layer is responsible for monitoring physical components (e.g., RFID patient tags, antennas and readers) and supports International Organization for Standardization (ISO) standard [6].

Given the space limitations, in the rest of paper we focus on illustrating the role of intelligent technology layer, sensemaking (cognitive) layer, situation adaptation layer using real-world application respectively.

4   RFID-Based Clinical Diagnostic System Application

Medical practitioners in the Inner-south East Melbourne Division of General Practice in Alfred hospital in Melbourne, Australia have traditionally used a check box (Yes/No) based patient symptom gathering form. However, this form among other aspects has been the subject of review in determining the inconsistencies in the diagnosis and prescription habits of medical practitioners in the hospital. In order to address this problem a RFID-based intelligent multi-agent multimedia clinical diagnostic and treatment support system has been developed with the following objectives: i) to develop an on-line adaptive diagnostic and treatment support based on multimedia diagnostic input data using mobile technology (e.g., RFID)., and ii) to develop capability in the system which can identify inconsistencies between treatments prescribed by practitioners and the corresponding guideline recom-mendations, on an ongoing basis.

Figure 3 shows a RFID-based automatic patient identification interface for an Intelligent Clinical Diagnosis and Treatment Support (ICDTS) System using C# in Microsoft Visual Studio.net 2003 environment. The ICDTS uses the unique ID transmitted by RFID patient tags as a key to information and perhaps other information (e.g. name, DOB, drug allergies, blood group, etc.) stored in the health centers back-end databases. For example, an RFID patient tag only contains a unique tag ID, which an ICDTS system application can use to retrieve a record stored in the patient database. When a patient appears with a wristband, which has an embedded RFID tag within a reader read range, the application read the patient ID and displays the patient information.

The interface is shown in Figure 6, 7, 8, and 9 are displayed by clicking Diagnostic Subsystem, Manual Selection, Suggested Diagnosis, and Potential Diagnosis buttons respectively.

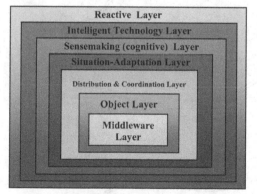
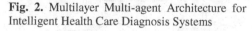
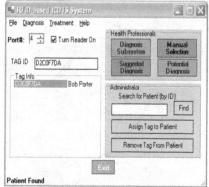

Fig. 2. Multilayer Multi-agent Architecture for Intelligent Health Care Diagnosis Systems

Fig. 3. RFID-based ICDTS System Application

4.1   Intelligent Diagnosis and Treatment Support Problem Solving Agents

Figure 5 shows the application of the sensemaking (cognitive) layer for modeling the cognitive structure employed by medical practitioners. Figure 5 captures the cognitive

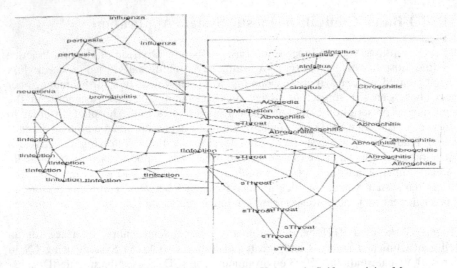

Fig. 4. Potential Diagnosis Clusters using Kohonen's Self-organizing Maps

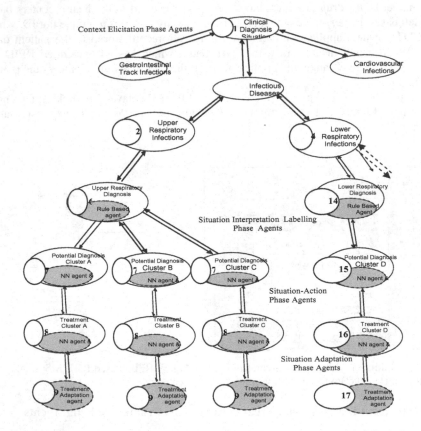

Fig. 5. Partial Computational Overview of a Medical Practitioner's Decision Path Based on Selection of Symptom to Diagnosis and Treatment Strategy

or semantic context in which clinical diagnosis is conducted and treatments prescribed by the medical practitioners.

The number labels shown in Figure 5 of context elicitation, situation interpretation, situation-action and situation adaptation agents are linked to Table 1 which depicts the abstraction hierarchy or decision pathways employed by medical practitioners for clinical diagnosis and treatment. The agents in Figure 5 also show the intelligent technologies (serviced by the intelligent technology layer) of CAHCS architecture.

The medical practitioners are generally expected to follow the therapeutic guidelines [9] provided by regulatory bodies for prescribing treatments to patients. However, in practice, based on their experience and patient situation they override the prescribed treatments in the guidelines for certain types of diagnosis. The treatment adaptation agents in Figure 5 enable the medical practitioners to override the recommended treatments by the systems in different patient-doctor situations.

The potential diagnosis cluster agents shown in Figure 5 are learnt using Kohonen's self-organizing maps. Figure 4 shows upper and lower respiratory infection diagnostic clusters learnt from historical symptom-diagnosis data provided by Inner-south East Melbourne Division of General Practice in Alfred hospital in Melbourne. The clusters from the cluster grid in Figure 4 are grouped into four clusters, namely, Cluster A (Generalized Upper Respiratory Tract Infection), Cluster B (Acute Sore throat), Cluster C (Acute Otitis Media, Otitis Media Effusion and Acute Sinusitis) and Cluster D (other Lower Respiratory Infections). These clusters have been validated by medical practitioners in Alfred Hospital as valid clusters. Theses four clusters are mapped into the situation construction structure employed by practitioners for medical diagnosis and treatment. The situation construction structure is based on the four situation construction phases defined in sensemaking (cognitive) layer.

In the process of diagnosis and treatment a medical practitioner may use the clinical and diagnosis system starting from symptoms to diagnosis to treatment or the practitioner may only like to check the symptoms for a particular predetermined diagnosis or they may like to go straight from diagnosis to treatment. The symptom to diagnosis to treatment pathway is shown in the Upper respiratory column in Table 1. The predetermined diagnosis decision pathway is shown under the Upper Respiratory

Table 1. Abstraction Hierarchy of Medical Practitioner's Diagnosis and Treatment Strategy

	Infectious Diseases	Upper Respiratory	Upper Respiratory (Bronchitis)	Lower Respiratory	Lower Respiratory (lung infection)
Context Elicitation	1	2	3	4	5
Situation Labeling (Control)		6	10	14	18
Situation-action (diagnosis)		7	11	15	19
Situation-action (Treatment)		8	12	16	20
Situation-adaptation (postprocessing)		9	13	17	21

(Bronchitis) column. Bronchitis represents a particular predetermined diagnosis chosen by the practitioner. Similarly decision pathways are shown in Table 1 for Lower respiratory infections.

5 Implementation Aspects of Clinical and Diagnosis System

Figure 6 represents the context elicitation of the sensemaking (cognitive) layer of the CAHSS architecture. It also to shows how the perceptual dimensions (reflecting the perceptual-action level shown in Table 1) of shape and location related to the upper and lower respiratory infection are used by the medical practitioner for cognitive modeling and problem solving. Figure 7 shows the interface for diagnosis to treatment decision path way (related to column 2 and 4 of Table 1) employed by the medical practitioner. Figure 8 shows the diagnostic and treatment information related to a predicted diagnosis (related to situation-action phase). The Treatment via Practitioner Experience "button is related to situation adaptation phase of the sensemaking (cognitive) layer of the CAHSS architecture where the medical practitioner overrides

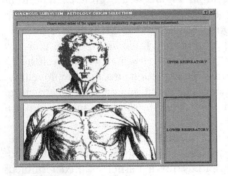
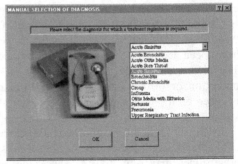

Fig. 6. Symptom-diagnosis-treatment Pathway (Etiology Selection)

Fig. 7. Diagnosis – treatment Decision Pathway - selecting Diagnosis for Which Treatment Support is Required

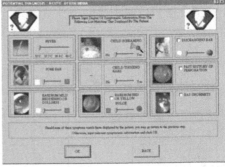

Fig. 8. Suggested Diagnosis and Treatment Information Including Adaptation

Fig. 9. Multimedia Based Symptomatic Data Gathering for Acute Otitis Media

the treatment prescription based on exiting Therapeutic guidelines. Figure 9 employs perceptual dimensions and multimedia artifacts used for designing a more practitioner-centred symptom data gathering interface related to Acute Otitis Media diagnosis (as against existing form which led to diagnostic and treatment inconsistencies by medical practitioner).

6 Conclusions

In this paper we have described a context-aware multi-layer health care system architecture for design of practitioner-centred RFID-based Intelligent Clinical Diagnosis and Treatment Support System The authors have shown the application and implementation of the perceptual, procedural (employing existing or learnt diagnostic and treatment knowledge) and construction level (employing various cognitive layer constructs and decision pathways) constructs for design of the above system. The prototype has been developed using real practitioner data. Efforts are being made to develop the complete system for use in medical practice.

References

1. Correa, F.A., Gil, M.J., Redín, L.B.: Benefits of Connecting RFID and Lean Principles in Health Care. Working Paper 05-4, Business Economics Series 10 (2005)
2. Adrian, P.: Sensors Have Expanding Opportunities for Use in Wearable Devices for Health Monitoring (2005) (accessed on September 25, 2006), http://www.sensorsmag.com/sta/sta1105.shtml
3. Belal, C., Rajiv, K.: RFID-based Real-time Hospital Patient Management System. In: Proceedings of the 6th IEEE/ACIS International Conference on Computer and Information Science, and International Workshop on e-Activity 2007, July 11-13, IEEE Computer Society, Los Alamitos (2007)
4. U.S. Government Accountability Office.: Radio Frequency Identification Technology in the Federal Government, 441 G Street NW, Room LM Washington, D.C. 20548 (2005)
5. Denis, L.: What is WiFi? An Introduction to Wireless Networks for the Small/Medium Enterprise (SME) (accessed on February 10, 2007), http://www.openxtra.co.uk/articles/wifi-introduction.php
6. LandMARC.: Integrated Sensor Radio Frequency Identification (ISRFID), Georgia Tech Research Institute Electro-Optics, Environment, and Materials Laboratory - GTRI Baker Building - Room 328 Atlanta, GA 30332-0834 (2002)
7. Rasmussen, J.: Information Processing and Human-Machine Interaction: An Approach to Cognitive Engineering. North-Holland, Amsterdam, The Netherlands (1986)
8. Adomavicius, G., Tuzhlin, A.: Toward the Next Generation of Recommender Systems: A Survey of the state-of-the-Art and possible Extensions (2005)
9. Therapeutic Guidelines Limited. Welcome to Therapeutic Guidelines (accessed on February 01, 2007), http://www.tg.com.au/

Quantitative Assessment of Pap Smear Cells by PC-Based Cytopathologic Image Analysis System and Support Vector Machine

Po-Chi Huang[1], Yung-Kuan Chan[2], Po-Chou Chan[3], Yung-Fu Chen[4],
Rung-Ching Chen[5], and Yu-Ruei Huang[5]

[1] Department of Pathology, Taichung Hospital, Department of Health, Executive Yuan,
403 Taichung, Taiwan
pchuanglin.tw@yahoo.com.tw
[2] Department of Management Information Systems, National Chung Hsin University,
402 Taichung
ykchan@nchu.edu.tw
[3] Department of Management Information Systems,
Central Taiwan University of Science and Technology, 411 Taichung
bjjem@ctust.edu.tw
[4] Department of Health Services Administration, China Medical University, 404 Taichung
yungfu@mail.cmu.edu.tw
[5] Department of Information Management, Chaoyang University of Technology,
413 Taichung, Taiwan
{crching,s9414636}@cyut.edu.tw

Abstract. Cytologic screening has been widely used for controlling the prevalence of cervical cancer. Errors from sampling, screening and interpretation, still concealed some unpleasant results. This study aims at designing a cellular image analysis system based on feasible and available software and hardware for a routine cytologic laboratory. Totally 1814 cellular images from the liquid-based cervical smears with Papanicolaou stain in 100x, 200x, and 400x magnification were captured by a digital camera. Cell images were reviewed by pathologic experts with peer agreement and only 503 images were selected for further study. The images were divided into 4 diagnostic categories. A PC-based cellular image analysis system (PCCIA) was developed for computing morphometric parameters. Then support vector machine (SVM) was used to classify signature patterns. The results show that the selected 13 morphometric parameters can be used to correctly differentiate the dysplastic cells from the normal cells (p<0.001). Additionally, SVM classifier has been demonstrated to be able to achieve a high accuracy for cellular classification. In conclusion, the proposed system provides a feasible and effective tool for the evaluation of gynecologic cytologic specimens.

1 Introduction

Cytology evaluation is a safe, efficient and well-established technique for the diagnoses of diseases. The most famous triumph in cytology is that it has successfully controlled the mortality and morbidity of cervical cancer by mass screening. The role of cytology aimed at early detection of dysplasia or pre-invasive cancer cells. Once

D. Zhang (Ed.): ICMB 2008, LNCS 4901, pp. 192–199, 2007.

the abnormal cells are detected, the patient will be arranged to undergo a biopsy examination, and then effective surgical treatments will be done. Consequently, the progression of the cancer will be stopped at its early stage.

Classical cytologic diagnosis is based on microscopic observation of the specialized cells and judged qualitatively by using descriptive criteria, which may be inconsistent because of subjective discrepancy of the personnel [1]. To prevent the false negative rate in screening, since 1990 many advanced technologies focusing on sampling, smear preparation, or screening quality control have been developed and introduced into the practical work [2,3]. These commercial devices can be divided into the following categories based on their approaches: (1) for a better slide preparation to reduce sampling error, such as thin-layered liquid based preparation (ThinPrepTM, SurePath, Tripath) [4,5]; (2) for reducing workload and screening error, such as autoscreening system (ThinPrep Imaging System, Cytyc, Boxborough, MA) and FocalPoint System (Tripath Imaging, Burlington, NC); (3) for laboratory quality control, such as rescreening (Papnet) [6]; and (4) for quality assurance, such as proficiency test [7]. However, most of these devices are not designed to assist diagnosis by supplying the calculable parameters to eliminate interpretation errors and inter-observer discrepancy [8]. In addition, it is not applicable for general cytological laboratory because of high cost and technical or linguistic gaps [3]. Thus, without a reproducible and quantitative tool, it is still an unsolved problem for a routine cytological laboratory to improve the diagnostic divergence caused by visual observation.

Earlier studies on quantitative methods for estimating the cytological specimen can be traced back to some 30 years ago, and is still continuing in developing [9-10]. Reliability, access, cost, efficiency, technical maintenance and linguistic communication may be the main considerations regarding the experimental design for the users. Owing to revolution and evolution of new technologies, enhanced power of computation, decreased cost of hardware and software, and prevalence of the Internet, more and more studies are engaged in developing system using computational algorithms for cellular image analysis for other variant diseases [11-13]. Such studies are optimistic and promising in helping resolving the limitation of the mankind, especially in the fields of bioinformatics, biology, and medicine.

2 Materials and Methods

As illustrated in Fig. 1, the experimental procedures can be divided into the following steps: (1) acquisition of cell images, (2) image editing and processing, (3) measurement and analysis of cellular morphology and texture, and (4) classification of cell types using SVM. Customized programs were designed in our laboratory to simplify analytic procedures, facilitate cellular image review, organize the file names of cell images, and calculate the morphmetric features of cells. Additionally, statistic significance of the selected morphometric variables and performance between the available SVM classifier and the Fisher linear discriminant classifier implemented using SPSS (Chicago, IL, USA) were also compared.

Acquisition of cell image: Cytological images were captured using a high-resolution digital camera (Olympus C-5060, Japan) mounted on a microscope (Olympus BX 51,

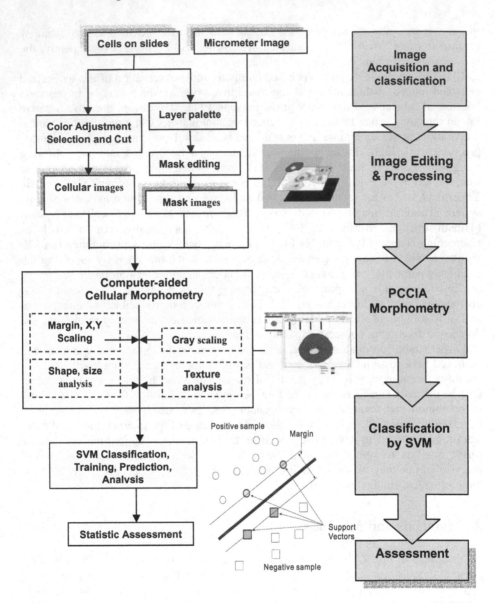

Fig. 1. Flowchart of the experimental procedure

Japan) and stored as digital format. Forty-two Papanicolaou-stained liquid-based cervical smears (Thin-Prep) from our gynecologic files were used for this investigation. We captured 1814 cell images (1556 × 1076 pixels) with different scales of magnification (100x, 200x, and 400x). Among them, 477 are classified as superficial cells, 499 as intermediate cells, 478 as parabasal cells, and 360 as abnormal cells including low grade (L) and high grade (H) squamous intraepithelial lesion (SIL). All the images were renamed using a scheme based on cell type, standardized sequence number, magnification, requesting pathological number, and diagnostic code, to be easily documented and retrieved by the analytical programs and SVM software. The digitized cellular images were reviewed by 3 certificated cytopathologists and 6 certificated cytotechnologists. By excluding the images with minimal magnification, extensive cellular overlapping, interference by other inflammatory cells or debris, and peer disagreement in classification, 503 images were finally selected for further analyses. Among them, 139 images were classified as superficial (S) cells (from 13 different cases), 178 as intermediate (I) cells (from 10 different cases), 128 as parabasal (P) cells (from 10 different cases), and 58 as low-grade and high-grade squamous intraepithelial lesion (SIL) (from 25 different cases with further biopsy confirmation). Classification of cell types was based on peer agreement assumed to be the golden standard for evaluating the efficiency of artificial intelligent classifiers. In addition to these cellular images, micrometer images at 400x magnification were also captured for calibration of the proposed system.

Image editing and processing: Semi-automated cellular extraction was done by using a commercial software package (Adobe Photoshop 7.0, USA). Image processing and editing can be easily operated by personnel. First, the program automatically adjusted the color of the image on the computer to a visual view very similar to the view using the microscope. Secondly, we selected individual cells using layer palette and mask technique supported by Adobe Photoshop package. After the image editing process, the colors of cytoplasm and nucleus of a cell image was converted into blue and green, respectively. Thus, each cell extracted from the background will be saved as an alternative image in another file (Graphics Interchange Format, GIF file, 1556 × 1076 pixels). The original image and its cell mask will be saved as two different but related files. In the automated analysis program, the image pair will be simultaneously analyzed and used for calculating nuclear parameters.

Measurement and analysis of cellular morphology and texture: A software program, namely personal computer-based cellular image analysis (PCCIA) system, was designed in our laboratory to perform cellular image analysis. In order to detect the cell contour from the mask, a method, namely circular seeded region growing (CSRG), has been proposed. CSRG automatically detects the contours of cell nucleus and membrane based on a 3x3 block. The block is shifted clockwise to detect connected pixels located at the boundaries of a cell nucleus or membrane.

PCCIA can automatically measure the morphometric parameters of the cells either individually or in a batch. With the help of internal calibration using the micrometer image, various parameters such as nuclear perimeter, area, maximum length, maximum width, ratio of nucleus and cytoplasm areas (N/C ratio), maximum length from axel center to perimeter (MAP), average length from axel center to perimeter (AAP), maximum length from center of gravity to perimeter (MGP), average length from center of gravity to perimeter (AGP) were obtained for the evaluation of the nuclear size and shape irregularity of a cell. Other parameters, including entropy of co-occurrence matrix (ECM), contrast of co-occurrence matrix (CCM), coarseness and contrast were also applied for analyzing the textural features of the nuclei.

Classification of cell types using SVM: The goal of SVM is to separate multiple clusters with a set of unique hyperplanes that have greatest margin to the edge of each cluster. In this study, the SVM software packages (LIBSVM) developed by Chang and Lin [14] was adopted for classification of different cell types. The whole dataset of morphometric parameters has been normalized to a serial standard setting based on the requirements of LIBSVM. We separated the dataset into training and testing sets. The training set contains 40 data sets, each consists of superficial, intermediate, parabasal and dysplastic cells and accounts for 160 cell data in total. The test group, including 18 data sets (72 cell data), was used to examine the prediction ability of the trained SVM.

3 Results

For dysplastic cells, the morphometric parameters including perimeter (40.2±8.1 μm), area (192.6±80.5 μm^2), maximum length (15.6±3.1 μm), maximum width (12.6±2.7μm), N/C ratio (0.48±0.75), MAP (107.8±24.0μm), AAP (99.1±19.8μm), MGP (99.1±19.8μm), and AGP (85.4±17.2μm) were all found to be significantly

Table 1. Accuracy and prediction power of SVM and a comparison with discriminant classification

Cell Type	SVM classification		Discriminant classification	
	Accuracy	Number of false interpretation	Accuracy	Number of false interpretation
Superficial cell (N=139)	96.40% (134/139)	I=4; P=1; D =0	94.24% (131/138)	I=7; P=1; D =0
Intermediate cell (N=178)	91.57% (163/178)	S=4; P=6; D =5	96.07% (171/178)	S=1; P=6; D =0
Parabasal cell (N=128)	93.75% (120/128)	S=3; I=1; D=2	93.75% (120/128)	S=0; I=7; D =1
Dysplastic cell (N=58)	100% (58/58)	S=0; I=0; P=0	89.66% (52/58)	S=0; I=3; P=3
All cells (N=503)	94.43% (475/503)	Total error=28	94.23% (474/503)	Total error= 29
Prediction Power	Sensitivity	100%		89.7%
	Specificity	98.5%		99.8%
	Positive predictive value	89%		98.1%
	Negative predictive value	100%		98.6%

Abbreviation: "S"=superficial cells, "I"=Intermediate cells, "P"=parabasal cells, "D"=dysplastic cells, including low and high grade squamous intraepithelial cells.

greater than the normal cells ($p<0.05$). Among the 13 morphometric parameters, except contrast, all other twelve parameters have been demonstrated to have statistical significance (p<0.001, t-test) in cellular differentiation. The statistic results show that the dysplastic cells have larger size (i.e. larger perimeter, area, maximum length and maximum width), higher nuclear proportion (i.e. larger N/C ratio), greater irregularity in nuclear shape (i.e. larger MAP, AAP, MGP, and AGP), greater chromatin density (i.e. less ECM), and higher nuclear irregularity (i.e. greater variation in CCM and coarseness).

The accuracy and the prediction power of SVM and a comparison with discriminant classification implemented by using statistic SPSS are summarized in Table 1. Classification using SVM reveals greater accuracy and sensitivity and less false negative cases (accuracy=94.43%, sensitivity=100%, specificity=98.5%, and false negative=0) in discriminating different cell types compared to the statistic methodology established using SPSS (accuracy 94.23%, sensitivity: 89.7% and specificity: 99.8%, false negative case=6). SVM presents high sensitivity with no false negative case while still attaining satisfactory accuracy, specificity, and positive predictive value.

4 Discussion and Conclusions

The merit of cytology in discriminating abnormal from normal cells has been widely recognized and accepted in cervical screening program. However, the false negative cases with postponement of the optimal treatment are the most unpleasant results.

Traditionally, cytoloic criteria set for differentiating normal cells from dysplastic cells are based on "change" in N/C ratio and nuclear size, "irregularity" of nuclear shape and nuclear membrane, and "density and granularity" of nuclear chromatin. Most of the criteria are descriptive and relatively subjective. In contrast, in computed morphometry, the subjective criteria are turned into quantitative parameters. In our study, the 13 morphometric parameters adopted in this study can be categorized into (1) nuclear size (perimeter, area, maximum length and maximum width), (2) shape (MAP, AAP, MGP and AGP), (3) nuclear texture such as density or distribution of chromatin pattern (ECM, CCM, coarseness, contrast), and (4) N/C ratio. The experimental results show that, except contrast, the other 12 parameters work well in the differentiation of the normal from the dysplastic cervical cells (p<0.001). These finding are all compatible to the personnel observation [15] and the previous computed morphometric data [16], i.e. the dysplastic squamous cells have larger nuclear size, more irregularly nuclear shape and hyperchromatia, and higher N/C ratio. Several previous studies [13,16] indicated that successful selection of morphometric parameters will affect the accuracy of cancer diagnosis. The most widely used parameters for cellular classification include mean nuclear area, perimeter, shape, and N/C ratio [11,17]. In addition to these basic morphometric parameters, Murata et al. [13] innovatively reported 27 morphological nuclear parameters which were then abstracted and categorized into more reasonable cytological features to achieving better clinical understanding of computed morphometric features.

In this study, SVM-based classifier has been used to train and predict the normality of the cervical squamous cells. The SVM algorithm was implemented using the

LIBSVM program (http://www.csie.ntu.edu.tw/~cjlin/libsvm). By using the model, we can quickly, easily, and automatically perform analysis, classification, and regression on our numerical datasets. The power of prediction of the dysplasia could also be assumed from the normal cells based on the accuracy and sensitivity analysis. The resulting prototype enabled us to effectively distinguish the normal cells from dysplastic cells without any false negative cases. The results of classification are compatible with the discriminant classification implemented using SPSS program and consistent to the personnel classification.

In conclusion, a semi-automated image analysis system has been developed for morphologic measurement and evaluation on cervical cells. By using this image analysis system, we can establish objective quantitative documentation leading to statistic analysis by individual laboratory. More sequential investigation with statistic measurements is needed to elucidate its practical utility in a laboratory and the capability to improve the diagnostic quality of a laboratory. It is expected to be able to help diminish the amount of the diagnosis in the gray zone on cervical smears, especially on the ASCUS (atypical squamous cells with undetermined significance) v.s. LSIL and the ASCUS v.s. HSIL; or assisting the cellular classification in other cytological fields. By combining the findings obtained from clinical, cytomorphological and morphometric parameters, we can resolve more problems arising from inter-observer variation and ambiguous diagnosis.

References

[1] DeMay, R.M.: Common problems in Papanicolaou smear interpretation. Arch. Pathol. Lab. Med. 121, 229–238 (1997)

[2] Hartmann, K.E., Nanda, K., Hall, S., Myers, E.: Technologic advances for evaluation of cervical cytology: is newer better? Obstet. Gynecol. Surv. 56, 765–774 (2001)

[3] Stoler, M.H.: Advances in cervical screening technology. Mod. Pathol. 13, 275–284 (2000)

[4] Dawson, A.E.: Can we change the way we screen? the ThinPrep Imaging System. Cancer 102, 340–344 (2004)

[5] Kardos, T.F.: The FocalPoint System: FocalPoint slide profiler and FocalPoint GS. Cancer 102, 334–339 (2004)

[6] Mango, L.J.: Reducing false negatives in clinical practice: the role of neural network technology. Am. J. Obstet. Gynecol. 175, 1114–1119 (1996)

[7] Taylor, R.N., Gagnon, M., Lange, J., Lee, T., Draut, R., Kujawski, E.: CytoView. A prototype computer image-based Papanicolaou smear proficiency test. Acta. Cytol. 43, 1045–1051 (1999)

[8] Doornewaard, H., van der Schouw, Y.T., van der Graaf, Y., Bos, A.B., van den Tweel, J.G.: Observer variation in cytologic grading for cervical dysplasia of Papanicolaou smears with the PAPNET testing system. Cancer 87, 178–183 (1999)

[9] Harris, M.V., Cason, Z., Benghuzzi, H., Tucci, M.: Cytomorphological assessment of benign and malignant dense hyperchromatic groups in cervicovaginal smears. Biomed. Sci. Instrum. 36, 349–354 (2000)

[10] Nunobiki, O., Sato, M., Taniguchi, E., Tang, W., Nakamura, M., Utsunomiya, H., Nakamura, Y., Mori, I., Kakudo, K.: Color image analysis of cervical neoplasia using RGB computer color specification. Anal. Quant. Cytol. Histol. 24, 289–294 (2002)

[11] Arora, B., Setia, S., Rekhi, B.: Role of computerized morphometric analysis in diagnosis of effusion specimens. Diagn. Cytopathol. 34, 670–675 (2006)

[12] Wang, S.L., Wu, M.T., Yang, S.F., Chan, H.M., Chai, C.Y.: Computerized nuclear morphometry in thyroid follicular neoplasms. Pathol. Int. 55, 703–706 (2005)

[13] Murata, S., Mochizuki, K., Nakazawa, T., Kondo, T., Nakamura, N., Yamashita, H., Urata, Y., Ashihara, T., Katoh, R.: Morphological abstraction of thyroid tumor cell nuclei using morphometry with factor analysis. Microsc. Res. Tech. 61, 457–462 (2003)

[14] Chang, C.C., Lin, C.J.: LIBSVM: a library for support vector machines. Software (2001), available at http://www.csie.ntu.edu.tw/ cjlin/libsvm

[15] Naib, Z.M.: Cytopathology, 4th edn., pp. 65–67. Little, Brown and Company, Bosten, New York (1996)

[16] Ramesh, B.V., Padaki, V.C., Hegde, K.S., Hazarika, D., Verghese, C.A.: An interactive image analysis system for quantitative cytology & to classify cervical cells. Indian J. Med. Res. 96, 338–343 (1992)

[17] Kirillov, V., Stebenyaeva, E., Paplevka, A., Demidchik, E.: A rapid method for diagnosing regional metastases of papillary thyroid cancer with morphometry. Microsc. Res. Tech 69, 721–728 (2006)

An Integrated MRI and MRS Approach to Evaluation of Multiple Sclerosis with Cognitive Impairment

Zhengrong Liang[1,3], Lihong Li[1,4], Hongbing Lu[1,5],
Wei Huang[1,6], Alina Tudorica[1], and Lauren Krupp[2]

[1] Departments of Radiology, [2] Neurology, and [3] Computer Science,
State University of New York, Stony Brook, NY 11794
jzl@mil.sunysb.edu, ltudoric@notes.cc.sunysb.edu,
lkrupp@notes.cc.sunysb.edu
http://www.sunysb.edu/iris
[4] Department of Engineering Science and Physics, College of Staten Island,
City University of New York, Staten Island, NY 10314
lil@mail.csi.cuny.edu
[5] Department of Biomedical Engineering, the Fourth Military Medical University,
Xi'An, Shaanxi 710032, China
luhb@fmmu.edu.cn
[6] Department of Medical Physics, Memorial Sloan-Kettering Cancer Center
1275 York Avenue, NY 10021
huangw2@mskcc.org

Abstract. Magnetic resonance imaging and spectroscopy (MRI/MRS) plays a unique role in multiple sclerosis (MS) evaluation, because of its ability to provide both high image contrast and significant chemical change among brain tissues. The image contrast renders the possibility of quantifying the tissue volumetric and texture variations, e.g., cerebral atrophy and progressing speed, reflecting the ongoing destructive pathologic processes. Any chemical change reflects an early sign of pathological alteration, e.g., decreased N-acetyl aspartate (NAA) in lesions and normal appearing white matter, related to axonal damage or dysfunction. Both MRI and MRS encounter partial volume (PV) effect, which compromises the quantitative capability, especially for MRS. This work aims to develop a statistical framework to segment the tissue mixtures inside each image element, eliminating theoretically the PV effect, and apply the framework to the evaluation of MS with cognitive impairment. The quantitative measures from MRI/MRS neuroimaging are strongly correlated with the qualitative neuropsychological scores of Brief Repeatable Battery (BRB) test on cognitive impairment, demonstrating the usefulness of the PV image segmentation framework in this clinically significant problem.

1 Introduction

Multiple Sclerosis (MS) is the most common inflammatory demyelinating disease of central nervous system (CNS), characterized by repeated cycles of white matter

D. Zhang (Ed.): ICMB 2008, LNCS 4901, pp. 200–207, 2007.

(WM) damage, recovery, and injury. More than half of the MS patients develop cognitive dysfunction. The deficits often manifest in early adulthood and can profoundly disrupt occupational and social functioning. The domains most commonly disturbed are learning/recent memory, attention/information processing speed, verbal fluency, executive functions, and visuospatial skills. In this study we related neuropsychological performance to neuroimaging measures of cerebral injury in a group of subjects selected for cognitive impairment.

Volumetric analyses by magnetic resonance imaging (MRI) have shown that MS patients have significant cerebral atrophy (CA), progressing faster, reflecting the ongoing destructive pathologic processes [2, 7]. Cerebral atrophy has been shown to correlate with a variety of cognitive functions, including those functions most commonly disturbed. For example, correlations have been demonstrated for overall intellectual functioning, learning/recent memory, attention/information processing speed, and executive functions, though results for verbal fluency specifically have been somewhat inconsistent.

Studies of MS by ^{1}H magnetic resonance spectroscopy (MRS) have shown decreased levels of N-acetyl aspartate (NAA) in lesions and normal appearing WM (NAWM), related to axonal damage or dysfunction [1, 3, 6]. Decrease in NAA, or ratios of NAA over creatine (Cr) (NAA/Cr), NAA over choline compounds (NAA/Cho), are associated with more advanced disease and associated with level of disability. Two preliminary studies indicate that NAA levels may relate to cognitive variables as well, but further research is necessary to assess it as a neurobiological marker of cognitive impairment.

Although ^{1}H MRS has provided quantitative information about major pathologic aspects, it doesn't enable us to obtain information on specific brain tissues.

On the other hand, volumetric MRI analysis has provided morphological processes of brain tissues, but it doesn't enable us to obtain pathologic information underline the morphological processes.

The goal of this study is to map MR spectroscopy of interested chemical compounds onto their corresponding cerebral tissues and to establish an effective means to explore the complementary information between these two MR neural measures.

2 Methods

2.1 Theory

In the use of both MRI and MRS for quantitative analyses, a major challenge is associated with the partial volume (PV) effect, especially for MRS (because of its extremely low resolution at a cubic voxel size of 10 mm, while MRI can offer a resolution at 1 mm level). A theoretical solution to eliminate the PV effect is by the use of an image segmentation algorithm which is capable to quantify the tissue mixtures or percentages inside each image voxel. We have proposed an algorithm [4] and further developed it to segment the multi-spectral MR images in this work.

By acquiring the patient data within a same session of a short time period, we expect both MRI and MRS data are registered spatially. In other words, we have obtained the tissue fractions within each MRS voxel (of 10 mm side size) from the segmented tissue mixtures inside each MRI voxel (of 1 mm side size) [5].

The metabolite changes of the chemical compounds inside the cerebral tissues, measured by ^{1}H MRS, can be mapped onto the image voxels for correlation studies by the following formula

$$NAA = w\,WM + g\,GM + s\,Lesion \tag{1}$$

where we have assumed that WM has a weight factor of w contributing to the NAA measure, grey matter (GM) with a factor of g, and cerebral spinal fluid (CSF) with a factor of $c = 0$ and lesion with a factor of s. The complementary information between MRI and MRS leads to quantitative measures on both spatial and temporal correlations. Because both MRI and MRS images are spatially registered, a correlation between atrophy and NAA can be performed globally and locally across the field-of-view (FOV).

2.2 Data Acquisition

Multi-voxel ^{1}H MRS data were acquired with a 1.5T Phillips scanner with a PRESS sequence, TE = 135 ms, TR = 1500 ms, 16 cm FOV, 2D phase encoding (16x16), and 2 scan averages. The slice of interest with 2 cm thickness was taken through the posterior and anterior aspects of the corpus callosum. For each MRS voxel (1x1x2 cm^3), three peaks of N-acetyl aspartate compounds (or NAA), choline compounds (or Cho), and total creatine (or Cr) were digitized. Then the output of the MRS data is an image and each voxel contains the three digital values. From the three values in each MRS voxel, a ratio of NAA over Cho or NAA over Cr was computed for a relative measure of NAA level.

Multi-spectral (T1, T2, and FLAIR) MR images were acquired by the same scanner in the same session with voxel size of 0.9x0.9x1.5 mm^3 on an image slice of 256x256 array. To cover the whole brain space, more than one hundred image slices are usually generated for each T1, T2 or FLAIR scan. The eight corners' coordinates of the MRS image array were recorded within the MRI image array. The three multispectral T1, T2, and FLAIR images, as well as the MRS image are assumed registered spatially because all the data were acquired in the same session while the patient was lying on the scanner couch.

In addition, each MS patient underwent a modified version of the neuropsychological scores of Brief Repeatable Battery (BRB) test on cognitive functions.

3 Results

Participants were 38 individuals (20-55 years old) with relapsing remitting (60.5%) and secondary progressive (39.5%) MS. Each patient underwent the MRI/MRS data acquisition session and followed by a modified Brief Repeatable Battery (BRB) of neuropsychological tests. Figure 1 shows an example of the segmentation of multi-spectral MR images of a patient. Figure 2 shows an example of MRS data acquisition.

Figure 3 shows an example of mapping the central 8x8 MRS voxels onto the segmented MRI array of seven slices. From the segmented tissue mixture distributions in Figure 1 and the mapped NAA distribution in Figure 3, a correlation between atrophy and NAA can be performed globally and locally across the FOV. In the following, a series correlation studies are presented with extension to include BRB neuropsychological tests.

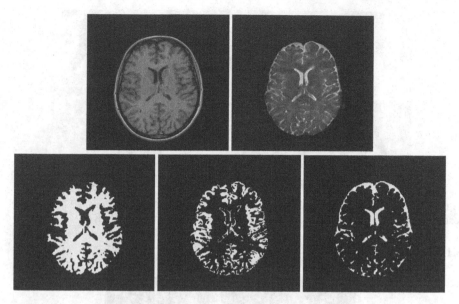

Fig. 1. Top left is a T1 image slice and top right is a T2 image slice at the same axial location. Bottom from left to right shows the segmented WM, GM, and CSF.

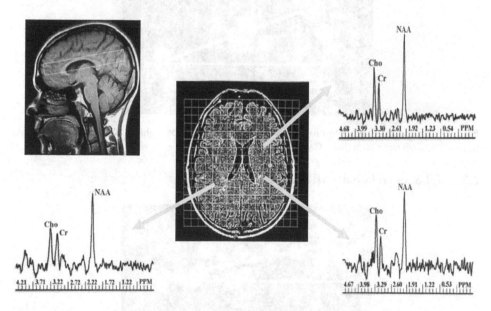

Fig. 2. Top left indicates the location of the MRS image volume taken through the posterior and anterior aspects of the corpus callosum. The middle shows a FLAIR image slice where the MRS voxel array was highlighted. Three MR spectra from three MRS voxels respectively are displayed.

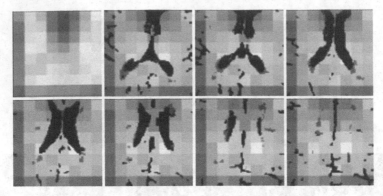

Fig. 3. A demonstration of mapping spectroscopic voxels (top left) to segmented image voxels, resulting in more accurate measure on both spatial and temporal correlations

3.1 Global Correlation – MRS and MRI

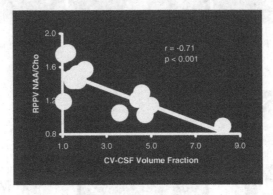

Fig. 4. Significant inverse relationship between NAA/Cho of right posterior periventricular (RPPV) and central ventricular (CV)-CSF volume fraction

3.2 Global Correlation – MRI and BRB

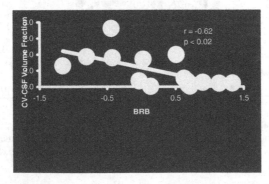

Fig. 5. Significant inverse relationship between central ventricular CV-CSF volume fraction and BRB scores

3.3 Global Correlation – MRS and BRB$_{Cho}$

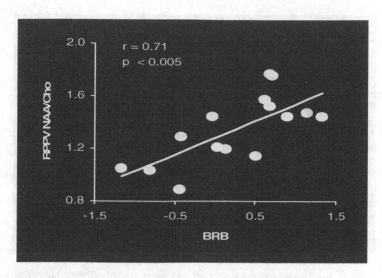

Fig. 6. Significant positive correlation between right posterior periventricular RPPV NAA/Cho and BRB scores

3.4 Global Correlation – MRS and BRB$_{Cr}$

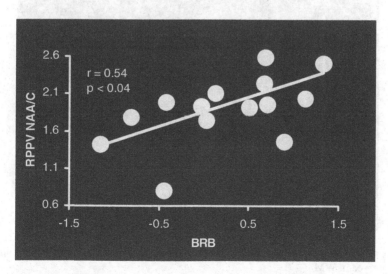

Fig. 7. Significant positive correlation between right posterior periventricular RPPV NAA/Cr and BRB scores

3.5 Local Correlation Study in WM$_{Cho}$

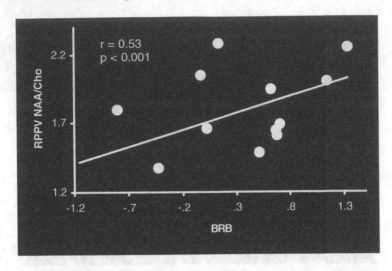

Fig. 8. A positive correlation between right posterior periventricular RPPV NAA/Cho and BRB scores in WM

3.6 Local Correlation Study in WM$_{Cr}$

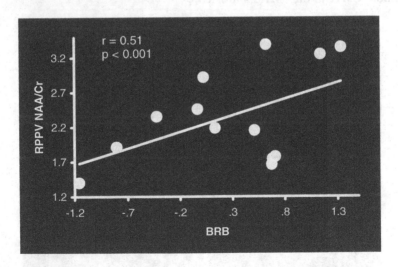

Fig. 9. A positive correlation between right posterior periventricular RPPV NAA/Cr and BRB scores observed in WM

4 Discussion and Conclusions

Mixture-based image segmentation is a theoretical solution to the PV effect and provides the most accurate result in quantifying tissue volumes and textures. Mapping the low-resolution MRS data onto the segmented high-resolution tissue distribution offers a unique way to study both structural and functional changes of the brain tissues.

Cerebral atrophy and brain metabolite level correlate with each other as well as BRB scores assessed by cognitive functions.

Brain metabolite level measured by ^{1}H MRS can be quantitatively mapped onto segmented tissue mixtures in each image voxel for correlation studies between MRI and MRS.

As both MRI and MRS are spatially registered, a correlation study can be performed both globally and locally across the FOV.

The integrated MRI/MRS framework shall open a new way to explore the MRS metabolic changes and MRI morphological processes for studying brain functions.

Acknowledgements

This work was supported in part by the National Institutes of Health Grant #CA082402 and Grant #CA120917. Dr. L. Li was supported in part by the PSC-CUNY award program. Dr. H. Lu was supported in part by the National Nature Science Foundation of China under Grant 30470490.

References

1. De Stefano, N., Narayanan, S., Francis, G., Arnaoutelis, R., Tartaglia, M., Antel, J., Matthews, P., Arnold, D.: Evidence of axonal damage in early stages of multiple sclerosis and its relevance to disability. Archives of Neurology 58, 65–70 (2001)
2. Fox, N., Jenkins, R., Leary, S., Stevenson, V., Losseff, N., Crum, W., Harvey, R.: Progressive cerebral atrophy in MS: A serial study using registered, volumetric MRI. Neurology 54, 807–812 (2000)
3. Gonen, O., Catalaa, I., Babb, J., Ge, Y., Mannon, L., Kolson, D., Grossman, R.: Total brain N-acetylaspartate: A new measure of disease load in MS. Neurology 54, 15–19 (2000)
4. Liang, Z., Li, X., Eremina, D., Li, L.: An EM framework for segmentation of tissue mixtures from medical images. In: International Conference of IEEE Engineering in Medicine and Biology, Cancun, Mexico, pp. 682–685 (2003)
5. Liang, Z., Li, L., Huang, W., Tudorica, A., Krupp, L.: An integrated MRI and MRS framework for studies of cognitive impairment. In: The 89th Annual Meeting of the Radiological Society of North America (RSNA), p. 593 (2003)
6. Pan, J., Krupp, L., Elkins, L., Coyle, P.: Cogsnitive function and NAA in multiple sclerosis. Applied Neuropsychology 8, 155–160 (2001)
7. Rudick, R., Fisher, E., Lee, J., Simon, J., Jacobs, L.: MS Collaborative Research Group: Use of brain parenchymal fraction to measure whole brain atrophy in relapsing remitting MS. Neurology 53, 1698–1704 (1999)

Using Modified Contour Deformable Model to Quantitatively Estimate Ultrasound Parameters for Osteoporosis Assessment

Yung-Fu Chen[1], Yi-Chun Du[2], Yi-Ting Tsai[2], and Tainsong Chen[2]

[1] Department of Health Services Administration, China Medical University, Taichung
yungfu@mail.cmu.edu.tw
[2] Institute of Biomedical Engineering, National Cheng Kung University, Tainan, Taiwan
{fresh.song,chents}@mail.ncku.edu.tw, eting.tsai@gmail.com

Abstract. Osteoporosis is a systemic skeletal disease, which is characterized by low bone mass and micro-architectural deterioration of bone tissue, leading to bone fragility. Finding an effective method for prevention and early diagnosis of the disease is very important. Several parameters, including broadband ultrasound attenuation (BUA), speed of sound (SOS), and stiffness index (STI), have been used to measure the characteristics of bone tissues. In this paper, we proposed a method, namely modified contour deformable model (MCDM), bases on the active contour model (ACM) and active shape model (ASM) for automatically detecting the calcaneus contour from quantitative ultrasound (QUS) parametric images. The results show that the difference between the contours detected by the MCDM and the true boundary for the phantom is less than one pixel. By comparing the phantom ROIs, significant relationship was found between contour mean and bone mineral density (BMD) with R=0.99. The influence of selecting different ROI diameters (12, 14, 16 and 18 mm) and different region-selecting methods, including fixed region (ROI_{fix}), automatic circular region (ROI_{cir}) and calcaneal contour region (ROI_{anat}), were evaluated for testing human subjects. Measurements with large ROI diameters, especially using fixed region, result in high position errors (10-45%). The precision errors of the measured ultrasonic parameters for ROI_{anat} are smaller than ROI_{fix} and ROI_{cir}. In conclusion, ROI_{anat} provides more accurate measurement of ultrasonic parameters for the evaluation of osteoporosis and is useful for clinical application.

1 Introduction

Osteoporosis is a systemic skeletal disease leading to bone fragility, which is characterized by low bone mass and micro-architectural deterioration of bone tissue. Finding an effective and inexpensive method for prevention and early diagnosis of the disease is very important. Bone mineral density (BMD) is generally used in dual-energy X-ray absoroptiometry (DEXA) for osteoporosis diagnosis. Although it is a convenient and precise method for BMD measurement, it is dangerous for patients to exposure to X-ray. Ultrasound, in contrast, embeds several advantages which include no exposure to

D. Zhang (Ed.): ICMB 2008, LNCS 4901, pp. 208–215, 2007.
© Springer-Verlag Berlin Heidelberg 2007

ionizing radiation, low cost, and great portability. Several parameters, including broadband ultrasound attenuation (BUA), speed of sound (SOS), and stiffness index (STI), have been used for measuring the characteristics of bone tissues. Previous studies showed that SOS and BUA have a great correlation with bone density in bovine [1, 2] and have been widely applied in bone quality assessment [3, 4]. Stiffness calculated from BUA and SOS is able to compensate for variations in heel width and heel temperature [5]. Some investigations demonstrated that it is more sensitive than SOS and BUA to identify post-menopausal women with bone fractures [6, 7].

Most commercialized ultrasonic devices only measure the parameters from a single point in a bone area without considering the heterogeneous difference of the bone. The accuracy will be affected by different measuring areas. In addition, the bone density is not uniform in the heel bone, so it is not objective to only observe a specific region or a point in the parametric image of the heel bone. Recent investigations demonstrated that the images could enhance the performance by assessing the heterogeneity of the bone or selecting similar region of interest (ROI) for each subject. The purpose of this study is to propose a fully automatic method to compute the parameters, including BUA, SOS, and STI of the entire calcaneus. A modified contour deformable model (MCDM) similar to the method proposed by a previous investigation [8] was used to detect calcaneus contour. MCDM was based on active shape model [9] and active contour model [10] for the detection of calcaneus contour that the whole heel bone area was used for generating parametric images. In order to increase the accuracy and automation of the system, active shape model has been used to replace Fourier descriptor [8] for obtaining the initial contour in this study. Furthermore, phantom experiment was used for validating the accuracy of the detected contours and the bone densities. The estimated parametric values, i.e. BUA, SOS and STI, were compared with the values obtained from manual or automatic ROI's [11].

2 Materials and Methods

Ultrasound parametric images were acquired using a QUS scanner, UBIS 5000 (DMS, Montpellier, France), with two 0.5 MHz transducers, one for transmitting and the other for receiving. Nine human subjects (5 female and 4 male) in total were recruited for experimental testing. The subjects were divided into two groups including young (7 subjects, age: 23-25) and middle-aged (2 subjects, age: 48). QUS parametric measurements may be influenced by the size and location of the ROIs because of heterogeneous property of calcaneus [12]. Hence, the parameters were averaged over a region selected by different modes, including fixed center (x: 26mm, y: 39mm) [12] with variable size (12, 14, 16, and 18mm), automatic selection based on the lowest attenuation [14] with variable size (12, 14, 16, and 18mm), and whole calcaneus detected by MCDM. Figure 1 shows the experimental setup and illustration of different ROI-selection modes. The regions enclosed by the detected contour were used to calculate mean parametric values. The experimental procedure is as follows: (1) re-sampling the UBIS images from 60x60 to 120x120 using linear interpolation to increase spatial resolution, (2) determining the

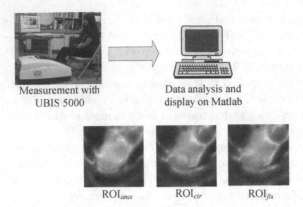

Measurement with   Data analysis and
UBIS 5000   display on Matlab

ROI$_{anal}$ ROI$_{cir}$ ROI$_{fix}$

Fig. 1. Experimental setup and illustration of different modes of ROI selection

initial contour by using ASM, and (3) deforming the contour by applying discrete ACM for calcaneal contour detection.

2.1 Active Contour Model

Recently, ACM has been used to detect whole calcaneus for reliable estimation of QUS parameters [8]. The convergence of ACM contour depends on the interaction of internal and external forces until the minimum force has been found [10]. The internal force is calculated based on the assumption that the contour is continuous and smooth, while the external force is used to extract the desired image features, such as lines or object boundaries. In this study, the discrete dynamic contour model was used to detect the calcaneus, in which a contour is composed of vertices connected by edges [13]. The total contour force is a combination of internal, external, and damping forces, as shown in Eq. (1).

$$f = w_i f_{\text{int}} + w_e f_{\text{ext}} + w_d f_{dam} \tag{1}$$

The internal force mentioned here is similar to the elasticity and rigidity of the traditional model to keep the contour continuous and smooth [10]. In this case, the deformation process will continue to move the vertices to a point. The external force is contributed by the combination of two types of features including local standard deviation and local co-occurrence matrix. It was found that great contrast could be found in heterogeneous area where the local standard deviation is significantly higher than the homogeneous area located inside the calcaneous. Applying an $n \times n$ mask to image I, the first type of external force can be obtained by calculating the local standard deviation according to the following equation:

$$I_{SD}(x, y) = \frac{1}{n^2 - 1} \sqrt{\sum_{i=x-(\frac{n-1}{2})}^{x+(\frac{n-1}{2})} \sum_{j=y-(\frac{n-1}{2})}^{y+(\frac{n-1}{2})} [I(i, j) - m(i, j)]^2} \tag{2}$$

in which $m(i,j)$ indicates the mean gray-scale value of the nxn mask with the pixel (i,j) located at its center. The local co-occurrence matrix can be obtained by considering 4 directions ($\theta=0°$, $45°$, $90°$, and $135°$) with unit distance ($d=1$) from Eq. (3).

$$I_{cont}(x, y) = \sum_{i=1}^{n}\sum_{j=1}^{n-1}\left|x_{i,j} - x_{i,j+1}\right| + \sum_{i=2}^{n}\sum_{j=1}^{n-1}\left|x_{i,j} - x_{i-1,j+1}\right|$$

$$+ \sum_{i=2}^{n}\sum_{j=1}^{n}\left|x_{i,j} - x_{i-1,j}\right| + \sum_{i=2}^{n}\sum_{j=2}^{n-1}\left|x_{i,j} - x_{i-1,j-1}\right| \tag{3}$$

Edge detection (GI_{cont}) of the co-occurrence image can then be obtained by applying Canny filter to the co-occurrence image (I_{cont}). Finally, after normalization of two types of images, the external image can be obtained from Eq. (4).

$$f_{ext} = -\Delta E \tag{4}$$

with
$$E = GI_{cont}^{*} - I_{SD}^{*} \tag{5}$$

in which GI_{cont}^{*} and I_{SD}^{*} represent the normalized images of GI_{cont} and I_{SD}, respectively.

During the deformation process, the force acts on each vertex iteratively and moves it to a new position. The deformation process will be terminated when it reaches an equilibrium situation that the acceleration and velocity on each vertex become zero.

2.2 Active Shape Model

In order to reduce the processing time and increase the accuracy of the system, in this study, the initial contour was determined using active shape model (ASM) by training a set of calcaneus instances. ASM has been widely used in applications that objects within the same class are not identical for deforming to fit the images consistent to the training set [9]. First of all, a set of landmark points depicting the significant parts along the calcaneus contour was built. Secondly, a point distribution model (PDM) was used to model variation of the landmarks. Thirdly, principal component analysis was used for determining the main modes from the covariance matrix. Finally, the pose and shape parameters was estimated and used for adjusting the model to best fit the calcaneus contour. In Figure 2, the mean shape of human calcaneus obtained using ASM and PDM is demonstrated.

2.3 Data Analysis

In this study, both the left and right feet had been scanned for each subject with 5 images were taken for each foot. Standard deviation of a parametric value for each subject was calculated according to the following equation.

$$SD_i = \sqrt{\sum_{j=1}^{n_i}(x_{ij} - \bar{x}_i)^2 /(n_i - 1)} \tag{6}$$

where n_i indicates the number of tests done for subject i. For each test group, the standard deviation can be obtained by

$$SD = \sqrt{\sum_{j=1}^{N_i} SD_i / N} \tag{7}$$

where N denotes the number of subject in a group. Finally, the precision error (PE) can then be obtained from the following equation:

$$PE = \frac{SD}{\bar{x}} \times 100\% \tag{8}$$

in which $\bar{x}$ indicates the mean of the evaluated parameter. All the software programs were implemented using MATLAB (The MathWorks, Natick, United States).

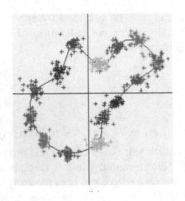

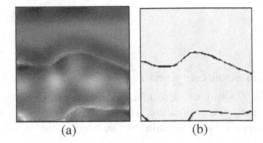
(a)   (b)

Fig. 2. Mean shape obtained by point distribution model for human calcaneus

Fig. 3. Contours obtained from (a) ultrasound image detected by MCDM and (b) phantom plate delineated by hand

3   Results and Discussions

Figure 3 shows an example of phantom contour detected by MCDM from the parametric image and the true boundary delineated by hand. The difference between two shapes is less than one pixel. Mean parameters obtained from the calcaneal area detected using MCDM were found to have great correlation with BMD, the correlation coefficients for BUA and SOS are 0.99 and 0.98 respectively. These results demonstrate that MCDM is efficient for detecting the calcaneus contour.

Figure 4 illustrates individual steps and their corresponding results for BUA parametric image enhancement and ACM pre-processing. The effects of selecting different ROI diameters (12, 14, or 18 mm) and different region-selecting methods, including fixed region (ROI$_{fix}$), automatic circular region (ROI$_{cir}$), and calcaneal contour region (ROI$_{anat}$), were evaluated for the subjects. The position errors induced by different ROI selection modes are compared in Table 1. As shown in this table, measurements using large ROI diameters, especially for using fixed region, result in high position errors (10-45%). In contrast, the calcaneus contour detected by using MCDM demonstrates a great improvement in localization with lower error (3%). The results show that MCDM is more reliable than the traditional ROI selection modes for automatically analyzing parametric image of osteoporosis.

The precision errors of the measured ultrasonic parameters for different ROI selection modes are shown in Figure 5. The precision errors of the measured ultrasonic parameters for ROI$_{anat}$ (1.02 for BUA, 0.07 for SOS, and 0.46 for STI) were significantly smaller than ROI$_{fix}$ (3.75-4.23 for BUA, 0.42-0.54 for SOS, and 1.79-2.71 for STI) and ROI$_{cir}$ (1.78-2.85 for BUA, 0.19-0.36 for SOS, and 1.60-1.91 for STI). It can be found that the parametric values obtained using MDCM have less variances compared with other modes. In addition, STI (3rd row in the figure) tends to be more immune to various selection modes, which might be the reason why it is more sensitive in detecting osteoporosis for post-menopausal women [6, 7]. As shown in Table 2, by comparing the measured BUA values of left foot and right foot for each individual, MDCM tends to have more consistent result than other two methods. It indicates that MDCM always considers the whole calcaneus while the values obtained by other two modes might be affected by different selected locations and inhomogeneity for left and right feet.

Table 1. A comparisons of position errors (%) using different ROI sizes and various modes of ROI selection for human test. The ground-truth contour was drawn manually by an expert.

ROI Selection	ROI$_{fix}$				ROI$_{cir}$				ROI$_{anat}$
Diameter (mm)	12	14	16	18	12	14	16	18	-
Position Error	10	12.8	25	45	0	0	0	37.8	3

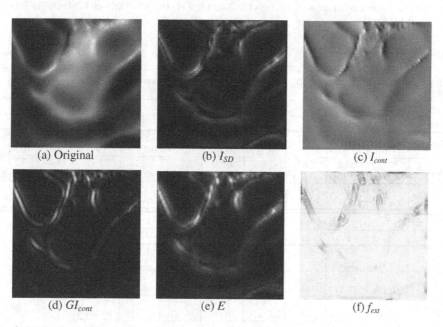

(a) Original   (b) I_{SD} (c) I_{cont}

(d) GI_{cont} (e) E (f) f_{ext}

Fig. 4. (a) Original BUA parametric image and two types of features used for the calculation of external forces: (b) local standard deviation and (c) co-occurrence matrix. (d) The image after applying Canny filter to image shown in (c). (e) Energy image and (f) external image obtained using Eq. (4).

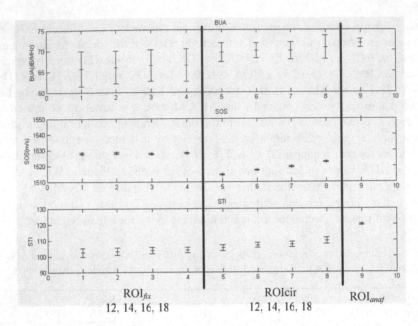

Fig. 5. Precision errors of the measured ultrasonic parameters in BUA, SOS and STI. The notation of numbers on the horizontal axis is: 1-fix12; 2-fix14; 3-fix16; 4-fix18; 5-cir12; 6-cir14; 7-cir16; 8-cir18; 9-MCDM.

Table 2. Measured BUA values of test subjects for both left and right feed using three ROI selection modes. Note that the parametric values of left foot and right foot using MDCM for individual subjects have more consistent results than other two modes.

Subject	1		2		3		4		5	
Foot	L	R	L	R	L	R	L	R	L	R
Fix12	63.7 (1.10)	62.3 (1.81)	73.7 (2.65)	71.0 (0.21)	62.6 (0.12)	60.3 (0.12)	68.2 (0.52)	67.3 (0.49)	70.7 (0.67)	68.7 (0.31)
Cir12	65.2 (0.67)	64.6 (0.40)	79.4 (0.67)	79.8 (1.22)	63.0 (0.15)	62.2 (0.1)	72 (0.91)	71.7 (0.99)	75.4 (0.7)	72.7 (0.35)
MDCM	70.0 (0.38)	70.0 (0.21)	76.3 (0.23)	74.8 (0.17)	69.2 (0.12)	68.2 (0.15)	75.7 (0.25)	75.7 (0.15)	78.3 (0.35)	78.1 (0.00)

Subject	6		7		8		9	
Foot	L	R	L	R	L	R	L	R
Fix12	61.4 (0.51)	63.4 (1.51)	60.6 (0.96)	74.7 (1.97)	64.8 (0.81)	66.8 (0.93)	61.3 (3.39)	65.8 (0.57)
Cir12	65.0 (0.15)	67.0 (0.1)	65.2 (0.44)	78.2 (0.50)	65.2 (0.96)	67.9 (0.49)	69.2 (0.44)	66.8 (0.36)
MDCM	68.6 (0.3)	64.4 (0.21)	62.5 (0.15)	71.1 (0.40)	68.4 (0.68)	69.9 (0.50)	68.7 (0.15)	66.9 (0.20)

4 Conclusions

ROI$_{anat}$ detected by MCDM provides a more accurate region for measurement of the ultrasonic parameters. When examining the position errors of ROI$_{fix}$, the error is high, because improper central position and size of the ROI might increase the position error and thereby elevating the precision error. In contrast, the ROI_{anat} could provide an automatic method to detect the whole calcaneus contour with less position and precision errors and more consistent results. In addition, the time needed for each MCDM operation takes only 2-3 seconds which is significantly less than the method combining Fourier descriptor and ACM. In conclusion, MCDM provides a more accurate method for measurement of ultrasonic parameters in the evaluation of osteoporosis. It is expected that the proposed method can have great potential in clinical application for evaluating osteoporosis in vivo.

References

1. Evans, J.A., Tavakoli, M.B.: Ultrasonic attenuation and velocity in bone. Phys. Med. Biol. 35, 1387–1396 (1990)
2. Serpe, L., Rho, J.Y.: The nonlinear transition period of broadband ultrasound attenuation as bone density veries. J. Biomechanics 29, 963–966 (1996)
3. Njeh, C.F., Saeed, I., Grigorian, M., Kendler, D.L., Fan, B., Shepherd, J., Mcclung, M., Drake, W.M., Genant, H.K.: Assessment of bone status using speed of sound at multiple anatomical sites. Ultrasound in Med. & Biol. 27, 1337–1345 (2001)
4. Toyras, J., Nieminen, M.T., Kroger, H., Jurvelin, J.S.: Bone mineral density, ultrasound velocity, and broadband attenuation predict mechanical predict mechanical properties of trabecular bone differently. Bone 31, 503–507 (2002)
5. UBIS 5000 Technical Manual (1999)
6. Han, S., Medige, J., Ziv, I.: Combined models of ultrasound velocity and attenuation for predicting trabecular bone strength and mineral density. Clinical Biomechanics 11, 348–353 (1996)
7. Hadji, P., Hars, O., Wuster, C., Bock, K., Alberts, U.S., Bohnet, H.G., Emons, G., Schulz, K.D.: Stiffness index identifies patients with osteoporotic fractures better than ultrasound velocity or attenuation alone. Maturitas 31, 221–226 (1999)
8. Lefebvre, F., Berger, G., Laugier, P.: Automatic detection of the calcaneus boundary from ultrasound parametric images using active contour model: Clinical assessment. IEEE. Trans. Med. Imaging 17, 45–52 (1998)
9. Cootes, T.F., Taylor, C.J., Cooper, D.H., Graham, J.: Active shape models- their training and application. CVGIP: Image Understanding 61, 38–59 (1995)
10. Kass, M., Witkin, A., Terzopoulos, D.: Snakes: Active contour models. Int. J. Comput. Vision, 321–331 (1988)
11. Njeh, C.F., Boivin, C.M., Langton, C.M.: The Role of Ultrasound in the Assessment of Osteoporosis: A Review. Osteoporosis Int. 7, 7–22 (1997)
12. van der Bergh, J.P.W., Noordam, C., Thijssen, J.M., Otten, B.J., Smals, A.G.H., Hermus, A.R.M.M.: Measuring skeletal changes with calcaneus ultrasound imaging in healthy children and adults: The influence of size and location of the region of interest. Osteoporos Int. 12, 970–979 (2001)
13. Lobregt, S., Viergever, M.A.: A discrete dynamic contour model. IEEE. Trans. Med. Imaging 14, 12–24 (1995)
14. Fournier, B., Chappard, C., Roux, C., Berger, G., Laugier, P.: Quantitative ultrasound imaging at the calcaneus using an automatic region of interest. Osteoporos Int. 7, 363–369 (1997)

Noninvasive Ultrasound Imaging for Bone Quality Assessment Using Scanning Confocal Acoustic Diagnosis, μCT, DXA Measurements, and Mechanical Testing

Yi-Xian Qin[1], Yi Xia[1], Wei Lin[1], Erik Mittra[1], Clint Rubin[1], and Barry Gruber[2]

[1] Department of Biomedical Engineering
[2] Department of Medicine
State University of New York at Stony Brook
Stony Brook, NY 11794-2580
yi-xian.qin@sunysb.edu

Abstract. Osteoporosis is a disease characterized by decreased bone mass and progressive deterioration of the microstructure, affecting both mineral density and bone's fragility. Current diagnoses are only measuring apparent bone mineral density (AppBMD). Using our newly developed scanning confocal acoustic diagnostic (SCAD) system, we evaluated the ability of quantitative ultrasound in noninvasively predicting bone's quantity and quality on 19 human cadaver calcanei. Results show that ultrasound attenuation image on intact calcaneus represents bone mass distribution. High correlation (R=0.82) exists between SCAD determined broadband ultrasound attenuation (BUA) and DXA determined AppBMD at the calcaneus, as well as in the AppBMD result at femoral neck (R=0.81). SCAD determined BUA and ultrasound velocity (UV) are highly correlated with the micro-CT and mechanical testing determined bone quantity and quality parameters. These results suggest that image-based quantitative ultrasound is able to identify ROI and predict both bone mass and strength.

1 Introduction

Osteoporosis is a systemic skeletal disease, which results in compromised bone quality and an increased susceptibility to chronic and traumatic fractures. Osteoporosis related fractures represent an important clinical challenge as they are associated with decreased mobility, prolonged disability and increased mortality. In the tissue level, osteoporosis is a reduction in bone mass that leads to deteriorated and fragile bones and is the leading cause of bone fractures in postmenopausal women and in the elderly population for both men and women. About 13 to 18 percent of women aged 50 years and older, and 3 to 6 percent of men aged 50 years and older, have osteoporosis in the US alone. These rates correspond to 4~6 million women, and 1~2 million men who suffer from osteoporosis[12]. One-third of women over 65 will have vertebral fractures and 90% of women aged 75 and older have radiographic evidence of osteoporosis[14,15,19]. Another 37 to 50 percent of women aged 50 years and older, and 28 to 47 percent of men of the same age group, have some degree of osteopenia. Thus, approximately a total of 24 million people suffer from osteoporosis in the United States alone, with an estimated annual direct cost of over $16

D. Zhang (Ed.): ICMB 2008, LNCS 4901, pp. 216–223, 2007.
© Springer-Verlag Berlin Heidelberg 2007

billion to national health programs. Hence, early diagnosis that can predict fracture risk and result in prompt treatment is extremely important.

With osteoporosis, fractures can occur without a singular traumatic event, and thus early detection and diagnostic of bone loss, or a skeleton at risk, will allow a more prompt and appropriate treatment, ultimately improving our ability to prevent fractures. Unfortunately, a skeleton at risk of fracture cannot simply be determined by the amount of bone that exists; the *quality* of the bone is a critical factor. This becomes apparent when considering that interventions of low bone mass may deteriorate mechanical properties of the skeleton. Most osteoporotic fractures occur in cancellous bone[13]. Hence, non-invasive assessment of trabecular strength and stiffness is extremely important in evaluating bone quality[18].

At present, osteoporosis is commonly assessed by measures of bone quantity using bone mineral density (BMD) measurements that reflect the *in vivo* conditions of bone density and mass. Noninvasive measurements of bone mass would be of value in predicting the risk of fracture, in assessing the severity of the disease, and in evaluating response to treatment. Several methods are available for the measurement of bone mass, with the most commonly used methods being DXA and computed tomography (CT). DXA is currently the most commonly used technique because of its relative precision (~2%), and multi-site imaging ability (spine, hip, wrist and total skeleton). However, a certain percent of bone mass must be lost before significant radiation attenuation occurs[7]. The measurements obtained do not provide information about the integrity of the trabecular architecture, nor the mechanical properties of the composing trabeculi. Due to these issues, the quality of bones, whether in normal or osteopenic, remains largely unknown (i.e. it is extremely difficult to monitor the strength and the conductivity *in vivo*). An improved diagnostic tool is needed to evaluate both the quantity and the quality of bone, which will help in the early detection and therefore the possible prevention and treatment of this disease.

Recently, new methods have emerged with the potential to estimate cancellous bone modulus more directly. Ultrasonic techniques (UT) provide an intriguing method for characterizing the material properties of bone in a manner, which is non-invasive, non-ionizing, non-destructive, and relatively accurate. The primary advantage of UT is its capability of measuring not only bone quantity, but also bone quality, i.e., estimation of the mechanical property of bone. Over the past 15 years, numerous research approaches have been developed to quantitate bone mass and structural stiffness using UT.[2,1,3]. Quantitative ultrasound (QUS) is an emerging physical modality in the evaluation of bone material properties because it is simple, inexpensive, non-invasive and free of ionizing radiation. Preliminary results for predicting osteoporosis using QUS are quite promising, and it has much greater potential for widespread application (including screening for prevention) than traditional X-ray bone densitometry methods. As such, many QUS technologies have been developed, and there are currently used[17]. Using several available clinical devices, studies *in vivo* have shown the ability of QUS to discriminate patients with osteoporotic fractures from age-matched controls[6,9,16]. It has been demonstrated that QUS predicts risk of future fracture generally as well as DXA[4,11,10,16]. However, there are several noted limitations, including the tissue boundary interaction, non-linear function of density associated with bone ultrasonic attenuation, single index covering broad range of tissues (including cortical and trabecular regions) and the interpolation of the results. Recently, using imaging based technology, ultrasound is used for evaluating region of interests of bone, e.g, using array plane ultrasound wave (GE-Lunar, Inc., USA) and focused wave[5,8,17]. These methods provide ultrasound images in the calcaneus region, in which the parameter compares to DXA data. Perhaps the major drawbacks of current ultrasound devices are low resolution and lack of physical interrelation with meaningful bone strength. While only showing the correlation between BUA data and BMD, these devices mostly provide qualitative information for assessment of osteoporosis, not the true prediction for bone structural and strength properties. Therefore, UT remains at an initial stage, as a screening tool, because of the non-uniformity of the porous structure in the bone tissue and its associated affects in resolution[17].

To overcome these hurdles and improve the specificity of non-invasive ultrasonic assessment, we have initiated a new modality of QUS by developing a scanning confocal acoustic diagnostic (SCAD) technology particularly for identifying the strength of trabecular bone. Our new design of SCAN system is intended to provide true images reflecting to bone's structural and strength properties at particular skeletal sites, which can provide a true diagnostic tool (instead of just for screening) that surpasses the radiation based DXA machines.

To evaluate the potential of ultrasound scanning in characterizing human trabecular bone properties in the region of interest, the principal goal of this study was to evaluate both bone mineral density and strength properties using ultrasound scanning, μCT determined bone mineral contents (BMC) and structural properties, and the mechanical testing in the human cadaver calcanei.

2   Methods

2.1   Specimen Preparation

Total of 19 human calcanei were harvested from cadavers with ages ranging from 66 to 97 years old. Samples were kept in freezer (-40C°) and thawed to room temperature before measurements. After cleaning of the soft tissue, ultrasound scanning was performed on the intact calcanei bone using SCAD system. Images and corresponding ultrasound parameters calculated from ROI were recorded for each bone sample. DXA measurement was performed after the SCAD measurement on these intact samples, after which a 10mm diameter trabecular cylinder was extracted from the back region of each calcaneus with cortical bone was removed. Ultrasound testing was then performed on these extracted cylinders followed by micro-CT scanning and mechanical testing.

2.2   Ultrasound Scanning System and Measurements

A developed SCAD system consisted of a computer-controlled 2-D moving stage unit with focused transmitter and receiver transducers (1MHz) attached on it (Fig.1). The transmitter was driven by pulse signals and the signals passed through bone were received by the receiver amplifier unit and digitized at 25MHz. The digitized waveform data were then transferred to computer (Dell Latitude, TX) for analysis. The control software was written using LabView software (National Instrument, TX).

Fig. 1. The setup of a laboratory SCAD system. Two confocal ultrasound transducers are attached on the computer controlled 2-D scanning stage. The tested calcaneus bone is positioned in the middle of two transducers and scanned by the system. Signal is transmitted to a computer for analysis.

In the SCAD measurement, signal transmitted through bone are recorded as testing wave over an approximate $40\times40mm^2$ image array (1 mm pixel size). All these waves were processed to calculate the ultrasound attenuation (ATT; dB), the logarithm of the ratio of the reference wave energy to testing wave energy, the BUA (dB/MHz), slope of the frequency-dependent attenuation between 300kHz and 700kHz, and the UV to generate ATT, BUA and UV images (Fig.2). For each ATT image, a suitable-sized ROI was determined and applied to corresponding BUA and UV images to calculate the average BUA and UV. The location of ROI for intact calcaneus was at the center of calcaneus back region with 15×15mm field of view and ROI location for extracted bone cylinder was at the center of the cylinder with 8×8mm field of view.

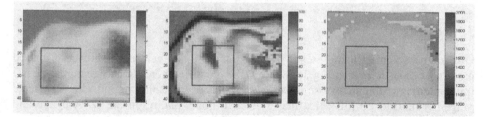

Fig. 2. ATT (left), BUA (middle), UV (right) images and the corresponding ROI determined in SCAD system. A suitable-sized ROI was determined to calculate the average BUA and UV.

2.3 DXA Measured Bone Mass Distribution and Apparent Density

By DXA scanning, a bone mass distribution image and apparent bone mineral density (AppBMD) can be obtained for each bone sample.

2.4 μCT Determining Microarchitecture and Density of Bone

Through a μCT 3-D reconstruction with a 20 μm resolution (μCT -20, Scanco Corp., USA), several parameters, such as the total volume (TV), bone volume (BV), bone mineral content (BMC), trabecular width (Tb.Th) and space, connectivity, and structural model index (SMI) were determined.

2.5 Tissue Mechanical Modulus

Contact force-displacement testing was used to determine the elastic modulus of trabecular bones. Using a mechanical testing machine (MTS Systems Corp., USA), the cylinders were uniaxially loaded in compression using displacement control. To overcome slight deviations from surface parallelism, a smoothly curved nail head was placed above the bone cylinder such that the force would be distributed evenly to the bone in the loading direction. An upper limit of 300 N – determined by prior loading of non-experimental but otherwise identical bone cylinders – was established to prevent the plastic yielding of any specimens while the loading was achieved in bone's elastic region. The loading rate was approximately 1000 με/s for the samples. Both displacement and force were digitized analyzed using MTS BasicTestware software.

The material properties studied was bulk modulus. Finally, the samples were compressively loaded up to their failure in the longitudinal direction and the yield strength and the ultimate strength were recorded.

ATT image from SCAD system and bone mass distribution image from DXA on intact calcaneus were compared. Correlation test was performed between QUS parameters and DXA determined AppBMD. For the extracted trabecular bone cylinders, interrelationships between QUS parameters and μCT determined structural values, and between QUS parameters and mechanical properties were evaluated through multiple correlations. Finally, while considering the complex structure of trabecular bone and its interactive influence on derived ultrasound signals, a new parameter that combined BUA and UV was determined by linear regression correlation between ultrasonic parameters and both μCT and mechanical properties. The data was analyzed using Pearson product moment correlation coefficients and the significance level was set at $p < 0.05$.

3 Results

Ultrasound scanning using SCAD system for the intact calcaneus showed a unique pattern of acoustic image (Fig.3). While DXA identified bone density features, SCAD image demonstrated distinct sound characteristics of trabecular region, i.e., ATT scale ranged from 0 to 60 (dB), that may reflect to bone quality. In the DXA image and SCAD ATT image (1mm resolution, 40×40 mm field of view) of the same human calcaneus, the ATT image clearly depicts the shape of calcaneus and the distribution of bone mass. The dark area in DXA image corresponds well to the dark region of the ATT image. This represents that ATT is proportional to bone density. All these distribution is similar to the configuration depicted in DXA image, which gives the AppBMD distribution of calcaneus.

Correlation analysis is done for ultrasound determined BUA in calcaneus ROI (Fig.4b) with DXA determined femoral neck AppBMD, and with calcaneus back region AppBMD (Fig.3a). Table.1 lists the correlation coefficients between BUA and AppBMD for SCAD.

Correlation analysis is also done for ultrasound determined BUA, UV in cylinder ROI with μCT and mechanical testing determined bone quantity and quality parameters. The individual ultrasound parameter, BUA or UV, is highly correlated with both bone density and modulus. After combining two ultrasound parameters in

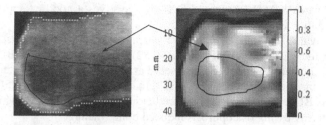

Fig. 3. DXA (a-left) and SCAD determined ATT (b-right) images of the same calcaneus. DXA image shows the AppBMD distribution and have a similar pattern with SCAD ATT image. Circled areas are the corresponding low bone mass area in DXA and ATT images.

Table 1. Correlation coefficient between SCAD determined BUA VS. DXA determined calcaneus and femoral neck AppBMD

	BUA
Calcaneus AppBMD	0.82
Femoral Neck AppBMD	0.81

Table 2. Correlation coefficient between SCAD determined parameters with μCT and mechanical testing determined bone quantity and quality parameters

	UV	BUA	Combined BUA & UV
Bulk Modulus	0.72	0.67	0.80
Yield Strength	0.89	0.80	0.93
Ultimate Strength	0.87	0.79	0.91
BV/TV	0.65	0.88	0.91
BMC	0.32	0.90	0.91
SMI	-0.63	-0.91	0.92
Connectivity	0.47	0.61	0.63
Trab. Thickness	0.33	0.71	0.71

the linear regression test, the correlation coefficients can be further improved to predict bone properties. Table 2 lists the correlation results.

Among the quantity and quality parameters, these trabecular bone samples showed a variety of values of density and stiffness. The value of BV/TV averaged 14±4% (mean ±s.d.), while the mechanical strength averaged 25±21 MPa for bulk modulus, 1.94±1.02 MPa for yield strength and 1.78±0.98 MPa for ultimate stress. Ultrasound scanning was capable of predicting the bone's quality parameters via multiple correlations.

4   Discussion

SCAD system can generate ultrasound images for the measured bone specimen, these images can provide us with the potential information not only on bone quantity, i.e., AppBMD, but also on bone property distribution. Based on detected images, the best representative ROI can be identified to characterize the bone properties. The similarity between SCAD image and DXA image gives a good example to demonstrate the capability and the reliability of this newly developed system.

The BUA value obtained from intact calcaneus using SCAD system is highly correlated to the calcaneus AppBMD (R>0.82). This indicates that BUA is a good indicator of bone density and it can also serve as a good indicator of osteoporosis. The high correlation exists between BUA and femoral neck AppBMD (R>0.81) implied that calcaneus BUA can also be a good predictor of hip bone density, which is a better skeletal site for assessing osteoporosis induced bone fracture.

Experiment results from extracted trabecular bone cylinders suggest that SCAD determined individual ultrasound parameter, BUA or UV, is able to predict bone quantity and quality, which is highly correlated with both bone structure and density parameters. Structural property parameters of trabeculae, e.g., BMC and BV/TV, are better represented by BUA, while ultrasonic wave velocity has a strong agreement with bone's strength property, e.g., modulus. This imply that overall bone quality is closely associated with both structure and stiffness of bone, in which combined BUA and UV has demonstrated significant performance in predicting mechanical characteristics of trabecular bone. All these results has shown the great potential of SCAD system to be used as *in vivo* diagnostic modality for assessing skeletal disorder, i.e., osteoporosis.

Ultrasound holds promise as an efficient and non-invasiveness assessment tool for bone status. These results suggest that SCAD can provide detailed information for the prediction of bone mass and strength. With the complex architecture of trabecular bone, combining BUA and UV can provide a better prediction of bone's quality for determining osteogenic conditions. As such, various ultrasound methods are available to optimize the correlations with the true mechanical properties of bone and ultimately fracture risk. Thus, a well-established database using this newly developed system may provide an insight into non-invasive diagnosis of osteoporosis and bone quality using ultrasound.

More generally, it is both interesting and promising, when looking at either mechanical properties or µCT parameters, to establish more global and clinically relevant properties that are best described by ultrasound. For example, yield and ultimate strength (the best indicators of true fracture risk) may be better correlated than elastic modulus (simply a measure of stiffness). In addition, the ultrasound values are best correlated with overall µCT parameters such as bone volume fraction and structural model index (which are again the best indicators of global quality of the bone), rather than specific parameters such as connectivity density and trabecular thickness.

5 Conclusions

SCAD holds promise as a new, non-invasive modality for assessing both density and quality. Acoustic mapping provides a true image for the region of interest, in which combining acoustic BUA and UV can provide better prediction of bone's quality in determining osteogenic conditions.

Acknowledgements

This work is kindly supported by the National Space Biomedical Research Institute through NASA Cooperative Agreement NCC 9-58, (TD00207 and TD00405, Qin), and New York Center for Biotechnology.

References

1. Ashman, R.B., Corin, J.D., Turner, C.H.: Elastic properties of cancellous bone: measurement by an ultrasonic technique. J.Biomech. 20, 979–986 (1987)
2. Ashman, R.B., Cowin, S.C., Van Buskirk, W.C., Rice, J.C.: A continuous wave technique for the measurement of the elastic properties of cortical bone. J.Biomech. 17, 349–361 (1984)
3. Ashman, R.B., Rho, J.Y.: Elastic modulus of trabecular bone material. J. Biomech. 21, 177–181 (1988)
4. Bauer, D.C., Gluer, C.C., Cauley, J.A., Vogt, T.M., Ensrud, K.E., Genant, H.K., Black, D.M.: Broadband ultrasound attenuation predicts fractures strongly and independently of densitometry in older women. A prospective study. Study of Osteoporotic Fractures Research Group. Arch. Intern. Med. 157, 629–634 (1997)
5. Calle, S., Remenieras, J.P., Bou, M.O., Defontaine, M., Patat, F.: Application of nonlinear phenomena induced by focused ultrasound to bone imaging. Ultrasound Med. Biol. 29, 465–472 (2003)
6. Cheng, S., Tylavsky, F., Carbone, L.: Utility of ultrasound to assess risk of fracture. J. Am. Geriatr. Soc. 45, 1382–1394 (1997)
7. Chesnut, C. H. I.: Non-Invasive Methods for Bone Mass Measurement, 77–87 (1993)
8. Gomez, M.A., Defontaine, M., Giraudeau, B., Camus, E., Colin, L., Laugier, P., Patat, F.: In vivo performance of a matrix-based quantitative ultrasound imaging device dedicated to calcaneus investigation. Ultrasound Med. Biol. 28, 1285–1293 (2002)
9. Gregg, E.W., Kriska, A.M., Salamone, L.M., Roberts, M.M., Anderson, S.J., Ferrell, R.E., Kuller, L.H., Cauley, J.A.: The epidemiology of quantitative ultrasound: a review of the relationships with bone mass, osteoporosis and fracture risk. Osteoporos. Int. 7, 89–99 (1997)
10. Hans, D., Schott, A.M., Arlot, M.E., Sornay, E., Delmas, P.D., Meunier, P.J.: Influence of anthropometric parameters on ultrasound measurements of Os calcis. Osteoporos. Int. 5, 371–376 (1995)
11. Hans, D., Schott, A.M., Meunier, P.J.: Ultrasonic assessment of bone: a review 2, 157–163 (1993)
12. Looker, A.C., Johnson, C.L.: Prevalence of elevated serum transferrin saturation in adults in the United States. Ann. Intern. Med. 129, 940–945 (1998)
13. Melton III, L.J., Orwoll, E.S., Wasnich, R.D.: Does bone density predict fractures comparably in men and women? Osteoporos. Int. 12, 707–709 (2001)
14. Melton, L.J.I.: How Many Women Have Osteoporosis Now? J. Bone Min. Res. 10, 175–177 (1995)
15. Melton, L.J.I.: Epidemiology Of Hip Fracture: Implications of the Exponential Increase With Age. Bone 18, 121S–125S (1996)
16. Njeh, C.F., Boivin, C.M., Langton, C.M.: The role of ultrasound in the assessment of osteoporosis: a review. Osteoporos. Int. 7, 7–22 (1997)
17. Njeh, C.F., Hans, D., Fuerst, T., Gluer, C.-C., Genant, H. K.: Quantitative Ultrasound Assessment of Osteoporosis and Bone Status. Munich (1999)
18. Orwoll, E.S., Bevan, L., Phipps, K.R.: Determinants of bone mineral density in older men. Osteoporos. Int. 11, 815–821 (2000)
19. Wahner, H. W., Fogelman, I.: The Evaluation of Osteoporosis: Dual Energy X-Ray Absorptiometry in Clinical Practice, London (1994)

Hierarchical Matching of Anatomical Trees for Medical Image Registration

Tobias Lohe[1], Tim Kröger[2], Stephan Zidowitz[2], Heinz-Otto Peitgen[2], and Xiaoyi Jiang[1]

[1] Department of Mathematics and Computer Science,
University of Münster, Germany
tobias.lohe@uni-muenster.de, xjiang@math.uni-muenster.de
[2] MeVis Research GmbH, Bremen, Germany
{tim,zidowitz,peitgen}@mevis.de

Abstract. Today, tomographic images are used in medical applications more and more. To support physicians in diagnosis and treatment, a registration of two images taken at different points in time or under different conditions is needed. As the structure of the vessel or airway trees is relatively stable between two image acquisitions, they provide a good basis for the automatic determination of landmarks. In this work, a hierarchical tree search algorithm is proposed, which efficiently computes a matching between branchpoints of anatomical trees, which can be used as landmarks for an elastic registration. The algorithm is designed to be general and robust in order to be applicable to a variety of different datasets, which are acquired by different sensors or under different conditions. The validation of the algorithm against manually created ground truth data leads to a 80.9% rate of correctly matched branchpoints. Allowing a tolerance of 5 mm, the rate increases to 89.9%. The runtime for 50–700 vertices is about 1–45 seconds.

1 Introduction

With the increasing amount of medical images available for diagnosis, planning treatment, and monitoring the patient's health, there is a need to automatically align these images [1]. This alignment or *registration* is the "process of overlaying two or more images of the same scene taken at different times, from different viewpoints, and/or by different sensors" [2]. Intensity- and landmark-based registration approaches have been recently combined, which leads to improved results in comparison to the single approaches [3].

As the image data varies strongly, registration approaches that are purely based on the voxel intensities do not yield optimal results. Extracted vessel or airway trees, however, are relatively stable between the two images, and can be used to automatically compute landmarks by the matching of branchpoints. This is the case for instance in progress analysis, where changes over time are investigated, and in a variety of other applications [4]. This work presents an algorithm for the automatic determination of landmarks by matching anatomical vessel or airway trees.

D. Zhang (Ed.): ICMB 2008, LNCS 4901, pp. 224–231, 2007.

2 Related Work

TSCHIRREN ET AL. [5] propose an algorithm for the matching of human airway trees based on the *association graph*. They use a hierarchical approach that matches major branchpoints first and afterwards the subtrees underneath the major branchpoints. The algorithm is applied to a total of 17 datasets of the human lung, which are acquired at different lung volumes. The validation leads to 92.9% correct matches. The runtime is given as 1–3 seconds for 200–300 vertices on a 1.2 GHz AMD Athlon computer. Another approach based on *association graphs* is proposed by METZEN ET AL. [6], which tries to match the complete trees in one step. The application to two trees, one comparing two bronchial trees of the lung in inhaled and exhaled state, the other comparing two trees of the liver portal vein from CT and MRI images, leads to 90.5% correct matches. The runtime for roughly 200 vertices is given as 200–370 seconds.

A further approach proposed by GRAHAM AND HIGGINS [7] tries to model the deformation of the two anatomical trees, which is due to differences between the underlying images or segmentation errors. Based on this model they propose a *dynamic programming* algorithm. Their algorithm is validated by visual inspection only. The runtime is given as five seconds for 130–340 vertices on a 3.4 GHz Pentium 4 computer. The algorithm proposed by CHARNOZ ET AL. [8] uses a *tree search* framework. Their algorithm starts with matching the root vertices and then processes both trees in parallel in depth-first order, top-down to the leaves. The application to one liver dataset, which is acquired at two different points in time, results in a 95% rate of correct matches. The runtime is given as roughly 240 seconds for 380 vertices on a 1 GHz computer.

KAFTAN ET AL. [9] try to match *complete paths* instead of single vertices, where a complete path is defined as any path from the root to a leaf vertex. Their algorithm is tested with airway trees from CT acquisitions. They achieve an average of 87% correct path matches. BÜLOW ET AL. [10] use *point shape features*, like the 3D shape context, to compare vertices. Applied to six bronchial trees, which are matched against a model tree, this method matches 69% of the points correctly. TANG AND CHUNG [11] propose an algorithm that is based on the minimization of the *tree edit distance* between two trees. Their results are only visually verified (using cerebral data with only 30 vertices).

3 Algorithm

The proposed *symmetric tree search* algorithm is based on the general tree search framework, which is used e. g. for object recognition in images. As a consequence, the algorithm is able to make use of the hierarchical structure of the trees. The symmetric search in both trees prevents problems arising by the use of wildcards.

Let $T^a = (V^a, E^a, r^a, A^a)$ and $T^b = (V^b, E^b, r^b, A^b)$ be two rooted trees, $C(v^a, v^b) \rightarrow [true, false]$ a *consistency constraint* that decides if two vertices form a valid match, and $S : (T^a, T^b, M) \mapsto x \in \mathbb{R}$ a *similarity measure* that evaluates the quality of the *matching* $M \subseteq V^a \times V^b$ for the given trees T^a and

T^b. The aim of the matching algorithm is to find the optimal matching M^*, with respect to the consistency constraint and similarity measure, i. e.

$$M^* = \arg\max_M S(T^a, T^b, M) .$$

Let $V^a = (v_1^a, \ldots, v_k^a)$ and $V^b = (v_1^b, \ldots, v_n^b)$ be the vertices of two trees T^a and T^b, sorted in top-down, breadth-first order. As an example, consider Figure 1 with the vertices $V^a = (a1, a2, a3, a4, a5)$ and $V^b = (b1, b2, b5)$.

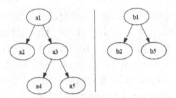

Fig. 1. Two example trees T^a (left) and T^b (right)

The symmetric search algorithm starts with the match of the root vertices (v_1^a, v_1^b). At any level l in the search tree, two non-assigned vertices v^a and v^b (one from each tree) are regarded simultaneously and the consistent matches are inserted as nodes at level $l + 1$ into the search tree. This search tree is built and searched using a depth-first search combined with backtracking (see pseudocode in Algorithm 1).

As an example, the two trees in Figure 1 are considered. It is assumed that the following vertex pairs are consistent with each other: $(a2, b2)$, $(a2, b5)$, $(a3, b2)$, $(a3, b5)$, $(a4, b5)$, and $(a5, b5)$. Furthermore, the evaluation is assumed to return the value 1.0 for a match (ai, bi) and the value 0.8 for a match (ai, bj) with $i \neq j$. The resulting search tree is shown in Figure 2. The algorithm is initialized with the root vertices $(a1, b1)$. In the first call of the search() function $a2$ and $b2$ are the next vertices which leads to the three consistent candidates $(a2, b2)$, $(a2, b5)$, and $(a3, b2)$. The respective similarity values are shown in brackets below the matches. The search recursively continues with the three extended matchings, which finally leads to the depicted search tree. The best matching is $[(a1, b1), (a2, b2), (a5, b5)]$ with a value of 3.0.

Possible choices for consistency constraints and similarity measures are discussed in Section 4. As these functions follow the STRATEGY design pattern [12], they are exchangeable and can be specially chosen for particular applications. In order to provide the possibility not to assign any of the both next vertices v^a and v^b, the next *two* vertices in each tree are considered. This procedure has the additional advantage to be able to choose only the best matches according to the similarity measure, which makes the result more stable.

The symmetric search algorithm is able to efficiently find the optimal solution for small trees. But for real data with some hundred vertices, an exhaustive search has exponential complexity and takes much too long. Consequently, the

---

Algorithm 1. Symmetric tree search algorithm.

Input: two anatomical trees (T^a and T^b)
Output: optimal matching M^*

$M = [(r_a, r_b)]$ // `initialize with root vertices`
$M^* = \text{search}(T^a, T^b, M)$ // `start algorithm`
return M^*

// `main function`
function search(T^a, T^b, M)
begin
    if T^a or T^b has no more vertices **then**
        M.value = evaluate(T^a, T^b, M) // `evaluate matching`
        return M // `stop search`
    end
    candidates = {} // `compute candidate set`
    v^a = next vertex in T^a
    v^b = next vertex in T^b
    $(v^a_{lma1}, v^b_{lma1}) = \text{leastMatchedAncestor}(v^a, M)$
    for each vertex v^b_i in children(v^b_{lma1}) **do**
        if consistent(v^a, v^b_i) **then** candidates.insert((v^a, v^b_i))
    end
    $(v^a_{lma2}, v^b_{lma2}) = \text{leastMatchedAncestor}(v^b, M)$
    for each vertex v^a_i in children(v^a_{lma2}) **do**
        if consistent(v^a_i, v^b) **then** candidates.insert((v^a_i, v^b))
    end
    for each match (v^a_i, v^b_j) in candidates with evaluate(v^a_i, v^b_j, M) > 0 **do**
        // `continue search with extended matching if value > 0`
        $M_{ij} = M + (v^a_i, v^b_j)$
        $M_{ij} = \text{search}(T^a, T^b, M_{ij})$
    end
    $M^* = \arg\max M_{ij}.\text{value}$ // `optimal matching has maximal value`
    return M^*
end

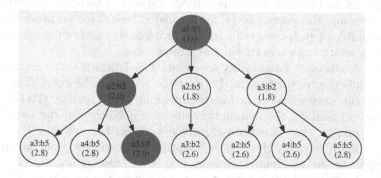

Fig. 2. Search tree for the symmetric algorithm

search space has to be further reduced. Unfortunately, this reduction implies that the algorithm no longer finds the optimal matching, but only a locally optimal solution, at least from a theoretical point of view.

Therefore, an iterative extension of the algorithm is proposed, which consists of the following steps:

1. Compute the complete search tree up to a given depth d of the search nodes.
2. Continue the search with a fixed number n of best matchings, according to the similarity measure, up to the depth $2d$.
3. Repeat steps 1. and 2. until the search tree is completely expanded.
4. Choose the best matching with respect to the similarity value.

The main advantage of the proposed algorithm in comparison to the association graph and dynamic programming approaches is the ability to use similarity measures, which are computed in relation to previously matched vertices. This ability is a direct consequence of the hierarchical approach. Another important advantage in comparison to [5] is the ability to compensate for errors in an early stage of the algorithm due to the stepwise extension and refinement of the matching. [8] suffers from the disadvantage that either vertex or edge attributes are used for the matching decision, while the proposed algorithm uses both. In contrast to all previous approaches, the proposed algorithm is explicitly designed for generality, i.e. no specific assumptions about the underlying tree data are made and the algorithm is not optimized for single applications.

4 Application to Anatomical Trees

The extraction of the vessel or airway trees from the three-dimensional images is carried out with the algorithm proposed in [13]. The algorithm may extract cyclic edges and therefore, in a formal sense, returns a graph and not a tree. The generated vessel graph is enriched by computed attributes like the position of the vertices/branchpoints or the length and volume of the edges/vessels.

As the matching algorithm needs rooted trees as input, cycles have to be removed. For a reliable and robust matching it is also important to prune spurious branches and to combine indistinguishable vertices, which are detected using subtree sizes and distances (see [4] for details). These three preprocessing steps serve two different purposes: reducing the problem size and removing segmentation errors, which improves runtime and robustness.

Several consistency constraints are used. The INHERITANCE constraint requires the inheritance relationship between the vertices to be equal. The LEAVES constraint guarantees that no leaf vertices are matched. The ROOTPATHLENGTH constraint is based on the assumption that the difference in the path lengths should be smaller than a certain threshold $t_L \in \mathbb{R}$, i.e. $\mathrm{rpl}(v^a, v^b) = true \Leftrightarrow |\mathrm{len}(p^a) - \mathrm{len}(p^b)| < t_L$. Here, t_L is adaptively chosen based on the tree data with respect to the maximal path length: $t_L = c_L \cdot \mathrm{max}_{\mathrm{rpl}}$ ($c_L \in [0, 1]$). Analogous, the ROOTPATHVOLUME constraint is based on the path volume.

In this work, only two similarity measures are presented, while a more comprehensive collection is provided in [4]. The similarity values are normalized in order to be able to combine different measures by $a_\sigma(r) = 2 \cdot 2^{\frac{1-r}{\sigma-1}} - 1$. The first similarity measure FIRST-PATHLENGTH compares the path lengths of the current match in relation to the first match:

$$\mathrm{fpl}(v_1^a, v_1^b, v_2^a, v_2^b) = a_\sigma \left(\max \left(\frac{\mathrm{len}(p^a)}{\mathrm{len}(p^b)}, \frac{\mathrm{len}(p^b)}{\mathrm{len}(p^a)} \right) \right).$$

The LEAST-PATHANGLE measure compares the angles between the two paths to the respective least matched ancestors:

$$\mathrm{lpa}(v_1^a, v_1^b, v_2^a, v_2^b) = \begin{cases} a_\sigma \left(\frac{1}{\cos \sphericalangle (p^a, p^b)} \right), & \text{if } \cos \sphericalangle (p^a, p^b) > 0, \\ -1, & \text{if } \cos \sphericalangle (p^a, p^b) \leq 0. \end{cases}$$

The total similarity value is determined by the weighted combination

$$s(v_1^a, v_1^b, v_2^a, v_2^b) = w_1 \cdot \mathrm{fpl}(v_1^a, v_1^b, v_2^a, v_2^b) + w_2 \cdot \mathrm{lpa}(v_1^a, v_1^b, v_2^a, v_2^b).$$

Two additional adaptations of the algorithm are made. First, not the root vertices are taken as first match, but the first branchpoints. Second, the branching factor is limited by another algorithm parameter b, i.e. at each node in the search tree only the b best child nodes are further analyzed.

5   Ground Truth Validation

For eleven datasets originating from real patients, ground truth data was created manually by human experts. These datasets come from different organisms (human and pig), different organs (lung and liver) and feature six different problem types and multitemporal as well as multimodal analysis: progress analysis, lung in different inhalation states, pre-/intra-operation, CT vs. MRI, different contrast agents, and contrast agent compared to cast model. The number of vertices ranges from 18 to 726, while the ground truth covers 4 to 54 matches.

The complete validation results are presented in [4], while in this work only the best configuration is presented, which is as follows: four consistency constraints INHERITANCE, LEAVES, ROOTPATHLENGTH ($c_L = 0.1$), and ROOTPATHVOLUME ($c_V = 0.46$); two similarity measures FIRST-PATHLENGTH ($\sigma = 1.50, w_1 = 0.25$) and LEAST-PATHANGLE ($\sigma = 1.61, w_2 = 0.75$).

This configuration leads to an average rate of 80.9% (72 right, 17 wrong), an error $E = 119.2$ (defined as the sum of all distances from a wrong to a right matched vertex), and a topological error $TE = 22$ (defined like E for topological distances). The runtime is on average 10.1 seconds and lies between 1–45 seconds for the individual datasets (measured on a 1.6 GHz AMD Sempron computer). The low error indicates that most wrong matches only differ by a few millimeter and a topological distance of 1 from the correct vertex, and that mostly neighboring vertices are confused. If the rate is measured with a tolerance of 5 mm for the distance and 1 for the topological distance, the rate increases to 89.9% (80 right and 9 wrong matches).

The total rate of 80.9% without tolerance is lower than for previous approaches but equally well with a small tolerance. With respect to the runtime, the proposed algorithm is much faster than [6] and [8], and lies in a similar range like [5] and [7]. Additionally, the presented algorithm has the major advantage to perform well for a variety of organs and applications. However, the algorithm can be adapted to special needs easily.

As a matter of course, no ground truth data is available in the daily clinical routine. Therefore, it is important to provide a descriptive visualization of the matching results. We propose a coloration of corresponding paths, i.e. of vessel segments. The idea is to consider the unique path from a matched vertex to the least matched ancestor, and to assign the same color to the corresponding paths. An example for the visualization is shown in Figure 3.

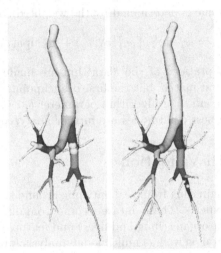

Fig. 3. Matching visualization for two airway trees of the human lung

6   Conclusion and Future Work

The proposed algorithm is able to efficiently compute a matching of corresponding vertices in anatomical trees. It achieves a rate of 80.9% correctly matched vertices and 89.9% with 5 mm tolerance. This rate might be further increased if the parameters are optimized for special applications. The runtime of 1–45 seconds is very low.

As an outlook, the registration based on the landmarks that are computed by the algorithm is regarded. The ground truth validation shows that most wrong matches only differ by a few millimeter from the correct match. As a consequence, the registration should be able to handle this tolerance and allow a small displacement of the landmarks. Using such a tolerating registration method in combination with the matching, the necessary displacement is a good indicator for the quality of the matching and could be used to optimize the matching configuration if no ground truth is available.

References

1. Hill, D.L.G., Batchelor, P.G., Holden, M., Hawkes, D.J.: Medical image registration. Physics in Medicine and Biology 46(3), R1–R45 (2001)
2. Zitová, B., Flusser, J.: Image registration methods: a survey. Image and Vision Computing 21(11), 977–1000 (2003)
3. Fischer, B., Modersitzki, J.: Combination of automatic non-rigid and landmark based registration: the best of both worlds. In: Medical Imaging 2003: Image Processing. Proceedings of SPIE, vol. 5032, pp. 1037–1048 (2003)
4. Lohe, T.: Hierarchical matching of anatomical trees for medical imaging applications. Master's thesis, Department of Mathematics and Computer Science, University of Münster, Germany (2007)
5. Tschirren, J., McLennan, G., Palgyi, K., Hoffman, E.A., Sonka, M.: Matching and anatomical labeling of human airway tree. IEEE Transactions on Medical Imaging 24(12), 1540–1547 (2005)
6. Metzen, J.H., Kröger, T., Schenk, A., Zidowitz, S., Peitgen, H.O., Jiang, X.: Matching of tree structures for registration of medical images. In: Graph-Based Representations in Pattern Recognition, 6th IAPR-TC-15 International Workshop. LNCS, vol. 4538, Springer, Heidelberg (2007)
7. Graham, M.W., Higgins, W.E.: Globally optimal model-based matching of anatomical trees. In: Medical Imaging 2006: Image Processing. Proceedings of SPIE, vol. 6144, 614415 (2006)
8. Charnoz, A., Agnus, V., Malandain, G., Soler, L., Tajine, M.: Tree matching applied to vascular system. In: Brun, L., Vento, M. (eds.) GbRPR 2005. LNCS, vol. 3434, pp. 183–192. Springer, Heidelberg (2005)
9. Kaftan, J.N., Kiraly, A.P., Naidich, D.P., Novak, C.L.: A novel multipurpose tree and path matching algorithm with application to airway trees. In: Medical Imaging 2006: Physiology, Function, and Structure from Medical Images. Proceedings of SPIE, vol. 6143, 61430N (2006)
10. Bülow, T., Lorenz, C., Wiemker, R., Honko, J.: Point based methods for automatic bronchial tree matching and labeling. In: Medical Imaging 2006: Physiology, Function, and Structure from Medical Images. Proceedings of SPIE, vol. 6143, 61430O (2006)
11. Tang, T.W.H., Chung, A.C.S.: Cerebral vascular tree matching of 3D-RA data based on tree edit distance. In: Yang, G.-Z., Jiang, T., Shen, D., Gu, L., Yang, J. (eds.) Medical Imaging and Augmented Reality. LNCS, vol. 4091, pp. 116–123. Springer, Heidelberg (2006)
12. Gamma, E., Helm, R., Johnson, R., Vlissides, J.: Design Patterns. Elements of Reusable Object-Oriented Software, Addison-Wesley, Reading (1995)
13. Selle, D.: Analyse von Gefäbetastrukturen in medizinischen Schichtdatensätzen für die computergestütze Operationsplanung. PhD thesis, Department of Mathematics and Computer Science, University of Bremen Germany (1999)

Interactive Deformable Registration Visualization and Analysis of 4D Computed Tomography

Burak Erem[1], Gregory C. Sharp[2], Ziji Wu[2], and David Kaeli[1]

[1] Department of Electrical and Computer Engineering, Northeastern University
Boston, MA 02115
[2] Department of Radiation Oncology, Massachusetts General Hospital
Boston, MA 02114

Abstract. This paper presents a new interactive method for analyzing 4D Computed Tomography (4DCT) datasets for patient care and research. Deformable registration algorithms are commonly used to observe the trajectories of individual voxels from one respiratory phase to another. Our system provides users with the capability to visualize these trajectories while simultaneously rendering anatomical volumes, which can greatly improve the accuracy of deformable registration.

1 Introduction

Radiation therapy is a method of treating patients with various types of cancerous tumors. The goal of the treatment is to kill cancerous cells by exposing them to radiation but, when exposed, enough radiation will kill healthy tissue as well. This becomes more of a concern for a physician planning a patient's treatment when the location of the tumor moves significantly due to cardiac activity or respiration, often leading to lower treatment success rates. For this reason, much research in this area focuses on minimizing exposure of healthy tissue to radiation while maximizing the coverage of the intended target. With a better understanding of internal anatomical motion, physicians can improve the accuracy and efficiency of the treatment of their patients.

One attempt at characterizing such motion is by using a deformable registration algorithm on 4DCT data to map, voxel by voxel, movement from one respiratory phase to another. Based on splines, this model of voxel trajectories can have undesirable results if the algorithm's parameters are not appropriately set. Furthermore, it can be difficult to determine what the proper parameters should be without some visual feedback and experimentation.

This paper introduces several new ideas for medical visualization that can help address this issue. For the visualization of anatomical motion in 4DCT image sets, we present the ability to display point trajectories. Specifically, we have developed a toolset that can simultaneously visualize vector fields and anatomy, provides interactive browsing of point trajectories, and allows for the improved identification of current trajectory position using node color. We also describe

D. Zhang (Ed.): ICMB 2008, LNCS 4901, pp. 232–239, 2007.

some additional interactive capabilities of our work, such as editing of deformation fields which can enable automatic and interactive registration.

2   Background

The analysis of anatomical trajectories relies heavily on mathematics, but also heavily relies on a visual interpretation of the data. Thus, because simultaneous mathematical and visual analysis is important, in this section we will discuss the registration and visualization background that has influenced the work presented in this paper.

2.1   Deformable Registration

Image registration is a process to determine a transformation that can relate the position of features in one image with the position of the corresponding feature in another image. Spline-based free-form registration is capable of modeling a wide variety of deformations and also, by definition, ensures a smooth deformation field. A deformation field is represented as a weighted sum of spline basis functions, of which B-splines are one of the most widely used. In the B-spline transformation model [1], the deformation vectors are computed using B-spline interpolation from the deformation values of points located in a coarse grid, which is usually referred to as the B-spline grid. The parameter space of the B-spline deformation is composed by the set of all the deformations associated with the nodes of the B-spline grid. A cubic B-spline in matrix form is:

$$\mathbf{S}_i(t) = \begin{bmatrix} t^3 & t^2 & t & 1 \end{bmatrix} \frac{1}{6} \begin{bmatrix} -1 & 3 & -3 & 1 \\ 3 & -6 & 3 & 0 \\ -3 & 0 & 3 & 0 \\ 1 & 4 & 1 & 0 \end{bmatrix} \begin{bmatrix} \mathbf{p}_{i-1} \\ \mathbf{p}_i \\ \mathbf{p}_{i+1} \\ \mathbf{p}_{i+2} \end{bmatrix}, t \in [0, 1] \tag{1}$$

where $\mathbf{p}_j$ are the control points. Note that B-splines have a finite support region. Thus changing the weight or contribution of each basis function affects only a specific portion of the overall deformation. By increasing the resolution of the B-spline grid, more complex and localized deformations can be modeled.

An alternative to the B-spline deformation model is landmark-based splines, typically implemented using thin-plate splines [2] or other radial basis functions. In this approach, a set of landmark correspondences matches is formed between points in a pair of images. The displacements of the correspondences are used to define a deformation map, which smoothly interpolates or approximates the point pairs. One approach of particular interest is radial basis functions that have finite support, such as the Wendland functions [3]. Because these functions only deform a small region of the image, the deformations can be quickly computed and updated for interactive applications. Given N points, located at x_i and displaced by an amount λ_i, the deformation $\boldsymbol{\nu}$ at location x is given as:

$$\boldsymbol{\nu}(x) = \sum_{i=1}^{N} \lambda_i \phi(|x - x_i|), \tag{2}$$

where ϕ is an appropriate Wendland function, such as:

$$\phi(r) = \begin{cases} \left(1 - \frac{r}{\sigma}\right)^2 & r \le \sigma \\ 0 & \text{otherwise.} \end{cases} \tag{3}$$

The variable σ controls the width of the adjustment, usually on the order of one to two centimeters for human anatomy. Several of these Wendland functions are used together to form a complete vector field, which defines the motion of organs of the anatomy.

2.2   Volume Visualization

Volume visualization is a way of viewing the structure of the anatomy in 3D. The main goal of volume visualization is to represent higher dimensional data on a two-dimensional computer screen for visual inspection. In this case, we use visualizations of the same 4DCT datasets which we have used for deformable registration calculations, providing a superimposed anatomical frame of reference for analysis.

While it is common to see 3D renderings of human anatomy in this field, it is important to note that there are several methods of obtaining these visualizations with important distinctions between them. We separate these into two categories: 1) direct volume rendering and 2) explicit volume rendering. With explicit volume rendering, the boundaries of the structure which are being visualized are explicitly defined, calculated, and then projected onto the 2D viewing plane of the user. On the other hand, direct volume rendering only calculates the surfaces which will be projected onto the 2D viewing plane, making it a faster alternative.

We chose to work with direct volume rendering in our analysis because of its inherent speed advantage. We note that there is no loss of information from the user's perspective with this method, especially from the standpoint of analyzing and editing deformable registration parameters. It is because the renderings act as a reference for visual comparison to the independent registration calculations that explicit surfaces are not necessary.

2.3   SCIRun

Developed by the Scientific Computing and Imaging (SCI) Institute at the University of Utah, SCIRun is a problem solving environment designed to allow researchers the freedom to build programs to perform various scientific computing tasks [4]. In our particular application, a dataflow network of modules already existed that allowed us to do direct volume rendering. The network is a simplified version of the SCIRun PowerApp called BioImage [5]. Enhancements were made to that network to allow for visualization of 4DCT datasets and point paths by cycling through them one phase at a time. Building on the existing tools, we can provide for more efficient and interactive ways of analyzing tumor motion.

The viewing window, the central module to which almost all dataflow eventually leads, is especially useful for our application. This graphical viewport allows navigation of the 3D environment in which we work by zooming, panning, and rotating. Furthermore, the viewing window passes back event callbacks to certain classes of objects that allow module developers to make interactive, draggable, clickable tools. However, movement of such tools is limited to the viewing plane. Thus, by rotating the viewing plane, one is able to change the directions of motion of the interactive tools.

3   Methodology

3.1   Viewing Trajectory Loops

To represent a 4D trajectory in a 3D graphical environment, we have developed a cursor that displays the path of movement of a single voxel over time. A user can move the cursor by clicking and dragging it in a motion plane parallel to the viewing plane. At its new location, the cursor displays the trajectory of the voxel at that point by showing a line path. The direction and magnitude of the motion during each time phase are indicated by a color transition from blue to red.

All trajectories start and end at the same shades of blue and red, but may display less of certain intermediate shades due to very low magnitude movements during those time phases. This can be very useful when comparing two trajectories of similar shape, but very different color patterns, indicating that despite having followed a similarly shaped path, each voxel followed the path at a different speed.

3.2   Editing Point Paths

Once a user has identified a region of interest using our tool, they can then explore the region in greater detail. Instead of displaying a line path, this tool displays several cursors to convey similar information without using lines. To prevent confusion about the order, the module connects to the same tool that allows the user to select the 4DCT phase currently being viewed, and then highlights the corresponding cursor with a different color. At each respiratory phase, the path of a voxel can be followed both through this tool and a volume visualization simultaneously.

If it is observed that the trajectory and the visualization do not agree, the user has the option of editing the trajectory by moving the cursors. It should be noted that this will not modify the 4DCT data itself, but only supplement the output of the registration algorithm. Also, moving the cursor will not only effect the voxel whose trajectory is being viewed, but will also have an attenuated effect on the surrounding area. To view the extent of this effect, the user can use several of the previously described tools to view the updated trajectory loops.

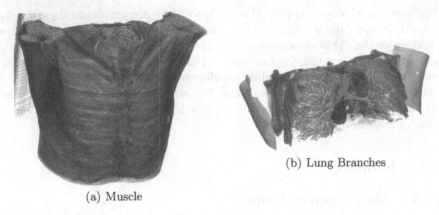

(b) Lung Branches

(a) Muscle

Fig. 1. (a) Visualization of bone and muscle. Although it is possible to analyze trajectories within this type of visualization, or (b) one showing the branches of the lungs, we provide examples showing only bony anatomy for visual clarity.

4   Results

The visual nature of these tools provides a definite improvement in the way tumor motion analysis is performed. The user has a rich set of visualization capabilities using our system; volume rendering of 4DCT datasets is capable of showing many different kinds of tissue. Figure 1 shows two examples of different kinds of tissue that can be visualized. In Figure 1(a) we show how muscle and bone can be displayed simultaneously and that our visualization tools are not strictly limited to bone. Figure 1(b) shows branches of a lung, an important kind of tissue whose motion is important to understand in order to treat tumors located within. However, for the rest of the figures, we use renderings of bony anatomy only to avoid cluttering the view of our tools. It should be noted that this is less of a concern when viewing them together in an interactive environment.

The trajectory loop tool's purpose is to facilitate rapid analysis of trajectories within the visual environment. We are able to run the trajectory loop at every position the cursor has been (see Figure 2), showing a trail of several loops that have been visualized. In this figure, the tool was used to analyze the extent to which the registration algorithm detected motion at various spatial locations within the lung. As expected, movements became smaller as the cursor was used to inspect areas closer to bone. On the other hand, trajectory loops closer to the lower lung showed significant motion.

If unsatisfied with analysis of the trajectories when compared to the visualization, the user can make adjustments within this environment to improve the registration. Figure 3 shows the path editing tool, where each of the individual points can be moved independently to adjust the path to the user's specifications. The point that is colored green highlights the current phase of the 4DCT that is being visualized. Thus, if the rest of the anatomy were visible, one could see the voxel to which that specific point path belonged. While Figure 3(a) shows

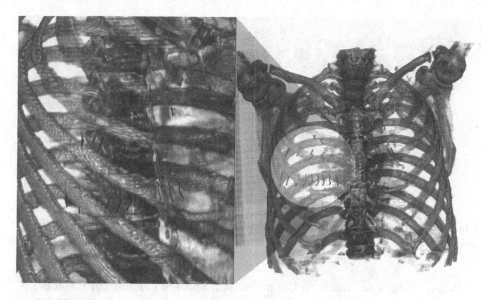

Fig. 2. Viewing several trajectories in the lung while visualizing surrounding bony anatomy (right) and while zoomed in (left). Trajectories are represented as line loops that make a smooth transition from blue to red in even increments across each of the respiratory phases.

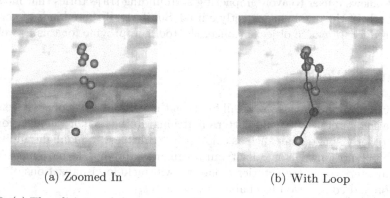

(a) Zoomed In   (b) With Loop

Fig. 3. (a) The editing tool shown alone with the current phase highlighted in green and (b) the same editing tool shown with the trajectory loop superimposed to demonstrate the relationship between the two tools. The point highlighted in green is edited while the others remain fixed to prevent accidental changes.

the editing tool alone, Figure 3(b) shows the trajectory loop tool and the path editing tool when used at the same point. This may not normally be a desired way to edit a path, but in this case it serves to illustrate the relationship between the two tools. Each has its own purpose for different intended uses, but this demonstrates that both represent the same registration information.

Fig. 4. A zoomed out (left) and more detailed (right) perspective of editing a point path while observing changes using the trajectory loop tool

When changes are made to the point path and are committed, the tool appends modifications to the previous registration results and refreshes the visualization. Changing the visible path affects the surrounding paths as well, in a way similar to how smudging tools work in image editing software. The effect of this range of influence can be seen by using the path editing tool and several trajectory loop tools simultaneously, as shown in Figure 4. This kind of visual feedback allows a user to avoid impacting surrounding trajectories that move independently of the one being directly edited. Similarly, if those kinds of changes are desired for an entire object at once, the tool can provide for this as well.

5   Future Work

Our future efforts with this work will focus on three major areas of advancement: visualization, interactivity, and pattern matching. In the area of visualization, we will use other visual queues such as color or line thickness to highlight additional attributes of motion such as velocity and regularity. Further, as movement is not fully characterized by trajectories alone, we will include visualizations of tissue expansion and contraction to enable new analyses.

To improve interactivity, we will explore more efficient means of marking regions whose trajectories have been deemed unreliable. One approach may be to paint a region in 3D and recompute the registration for that region alone. Additionally, we plan on learning registration algorithm parameters from the way researchers use these interactive tools.

Lastly, we will explore motion correlation measurement and analysis between different regions of the anatomy using a combination of the visualization and interactive tool creation capabilities that we have shown and the pattern matching mentioned above.

6   Conclusion

In this paper we have introduced a set of tools that allow researchers characterizing anatomical motion to visualize and edit deformation fields in a 3D environment. While it is clear that deformable registration is a valuable research tool for the area of anatomical motion research, we have been able to improve the usefulness of the algorithm by providing an intuitive interface that displays information more efficiently, encourages more integration with other forms of visualization, and provides a way of interacting with the data to make changes to the model in the same environment. We have also described some of the future directions for this project.

Acknowledgments

This work was supported in part by Gordon-CenSSIS, the Bernard M. Gordon Center for Subsurface Sensing and Imaging Systems, under the Engineering Research Centers Program of the National Science Foundation (Award Number EEC-9986821). This work was made possible in part by software from the NIH/NCRR Center for Integrative Biomedical Computing, P41-RR12553-07.

References

1. Rueckert, D., Sonoda, L.I., Hayes, C., Hill, D.L.G., Leach, M.O., Hawkes, D.J.: Non-rigid registration using free-form deformations: Application to breast MR images. IEEE Trans. on Med. Imag. 18(8), 712–721 (1999)
2. Bookstein, F.L.: Principal warps: Thin-plate splines and the decomposition of deformations. IEEE Trans. Pattern Anal. Mach. Intell. 11(6), 567–585 (1989)
3. Fornefett, M., Rohr, K., Stiehl, H.S.: Radial basis functions with compact support for elastic registration of medical images. Image and Vision Computing 19(1–2), 87–96 (2001)
4. SCIRun.: A Scientific Computing Problem Solving Environment, Scientific Computing and Imaging Institute (SCI)
5. BioImage.: Volumetric Image Analysis and Visualization. Scientific Computing and Imaging Institute (SCI)

Pinhole SPECT vs. Cone-Beam SPECT

Gengsheng L. Zeng

Utah Center for Advanced Imaging Research (UCAIR),
University of Utah, 729 Arapeen Drive,
Salt Lake City, UT 84108, USA
larry@ucair.med.utah.edu

Abstract. In single photon emission computed tomography (SPECT), pinhole and cone-beam collimators are used for small object imaging. It is accepted that a pinhole collimator should be used if the object is very small, and the cone-beam collimator should be used if the object is larger. This paper presents criteria to determine which collimation geometry is more advantageous in terms of spatial resolution and detection sensitivity.

1 Introduction

SPECT (single photon emission computed tomography) is a medical imaging technique that creates images of the distribution of radiopharmaceuticals inside the patient (or other objects) [1]. The radiation source is injected into the patient. The gamma photons emitted from the patient body are acquired by a gamma camera outside the patient. The camera rotates around the patient (see Figure 1), and the computer processes the projections acquired by the camera from different views and produces a three-dimensional reconstructed image. The SPECT images are important in understanding of human organ's biological processes.

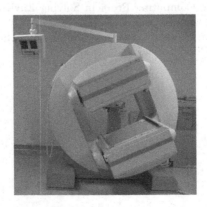

Fig. 1. A SPECT system that has two gamma cameras. A collimator is mounted on each camera. The two cameras rotate with the system gantry during data acquisition.

D. Zhang (Ed.): ICMB 2008, LNCS 4901, pp. 240–247, 2007.
© Springer-Verlag Berlin Heidelberg 2007

Due to the fact that the gamma ray energies are much higher than those of visible lights, the conventional lens does not function in a gamma camera. Instead, the "selective" collimators are used in gamma cameras to determine which photons are to be received and which photons are to be rejected.

Parallel-hole collimators are commonly used for patient imaging. Pinhole collimators are routinely used for small animal imaging and for patient thyroid imaging. Cone-beam collimators are sometimes used for patient brain imaging and cardiac imaging [2]. Recently, multi-pinhole collimators have been applied to patient cardiac imaging as well [3]. The purpose of this paper is to compare the pinhole and cone-beam collimators and provide criteria to determine which collimator should be used in a particular imaging application.

2 Theory

Figure 2 illustrates a pinhole collimator and a cone-beam collimator. In this paper, we assume that these two systems have the same focal-length f and same distance b from the focal point to the point-of-interest (POI). The goal of this paper is to compare these two systems by placing a small object at the POT position and requiring that they give the identical spatial resolution (or detection sensitivity) on the detectors. Since we fix the resolution (or the sensitivity) of the two systems, the superior system is the one that provide larger detection geometric efficiency (or the better resolution). Larger detection sensitivity means that more gamma photons can be detected and this results in lower Poisson noise in the data. Better resolution means smaller objects (e.g., lesions) can be resolved. We use the equations from [4] to derive the results. We further assume that the POI is at the central axis of the cone of projection rays.

For the pinhole geometry, we have these two relations:

$$\text{Resolution: } R_{ph} \approx d\,\frac{f+b}{f} \qquad (1)$$

Geometric Efficiency: $g_{ph} \approx \dfrac{d^2}{16b^2}$. (Note: There is a typo in the book, where d^2 is

printed as d.) $\qquad (2)$

For the cone-beam geometry, we have:

$$\text{Resolution: } R_{cb} \approx d_c\,\frac{f-b}{L}(1-\frac{1}{2}\frac{L}{f}) \qquad (3)$$

$$\text{Geometric Efficiency: } \quad g_{cb} \approx K^2(\frac{d_c}{L})^2(\frac{f-L}{b})^2. \qquad (4)$$

where the septa thickness t is ignored for simplicity, otherwise there is a $(\dfrac{d_c}{d_c+t})^2$

factor in g_{cb}.

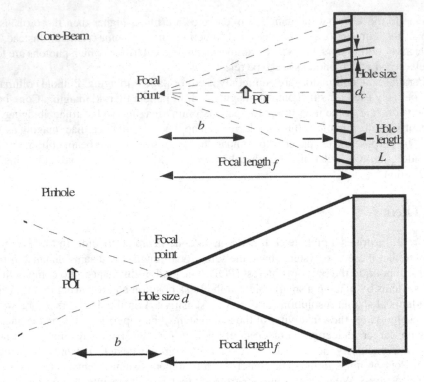

Fig. 2. Parameters in a pinhole and cone-beam systems

2.1 Resolution Comparison

The requirement of the two system having the identical spatial resolution on the detectors implies

$$R_{ph} = R_{cb},$$ (5)

and from (1), (3) and (5), we have

$$d\frac{f+b}{f} = d_c\frac{f-b}{L}(1-\frac{1}{2}\frac{L}{f}).$$ (6)

In order to satisfy (6) the hole-length L of the cone-beam collimator must satisfy

$$L = \frac{f}{\frac{1}{2}+\frac{d}{d_c}\frac{f+b}{f-b}} = \frac{f}{\frac{1}{2}+\frac{1}{\beta}\frac{f+b}{f-b}}$$ (7)

where $\beta = d_c/d$.

Comments. Pinhole and cone-beam collimators with the same f and b can have different performances in terms of resolution. When cone-beam collimator hole-length L

satisfies (7), both collimators give the same spatial resolution on the detectors for an object at the POI. If

$$L > \frac{f}{\frac{1}{2} + \frac{1}{\beta}\frac{f+b}{f-b}}$$

(8)

the cone-beam collimator will provide better resolution than the pinhole. If

$$L < \frac{f}{\frac{1}{2} + \frac{1}{\beta}\frac{f+b}{f-b}}$$

(9)

the pinhole collimator will provide better resolution than the cone-beam.

Example 1: As a numerical example, let $d = 1$ *mm*, $d_c = 1$ *mm*, $f = 200$ *mm*, and $b = 100$ *mm*, we have that if $L = 57$ *mm* the two collimators will have the same spatial resolution on the detectors for an object at the POI. If $L > 57$ *mm*, the cone-beam collimator has better resolution. If $L < 57$ *mm*, the pinhole collimator has better resolution.

If we change the hole size of the cone-beam collimator to $d_c = 0.5$ *mm*, we have that if $L = 31$ *mm* the two collimators will have the same spatial resolution on the detectors for an object at the POI. If $L > 31$ mm, the cone-beam will have better resolution than the pinhole.

If we change the hole size of the cone-beam collimator to $d_c = 2$ *mm*, we have that if $L = 100$ *mm* the two collimators will have the same spatial resolution on the detectors for an object at the POI. However, in this particular situation the L is too long to be practical; the pinhole always has better resolution than the cone-beam.

2.2 Sensitivity Comparison

Next we consider the ratio of the geometric efficiencies (2) and (4):

$$\frac{g_{cb}}{g_{ph}} = \frac{K^2 (\frac{d_c}{L})^2 (\frac{f-L}{b})^2}{\frac{d^2}{16b^2}}$$

(10)

where K is a constant that depends on the hole shape (~0.24 for round holes and ~0.26 for hexagonal holes). We assume $K = 0.25$. Thus,

$$\frac{g_{cb}}{g_{ph}} = \frac{(\frac{d_c}{L})^2 (f-L)^2}{d^2} = [\frac{d_c(f-L)}{Ld}]^2 = [\beta \frac{(f-L)}{Ld}]^2$$

(11)

where $\beta = d_c / d$.

Let the ratio in (11) be unity, solving for L yields

$$L = \frac{f}{1 + 1/\beta}. \tag{12}$$

Comments. Pinhole and cone-beam collimators with the same f and b can have different performances in terms of detection sensitivity. When (12) is satisfied, both collimators give the same sensitivity for an object at the POI. If

$$L < \frac{f}{1 + 1/\beta} \tag{13}$$

the cone-beam collimator will provide better sensitivity than the pinhole. If

$$L > \frac{f}{1 + 1/\beta} \tag{14}$$

the pinhole collimator will provide better sensitivity than the cone-beam.

Example 2: As a numerical example, let $d = 1$ *mm*, $d_c = 1$ *mm*, $f = 200$ *mm*, and $b = 100$ *mm*, we have from (13) that if $L < 100$ *mm* the cone-beam will have better sensitivity than the pinhole. From Example 1, we learn that if $L > 57$ *mm*, the cone-beam collimator has better resolution. Therefore, if 57 *mm* $< L < 100$ *mm*, the cone-beam collimator will outperform the pinhole collimator in both resolution and sensitivity. At the "equal resolution" case of $L = 57$ *mm*, the sensitivity gain of the cone-beam over the pinhole, according to (11), is 6.3.

If we change the hole size of the cone-beam collimator to $d_c = 0.5$ *mm*, we have from (13) that if $L < 67$ *mm* the cone-beam will have better sensitivity than the pinhole. From Example 1, we learn that if $L > 31$ *mm*, the cone-beam collimator has better resolution. Therefore, if 31 *mm* $< L < 67$ *mm*, the cone-beam collimator will outperform the pinhole collimator in both resolution and sensitivity. At the "equal resolution" case of $L = 31$ *mm*, the sensitivity gain of the cone-beam over the pinhole, according to (11), is 7.4.

Now, we change the hole size of the cone-beam collimator to $d_c = 2$ *mm* (i.e., $\beta = 2$), and the "equal sensitivity" condition requires that $L = 133$ *mm*. When $L < 133$ *mm* the cone beam always has better sensitivity. From Example 1, when $L < 100$ *mm* the pinhole always has better resolution. Therefore, in this case, for any practical values of L, the cone-beam collimator always has a better sensitivity and worse resolution than the pinhole collimator.

2.3 Sensitivity Comparison with Equal Resolution

If we substitute the "equal resolution" condition (7) in the sensitivity ratio equation (11), we have

$$\frac{g_{cb}}{g_{ph}} = [\beta(\frac{1}{\beta}\frac{f+b}{f-b} - \frac{1}{2})]^2. \tag{15}$$

From (15), we have our main result:

$$\frac{g_{cb}}{g_{ph}} > 1 \text{ if and only if } f < (1+\frac{4}{\beta})b. \tag{16}$$

If we further restrict to the case of

$$\beta= 1, \text{ i.e., } d = d_c, \tag{17}$$

(16) becomes:

$$\frac{g_{cb}}{g_{ph}} > 1 \text{ if and only if } f < 5b. \tag{18}$$

Example 3: As a numerical example, let $d = 1$ *mm*, $d_c=1$ *mm*, and $f = 200$ *mm*, the cone-beam system is more efficient if $b > 40$ *mm*, otherwise the pinhole system is more efficient, given that they have the same spatial resolution of an object at the POI.

2.4 Resolution Comparison with Equal Sensitivity

If we substitute the "equal sensitivity" condition (12) in the resolution ratio of equation (3) over equation (1), after simplification, we have

$$\frac{R_{cb}}{R_{ph}} = (1+\frac{1}{2}\beta)\frac{f-b}{f+b}. \tag{19}$$

From (19), we have another main result:

$$\frac{R_{cb}}{R_{ph}} < 1 \text{ if and only if } f < (1+\frac{4}{\beta})b. \tag{20}$$

If we further restrict to the case of

$$\beta= 1, \text{ i.e., } d = d_c, \tag{21}$$

(20) becomes:

$$\frac{R_{cb}}{R_{ph}} < 1 \text{ if and only if } f < 5b. \tag{22}$$

Example 4: As a numerical example, let $d = 1$ *mm*, $d_c=1$ *mm*, and $f = 200$ *mm*, then the cone-beam system has better resolution if $b > 40$ *mm*, otherwise the pinhole system has better resolution, given that they have the same detection sensitivity of an object at the POI.

If $\beta= 1$, then $L = f/2$. This L is too long to be practical. If $\beta= 1/6$, then $L = f/7$ is a more practical length to build a cone-beam collimator. We can build a cone beam collimator that is superior to the pinhole collimator in terms sensitivity and resolution. The following is an example for human cardiac application.

Example 5: In a human cardiac pinhole SPECT [6], the diameter of the pinhole is chosen as 6 *mm* and the focal length f_{ph} is chosen as 120 *mm*. This pinhole collimator is reported to provide compatible cardiac SPECT images as a standard low-energy general-purpose (LEGP) parallel-hole collimator. In this example, we will see if we can design a cone-beam collimator to do a better job than this pinhole collimator.

If a cone-beam collimator is used to perform the same task, it is reasonable to assume β= 1/6 that is, cone-beam collimator's hole-size is 1 mm. Since a human is used for cardiac imaging, the cone-beam focal-length cannot be too short, and select it as f_{cb} = 640 *mm*. For a practical cone-beam collimator, let L = 45 *mm*.

We first consider their detection sensitivities using (2) and (4):

$$\frac{g_{cb}}{g_{ph}} = \frac{(\frac{d_c}{L})^2 (\frac{f-L}{b})^2}{\frac{d^2}{b^2}} = (\frac{\beta}{L})^2 (f_{cb} - L)^2 = 4.8563 . \tag{23}$$

Then we compare their resolution using (1) and (3):

$$\frac{R_{ph}}{R_{cb}} = \frac{d \frac{f_{ph}+b}{b}}{d_c \frac{f_{cb}-b}{L}(1-\frac{1}{2}\frac{L}{f_{cb}})} = \frac{6 \cdot \frac{120+b}{b}}{\frac{640-b}{45}(1-\frac{1}{2}\cdot\frac{45}{640})} > 1 \text{ for } 0 < b < 640 \text{ } mm. \tag{24}$$

The above two expressions mean that the designed cone-beam collimator has better spatial resolution than the pinhole collimator, and the cone-beam collimator has a approximately 5-fold sensitivity gain over the pinhole collimator for any object in the field-of-view.

3 Discussion

This paper compares a cone-beam collimator and a pinhole collimator with the same focal-length f and object-to-focal-point-distance b. A few relations have been derived. We further fix the hole-size d of the pinhole collimator and the hole-size d_c of the cone-beam collimator, we leave the cone-beam collimator hole-length L as a free parameter to vary. There may exist a range of values of L where the cone-beam outperforms the pinhole in both spatial resolution and detection sensitivity. However, if the hole size of the cone-beam collimator is larger than the hole size of the pinhole collimator, there may not exit a range of L to make the cone-beam resolution better than that of the pinhole, even though the cone-beam can have better sensitivity.

If the hole size of the cone-beam collimator d_c is chosen to be the same as the hole size d of the pinhole collimator, we have the following criteria:

In the equal-resolution case, if $f < 5b$, the cone-beam will have better sensitivity.
In the equal-sensitivity case, if $f < 5b$, the cone-beam will have better resolution.

If the hole size of the cone-beam collimator d_c is chosen to be 1/6 of the hole size d of the pinhole collimator, we have the following criteria:

In the equal-resolution case, if $f < 25b$, the cone-beam will have better sensitivity.
In the equal-sensitivity case, if $f < 25b$, the cone-beam will have better resolution.

Since larger objects demand a larger distance b, the condition $f < 5b$ (or $f < 25b$) is easily satisfied. However, for very small objects, these conditions may not be satisfied because the objects should be placed as closed to the focal point as possible to obtain sufficient magnification. Our criteria agree with the computer simulation results [5] that for a larger object, the cone-beam collimator is a better choice, while for a smaller object, the pinhole collimator is a better choice.

We must point out that even in many cases the cone-beam collimator outperforms the pinhole collimator, the cone-beam collimator is much more difficult to build than the pinhole collimator. Sometimes a cone-beam collimator with a very small hole size or a very long hole length is impossible to build using today's technology.

Pinholes find more applications these days. This is partially due to another advantage of the pinhole — the multiple-pinhole collimation. On the other hand, it is difficult to build a multiple-focal-point cone-beam collimator.

References

1. Zeng, G.L., Galt, J.R., Wernick, M.N., Mintzer, R.A., Aarsvold, J.N.: Single-photon emission computed tomography. In: Wernick, M.N., Aarsvold, J.N. (eds.) Emission Tomography: The Fundamentals of PET and SPECT, ch. 7, pp. 127–152. Elsevier Academic Press, Amsterdam (2004)
2. Gullberg, G.T., Christian, P.E., Zeng, G.L., Datz, F.L.: Cone beam tomography of the heart using single-photon emission-computed tomography. Invest. Rad., 681–688 (1991)
3. Kirch, D.L., Koss, J.E., Steele, P.P.: Dual-peak attenuation compensation (DPAC) using the upper and lower Tl-201 peaks during simultaneous stress/rest multi-pinhole SPECT (MP-SPECT) for myocardial perfusion imaging (MPI). J. Nucl. Med. 48, 99 (abstract, 2007)
4. Cherry, S.R., Sorenson, J.A., Phelps, M.E.: Physics in Nuclear Medicine, 3rd edn. Elsevier, Philadelphia (2003)
5. Qi, Y., Tsui, B.M.W., Zeng, G.L.: Optimizing collimator designs for small animal SPECT imaging using a scintillation camera. Annual Meeting of Society of Nuclear Medicine, Toronto (2005)
6. Funk, T., Kirch, D.L., Koss, J.E., Botvinick, E., Hasegawa, B.H.: A novel approach to multipinhole SPECT for myocardial perfusion imaging. J. Nucl. Med. 47, 595–602 (2006)

Constructing the Histogram Representation for Automatic Gridding of cDNA Microarray Images

Hong-Qiang Wang[1], Hau-San Wong[2], and Hailong Zhu[1]

[1] Department of RIIPT, The Hong Kong Ploytechnic University, Hong Kong, China
{rihqwang,rihlzhu}@inet.ployu.edu.hk
[2] Department of Computer Science, City University of Hong Kong, Hong Kong, China
cshswong@cityu.edu.hk

Abstract. This paper proposes an novel approach for automatic gridding of cDNA microarray images based on histogram representation. The approach constructs histogram representation to characterize microarray images and use it, instead of raw signal intensities used in previous gridding methods, to identify spots. The histogram representation can efficiently reduce noise and the influence from low raw signal intensities and local contaminations. The proposed approach is successfully tested on different types of microarray images and is compared with several previous algorithms.

1 Introduction

Currently, gene expression analysis has become a widely used tool in scientific and industrial researches, which has a large impact in many application areas such as diagnoses and treatments of human diseases, agricultural development or quantification of GMOs, drug discovery and design [1,2]. Gene expression analysis greatly depends on microarray technology which can simultaneously monitor expression levels of tens of thousands of genes and provide plenty of gene expression data used for the researches on diseases and biology [3,4]. Briefly speaking, microarray image processing includes three main steps in turn: gridding, segmentation and intensity extraction [5,6]. Of them, the gridding step plays a key role since the latter two steps, segmentation and intensity extraction, are performed only by simple computations based on the gridding results. The gridding problem can be formulated as how to accurately and automatically identify the hybridization area in a microarray image and assign the coordinates to each spot in the image. It is not easy to efficiently grid a microarray image. Although, from the manufacture process of microarrays, each probe can be accurately located on the microarray slide by a robot hand, it is inevitable that the slide is deformed by heat and pressure so that the sequent hybridization spots are moved and distorted. On the other hand, the sites and shapes of the hybridization spots are also affected by the variation of the hybridization process. These are the reasons that recently the gridding of microarray image becomes one of the considerable research focuses in both biological area and intelligent computation society [7,8].

As a result of gridding, a microarray image is reduced into a number of arrays or tables to be ready for extracting expression levels of each gene [8]. Traditionally, gridding is manually done by eye, or by a semi-automatic system. For example, ScanAlyze

D. Zhang (Ed.): ICMB 2008, LNCS 4901, pp. 248–255, 2007.
© Springer-Verlag Berlin Heidelberg 2007

and GenePix are two widely used semi-automatic softwares [9,10]. These traditional methods are mainly focused on the accuracy of finding positions of spots. However, for these methods, extensive human interaction can lead to unnecessary variations in the derived parameters due to the bias or fatigue of a human operator, and the process can be very time-consuming. Ease of use and high automation are always pursued for developing the gridding approaches. Following this line, Buhler et al. presented a soft package called Dapple to realize gridding [11]; Jain et al. proposed to optimize the positions of spots using a scoring function based on integrated image intensities [12]; Angulo and Serra proposed to use morphological operators to extract spot data from microarray images [13]. Another gridding approach worthy of mentioning is the Bayesian grid matching model proposed by Hartelius et al. [14]. The approach is derived from the theories of template matching and Bayesian image restoration. The apparent advantage is that it is good at identifying the location of distorted grid structures in images. Except the above separate gridding methods, there are some gridding methods built in an integrated processing system, such as the Stienfath's model [15], the Jain's model [12], and the Katzer's model [16,17]. For most of the above gridding approaches, a common disadvantage is that they often make assumptions about the size and shape of spots, or even impose some restrictions on the array print layout or materials used. For example, the Jain's model requires the rows and columns of all grids to be strictly aligned and the Katzer's model requires gaps between the grids. The imposition of the assumptions not only degrades the accuracy of gridding but also the automation level. Another nuisance is that one has to manually put into computers many assumed parameters. This paper proposes a novel histogram-based approach for automatically gridding microarray images. The approach adopts a histogram representation to characterize microarray images and implement gridding in an unsupervised and high-automated way. The approach can efficiently overcome noise and local contaminations, and can efficiently deal with microarray images with low signal intensities. Experimental results on different types of microarray images show that it is effective and efficient to use the histogram representation to characterize microarray images.

The rest of the paper is organized as follows: Section 2 describes our proposed approach for the gridding problem of microarray images in detail. In Section 3, the proposed approach is tested on real microarray images from different laboratory systems and is compared with several previous methods. An additional investigation is conducted to prove the superiority of the histogram representation over raw signal intensities. Section 4 concludes this paper.

2   Algorithm

2.1   Constructing Histogram Vectors for Rows and Columns of Microarray Images

A typical microarray image consists of a set of subgrids (sub-arrays), and each subgrid contains a set of spots. Both the subgrids in a microarray image and the spots in each subgrid are tiled in a rectangular way. For example, a mcroarray image can consist of 4×4 subgrids and 21×18 spots for each subgrid. A microarray image (matrix) can be represented as $A = \{a_{i,j}\}, i = 1...m$ and $j = 1...n$, where $a_{i,j} \in Z^+$ (usually

$a_{i,j}$ is in the range $[0...65,535]$ in a TIFF image). From the viewpoint of the function representation, such a microarray image can be seen as a two-dimensional gray intensity function:

$$a = p(x, y) \tag{1}$$

where $x = 1...n$ represents the column locations and $y = 1...m$ represents the row locations. If each row (or column) of a microarray image is viewed as a function $p_y(x)$ (or $p_x(y)$), we can characterize each row (or column) using the derivatives of the function to accurately and conveniently identify the borders of each spot. For the function $p_x(y)$, the derivatives with respective to the variable y can be computed by

$$\frac{d(p_x(y))}{dy} = \frac{\partial(p(x, y))}{\partial y} \tag{2}$$

Given the matrix $A = \{a_{i,j}\}$, for any column $x = x0$, we can get a series of approximate derivatives with respective to y:

$$\{\Delta a_{.,x0}\} = A_{\{2...m\},x0} - A_{\{1...(m-1)\},x0}. \tag{3}$$

Likewise, for any row $y = y0$, we can get a series of approximate derivatives with respective to x:

$$\{\Delta a_{y0,.}\} = A_{y0,\{2...n\}} - A_{y0,\{1...(n-1)\}}. \tag{4}$$

Compared with the raw intensity, the first-order derivatives can reduce noise and effectively capture the change of intensities. It can be imaginable that the change rates of the intensities near the boundaries tend to smaller than those in other areas. This means that boundaries meet the condition that the first-order derivatives of the intensity functions along them tend to be smaller than those in other areas. Thus, to make use of the hidden property, we construct the following two histogram vectors to efficiently characterize each row or column:

$$Colum : x \rightarrow C :$$
$$(\sum_{k=1}^{m-1} I(\Delta a_{k,x} > \delta)) \Big/ m - 1, \sum_{k=1}^{m-1} I(|\Delta a_{k,x}| < \delta) \Big/ m - 1,$$
$$\sum_{k=1}^{m-1} I(\Delta a_{k,x} < -\delta) \Big/ m - 1) \tag{5}$$

and

$$Row : y \rightarrow R :$$
$$(\sum_{k=1}^{n-1} I(\Delta a_{y,k} > \delta)) \Big/ n - 1, \sum_{k=1}^{n-1} I(|\Delta a_{y,k}| < \delta) \Big/ n - 1,$$
$$\sum_{k=1}^{n-1} I(\Delta a_{y,k} < -\delta) \Big/ n - 1) \tag{6}$$

where $I(\cdot)$ represents an indication function whose value equals 1 if true and 0 otherwise, and δ is, called derivative cutoff, a positive constant which bounds the derivatives near the rectangular boundaries of a spot, respectively. The parameter δ is chosen by the percentiles of the derivatives. From Eqs.(5) and (6), it can be found that the first-order derivative information contained in all the pixels on a row or column is used to characterize the row or column. The global consideration can efficiently overcome the local contamination and noise.

2.2 Spot Gridding Based on First-Order-Derivative Histogram Vectors

In view of the hierarchical built-in structure of a microarray image, our gridding approach grids spots through two stages: 1) drawing boundaries of each subgrid; 2) locating spots within each bounded subgrid. In the first stage, we optimize the boundaries of subgrids using the following quantities: For finding the column borders of subgrids,

$$S_{x0} = \sum_{i=1}^{m-1} |\Delta a_{i,x0}|, 1 \le x0 \le n; \tag{7}$$

for finding the row borders of subgrids,

$$S_{y0} = \sum_{j=1}^{n-1} |\Delta a_{y0,j}|, 1 \le y0 \le m. \tag{8}$$

For a microarray image with $(p \times q)$ subgrids, local optimization algorithms based on the quantities S_{x0} (S_{y0}) are constructed to find $q+1$ column borders ($p+1$ row borders) of subgrids. Take as an example the identification of column borders. First, we initialize the $q+1$ column borders as follows:

$$\begin{cases} x = B_i = 1 & i = 1 \\ x = B_i = round((i-1) \times (n/q)) & i = 2...(q+1) \end{cases} \tag{9}$$

where $round(\cdot)$ represents the function for solving the nearest integer. The $q+1$ actual borders can be sought in the following corresponding local ranges:

$$\eta_i = \begin{cases} \{B_i...C\} & i = 1 \\ \{(B_i - C)...(B_i + C)\} & i = 2...q \\ \{(B_i - C)...B_i\} & i = q+1 \end{cases} \tag{10}$$

where $C = round(n/(2q))$ is the integer nearest to n/(2q). The searching is performed by a local minimization algorithm which has the following objective function:

$$g_i(x) = \bar{S}_{j\in[x-b,x+b]}, x \in \eta_i \tag{11}$$

where $\bar{S}$ represents the average of S and b is a small positive integer. The ith optimized column border can be expressed as

$$x = \arg_{r\in\eta_i}\{\min(\bar{S}_{j\in[r-b,r+b]})\}, i = 1..., (q+1). \tag{12}$$

Likewise, the $p+1$ row borders of $(p \times q)$ subgrids can be located using a similar procedure.

Next, an unsupervised clustering method is employed to cluster these histograms into two clusters, of which one cluster with the center closer to (0,1,0) is chosen as candidate boundaries. Various versions of clustering algorithms can be employed for this task [18]. Here we adopt the k-means algorithm with $k = 2$. In order to overcome the clustering randomness, the clustering results of many times are integrated to extract boundaries which appear at frequency of above 80% in all the clustering results. For the clustering boundaries, a two-step sub-procedure is adopted for further refinement. First, an extraction process is applied to filter out the fake boundaries from the candidates, in which the distances between two contiguous candidates are calculated and the median distance is taken as a pseudo spot width. By the width, a set of back boundaries $E_i, i = 1...k$, which have a larger distance to its previous contiguous candidates than the pseudo width, are extracted. For each E_i, the corresponding front boundary $F_i, i = 1...k$, is estimated as its previous contiguous candidates. From these boundaries, a set of new boundaries can be obtained as follows:

$$L_i = \begin{cases} (F_1 + 1)/2 & i = 1 \\ (F_i + E_{i-1})/2 & k + 1 > i > 1 \\ (\Phi + E_{i-1})/2 & i = k + 1 \end{cases} \tag{13}$$

where Φ represents the total width of the subgrid. The spot width ω is re-evaluated as the median values of the new distances between two contiguous L_i. Secondly, any two contiguous L_i with the gaps beyond the cutoff $\tau = \xi\omega, 1 < \xi < 1.5$ are deleted, and uniformly divide the left space by ω.

3   Experimental Results

We test our proposed gridding approach on several real microarry images from three different laboratory systems: the Snijders's experiment [19], the gene expression omnibus (GEO) database (http://www.ncbi.nlm.nih.gov/geo/index.cgi) and the Stanford microarray database (SMD) (http://genome-www5.stanford.edu/).

3.1   Comparison of the Gridding Performances of the Histogram Representation and the Raw Intensities

Fig.1 illustrates the changing curves of the respective sums of the first-order derivatives and the raw signal intensities along one image dimension from a real microarray image, of which the top subfigure is for the first-order derivatives and the bottom is for the raw intensities. Fig.1 shows that the peaks for the raw intensities are not true peaks, non-symmetrical, plat and even sometimes something like irregular sawteeth as shown in the bottom subfigure. The fact will make it ineffective and even infeasible to construct a gridding optimization method based on the raw intensities. Inversely, the benign peaks of the first-order derivatives shows the good optimization performance of our histogram representation, as shown in the top subfigures in Fig.1.

3.2   Application to the Microarray Images from the Snijders' Experiment

Jain et al. validated their gridding method (UCSF Spot) on the Snijders's images [12]. The Jain's method accomplishes the location of spots mainly by two integrated images by summarizing the signal intensities in both image dimensions respectively. The combination of spot offsets and spacings in both X and Y directions is optimized such that the nominal spot locations correspond to the peaks in the integrated images. The software package of the Jain's method can be downloaded on the website,

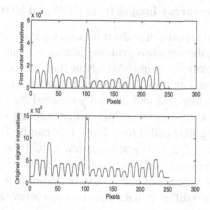

Fig. 1. Comparison of the 1st-order derivatives (top) and the original intensities (bottom)

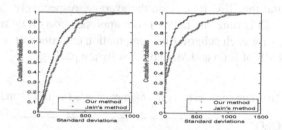

Fig. 2. Comparison of cumulative distributions of standard deviations of intensities of the replicate spots on the micorarray image, bt474a-CY3, between our approach and the Jain's method

http://cc.ucsf.edu/jain/public. Based on the image, bt474a-CY3, we compare our gridding approach with the Jain's method. From the detail of the Snijders's experiment, we know that three horizontal sequent spots in the image bt474a-CY3 correspond to a same clone of the genome and during hybridization some measures were taken to make sure the same hybridization condition for them. Based on the fact, we can evaluate a gridding method by checking the degrees of the differences of the expression measurements of the same clones from three replicate spots. Here, considering all the hybridized clones in each subgrid, we take the cumulative proportions of the standard deviations of the expression levels of the triple spots for a same clone as an index to compare our gridding approach with the Jain's method. For the comparison, we use the histogram foreground-background segmentation algorithm to calculate the expression measurements of each spot after gridding. For the detail of the segmentation algorithm, readers can refer to [12]. Fig. 2 shows the cumulative proportion curves for our gridding approach and the Jain's mehtod based on two subgrids of the microarray image bt474a-CY3. From this figure, it can be found that the less measurement differences of the same clones are obtained using the gridding results by our approach.

3.3   Application to Microarray Images from GEO and SMD

We also apply our gridding approach to the microarray images from the GEO and SMD database. Table 1 report the obtained gridding accuracies and the computational expenses for these images from GEO and SMD. Note that the accuracies are estimated by comparing with our manual analysis. Following [8], we have visually inspected each image with its corresponding grid and manually counted the number of full spots inside its grid cell, as well as the number of pixels that belong to the spot but are located outside the corresponding grid cell. From Table 1, it can be found that our approach is quite accurate in finding the grids and takes few CPU time for the microarray images. The columns, "Spot accuracy", indicate the percentage of spots which contain all their pixels in the corresponding cell. It can be found that for the microarray images from either of the two different databases of microarray images, SMD and GEO, the accuracies of spot identification are very high, exceeding 99 percent. Regarding the percentage of pixels which fall outside the grid cell, the results in the columns, "Pixel error", show that our approach is quite efficient, yielding around 0.1% and 0.06% for the SMD images and the GEO images on the average, respectively. In addition, seen from the columns, "CPU time" in Tables 1, our approach costs little time to complete the gridding process for each subgrid (the computation environment is Intel Pentium 4 CPU 3.00Ghz, 504MB of Ram and Matlab 7.0 software package).

Table 1. Gridding accuracies for microarray images from GEO and SMD

GEO			
Image/Subgrid	Spot accuracy	Pixel Error	CPU time
GSM17137/(2,3)	99.64%	0.032%	0.8542
GSM17163/(1,2)	100%	0	0.8538
GSM17186/(3,4)	97.28%	0.318%	0.8512
GSM17190/(4,4)	100%	0	0.8498
GSM17192/(2,1)	100%	0	0.8502
GSM17193/(1,4)	99.5%	0.028%	0.8433
Average	99.4%	0.0105%	0.8504
SMD			
632-CH2/(1,2)	99.50%	0.088%	0.8126
634-CH2/(2,2)	99.89%	0.033%	0.8095
1674-CH2/(2,1)	98.24%	0.115%	0.8175
1679-CH2/(2,3)	99.84%	0.041%	0.8204
2141-CH2/(2,2)	99.94%	0.031%	0.8125
Average	99.48%	0.0616%	0.8145

4   Conclusions

In this paper, we have proposed a novel approach based on the histogram representation for automatically gridding cDNA microarray images. In the approach, a microarray image is represented by the histogram representation which is formed using the first-order derivatives, and then the spot boundaries are identified by clustering the histograms.

The histogram representation has the ability to reduce the influence from noise and local contaminations and low gray intensities owing to the use of the first-order derivative information. Compared with the previous methods, our approach only needs inputing the size (the parameters, p and q) of subgrid arrays, and runs in the unsupervised way. The experimental results show the effectiveness and efficiency of the approach to automatically gridd microarray images, irrespective of image systems, the quality of signal intensities as well as image size.

References

1. Schena, M., Shalon, D., Davis, R.W., Brown, P.O.: Quantitative monitoring of gene expression patterns with a complementary microarray. Science 270, 467–470 (1995)
2. Baldi, P., Hatfield, G.W.: DNA microarrays and gene expression. Cambridge University Press, Cambridge (2002)
3. Schena, M.: Microarray analysis. John Wiley & sons, Inc., New York, USA (2003)
4. Antoniol, G., Ceccarelli, M.A.: Markov Random Field Approach to Microarray Image Gridding. In: Proc. 17th Int'l Conf. Pattern Recognition, pp. 550–553 (2004)
5. Bassett, D.E., Eisen, M.B., Boguski, M.S.: Gene expression informatics-it's all in your mine. Nat. Genet. 21(Suppl.), 51–55 (1999)
6. Antoniol, G., Ceccarelli, M.: Microarray image gridding with stochastic search based approaches. Image and Vision Computing 25, 155–163 (2007)
7. Yang, Y., Buckley, M., Dudoit, S., Speed, T.: Comparison of Methods for Image Analysis on cDNA Microarray Data. J. Computational and Graphical Statistics 11, 108–136 (2002)
8. Rueda, L., Vidyadharan, V.: A Hill-Climbing Approach for Automatic Gridding of cDNA Microarray Images. IEEE/ACM Transactions on Computational Biology and Bioinformatics 3, 72–83 (2006)
9. Axon Instruments, IncGenePix Pro 4.0, Documentation (2002), http://www.axon.com/
10. Eisen, M.B.: ScanAlyze, Software and Documentation (1999), http://rana.lbl.gov/EisenSoftware.htm
11. Buhler, J., Ideker, T., Haynor, D.: Dapple: Improved Techniques for Finding Spots on DNA Microarrays, UW CSE Technical Report UWTR, 12 (2000)
12. Jain, A., Tokuyasu, T., Snijders, A., Segraves, R., Albertson, D., Pinkel, D.: Fully Automatic Quantification of Microarray Data. Genome Research 12, 324–335 (2002)
13. Angulo, J., Serra, J.: Automatic analysis of DNA microarray images using mathematical morphology Bioinformatics. 19, 553–562 (2003)
14. Hartelius, K., Carstensen, J.M.: Bayesian grid matching. IEEE Transactions Pattern Analysis and Machine Intelligence 25, 162–173 (2003)
15. Steinfath, M., Wruck, W., Seidel, H.: Automated Image Analysis for Array Hybridization Experiments. Bioinformatics 17, 634–641 (2001)
16. Katzer, M., Kummer, F., Sagerer, G.: A Markov Random Field Model of Microarray Gridding. In: Proc. 2003 ACM Symp. Applied Computing (2003)
17. Katzer, M., Kummer, F., Sagerer, G.: Methods for automatic microarray image segmentation. IEEE Trans. Nanobioscience 2, 202–214 (2003)
18. Webb, A.R., Ltd., Q., Malvern, U.: Statistical pattern recognition. John Wiley & Sons, LTD., Chichester (2002)
19. Snijders, A.M., Nowak, N., Segraves, R., Blackwood, S., Brown, N., Conroy, J., Hamilton, G., Hindle, A.H., Huey, B., Kimura, K.: Assembly of microarrays for genome-wide measurement of DNA copy number by CGH. Nat. Genet. 29, 263–264 (2001)

Compression of Medical Images Using Enhanced Vector Quantizer Designed with Self Organizing Feature Maps

Yogesh H. Dandawate[1], Madhuri A. Joshi[2], and Shrirang Umrani[3]

[1] Department of Electronics and Telecommunications,
Vishwakarma Institute of Information Technology, Pune-48
yhdandawate@gmail.com
[2] Department of Electronics and Telecommunications,
College of Engineering, Pune-05
punemajoshi@gmail.com
[3] Vishwakarma Institute of Information Technology, Pune-48
shrirang.umrani@viit.ac.in

Abstract. Now a days all medical imaging equipments give output as digital image and non-invasive techniques are becoming cheaper, the database of images is becoming larger. This archive of images increases up to significant size and in telemedicine-based applications the storage and transmission requires large memory and bandwidth respectively. There is a need for compression to save memory space and fast transmission over internet and 3G mobile with good quality decompressed image, even though compression is lossy. This paper presents a novel approach for designing enhanced vector quantizer, which uses Kohonen's Self Organizing neural network. The vector quantizer (codebook) is designed by training with a neatly designed training image and by selective training approach .Compressing; images using it gives better quality. The quality analysis of decompressed images is evaluated by using various quality measures along with conventionally used PSNR.

1 Introduction

Images are very important in medicine for diagnostic and therapeutic use. Now days all images are in digitized form, and number of images per patient is more. For archiving, large memory space for storage is required. In today's era of telemedicine, the recent and archived images are to be transmitted over internet for the purpose of expert opinions and consultation. If images are large, it takes long time for transmission and reception. To store in less memory space and transmit with fast speed these images need to be compressed by some means. For example, a single digitized X-ray image of 2000x2000 pixel size with 8 bit per pixel requires 4MB of storage and with favorable speed of 8 KBps for transmission, requires approximately 10 minutes, which is very much.

Digital Imaging and Communications in Medicine (DICOM) is a standard used for distribution and viewing of medical images from different modalities. It is developed due to the requirement of the standards for the purpose of storage and transmission. Currently, DICOM standard supports run-length coding (RLE), lossy JPEG, lossless

D. Zhang (Ed.): ICMB 2008, LNCS 4901, pp. 256–264, 2007.
© Springer-Verlag Berlin Heidelberg 2007

JPEG, JPEG-LS (lossless and near lossless) and JPEG-2000 for compression of the image data. S. Hludov and Chr. Meinel [18] in their paper evaluated the performance of the LZW-JPEG compression scheme. B.Ramakrishnan and N.Shriram [19] proposed compression scheme for DICOM images based on well known Set Partitioning in Hierarchical Trees (SPIHT), which possess the progressive transmission capabilities useful for telemedicine applications.

In this paper, we are proposing medical image compression using vector quantization (VQ), which is one of the powerful techniques used over last two decades. We have developed an enhanced vector quantizer (codebook) for compression, which is optimized to reduce blockiness in the decompressed images and improve the quality of reconstructed image. Since VQ is a lossy compression technique, analysis of a reconstructed image with quality perspective is highly essential. Especially for medical images, some regions/ textures must be analyzed clearly. The motivation behind designing enhanced vector quantizer and evaluating its performance in terms of quality measures, aims towards simplicity in hardware design, if compared with its counterpart block based method JPEG and wavelets. This may be, used in dedicated imaging applications in medicine.

The performance of the developed Vector quantizer is evaluated by using quality measures like Structural content (SC), mean structural similarity index (MSSIM), a vital measure in medical images, image fidelity (IF), normalized cross correlation (NK) ,average difference in pixel values along with conventionally used Peak signal to noise ratio (PSNR). The compression ratio with run length encoding (RLE) is, also presented and file sizes are compared with JPEG.

2 Vector Quantizer

R.M. Gray [1] [3], N.M. Nasarabadi and R.A. King [2] in their paper presented an excellent review of Vector Quantization.

A vector quantizer (VQ) can be defined as mapping Q of L dimensional Euclidean space R^L into a finite subset Y of R^L,thus

$$Q : R^L \to Y \tag{1}$$

Where $Y = \left\{ \hat{X_i} \; ; i = 1,2,3....., \; N \right\}$ the set of reproduction vectors (code vectors) and N, is number of vectors in Y (codebook).

The codebook can be designed by various techniques. The early algorithm was proposed by Lloyd [4], and modified by Linde *et al.* [3] [4]. This is popularly known as LBG algorithm. Mean shape VQ, classified VQ, predictive VQ, adaptive hierarchical VQ (AHVQ). [2][3] and address VQ [5] are the other few used in design of VQ. This paper uses Kohonen's self organizing feature map neural network techniques.

Simon Haykin *et al.* [6] in their review on neural net approaches, described other methods in detail. Once the codebook is designed, an image to be compressed is divided into vectors. The vectors are generated either by clustering techniques(classification) or by dividing an image into blocks of 4x4, 4x8 or 8x8 pixels and then they are matched with the codebook vector (code vector)such that the distortion (Euclidean distance) is minimum. The addresses of the code vectors are, either transmitted or stored as a compressed data.

Thus, the VQ compression process comprises of two functions, an encoder, which views the input vector X and generate the address of reproduction vector Xi from the codebook. Second function is decoder, which has the same codebook as in encoder and it uses the address (index) and reproduces the codevectors and map the image.

3 Design of Vector Quantizer Using Kohonen's Self Organizing Feature Maps (SOFM)

According to Kohonen [7] [8] [9], self-organizing map has special property of effectively creating spatially organized "internal presentations" of various features of input signals and their abstractions. Self-organizing feature maps (SOFM) learn to classify input vectors according to how they are grouped (pattern) in the input space.

The network consist of N input nodes corresponding to the number of input vector elements and the output nodes which are arranged in two dimensional array with neighboring nodes designed to have similar responses to the inputs. Each output has connection with input and its weight.

Chung Wei *et al.* [10] in his paper clearly described Kohonen's algorithm. The summary of it is

For each vector x in the training set:

1) Classify x according to

$$\mathbf{x} \in C_i \ \text{ if } \ \|\mathbf{x} - \mathbf{w}_i\| = \min_j \|\mathbf{x} - \mathbf{w}_j\| \tag{2}$$

2) Update the features $\mathbf{w}_j$ according to

$$\mathbf{w}_j(t+1) = \left\{ \begin{array}{l} \mathbf{w}_j(t) + \alpha(t)[\mathbf{x} - \mathbf{w}_j(t)], \\ \mathbf{w}_j(t), \end{array} \right. \tag{3}$$

Where $\mathbf{w}$ is the feature vector (weights), α is a learning parameter in the range $0 < \alpha < 1$. Ci is the class.

The network is trained by using an image that contents rich features for image processing applications. Many researchers used Lena image for training SOFM network for codebook design. Anna Durai *et al.* [11] in their research paper clearly described the procedure. The same procedure is employed with modifications in the weight initialization for further improving the performance.

Guy Cazuguel [12]-[13] have successfully used SOFM in compression of medical images.

One of the advantages of SOFM in medical image perspective is that quantization is performed in the gray level pixel space, so that visual aspect of images is preserved which is very important for heavily textured images.

The experimentation with codebook trained using Lena image was carried out and it has been observed that this codebook do not perform well for medical images. It suffers through the drawback of SOFM that due to the neighborhood principle, the weights are changed for perfect black and white, with the blocks with very less or no variation in gray scale, which changes the texture and structure of image and this is responsible for the degradation of medical image in terms of quality.

In order to improve the quality of reconstruction we propose a different way of training the codebook. The training image as developed by combining different images, which includes some medical images also. This combination was done after studying the behavior of SOFM algorithm for different training images and also using selective training approach for selected gray level combination which represents black, white color and edges.

4 Quality Measures Used for Evaluation of Decompressed Images

I. Avicibas *et al.* [16], M. Mrak *et al.* and A.M. Eskicioglu [14] in their papers have described the statistical quality measures. This paper uses few quality measures, which are normally used for quality analysis of medical images.

4.1 Mean Square Error (MSE) and Peak Signal to Noise Ratio (PSNR)

The MSE is given by

$$\sum_{j=1}^{M} \sum_{k=1}^{N} [X(j,k) - \hat{X}(j,k)]^2 / MN \tag{4}$$

Where x is input vector and X^ is a codebook vector. MSE should be low for less distortion, means better quality. MxN is image size in pixels.

The PSNR is given by

$$PSNR = 10 \log \frac{255 * 255}{MSE} dB \tag{5}$$

For perfect reconstruction, it should approach to infinity. Normally it is in the range of 25 to 40dB.

4.1.1 Average Difference (AD)

$$\sum_{j=1}^{M} \sum_{k=1}^{N} [X(j,k) - \hat{X}(j,k)] / MN \tag{6}$$

This measure shown the average difference between the pixel values, ideally it should be zero.

4.2 Structural Content (SC), Image Fidelity (IF) and Normalized Correlation Coefficient (NK)

These are the co relational based quality measures, which normally look at correlation features between the pixels of original and reconstructed image. They are given as

$$SC = \sum_{j=1}^{M} \sum_{k=1}^{N} X(j,k)^2 / \sum_{j=1}^{M} \sum_{k=1}^{N} \hat{X}(j,k)^2 \tag{7}$$

$$IF = 1 - \sum_{j=1}^{M}\sum_{k=1}^{N}[X(j,k) - \hat{X}(j,k)^2]/\sum_{j=1}^{M}\sum_{k=1}^{N}[X(j,k)^2] \qquad (8)$$

$$NK = \sum_{j=1}^{M}\sum_{k=1}^{N}[X(j,k)\hat{X}(j,k)\ ]/\sum_{j=1}^{M}\sum_{k=1}^{N}[X(j,k)^2] \qquad (9)$$

Normally SC, IF and NK are in the range of 0 to 1, very near or one is the best.

4.3 Mean Structural Similarity Index (MSSIM) and Universal Quality Index (UQI)

Zhou Wang *et al.* [17] in their paper proposed a new quality measures, viz mean structural similarity index and Universal Quality Index. This compares local patterns of pixel intensities, which have been normalized for luminance and contrast. It is given by

$$SSIM = \frac{(2\mu_x\mu_y + C_1)(2\sigma_{xy} + C_2)}{(\mu_x^2 + \mu_y^2 + C_1)(\sigma_x^2 + \sigma_y^2 + C_2)} \qquad (10)$$

Where μ and σ are the mean and variance respectively, x and y are for original and reconstructed images. The Mean Structural Similarity index is calculated by taking mean of SSIM and UQI is calculated by substituting C_1 and $C_2 = 0$.

The Mean Opinion Score also plays an important role in the analysis, since many times measures like PSNR do not give clear indication of quality.

5   Experiments and Results

The experimentation was carried out on Pentium 4, 1.73GHz with 512 M RAM machine and using MATLAB 7.1 with Image Processing and Neural Network Toolboxes. The size of codebook is taken be 1K, since it gives better performance and cost effective in today's VLSI era. The size of images are taken to be 256x256.

The codebook was designed using Lena image, but as discussed it shows poor compression performance. The codebook is designed using a training image specially developed to enhance the performance. Selective training, training is done by varying different parameters of SOFM network based on the contents of the input image blocks. For sharp edges, network is not completely trained, for not variation in gray scale, it's completely trained. The decision for training were taken from the rigorous.

Experimentation and observations regarding network behavior for different inputs.

Being texture is important in medical images; textural analysis is performed to observe effect of compression on it. In our experimentation run length encoding (RLE) for the addresses (indexes) is applied in order to achieve further compression. The results with our training image codebook are presented in Table 1. Images used are CT scan of abdomen, head, angio, MRI, Ultrasound of abdomen lymphoma, cardiomypathy, liver cyst and X-ray of chest and fractures. Fig. 2 shows the original and decompressed images.. The comparison for file size with baseline JPEG is presented in Fig. 1.

Table 1. Quality analysis of images of 256x256 size compressed with our enhanced codebook of 1 K size. CR: Compression ratio.

Images	MSE	PSNR	AD	SC	NK	IF	MSSIM	UQI	CR
CTscan	32.204	33.05	4.68	0.902	0.993	0.64	0.96616	0.508	25.15
CThead	28.648	33.56	4.4	0.932	0.978	0.65	0.96801	0.423	27.02
CTabdomen	28.05	33.65	3.6	0.995	1	0.88	0.95849	0.968	13.3
CTangio	47.769	31.34	5.69	1.00	0.998	0.81	0.97483	0.995	13.01
MRI	32.249	33.05	4.52	0.953	0.995	0.73	0.97585	0.62	21.58
MRIknee	33.033	32.94	4.35	1.00	0.997	0.87	0.95884	0.994	14.71
Ultrasound	33.595	32.87	3.8	1.00	0.999	0.87	0.96268	0.996	13.61
Ultsnd abdolymphoma	32.494	33.01	3.83	0.956	1.00	0.76	0.95983	0.622	19.88
Ultsnd cardioiomypa	20.619	34.99	2.91	0.896	0.997	0.68	0.93246	0.327	32.42
Ultsndlivercyst	30.202	33.33	3.76	0.941	1.00	0.72	0.93761	0.352	24.01
Xray abnormalchest	10.23	38.03	1.69	0.999	1.00	0.96	0.99486	1	12.43
Xray normalchest	35.322	32.65	3.93	0.999	0.999	0.86	0.96828	0.997	12.52
Xrayfract	65.775	29.95	7.18	0.916	0.982	0.68	0.96767	1.0	14.41

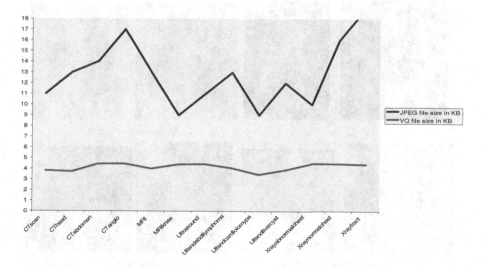

Fig. 1. Comparison of JPEG and VQ file sizes

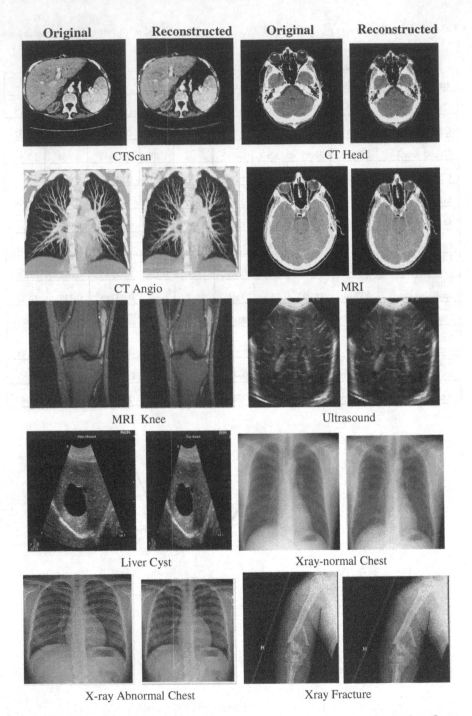

Fig. 2. Original and reconstructed (decompressed) images used in experimentation (Images courtesy: www.philips.com and www.wikipedia.com)

6 Discussion and Conclusions

From Table 1 it has been observed that the PSNR is adequate but the structural content and mean structural similarity index is significantly improved. The normalized correlation coefficient is approaching to one as well as except few images the image fidelity is also good. Even though not presented, the results are much better than other VQ methods. The images shown are without any post processing. The post-processing can also used for smoothing of the images, but it may not work well with all images. Another approach tried was, the decompressed image was applied to the well-trained backpropogation neural network, and loss is predicted out. It improves the quality measures by 10 %. From Fig.1, it is clear that VQ takes less space in the i.e. in the range of 3-4 KB which is nearly 3 times less than JPEG. The JPEG image used is baseline. If 50% quality JPEG is used, the file size range from 5-6KB and quality is lightly less than the proposed VQ. The contrast in the texture is degraded in compression and needs to be recovered by proper post processing.

References

1. Gray, R.M.: Vector quantization. IEEE ASSP Magazine 1, 4–29 (1984)
2. Nasrabadi, N.M., King, R.A.: Image coding using vector quantization: A review. IEEE Trans. on Communications 36(8), 957–971 (1988)
3. Gersho, A., Gray, R.M.: Vector Quantization and Signal Compression. Kluwer, Norwell, MA (1992)
4. Linde, Y., Buzo, A., Gray, R.M.: An algorithm for vector quantizer design. IEEE Trans.on Communications 28(1), 84–95 (1980)
5. Nasrabadi, N.M., Feng, Y.: Image Compression using address vector Quantization. IEEE Trans. On Communications 38(2), 2166–2173 (1990)
6. Dony, R., Haykin, S.: Neural Network approaches to image compression. Proceedings of IEEE 83(2), 288–303 (1995)
7. Kohonen, T.: The Self Organizing Maps Invited Paper. Proceedings of IEEE 78(9), 464–1480 (1990)
8. Kohonen, T.: Self-Organization and Associative Memory, 2nd edn. Springer, Heidelberg (1988)
9. Laha, A., Pal, N.R., Chanda, B.: Design of Vector Quantizer for image compression using Self Organizing Feature Map and Surface Fitting. IEEE Trans. On Image processing 13, 1291–1302 (2004)
10. Wei, H.-C., et al.: A kohonen based structured codebook design for image compression. IEEE Tencon Beijing (1993)
11. Durai, A., Rao, E.A.: An improved image compression approach with self organizing map using cumulative distribution function. GVIP Journal 6(2) (2006)
12. Cazuguel, G., Czihó, A., Solaiman, B.: Christian Roux Medical Image Compression and Feature Extraction using Vector Quantization, Self-Organizing Maps and Quad tree Decomposition Information Technology Applications in Biomedicine. In: ITAB IEEE Conference, pp. 127–132 (May 1998)
13. Cazuguel, G., Czihó, A., Solaiman, B., Roux, C.: Christian Roux Medical image compression and characterization using Vector Quantization: an application of Self-organizing Maps and quadtree decomposition, Information Technology Applications in Biomedicine, 1998. In: ITAB IEEE Conference (1998)

14. Eskicioglu, A.M., Fisher, P.S.: Image Quality Measures and their performance. IEEE Transactions on Communications 43(12) (December 1995)
15. Mrak, M., Grgic, S., Grgic, M.: Picture Quality Measures in Image Compression Systems. In: EUROCON 2003, Ljuijana, Slovenia (2003)
16. Avicibas, I., Sankur, B., Sayood, K.: Statistical Evaluation of Image Quality Measures. Journal of Electronic Imaging 11(2), 206–223 (2002)
17. Wang, Z., Bovik, A.C., Sheikh, H.R., Simoncelli, E.P.: Image Quality Assessment: From Error Visibility to Structural Similarity. IEEE Transactions on Image processing 13(4) (April 2004)
18. Hludov, S.: Chr. Meinel DICOM Image Compression.
19. Ramakrishnan, B., Shriram, N.: Compression of DICOM images based on wavelets and SPIHT for telemedicine applications.

Indicator and Calibration Material for Microcalcifications in Dual-Energy Mammography

Xi Chen[1], Xuanqin Mou[1], and Lei Zhang[2]

[1] Institute of Image Processing and Pattern Recognition, Xi'an Jiaotong University
Xi'an, Shaanxi, 710049, China
chenxi@mailst.xjtu.edu.cn, xqmou@mail.xjtu.edu.cn
[2] Deptartment of Computing, Hong Kong Polytechnic University, Hung Hom,
Kowloon, Hong Kong
clszhang@comp.polyu.edu.hk

Abstract. Dual-energy mammography can suppress the contrast between adipose and glandular tissues and improve the detectability of microcalcifications (MCs). In the published papers, MCs were calibrated by aluminum and identified by their thickness. However, the variety of compositions of MCs causes the variety of attenuation differences between MCs and MC calibration material which bring about huge calculation errors. In our study, we selected calcium carbonate and calcium phosphate as the most suitable MC calibration materials and the correction coefficient was reasonably determined. Area density was used as MC indicator instead of thickness. Therefore, the calculation errors from MC calibration materials can be reduced a lot and the determination of MCs will become possible.

1 Introduction

MCs are one of the earliest and the main indicator of breast cancer which is a deadly disease that adversely affects the lives of far too many people, primarily women. Thus the visualization and detection of MCs in mammograms play a crucial role in reducing the rate of mortality of breast cancer.

MCs are often microscopic and the size of 50 μm to 300 μm is of great importance in clinical diagnosis. The usual ones, mostly seen on mammograms, are not larger than 500 μm. Although MCs are small in size, they have greater x-ray attenuation than the surrounding breast tissue. This makes MCs relatively apparent on homogeneous soft-tissue backgrounds. However, visualization of MCs could be obscured in mammograms by overlapping tissue structures. Therefore, the small MCs can be extremely difficult to discriminate even if they have adequate intrinsic detail signal to noise ratio (SNR).

In dual-energy digital mammography, high- and low-energy images are acquired and synthesized to suppress the contrast between adipose and glandular

D. Zhang (Ed.): ICMB 2008, LNCS 4901, pp. 265–272, 2007.

tissues and improve the detectability of MCs. Under ideal imaging conditions, the thickness of MC and the glandular ratio can be well determined. However, quantitative dual-energy imaging can be influenced by many factors in practical application.

In clinical dual-energy mammography, imaging object is human breast; while in calibration measurements, only phantoms of breast-tissue-equivalent materials can be used. The composition and density differences between the calibration materials and human breast bring the differences of attenuation which lead to the calculation errors in dual-energy imaging. However, this type of error had not been discussed before our investigation [1]. In Ref.[1], we analyzed the MC thickness errors from calibration phantoms of glandular and adipose tissues. This analysis shows that the MC thickness errors from calibration phantoms of glandular and adipose range from dozens to thousands of microns which decrease the precise of dual-energy calculations seriously. Hence, we consider that the attenuation differences between MCs and *MC calibration material* may also bring about MC thickness errors. However, the errors of MC calibration are very different from glandular and adipose calibration. For an imaged person, the composition of MCs in breast is in diversity, so the attenuation differences between MCs and MCs calibration materials are variable. For the given MC calibration material and the given MC composition, the dual-energy calculation result can be corrected by a parameter *correction coefficient* [2]. How to select this correction coefficient for different MC compositions is still a problem.

The published papers showed that the works mentioned above had not been carried on. In most investigations [3], people always adopted aluminum as MCs and MC calibration material simultaneity. However, such ideal conditions could not be obtained in practical dual-energy mammography. In some investigations [2][4], aluminum was adopted as MC calibration material and the only one MC composition, calcite ($CaCO_3$), were investigated. Then, the resultant MC thickness was simply corrected by one coefficient between 0.6 and 0.8 due to the attenuation differences between aluminum and calcite. On the other hand, all of investigators adopted thickness as the assessment indicator of MCs.

Actually, the formation and composition of MCs are complicated. Types of MCs have been identified by means of pathologic examination in breast tissue and have been described in the pathology literature [5]. Apatite ($Ca_5(PO_4)_3(OH)$), calcium oxalate (CaC_2O_4)and calcite ($CaCO_3$) are the three main compositions of MCs.

MCs are the most important parameter for early diagnosis of breast cancer. The determination of the MC appearance is a metrics issue which should have an accurate and uniform criterion. In the published paper, the criteria, used to differentiate MCs from background, is MC thickness. However, MC thickness used for determination may not be a good choice since the densities of different types of MCs are far apart.

In this paper, we adopted area density instead of thickness as the indicator of MCs, studied different MC calibration materials and selected the most suitable ones for MC calibration.

2   Physical Model

In mammography, the breast is compressed to the thickness T which is to be composed of adipose tissue (thickness t_a), glandular tissue (thickness t_g) and MC (thickness t_c). As the total breast thickness T is known and the contribution of MCs to the total breast thickness can be ignored, the three unknowns of t_a, t_g, t_c can be expressed as two: glandular ratio $g = t_g/(t_a + t_g) \cong t_g/T$ and MC thickness t_c.

In dual-energy imaging calculations, a reference signal I_r is needed to increase the dynamic range of the logarithmic intensity value. Now we define the exposure data f as the log-value of ratio of the transmitted exposure I and reference signal I_r. The low- and high-energy log-value $f_l(t_c, g)$, $f_h(t_c, g)$ are measured independently using x-ray beams of different kVps:

$$
\begin{cases}
f_l = \ln(I_{rl}) \\
\quad - \ln\{\int P_{0l}(E) \exp[-\mu_a(E)T - g(\mu_g(E) - \mu_a(E))T - \mu_c(E)t_c] Q(E)dE\} \\
f_h = \ln(I_{rh}) \\
\quad - \ln\{\int P_{0h}(E) \exp[-\mu_a(E)T - g(\mu_g(E) - \mu_a(E))T - \mu_c(E)t_c] Q(E)dE\}
\end{cases}
\tag{1}
$$

$\mu_a(E)$, $\mu_g(E)$ and $\mu_c(E)$ are the linear attenuation coefficients of adipose tissue, glandular tissue and MCs, respectively. $Q(E)$ is the detector response.

The goal of dual-energy mammography is to convert the log-value functions $f_l(t_c, g)$ and $f_h(t_c, g)$ to MC thickness $t_c(f_l, f_h)$ and $g(f_l, f_h)$. Polynomials are often used to describe the relationship between (f_l, f_h) and (t_c, g) in diagnostic dual-energy imaging calculations. In this paper, cubic polynomials were used to describe the inverse-map functions:

$$
\begin{cases}
t_c = k_{c0} + k_{c1}f_l + k_{c2}f_h + k_{c3}f_l^2 + k_{c4}f_h^2 + + k_{c5}f_l f_h + k_{c6}f_l^3 + k_{c7}f_h^3 \\
g = k_{g0} + k_{g1}f_l + k_{g2}f_h + k_{g3}f_l^2 + k_{g4}f_h^2 + + k_{g5}f_l f_h + k_{g6}f_l^3 + k_{g7}f_h^3
\end{cases}
\tag{2}
$$

Coefficients $k_{ij}(i = c, g; j = 0, 1, \cdots, 7)$ are approximated numerically by least-squares technique according to calibration data. The attenuation differences between calibration materials and imaged human breast bring about errors of dual-energy calculation. When using calibration materials, in Eq.1, $f_l(t_c, g)$ and $f_h(t_c, g)$ are log intensities of imaged human breast and $\mu_a(E)$, $\mu_g(E)$ and $\mu_c(E)$ are are attenuation coefficients of calibration materials for adipose, glandular and MCs. And then, the computational results t_c' and g' have errors Δt_c and Δg. We have derived the error expressions [6]:

$$
\begin{cases}
\beta_l^c \times \Delta t_c + \beta_l^g \times T \times \Delta g = \alpha_l^c \times t_c + \alpha_l^g \times T \times g + \alpha_l^a \times T \times (1 - g) \\
\beta_h^c \times \Delta t_c + \beta_h^g \times T \times \Delta g = \alpha_h^c \times t_c + \alpha_h^g \times T \times g + \alpha_h^a \times T \times (1 - g)
\end{cases}
\tag{3}
$$

where

$$
\beta_{l,h}^c = \frac{\int R_{l,h}(E)\mu_c^{ph}(E)dE}{\int R_{l,h}(E)dE} \qquad \beta_{l,h}^g = \frac{\int R_{l,h}(E)(\mu_g^{ph}(E) - \mu_a^{ph}(E))dE}{\int R_{l,h}(E)dE}
$$

$$
\alpha_{l,h}^{a,g,c} = \frac{\int R_{l,h}(E)\Delta\mu_{a,g,c}(E)dE}{\int R_{l,h}(E)dE}
$$

$$R_{l,h}(E) = P_{0l,0h}(E)\exp\left[-\mu_a^{ph}(E)T - g(\mu_g^{ph}(E) - \mu_a^{ph}(E))T - \mu_c^{ph}(E)t_c\right]Q(E)$$

$\mu_a^{ph}(E)$, $\mu_g^{ph}(E)$, $\mu_c^{ph}(E)$ are attenuation coefficients of calibration materials for adipose, glandular and MCs.$\Delta\mu_{a,g,c}(E)$ are differences of attenuation coefficients between human breast and calibration materials for adipose, glandular and MCs. The deduction procedure was detailed in Ref.[6].

In Ref. [1][6], we have investigated the errors introduced by calibration phantoms of glandular and adipose. In this paper, only the errors introduced by MC calibration material are investigated, so α_l^a, α_h^a, α_l^g and α_h^g are zeros. Eq.3 can be rewritten as:

$$\begin{cases} \beta_l^c \times \Delta t_c + \beta_l^g \times T \times \Delta g = \alpha_l^c \times t_c \\ \beta_h^c \times \Delta t_c + \beta_h^g \times T \times \Delta g = \alpha_h^c \times t_c \end{cases} \tag{4}$$

3   Traditional MC Calibration

In traditional dual-energy calculation for mammography, aluminum was used for MC calibration and thickness was adopted as the indicator of MCs. The ratios of linear attenuation coefficients of aluminum and MCs, $\mu_{Al}/\mu_{calcite}$ and $\mu_{Al}/\mu_{calcium-oxalate}$, are about 0.6–0.8 for energies between 20 keV and 50 keV. Then, the calculation result t_c' was corrected by a coefficient between 0.6 and 0.8 [2][4].

Table 1 lists the percentage errors induced by aluminum calibration using the traditional method, the true MC thickness ranges from 100 μm–500 μm with glandular ratio 60%, and correction coefficient is 0.7. Three types of MCs were investigated, apatite, calcium oxalate and calcite. The imaging conditions in this paper are as same as those in papers of Kappadath and Shaw [2][4] which are in accordance with the clinical equipments. The x-ray spectra used for low- and high-energy measurements were 25kVp and 50kVp, respectively, using Mo anode and 0.03 mm Mo filter. The spectra data were taken from *Handbook of Mammographic X-ray Spectra* [7] with resolution of 1 keV. The detector consisted of a CsI:Tl converter layer coupled with an aSi:H+TFT flat-panel detector. All photons transmitted through the imaged object were assumed to be absorbed completely in the perfectly efficient converter layer. The elemental compositions of glandular and adipose tissue in a human breast were determined by Hammerstein [8]. The breast thickness is 5cm. Mass attenuation coefficients of the materials in this paper were computed by XCOM software from NIST [9].

In Table 1, the errors introduced by aluminum are big. When MC is calcium oxalate, the error is about −14%. When MC is calcite or apatite, the error is about 71% or 160%. Such huge errors will make the calculated MC thickness nonsense. When differentiating MCs from background, we always need a thickness threshold. However, the heavily variable errors will make the selection of threshold impossible.

Table 1. Percentage errors $\Delta t_c / t_c (\%)$ by aluminum calibration, correction coefficient 0.7

MC	MC thickness (μm)				
	100	200	300	400	500
CaC_2O_4	-14.55	-14.30	-14.06	-13.82	-13.59
$CaCO_3$	70.64	71.12	71.60	72.06	72.50
$Ca_5(PO_4)_3(OH)$	159.0	159.6	160.2	160.7	161.3

4 New Indicator and Calibration Materials

4.1 New Indicator for MCs

As seen in section 3, the calculation errors are huge and vary heavily when aluminum was used for calibration, that make the selection of threshold and determination of MCs impossible. The better calibration material for MCs must be found out. First, we noticed that thickness is not a good indicator for MC assessment.

For the three types of MCs, the mass attenuation coefficient of apatite is the biggest, while the calcium oxalate's is the smallest. However, the density of apatite is also the biggest, 3.06 g/cm^3, while the density of calcite is 2.71 g/cm^3 and calcium oxalate is 2.20 g/cm^3. Therefore, the differences of linear attenuation coefficients of the three types of MCs are bigger than those of mass attenuation coefficients. When dual-energy mammography imaging , we have no knowledge of the exact composition of MCs, so the attenuation differences between MCs and calibration materials would not be known and eliminated. If we adopted thickness as MC indicator, the big differences of linear attenuation coefficients will cause big calculation errors. On the contrary, the differences of mass attenuation coefficients of the three types of MCs are smaller. If we adopted area density ($area\ density = thickness \times density$) as MC indicator, mass attenuation coefficients should be used. The smaller differences of mass attenuation coefficients will cause smaller calculation errors. So area density is used as MC indicator in this investigation.

4.2 Correction Coefficient Determination

Considering MCs composed of calcium compound, we select aluminum, calcium, calcium phosphate, calcium oxalate and calcium carbonate as the candidates for MC calibration material. The correction coefficient is also necessary. The determination of correction coefficient should balance the differences of mass attenuation coefficient of different MC compositions and then the whole calculation errors will be decreased.

The procedure of correction coefficient determination is followed. For example, calcium is the candidate material. First, we calculate the ratios of mass attenuation coefficients between calcium and MCs. The ratios change as energy varying. Since the primary energy in dual-energy mammography is in 16–40keV, the ratios were studied in this energy range. In the range of 16–40keV, the ratio $\mu_{Ca}/\mu_{apatite}$ is 1.996–1.848, then we get the mean ratio 1.942. In the same way, the mean ratio is 2.700 for $\mu_{Ca}/\mu_{calcium-oxalate}$, 2.212 for $\mu_{Ca}/\mu_{calcite}$. Secondly, we average the three mean ratios to get the correction coefficient 2.285. The correction coefficient for each candidate material was computed and listed in Table 2.

4.3   New MC Calibration Materials

Now, we can select the new MC calibration material from these candidates. For each candidate material, we calculated α_l^c and α_h^c in Eq.4 for each of the fifty combinations of (t_c, g). Glandular ratio was in ten steps 5%, 15%, 25%, 35%, 45%, 55%, 65%, 75%, 85% and 95%, MC thickness was in five steps 100, 200, 300, 400 and 500μm. S_l and S_h are the sums α_l^c of α_h^c and of the fifty (t_c, g) for the given MC type, respectively. SS_l is the sum of absolute values of the three S_l. SS_h is those of the three S_h. The sums, SS_l and SS_h, are listed in Table 2, respectively. We also considered three added candidate materials, they are calcium phosphate, calcium oxalate and calcium carbonate without coefficient correction.We adopted SS_l and SS_h as the indicators of the most suitable calibration material. Calcium carbonate without coefficient correction has the smallest SS_l and SS_h, so we take calcium carbonate as the most suitable calibration material for all MCs. Calcium oxalate and calcium phosphate without coefficient corrections have the biggest SS_l and SS_h, they are not suitable for MC calibration. SS_l and SS_h of the other five candidate materials, including aluminum, are little more than those of calcium carbonate. So these five candidates can also be considered as the potential calibration materials.

Table 2. Correction coefficient, SS_l and SS_h for each candidate material

Candidate material	Correction coefficient	SS_l	SS_h
$CaCO_3$	1.0000	111.1	22.87
Ca	2.2848	112.6	26.30
$Ca_5(PO_4)_3(OH)$	1.1762	117.6	25.47
$CaCO_3$	1.0328	121.4	25.21
Al	0.6358	126.1	24.20
CaC_2O_4	0.8465	126.2	24.80
$Ca_5(PO_4)_3(OH)$	1.0000	159.8	32.57
CaC_2O_4	1.0000	173.8	36.16

5   Experiments and Discussion

We evaluated the percentage errors introduced by MC calibration materials here. Area density was used as MC indicator; six MC calibration materials were adopted.

In Table 3, calcium carbonate was used as MC calibration material. The calibration error is about -38% for MC of calcium oxalate, 34% for MC of apatite, zero for MC of calcite. Compare the data in Table 3 with data in Table 1, the maximum error in Table 1 is 161% which is unacceptable, while the maximum in Table 3 is 38% which is in a reasonable error range. In Table 3, errors for calcium oxalate have increased a little, but errors for calcium and apatite have decreased a lot. The error range in Table 3 is acceptable. Here, we take the *whole error* which is the sum of absolute values of the errors for the three types of MCs for comparison. The whole error of calcium carbonate calibration in Table 3 is $38\% + 34\% = 72\%$, while the whole error in Table 1 is 246%. The calculation errors introduced by MC calibration materials have been reduced greatly when using calcium carbonate for calibration and area density as indicator.

Comparing the whole errors of the six candidate materials, we found that the whole error in Table 3 is the smallest, so calcium carbonate is the best calibration material which agrees with the conclusion in section 4. In Table 4, calcium phosphate with correction coefficient was used as MC calibration material. The whole error in Table 4 is 76%, just a little more than that in Table 3. However, the error for apatite in Table 4 is about 18%, which is smaller than that in Table 3 which is 34%. Apatite is the chief component of MCs. If we adopt calcium phosphate as calibration material with correction coefficient 1.1762, the error for apatite will be reduced a lot. And then, the whole accuracy of MC determination will be increased in view of the importance of apatite. On the other hand, the often used calibration material aluminum has the highest whole error in these six candidate materials and its maximum error is 110% even after its correction coefficient was optimized, which means that aluminum is not suitable for MC calibration.

Table 3. Percentage errors $\Delta t_c/t_c(\%)$ by calcium carbonate calibration without correction

MC	MC thickness (μm)				
	100	200	300	400	500
CaC_2O_4	-38.25	-38.19	-38.13	-38.07	-38.01
$CaCO_3$	0.0000	0.0000	0.0000	0.0000	0.0000
$Ca_5(PO_4)_3(OH)$	34.32	34.14	33.96	33.80	33.63

Table 4. Percentage errors $\Delta t_c/t_c(\%)$ by ccalcium phosphate calibration with correction coefficient 1.1762

MC	MC thickness (μm)				
	100	200	300	400	500
CaC_2O_4	-45.97	-45.88	-45.78	-45.70	-45.61
$CaCO_3$	-12.46	-12.37	-12.28	-12.20	-12.11
$Ca_5(PO_4)_3(OH)$	17.62	17.62	17.62	17.62	17.62

6   Conclusions

Calculation errors introduced by MC calibration material were analyzed in this paper. The calculation errors are huge and variable seriously when adopting aluminum for MC calibration and using thickness as MC indicator, which is currently used in published literatures. In our investigation, we selected calcium carbonate and calcium phosphate as the most suitable MC calibration materials and the correction coefficient was reasonably determined. Area density was used as MC indicator instead of thickness. Therefore, the calculation errors from MC calibration are reduced a lot and the determination of MCs will become possible.

Acknowledgments. The project is partially supported by National Nature Science Fund of China (No.60472004 and No.60551003), and the fund of the Ministry of Education of China (No. 106143).

References

1. Mou, X.Q., Chen, X.: Error Analysis of Calibration Materials on Dual-Energy Mammography. In: Accepted by the 10th International Conference on Medical Image Computing and Computer Assisted Intervention, Brisbane, Australia,
2. Kappadath, S.C., Shaw, C.C.: Dual-energy Digital mammography: Calibration and Inverse-mapping Techniques to Estimate Calcification Thickness and Glandular-tissue Ratio. Med. Phys. 30, 1110–1117 (2003)
3. Kappadath, S.C., Shaw, C.C.: Quantitative Evaluation of Dual-energy Digital Mammography for Calcification Imaging. Phys. Med. Biol. 49, 2563–2576 (2004)
4. Kappadath, S.C., Shaw, C.C.: Dual-energy Digital Mammography for Calcification Imaging: Scatter and Nonuniformity Corrections. Med. Phys. 32, 3395–3408 (2005)
5. Fandos-Morera, A., Prats-Esteve, M., Sutas-Sotera, J.M., Traveria-Cros, A.: Breast Tumors: Composition of Microcalcifications. Radiology 169, 325–327 (1988)
6. Mou, X.Q., Chen, X.: Influence of Calibration Phantom on Dual-Energy Mammography. Submitted to Phys. Med. Biol.
7. Fewell, T.R., Shuping, R.E.: Handbook of Mammographic X-ray Spectra. HEW Publication (FDA) Washington. D.C (1978)
8. Hammerstein, G.R., Miller, D.W., White, D.R., Masterson, M.E., Woodard, H.Q., Laughlin, J.S.: Absorbed Radiation Dose in Mammography. Radiology 130, 485–491 (1979)
9. XCOM, http://physics.nist.gov/PhysRefdata/Xcom/Text/XCOM.html

Tongue Image Matching Using Color and Texture

Zhenhua Guo

Shenzhen Graduate School of Harbin Institute of Technology, China
denis@hit.edu.cn

Abstract. Tongue image matching is an important part for a tongue diagnosis system. Unlike common pattern recognition problems, it is hard to define the ground truth for tongue image matching because visual inspection of tongue by doctors is determined by the experience and knowledge of them. Here we propose to use, Mean Rank, as an objective and scientific criterion to evaluate matching performance. Instigating from color demosaicking, a new color texture operator, Primary Difference Signal Local Binary Pattern is proposed. The matching performance is evaluated on color, gray-scale and color texture, and fusion of color and texture features.

1 Introduction

Tongue diagnosis is a method to analyze diseases by observing tongue, which is composed of observing tongue's color and shape and observing tongue coating's color and texture, etc. It holds many advantages: non-invasive, simple and cheap. However, tongue diagnosis is based on clinician's experience and knowledge. The examination outcome could not be described scientifically and quantitatively.

Quantitative analysis of tongue images by using image analysis was firstly attempted by the University of Science and Technology of China in 1985[1]. Since then automatic tongue diagnosis has drawn more and more attention [2-8].

Content-based image retrieval (CBIR) make used of image features, such as color and texture, to index images with minimal human intervention [9]. Tongue image matching, a kind of CBIR techniques, could play an important role in tongue diagnosis [6]. It could be used to locate medical images in large database; it could be used to help rookie doctor compare old cases and make final decisions, etc. Although, many papers related tongue diagnosis have been published, tongue image matching is a less explored field. To our knowledge, there are very few papers related with this field [6-8]. However, [7-8] are using the whole tongue image as the query image. According Traditional Chinese Medicine (TCM) theory, different regions on tongue may provide different information, thus using the whole tongue image instead of small blocks may lost some valuable information. Li [6] proposed an objective criterion to evaluate different color metric' performance; however the criteria sometimes may fail, which is showed in Section 4. Also, the author did not compare texture feature, which could play an important role in tongue matching [7]. In this paper, we proposed a new tongue image matching performance evaluation criteria, Mean Rank (MR), which is rooted from mean match percentile [10]. According to

D. Zhang (Ed.): ICMB 2008, LNCS 4901, pp. 273–281, 2007.

this framework, experiments of tongue image matching using color, texture and fusion are reported and analyzed.

The rest of the paper is organized as follows. Section 2 reviews some color matching algorithms. Some texture features are introduced in Section 3, and a new color texture operator Primary Difference Signal Local Binary Pattern (PDSLBP) which is rooted from color demosaicking is proposed. MR is proposed in Section 4. Some experiments are reported and analyzed in Section 5. Finally, some conclusions are drawn in Section 6.

2   Color Based Matching Algorithms

Here we reviewed some commonly used color based image matching algorithms.

The color histogram of a color image is a three-dimensional array of integers storing the frequency of occurrence of the color pixels having the three color attributes as specified by the histogram bins.

One-dimensional projected histogram is a kind of simple representation for the three-dimension color histogram. The relation between projected histogram p^c with the color histogram P of one image is given by:

$$p_k^1 = \sum_{i=1}^{L}\sum_{j=1}^{L}P_{ijk}, p_k^2 = \sum_{i=1}^{L}\sum_{k=1}^{L}P_{ijk}, p_k^3 = \sum_{j=1}^{L}\sum_{k=1}^{L}P_{ijk} \tag{1}$$

Li [6] proposed a new metric, sorted metric, to compute the distance between two images. Instead of comparing each pixel in an image with all pixels in another image, all the pixels in each image are sorted first by one color channel, and then the comparison is performed on the sorted pixel lists. The *L1* distance norm is defined as:

$$D2_s(x, y) = \sum_{i=1}^{N}\sum_{c=1}^{3} \} x_{ic}^s - y_{ic}^s \mid \tag{2}$$

where x^s and y^s be the sorted pixels of image x and y in an ascending order of the color coordinates and N is the number of pixels in the image.

When we can take images as a very high dimension point, an intuitive metric is to compute point-to-point distance from image **x** and image **y**. However, the above method is very time consuming, about O(N^2). Alternatively, a point-to-cluster-center distance between x and y is proposed:

$$D2_c(x, y) = \sum_{i=1}^{N}\sum_{c=1}^{3} \left\{ [x_{ic} - m_c(y)]^2 + [y_{ic} - m_c(x)]^2 \right\} \tag{3}$$

$m_c(x)$ and $m_c(y)$ are the mean values of the cth color channel in images **x** and **y**.

A more simple and fast color coordinate distance is based on joint image statistics, which include mean and standard deviation value. The distance in *L1* norm is as:

$$D2_j(x, y) = \sum_{c=1}^{3} \left\{ |m_c(x) - m_c(y)| + |s_c(x) - s_c(y)| \right\} \tag{4}$$

$s_c(x)$ and $s_c(y)$ are the standard deviation values of the cth color channel in images.

3 Texture Based Matching Algorithms

In this section, we briefly introduce some widely used texture operator and their matching algorithms.

As gray-scale texture operators, the Gabor filter [13] and the Local Binary Pattern (LBP) [13] were selected because they have been applied successfully on texture classification and image retrieval.

A Gabor filter bank with four scales and six orientations was used [13]. A vector which is composed of mean and standard value of each filtered input image is used as representative feature.

A *L1* norm like distance between image **x** and **y** is utilized as dissimilarity measurement:

$$d(x, y) = \sum_{m=0}^{3} \sum_{n=0}^{5} \left\{ \left| \frac{\mu_{mn}^x - \mu_{mn}^y}{\alpha(\mu_{mn})} \right| + \left| \frac{\sigma_{mn}^x - \sigma_{mn}^y}{\alpha(\sigma_{mn})} \right| \right\} \tag{5}$$

where each μ_{mn} and σ_{mn} represent the mean and standard deviation of the input image convolved by the Gabor filter at scale m and orientation n, $\alpha(\mu_{mn})$ and $\alpha(\sigma_{mn})$ are the standard deviation of the features over the entire database.

The LBP is a global texture feature based on statistics gray scale texture primitive [13]. In the following experiments, $LBP_{P,R}$ stands for the variation of LBP, where R denoted the radius and P denoted the number of points nearby. Multi-scale LBP is created by concatenating the histograms produced by different operators. For example, $LBP_{(8,1+16,2)}$ stands for a multi-scale operator which is fusion of $LBP_{8,1}$ and $LBP_{16,2}$. To reduce dimension and speed up matching, a "uniform" LPB is proposed [13], such as $LBP_{16,2}^{u2}$ contains 243 bins only. For the dissimilarity measure of LBP, to compare different algorithms fairly, the L1 norm and L2 norm are used here.

Most gray-scale texture operators can be straightforwardly applied on color image by combining the results of channel-wise operations. The feature vectors obtained from different channels are simply concatenated into a color texture description.

Opponent color Gabor filter (OCGabor) [13], which takes inter channel into consideration. In addition to unichrome features derived from filtered color channels, OCGabor also uses differences between filtered color channels to mimic the opponent color processing of eye. The unichrome color feature is computed one each color channel by every filter, there are totally 36 (3*4*3) unichrome features. While Opponent color features are cal-culated from the difference of filtered color channels, the differences are calculated between different color channels, same orientations, same or adjacent scales. Thus the total number of opponent color features is 84 (3*4*7).

The unichrome and opponent color features are concatenated into one vector. For computing distance, a L2 norm like distance with feature variances is used:

$$d(s, m) = \sum_{i=0}^{N-1} \frac{(s_i - m_i)^2}{\sigma_i^2} \tag{6}$$

where σ_i^2 is the variance of feature i.

The LBP operator can be extended to color image to form opponent color LBP (OCLBP) [13] in a similar way. For an input image, separated color channel LBP features are extracted first. Then each pair of color channels is used to extract opponent color pattern. When extracting opponent LBP, the center pixel for a neighborhood and the neighborhood itself are taken from different color channels. Some opponent pairs, such as R-G and G-R are highly correlated, only half of opponent pairs are used in fact. Finally, six LBP histograms are concatenated into one feature vector.

PDS which is denoted by (8) has been applied on color demosaicking and has achieved very good SNR [12]. The correlations of green-red and green-blue are very consistent in the image, and $\Delta_{g,r}$ and $\Delta_{g,b}$ could be assumed as smooth signals. This instigated us to apply LBP operator on PDS directly.

$$\Delta_{g,r}(x, y) = G(x, y) - R(x, y); \quad \Delta_{g,b}(x, y) = G(x, y) - B(x, y) \tag{7}$$

Similar to OCLBP, three unichrome LBP features are extracted first. After getting two new pseudo-color channels by subtracting G from R and G from B, LBP operator is applied on these channels. Finally, five LBP histograms are concatenated into one feature vector.

4 MR

Unlike many pattern recognition problems, it is hard to define ground truth for tongue image matching. Usually, ground truth is based on TCM doctors' judgments [7-8]. However, different TCM doctors may have different judgments on the same block. In same cases, the deviation is up to 40% [6].

Li [6] proposed to employ the consensus of all metrics in all color spaces together with the ranked percentile pairs as the ground truth. Totally 189 tongue blocks were used in their research, therefore there were 17,955 (189*188/2) distance between these blocks. For example, a threshold for 5% match is obtained by sorting these 17,955 distances to find the 898th smallest distance. All those image pairs with distance smaller than this threshold value are declared as matches. However, this criterion will work well only when the following two assumptions meet:

1) Each metric's distance is really related to dissimilarity between images;
2) Each metric's discriminative capacity is comparable.

Fig 1 and Fig 2 show an example that this criterion may have problem sometimes.

From Table 1&2, we could see that if we set a strict threshold, Fig. 2-a) and b), Fig. 2-a) and c) could not be declared as matches; but if we set a loose threshold, Fig. 1-a) and Fig.1-d) could be declared as a match. Thus, declared matches using above method may include some mismatches or miss some true matches.

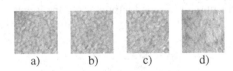

a)   b)   c)   d)

Fig. 1. Some tongue blocks extracted from jtongue image. a), b) and c) are extracted from the same tongue, d) is extracted from another tongue image.

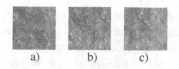

a)   b)   c)

Fig. 2. Some tongue blocks extracted from one tongue image

Table 1. The distances between Fig. 1-a) and the other three blocks

	Fig. 1-b)	Fig. 1-c)	Fig. 1-d)
Sorted (L1 Norm)	61674	73418	52189
Histogram (32^3, L1 Norm)	2100	3092	3992

Table 2. The distances between Fig. 2-a) and the other two blocks

	Fig. 2-b)	Fig. 2-c)
Sorted (L1 Norm)	123566	195427
Histogram (32^3, L1 Norm)	3696	4016

To circumvent the problem of ground truth, we proposed to use MR, which is rooted from Mean Match Percentile, as a criterion to evaluate tongue image matching performance. The main steps of MR are as follows:

1) Some tongue blocks are cropped from our tongue database manually; these blocks are composed of similar color and texture;

2) 4 sub-blocks, as showed in Fig. 3) with overlapping are extracted from every tongue block to create a sub-block database, the four sub-blocks extracted from the same block are declared as one group;

3) Select one of sub-block as a query block, compute distances between it with the remaining sub-blocks, rank these sub-blocks according to the distance and record the rank of three sub-blocks which are in the same group with the query block;

4) Iteratively running 3) until all the sub-blocks are queried;

5) Compute the mean of all the rank, MR.

Fig. 3. A block with its four sub-blocks' position

The idea of MR is that a good tongue matching algorithm should cluster overlapping blocks extracted from the same tongue as near as possible. The smaller MR, the better algorithm and a perfect algorithm will get MR=2.

5 Experiments

In this section, we will investigate different matching methods using color and texture information. Later, some tests on fusing color and texture information are evaluated.

In the following, all experiments are based on one tongue block database: firstly, 500 blocks from 500 different tongue image, 112*92 size, 24 bit RGB color image, are cropped from our tongue image database captured by 3CCD Digital Video; then, 2000 sub-blocks, 64*64 size, 24 bits RGB color, as showed in Fig. 3 are composed of the test database.

5.1 Performance Comparison Using Color Information only

Table 3 listed the result using different color metrics.

Table 3. MR using different color features

	L1	L2
Projected Histogram (256*3)	182.5733	169.1118
Projected Histogram (128*3)	187.9991	170.0188
Mean+Std	232.9348	218.1316
Point to cluster center distance	324.1548	326.6440
Sort Matrix (sort by R Channel)	243.0658	214.9146
Color Histogram (64^3)	19.1663	45.4200
Color Histogram (32^3)	26.0082	32.1918

where, L1 and L2 are two different distance norms. Sort Matrix (sort by R Channel) means sort the color pixels according to R channel.

We can see color histogram gets the best result among all the color metrics. High dimension color histogram could decrease MR also, however, its high dimension impede its application in large-scale image matching.

5.2 Performance Comparison Using Texture Information only

Firstly, we tested on using gray-scale texture feature. The results are showed in Table 4. With gray-scale operator, only the luminance information was considered. Here the formula we adopted to compute to luminance from RGB color space was Y=0.2989R+ 0.5870G+ 0.1140B.

Table 4. MR using gray-scale textures

	L1	L2
Gabor (48-dimension)	178.1623	188.4668
$LBP_{8,1}$	84.5021	113.1455
$LBP^{u2}_{16,2}$	99.6806	199.3581
$LBP^{u2}_{24,3}$	125.8430	243.0453
$LBP_{(8,1+{}^{u2}16,2)}$	74.4121	117.2068
$LBP_{(8,1+{}^{u2}16,2+{}^{u2}24,3)}$	76.7891	130.5615

Usually Gabor's performance is comparable to LBP [13]. But for tongue image, Gabor filter's performance is much worse than LBP, the possible reason is that tongue images are composed of fine texture, unlike some natural scenes, which cover only a very small region. Large radius LBP operator's performance also certificates this.

Then, we tested on color-texture features, results are listed in Table 5. Here we considered single color channel information only. Then three color channels' features were concatenated into one vector.

Table 5. MR using color textures

	L1	L2
Gabor (36-dimension)	212.5938	180.6935
$LBP_{8,1}$	77.2501	103.4506
$LBP^{u2}_{16,2}$	91.7755	185.5135
$LBP^{u2}_{24,3}$	116.7415	230.5698
$LBP_{(8,1+{}^{u2}16,2)}$	68.4781	108.4315
$LBP_{(8,1+{}^{u2}16,2+{}^{u2}24,3)}$	71.6020	124.1826

Similar to Gray-scale LBP, multi-scale color LBP could improve the matching performance [13]. Finally, we combined unichrome features with inter-color-channel features together. The results are showed in Table 6.

Table 6. MR using opponent color and PDS textures

	L1	L2
Gabor (120-dimension)	87.7300	103.0286
$OCLBP_{8,1}$	60.1521	165.3570
$PDSLBP_{8,1}$	41.7645	96.3685
$OCLBP^{u2}_{16,2}$	58.3190	127.6926
$PDSLBP^{u2}_{16,2}$	48.4680	117.3146
$OCLBP^{u2}_{24,3}$	74.1648	128.9686
$PDSLBP^{u2}_{24,3}$	49.3616	92.9410

From Table 4-6 we can see color texture performs better than gray-scale texture. Also additional inter-color-channel information could improve performance. L1 norm is better than L2 norm in most of cases.

We have also tested several simple fusion strategies to see whether color information plus texture could improve the performance of matching. Three different fusion were tested, product of two distance, board count [11] and Probabilistic Combined metric [6]. Fusing with 32^3 color histogram, all texture-based features have much improvement. PDSLBP got the best result no matter which fusion strategy was used. $PDSLBP_{8,1}$ combined with color histogram by product of two distance could get 10.8530 MR, which is the best result we can get from all the experiments. Due to page limit, we omitted the detailed results.

Although PDSLBP is the best one, we can see MR is far away from ideal result, 2. Except the features are not discriminative enough, there are two reasons why the MR is so big:

1) We extracted four sub-blocks from one block, sometimes these sub-blocks have different color or texture. Fig. 4 shows an example;
2) Although some tongue sub-blocks are not extracted from the same block, their color and texture are almost the same.

a) Query   b) 1st Rank   c) 2nd Rank   d) 77th Rank   e) 252nd Rank

Fig. 4. a-d) are extracted from one tongue image. c) is extracted from another image.

6   Conclusions

To circumvent the problem of ground truth, we proposed a new objective evaluation for tongue image matching, MR, which is also applicable to general image matching evaluation. A new LBP operator, PDSLBP, is proposed for color image. After a series of experiments evaluated by MR, we found PDSLBP was the best texture feature for tongue image matching, we also verified that tongue image matching was more suitable by combining color and color texture. Experiments on more fusion and color space such as CIELab, HSV will be investigated and tested in the future.

References

1. Li, M.M., et al.: The contemporary investigations of computerized tongue diagnosis. In: The Handbook of Chinese Tongue Diagnosis, Peking, pp. 1315–1317. Shed-Yuan Publishing (1994)
2. Yang, C.: A novel imaging system for tongue inspection. In: Proc. IEEE-IMTC, pp. 159–163 (2002)
3. Chiu, C.C.: A novel approach based on computerized image analysis for traditional Chinese medical diagnosis of the tongue. Comput. M. PR. 61(2), 77–89 (2000)
4. Yuen, P.C., Kuang, Z.Y., Wu, W., Wu, Y.T.: Tongue texture analysis using opponent color features for tongue diagnosis in traditional Chinese medicine. In: Proc. TAMV, pp. 21–27 (1999)
5. Pang, B., Zhang, D., Li, N.M., Wang, K.Q.: Computerized Tongue Diagnosis Based on Bayesian Networks. IEEE Trans. Biomedical Engineering 51(10), 1803–1810 (2004)
6. Li, C.H., Yuen, P.C.: Tongue image matching using color content. Pattern Recognition 35(2), 407–419 (2002)
7. Zhu, W., Zhou, C., Xu, D., Xu, J.: A multi-feature CBIR Method Using in the Traditional Chinese Medicine Tongue Diagnosis. In: Proc. ISPCA, pp. 831–836 (2006)
8. Qin, J., Meng, J., Wu, G., Liu, H.: The retrieval of the medical tongue-coating images using fuzzy CMAC neural network. In: Proc. ICIT, pp. 14–17 (2005)

9. Wei, C.H., Li, C.T., Wilson, R.: A content-based approach to medical image database retrieval. Database Modeling for Industrial Data Management, pp. 258–292. Idea Group publishing, USA (2005)
10. Funt, B.V., Finlayson, G.D.: Color Constant Color Indexing. IEEE Trans. Pattern Anal. Mach. Intell 17(5), 522–529 (1995)
11. Ho, T., Hull, J., Srihari, S.: Decision combination in multiple classifier systems. IEEE Trans. Pattern Anal. Mach. Intell 16(1), 66–75 (1994)
12. Zhang, L., Wu, X.: Color Demosaicking Via Directional Linear Minimum Mean Square-Error Estimation. IEEE Trans. Image Processing 14, 2167–2178 (2005)
13. Maenpaa, T., Pietikainen, M.: Classification with color and texture: jointly or separately. Pattern Recognition 37, 1640–1692 (2004)

Pixel Based Tongue Color Analysis

Bo Huang and Naimin Li

Department of Computer Science and Technology
Harbin Institute of Technology Shenzhen Graduate School, Shenzhen, China
7413762@126.com

Abstract. Tongue diagnosis is a distinctive and essential diagnostic measure in Traditional Chinese Medicine (TCM), and chromatic information is its most decisive characteristic which is utilized to unearth pathological changes for identifying diseases. In this paper, a computerized medical biometrics scheme is established which classify all pixels in tongue into various color classes. For train specimens, both a forward and a backward selection are employed to pick up the correct labeled pixel specimens and screen out the wrong, and then various pixels of diversified colors are classified for the tongue color analysis. The experimental outcomes are more applicable to tongue color analysis.

1 Introduction

Tongue diagnosis is a distinctive diagnostic measure, and computerized tongue diagnosis (CTD) is also being a prosperous application of medical biometrics [2]. A doctrine has been authorized that various tongue colors correspond to various health states. Therefore, as a sensitive indicator of internal pathological changes, the chromatic perception serves as an indispensable guideline for differentiating diseases.

As color plays such a prominent role in diagnosis, it has attracted increasing CTD researcher's attention. Pang [1] presented a approach based on quantitative features. Li [3] proposed a regularized algorithm to extract important color with few populations, and [4] analyzed the matching issue. Wang [5] developed a JSEG approach to distinguish color. All approaches mentioned above are a kind of sub-image based approaches. They are analogous with the flow in Fig.1: Firstly, sub-images are cut from intact tongue. Then features are enumerated. Finally color classes of sub-images are classified. However, these approaches may be more reasonable if they have preserved global information and abandoned irrelevant local specimens.

Obviously, except only an irregular sub-image approach [5], other regular sub-image approaches ignored the global information out of the selected sub-images. Fig.1 is a typical example. The blocks only correspond to the sectional chromatic material, and most are neglected, especially the marginal with the most important pathologic significance. From Fig.2, it can be concluded that the color distribution and the peaks of distributions in different blocks are distinctive. Intuitively, different distributions predicate various pathologic significance, but the sub-image based approach discards the valuable cue, and drop down the accuracy of final analysis.

Even for local information in sub-images, irrelevant specimens are imported. All these approaches regard pixels in a given sub-image as a whole, and bring in noises

D. Zhang (Ed.): ICMB 2008, LNCS 4901, pp. 282–289, 2007.

Fig. 1. Outline of sub-image based methods

Fig. 2. Four different regions of tongue image and corresponding histograms

consequently. In most cases, there are many kinds of pixels belongs to various classes whose difference can't be neglected. As for pixels belong to one class, the pixels belong to others are irrelevant noises, and vice versa. In the third sub-image of Fig.2, there are lots of red points whose visual effect are far from the rest. So the sub-image based approaches ignore the difference between pixels with various colors, and treat sub-images as monolithic objects. Finally, these methods deteriorate the accuracy.

So a reasonable analysis object of tongue color should be the every pixel, other than sub-images. And the paper is organized as follows. Section 2 and 3 describes the training and the testing part of pixel classification model. Section 4 carries on the performance analysis. Finally, Section 5 concludes this paper.

2 Training Part

The training part is two steps: forward and backward selection which are two kinds of data refining and subset selection in statistics used for eliminating redundant.

2.1 Forward Selection

For an image X, the class number is not fixed: 12 (4 coating classes and 8 substance classes), and can not be ascertained in advance. It is imputed to uncontrollability of the unsupervised classifier, and every image's c is derived empirically and evaluated to various integers between a range. c value can be affirmed in the following four procedures: dividing, selecting candidate, building compare objects and comparing.

Firstly, X can be divided into c clusters by FCM 5 times, and c value of every time is a different integer between [6, 10]. Here, this time and this range are derived empirically. Then X is divided into c images: $X^1, X^2, \cdots X^c$ as (a) in Fig.3. Secondly, some tongue cluster images are selected by whether the tongue cluster images belong to the wanted color classes. In (b) of Fig.3, cluster images X^6 and X^7 are selected as the input of the follow procedure and others are discarded. Thirdly, the selected tongue cluster images are "added" as the requisite compared objects. This procedure is a kind of image adding, the pixels which are not pure green ($[0, 255, 0]$) are added into an image $X^{C,ADD}$ like this: Where x_k^i is the color of a cluster image X^i, x_k^j is the color of another X^j, and $x^{c,add}$ is the color of the c added image $X^{C,ADD}$. When c is equal with 7, 8, 9, 10, two clusters are "added" into a training set $X^{C,ADD}$, as shown as in (c) of Fig.3. Fourthly, these 5 "added" cluster images (Including $X^{6,ADD}$, though it is without image adding) are the compare image objects. These training set, $X^{6,add}, X^{7,add}, X^{8,add}, X^{9,add}$ and $X^{10,add}$, are used to compare to a best yellow coating training set $X^{C,ADD}$. In (c) of Fig.3, when c is 6, the yellow coating pixels' location in tongue image X is closest to the subjective feeling, so 6 is the final c value of forward selection to this image.

These pixels in selected "tongue cluster" image $X_i^{C,ADD}$ can combine a "pixels set" image Y_j. Fig.4 reveals the combining from N representative labeled tongue images specimens to the yellow coating "pixels set" image by sorting all pixels in a color class into a pixel set block image. In Fig.4, the first line is the origin tongue images X_i, and the second line is the selected representative yellow coating pixels images $X_i^{C,ADD}$ after image adding,. Then these "tongue cluster" images constitute the initial yellow coating "pixels set" image Y_j. After selected "tongue cluster" images are labeled into various classes, 12 initial "pixels set" images Y_j are buildup.

2.2 Backward Selection

Though forward selection is executed, there are some failures. Observe carefully, it can be found that top of yellow coating initial "pixel set" is much dark than most, and bottom is much bright. This failure also should impute to the uncontrollability of unsupervised classifier, which labels many wrongs. After combination, these wrongs will occupy a certain ratio. So another riddling is prerequisite.

Contrary to the forward selection, the least representative subset is dropped out, so long as it is not representative at our chosen critical level. We continue by successively re-fitting reduced training pixel set and applying the same rule until all remaining subsets are visible representative. This riddling can be seen as three procedures: dividing, building compare objects and comparing.

Firstly, all pixels in the initial "pixel set" images Y_j are treated as the input, and FCM is applied on them. Y_j is also divided into c clusters $Y_j^1, Y_j^2, \cdots Y_j^c$ by FCM 5 times, and c value of every time is a different integer between [6, 10]. Just as (a) of Fig.5, the initial "pixel set" image is divided into c small pixels cluster.

Secondly, for each cluster in each initial "pixel set" images, an image with highest ratio of this cluster is searched in the training image set mechanically like (b) of Fig.5. Here the ratio is the pixels which belongs to this cluster to the all pixels like this:

$$Ratio = Num(x_k \in Y_j^q) / Num(x_k \in X_i) , \quad i = 1, 2, \cdots, T$$ (Here, Y_j^q is the divided cluster image from Y_j, X_i is the training set used to search, T is the

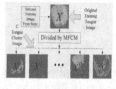
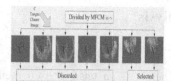
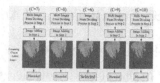

(a) Dividing   (b) Searching candidate   (c) Building compare objects

Fig. 3. Three procedures in forward selection

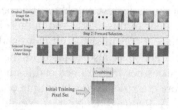

Fig. 4. Building initial training pixel set

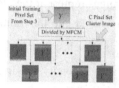
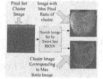
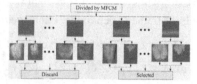

(a) Dividing   (b) Searching candidate   (c) Building compare objects

Fig. 5. Three procedures in backward selection

training set's number), and the ratio is deduced by the following RKNN algorithm. A top ratio specimen will be found for each cluster, and be used to compare.

Thirdly, this top ratio image is compared to decide whether keep down. First it is judged whether the cluster in top ratio specimen is a pure cluster (the pure cluster means it only include pixels belongs to a class, and the pixels belongs to others is few). If the answer is no, the image is discarded. Otherwise, it is kept down. Second it is judged whether the cluster is a cluster belongs to corresponding class. Just like the second pixel set cluster image in (c) of Fig.5, it is with the highest pixels ratio of "darkest" yellow cluster in yellow coating "pixels set" image. Apparently, this cluster doesn't belong to this class, so this cluster is discarded. And the third pixel set cluster image in (c) of Fig.5 conform the human being's subjective visual feeling, so it is kept down. In this way, the right labeled sets in each "pixels set" images are selected, and the wrong labeled ones are discarded.

Finally, eight clusters in them are kept down for constituting final yellow coating color class. Of course, clusters which consisted of most wrongs are thrown out. After all pixels of selected residual "tongue cluster" images are labeled into various color classes, 12 final "pixels set" images with various sizes are buildup.

3 Experiments and Analysis

3.1 Testing Procedure

For this pixel classification scheme, if an unsupervised method is applied to final pixel classification directly, the classifier's behavior can not be freely controlled as the requirement of clinic diagnosis. So a supervised classifier is determined to classify all pixels of the testing specimens when the trained pixel sets have got their class labels. K Nearest Neighbor is a classical supervised classifier in common use. Its idea is simple: if the majority of the K nearest neighbor of a specimen belongs to a certain class, then this specimen is a one of this class. And in this classification, final decision is only related with the adjacent specimens, so it can handle imbalance between the numbers of various classes, and it is also applied to the specimen sets with some extent overlap. But all distances between trained and testing specimens are calculated in the KNN arithmetic before classification, so the time complexity will be huge with plentiful pixel specimens. A Reduced K Nearest Neighbor, which can be named RKNN, is proposed to solve this speediness headache as follows.

Firstly, the trained specimens are transformed to a 3D array. Its indexes represent the feature of each pixel specimen respectively, and the cell values represent the class labels of trained specimens. Each specimen $< x_k, f(x_k) >$ is added into the training sets. Here, x_k is the feature vector of the specimen; $f(x_k)$ is the class label of the specimen; $f(x_k) \in C$, $C = \{c_1, c_2, ..., c_n\}$ is the class set. Secondly, giving a unlabeled testing specimen x_q, then select the h most similar specimen $x_1, x_2, \cdots, x_h$ in the cube with the size of m^3, and this cube's center is x_q; Thirdly, the δ between the trained specimens nears the testing specimens will be calculated by the traversing array. Then $\hat{f}(x_q) = \arg\max_{c \in C} \sum_{i=1}^{h} \delta(c, f(x_i))$; here $\hat{f}(x_q)$ is the classification decision of the unlabeled x_q. Apparently, the time complexity is down sharply. So RKNN transforms the global arithmetic to a local optimization. Finally, x_k^c belonging to each class can constitute some labeled pixels image X^c.

Searching top ratio images in backward selection is similar with two classes RKNN. It considers each cluster as a class, the others as another class, and the pixel ratio is calculated to find the highest one.

3.2 Testing Results

After RKNN classification, every pixel can get one label. Because pixels can not be distinguished manually, the accuracy only can be drawn from subjective judgment.

Obviously, our method divided pixels sets. Fig.6 shows the training results' pixel distribution of 4 coating and 8 substance classes in the RGB space and the next 6 small figures give clearer impression of every two color classes' location.

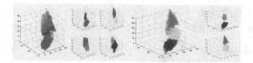

Fig. 6. All substance and coating color classes' distribution in the RGB color space

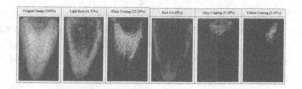

Fig. 7. A yellow coating tongue image classification results images

Fig.7 illustrates a tongue classification result images. Intuitively, the classifier distinguishes all pixels to corresponding color classes correctly, and the location and quantity are also conformed to the subjective feeling. In these images, all pixels in each image belong to one color class, and the pixel ratio is given in each labeled tongue pixels image's top. White coating could be found in the central section of tongue body, and the substance of this tongue is a mixture of light red. Therefore, the global color distribution can be deduced quickly that, this tongue's coating is white coating, and its substance's color is light red. In the same time, local information haven't been neglected by this method, the yellow coating's distribution also conform visual feeling. So the tongue color analysis of this tongue image is achieved effortlessly.

So it can be concluded from these figures that classification has accomplished the pixels distinguishing. All pixels are endowed with their color class labels. And all these images conformed to human's subjective feeling.

4 Performance Analysis

4.1 Comparison with Initial Training Results

In the manual assistant labeling, a pixel can't be labeled manually, even if small local block regions are zoomed to magnified ones. On the contrary, a cluster can be labeled into a class together. In the forward selection, it will bring in noises. On the other hand, it will bring correct specimens out in the backward selection. But have no alternative to label so huge pixels. So this riddling method became the preferred way.

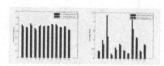

Fig. 8. Advantage ratio and variation coefficient of all color classes

For evaluated the classifier's accuracy, two metrics are calculated: advantage-ratio (AR) and variation-coefficient (VC).AR is the ratio of the within-class to the between-class distance: $AR = \sum_{x_k \in X_i} [(x_k - u_i)(x_k - u_i)^T]/N_i(u_i - u)(u_i - u)^T$.

VC is defined as the ratio of standard deviation to the mean of the distances from samples within the cluster to the samples outside the cluster: $VC_i = Std_i / Mean_i$.

Fig.8 is the AR and VC of 12 color classes for evaluated the classifier's accuracy. Obviously, under the same mean diameter, the lower the advantage ratio and variation coefficient values, the better the quality of the cluster is. It can be seen that the AR and VC of the prior one is overmatch the posterior one. These can be also considered as an objective evidence of the necessity of riddling on training part.

4.2 Comparison with Sub-image Based Method

The accuracy of sub-image based method is affected by the global information ignorance between color classes mainly, but pixel based method can handle this case. The most visible difference is the color difference between coating and substance. (a) in Fig.9 is four samples which are divided into coating pixel color class and substance pixel color class by our methods. Every sample after this two class (coating and substance) pixels classification is visual and apprehensible. From subjective perceptivity, coating and substance are divided completely.

On the other hand, local difference can be distinguished by our method. There are three kinds of tongues: thin coating, thick coating and no coating. (b) in Fig.9 is three samples corresponding to three kinds of tongue sub-images. From the visual effects and their histogram distribution, all these tongues can be distinguished easily.

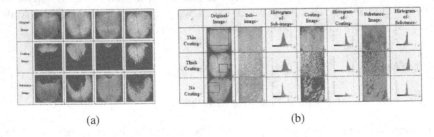

(a)   (b)

Fig. 9. Coating and substance separation

So sub-image based method is not applicable to tongue color analysis, and pixel based tongue color analysis will classify all pixel in tongue images, and solve the problem above mentioned.

5   Conclusions

Though the manual labeling process is tedious, this training part facilitates the next testing part. From what has been discussed above, pixel based method accord with

TCM philosophic macroscopically ideology, and this method is also more appropriate than sub-image based method for tongue color analysis.

Acknowledgement

This work is partially supported by the National Natural Science Foundation (NSFC) key overseas project under the contract no. 60620160097.

References

1. Pang, B., Zhang, D., Li, N., Wang, K.: Computerized Tongue diagnosis Based on Bayesian Networks. IEEE Tran. On Biomedical Engineering 10(51), 1803–1810 (2004)
2. Zhang, D.: Automated Biometrics: Technologies & Systems. Kluwer Academic Publishers, USA (2000)
3. Li, C.H., Yuen, P.C.: Regularized Color Clustering in Medical Image Database. IEEE Tran on Medical Imaging 19(11), 1150–1155 (2000)
4. Li, C.H., Yuen, P.C.: Tongue Image Matching Using Color Content. Pattern Recognition 35(2), 407–419 (2002)
5. Wang, Y.G., Yang, J., et al.: Region partition and feature matching based color recognition of tongue image. Pattern Recognition Letter 28(1), 11–19 (2007)

Gradient Direction Edge Enhancement Based Nucleus and Cytoplasm Contour Detector of Cervical Smear Images

Shys-Fan Yang-Mao[1], Yung-Fu Chen[2], Yung-Kuan Chan[3],
Meng-Hsin Tsai[3], and Yen-Ping Chu[4]

[1] Department of Computer Science and Engineering,
National Chung Hsing University, Taichung, Taiwan
`wool@cs.nchu.edu.tw`
[2] Department of Health Services Administration, China Medical University, Taichung
`yungfu@mail.cmu.edu.tw`
[3] Department of Management Information Systems, National Chung Hsing University,
Taichung, Taiwan
`{ykchan,mht}@nchu.edu.tw`
[4] Department of Computer and Information Engineering, Tunghai University, Taichung
`ypchu@thu.edu.tw`

Abstract. This paper presents a gradient direction edge enhancement based contour (GDEEBC) detector to segment the nucleus and cytoplasm from each cervical smear image. In order to eliminate noise from the image, this paper proposes a trim-meaning filter that can effectively remove impulse and Gaussian noise but still preserve the edge sharpness of an object. In addition, a bi-group enhancer is proposed to make a clear-cut separation for the pixels lying between two objects. Finally, a gradient direction (GD) enhancer is presented to suppress the gradients of noise and to brighten the gradients of object contours as well. The experimental results show that all the techniques proposed above have impressive performances. In addition to cervical smear images, these proposed techniques can also be utilized in object segmentation of other types of images.

1 Introduction

Cervical cancer is the leading cause of mortality for women. Unlike other cancers that have distinguished symptoms, such as pain, noticeable lumps, etc., cervical cancer has no telltale symptoms until it is so advanced that is usually unresponsive to treatment [3]. Currently, cervical smear screening is the most popular method used to detect the presence of abnormal cells arising from the cervix. The purpose of the smear screening is to diagnose pre-malignant cell changes before they progress to cancerous stage.

Current manual screening methods are costly and are very likely to result in inaccurate diagnosis due to human error. The introduction of machine assisted screening will therefore bring significant benefits to the community, not only reduction of financial costs but increase of screening accuracy. An effective boundary detection algorithm, locating the contours of cytoplast and nucleus, plays an important role in developing a useful computer-assisted diagnostic system.

D. Zhang (Ed.): ICMB 2008, LNCS 4901, pp. 290–297, 2007.
© Springer-Verlag Berlin Heidelberg 2007

Wu et al. [10] introduced a parametric optimal segmentation approach which is suitable for images of non-overlapped cells with smooth cell boundaries or contours. Mat-Isa et al., based on thresholding, [5] utilized the region growing algorithm as a feature extraction technique. This proposed algorithm is called seeded region growing features extraction (SRGFE), which is used to extract the size and grey level of certain region of interest on a digital image. Walker [11] used a series of automated fast morphological transforms with octagonal structuring elements. Martin [4] and Norup [6] also take the CHAMP Digital image software to segment and classify cervical smear images.

Most image segmentation methods perform well when the image has good quality and the object contours are distinct. However, cervical smear images are frequently contaminated and the cytoplasm and nucleus contours of cervical cells are often vague, especially for abnormal cervical cells.

The principal objective of image preprocessing techniques is to process an image to make it more suitable than the original image for further application. To resolve the problems mentioned above, this paper proposes a gradient direction edge enhancement based contour (GDEEBC) detector to segment the cytoplasm and nucleus from cervical smear images. In the image preprocessing stage, three techniques, including trim-meaning filter, bi-group enhancer, and gradient direction weight (GDW) enhancer, are presented and used to eliminate the noises on an image and to sharpen the contours of objects before extracting the object. In addition to cervical smear images, the three proposed techniques are also effective for detecting object contours of other types of images. The aim of this paper is to develop an image segmentation system to sever the cytoplast and nucleus from a cervical smear image. This system is very helpful for developing an automated cervical cancer screening system without a priori knowledge of the image objects.

2   The GDEEBC Detector

The proposed GDEEBC detector contains four procedures, as described below, including trim-meaning, bi-grouping, GDW enhancing, and contour extracting. The objectives of these individual steps are to eliminate noise, to discriminate the pixels adjacent to the object contour between the background and the object, to suppress the gradients of noises and to brighten the gradients of object contours, and to draw the contours of cytoplasm and nucleus, respectively. The proposed trim-meaning and bi-grouping enhancers are used to preprocess the images to eliminate noise and to intensify the contours of object to be detected on an image, while the gradient direction (GD) enhancer is applied to enrich the gradients of cytoplast and nucleus contours and to suppress the gradients of noise.

2.1 Trim-Meaning Method

Image segmentation task mainly depends on the image quality. It is well known that the generation of an accurate edge map becomes a critical issue when the images are corrupted by noises. Impulse (also known as salt & pepper) and Gaussian noises are very often encountered during image acquisition. A pixel corrupted by Gaussian noise has amplitude slightly different from that of its neighbors, while impulse noise makes the amplitude of a pixel much larger or much smaller than that of its neighbors.

There are several denoising techniques presented in previous studies, such as mean filter [2], Gaussian filter [2], and type-B filter [8]. Figure 1(a) and 1(b) show a simulated image and the same image corrupted by adding impulse noise on the left and Gaussian noise on the right of the simulated image, respectively. The results obtained using trim-meaning approach with different parameter settings adopting 5x5 blocks are shown in Fig. 1(d). Figures 1(e), 1(f), and 1(c) demonstrate the images after being processed by mean, Gaussian, and type-B filters. Figure 1(c) indicates that type-B filter can eliminate only impulse noise but Gaussian noise, while Figures 1(e) and 1(f) depict that mean and Gaussian filters are unable to remove the noise efficiently which in turn make the object contours even vaguer.

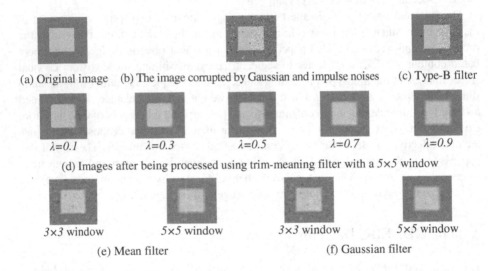

(a) Original image   (b) The image corrupted by Gaussian and impulse noises   (c) Type-B filter

$\lambda=0.1$ $\lambda=0.3$ $\lambda=0.5$ $\lambda=0.7$ $\lambda=0.9$

(d) Images after being processed using trim-meaning filter with a 5x5 window

3x3 window   5x5 window   3x3 window   5x5 window

(e) Mean filter   (f) Gaussian filter

Fig. 1. Denoised images obtained after being processed by Mean, Gaussian, Type-B, and Trim-meaning filters

In order to dispose both the impulse and Gaussian noises, trim-meaning filter is proposed in this paper. Let $p_{i,j}$ be the pixel located at the position (i, j) on a cervical smear image f_0, and $W_{i,j}$ be a $m{\times}m$ window with $p_{i,j}$ located at its center. Assume that $C_{i,j}=\{c_1, c_2, ..., c_m\}$ are the colors of the pixels in $W_{i,j}$, and then the color values in $C_{i,j}$ are sorted in ascending order, that is $c_1 \leq c_2 \leq ... \leq c_m$. The trim-meaning filter removes the lower and upper tails of $C_{i,j}$'s to eliminate the impulse noise and Gaussian noise by replacing the value of $p_{i,j}$ with the mean, c', obtained by averaging the remainders of $C_{i,j}$'s. Therefore, trim-meaning filter is expected to be able to dispose both impulse and Gaussian noise effectively. Let the trimmed lower and upper tails of $C_{i,j}$'s be $100{\times}\lambda$ % of $C_{i,j}$'s, c' can be defined as:

$$c' = \frac{1}{(1-2\lambda)m^2}\sum_{h=\lambda\times m^2+1}^{m^2(1-\lambda)}c_h \qquad (1)$$

As shown in Figure 1, it can be found that the trim-meaning filter can significantly abate the amplitudes differences between the noisy pixel and its neighboring pixels for a given window with $m \times m = 5 \times 5$, especially for $\lambda = 0.5$. The trim-meaning filter not only can effectively eliminate impulse and Gaussian noise, but also can achieve better performance than the mean and Gaussian filters in terms of edge sharpness.

2.2 Bi-grouping Approach

The term "edge" stands for a local luminance change, where the gradient of sufficient strength is considered important in a given task. Other contextual edge detection techniques based on suppression have been previously proposed. Type-A filter [8] is provided to enhance the contours of objects, which takes into account the differences between the pixel to be processed and its neighbors. Small differences are considered as noise to be reduced while large differences as edges to be preserved.

Yina [13] also presented an automatically adaptive window-level selection algorithm, namely adaptive image optimization (AIO), to improve the performance. Adopting AIO, the quality of an image can be improved by adaptively increasing the maximum dynamic range.

Figures 2 compare examples of cell images and their corresponding gradient images after being processed by AIO algorithm, type-A pre-filtering, and bi-group approach, respectively. The gradient images were obtained using Sobel operator [1]. In figure 2, it was found that for AIO algorithm and Type-A filter, suppression has no effect on nearby edges which have equally strong gradients. In order to improve the shortage, the bi-group approach has been proposed to effectively isolate pixels located on the object contour from the background pixels, as demonstrated in Fig. 2(d).

After being processed by the trim-meaning filter, image f_t is generated from f_o. We explain as follows. Let $p_{i,j}$ be the pixel located at the coordinates (i, j) in f_t, and $W_{i,j}$ be the corresponding window of $p_{i,j}$ where $p_{i,j}$ is the central pixel of $W_{i,j}$ consisting of $m_b \times m_b$ pixels. Assume that $C_k = \{c_1, c_2, ..., c_{m_b^2}\}$ are the colors of the pixels on $W_{i,j}$, and the color values in $C_{i,j}$ are sorted exponentially, $c_1 \le c_2 \le ... \le c_{m_b^2}$.

Let $mid = (m_b^2 + 1)/2$ with m_b as an odd number, The bi-group approach defines two intervals as $[c_1, c_{mid}]$ and $[c_{mid+1}, c_{m_b^2}]$. Hence, the bi-group approach replaces c with c', where c' is defined as follows:

$$c' = \begin{cases} \dfrac{1}{mid} \sum_{i=1}^{mid} c_i, & \text{if } \dfrac{1}{mid} \sum_{i=1}^{mid} c_i \le c \le c_{mid}, \\[2ex] \dfrac{1}{mid-1} \sum_{i=mid-1}^{m^2} c_i, & \text{if } c_{mid} < c \le \dfrac{1}{mid-1} \sum_{i=mid+1}^{m^2} c_i \\[2ex] c, & \text{otherwise} \end{cases} \quad (2)$$

If c is within the indefinite intervals, the bi-group enhancer changes c into the average colors c_f of the first half of $C_{i,j}$'s when c is closer to c_f, or c is supplanted by the average color of the latter half of $C_{i,j}$'s. Figure 2 illustrates that a bi-group enhancer can more effectively separate the object pixels from the background pixels.

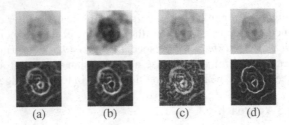

(a)	(b)	(c)	(d)

Fig. 2. (a) A cell image (upper row) and its gradient image (bottom row). Images preprocessed using (b) AIO, (c) type-A filter, and (d) bi-group enhancers and their corresponding gradient images.

2.3 Gradient Direction Enhancing

Usually, the gradients of pixels in an edge tend to have more uniform orientation, while the gradients for pixels corrupted by noise are more non-uniform and irregular. As shown in Figure 3(a), the pixels located close to the object contour direct from the object to its adjacent area or vise versa, in which the blue arrow indicates an edge while the red arrows denote gradient directions. As shown in the figure, the gradients direct from a darker area to a brighter area by intersecting the object edge with a right angle. However, in Figure 3(b), the gradient of noise demonstrates more non-uniform orientation compared to an object edge. Based on the aforementioned characteristics, this paper proposes a method, namely gradient direction weighting (GDW) method, to enhance gradient direction to decrease edge gradient of noise, thereby enhance the object edges for efficient segmentation.

(a)	(b)

Fig. 3. Comparisons of gradient directions between (a) object and (b) noise

For a pixel $p(i, j)$ on a image, GDW method uses a scheme similar to noise suppression approach by considering its adjacent pixels in a 5x5 block with $p(i, j)$ as the central pixel for calculating the orientation θ of a candidate edge L. Then Sobel operator is used to calculate the gradient directions for individual adjacent pixels of $p(i, j)$. Denote the gradient direction of the i-*th* adjacent pixel as θ_i, the probability of $p(i, j)$ to be an edge point increases when $|\theta - \theta_i|$ approximates to $90°$. Hence, by incorporating GDW for noise suppression, $c'(i, j)$ can be modified according to the equation shown below:

$$c''(i, j) = c'(i, j) \times \frac{1}{25} \times \sum_{k=1}^{25} \sin |\theta - \theta_k| \qquad (3)$$

Then the Sobel gradient image f_g now weighted with GDW weight to the enhanced gradient image f_m.

2.4   Contour Extracting Approach

The color intensity of a pixel p_{ij} in f_m represents the possibility of the pixel located at the coordinates (i, j) in f_0 to be an edge pixel. To successfully segment the cytoplast and nucleus, given an adaptive threshold to isolate possible edge pixels is the prerequisite. Otsu's method [7] is one of the commonly used threshold decision methods and is utilized by GDEEBC for obtaining the threshold. Assume that the threshold Th is obtained by Otsu's method, the GDEEBC detector sweeps each pixel p_{ij} in f_m to generate a binary image f_b. If the color intensity of p_{ij} is greater than or equal to Th, the GDEEBC detector assigns 1 to the pixel located at the coordinates (i, j) on f_b; otherwise 0 is given. The pixels in f_m with the value 1 in f_b are called candidate edge pixels.

The expected edge should be of one-pixel thick. The GDEEBC detector hence adopts a hit-and-miss transform based skeletonization (HMTS) algorithm [2] to build the edges with thickness of one pixel. The HMTS algorithm is performed to trim the redundant-edge pixels, so that the edges are only one pixel in width. It guarantees that connectivity is preserved and the overall geometric structure of the object in the image is preserved. Nonetheless, uneven object edges tend to cause small spurs on a skeletonized edge, a pruning algorithm is required to remove them.

Finally, the biggest closed loop L_c on f_b is used to describe the contour of the cytoplasm, while the darkest region on f_0 surrounded by a loop which corresponds to L_n on f_b. It means that L_c and L_n are the contours of the cytoplasm and the nucleus of the cervical cell on f_0. Figure 4 shows the f_g, GWD, f_m, f_b, and the cytoplasm (L_c) and nucleus (L_n) contours of image f.

3   Experimental Results

In this section, the experimental result of GDEEBC detector is compared to those obtained by GVF-ACM method [12] and CHAMP software [4, 6]. Five error measures of segmentation performance, including misclassification error (ME), edge mismatch (EMM), relative foreground area error (RAE), modified Hausdorff distance (MHD), and region nonuniformity (NU), were used for performance evaluation [9]. There are 25 Pap smear images with size of 64×64 pixels provided by Taichung Hospital, were used for experiments. Each image was transformed into a gray-level image before further processing. As shown in Figure 5, row 1 and row 2 display the test images and their target cytoplasm and nucleus contours drawn manually by an experienced doctor.

In this investigation, the GDEEBC detector is employed to extract the cytoplasm and nucleus contours of the test images. The parameter settings for individual steps are: $m=5$ and $\lambda=50$ for trim-meaning, $m=5$ for bi-grouping, and $m=5$ for GDW approach. For comparisons, GVF-ACM method and CHAMP are also adopted to segment the cytoplasts and nucleuses from the test images. For ACM, all the parameters including α, β, and κ have been set to 1. Figure 5 gives the cytoplasm and nucleus contours obtained by using GDEEBC detector, GVF-ACM method, and CHAMP software.

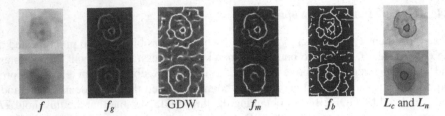

$$f \qquad f_g \qquad GDW \qquad f_m \qquad f_b \qquad L_c \text{ and } L_n$$

Fig. 4. Illustration of images f_g, GWD, f_m, f_b, and contours of cytoplasm (L_c) and nucleus (L_n) for original images f

Table 1 compares the average performance measures of the extracted cytoplasm and nucleus contours for **25** test images. Table 1 shows the segmentation errors of the extracted contours in Figure 10 evaluated by six error measures. In this table, ME, EMM, REA, and MHD, all show that GDEEBC detector can give a much better performance than GVF-ACM method and CHAMP software. Only NU indicates that GDEEBC detector is slightly inferior to GVF-ACM method.

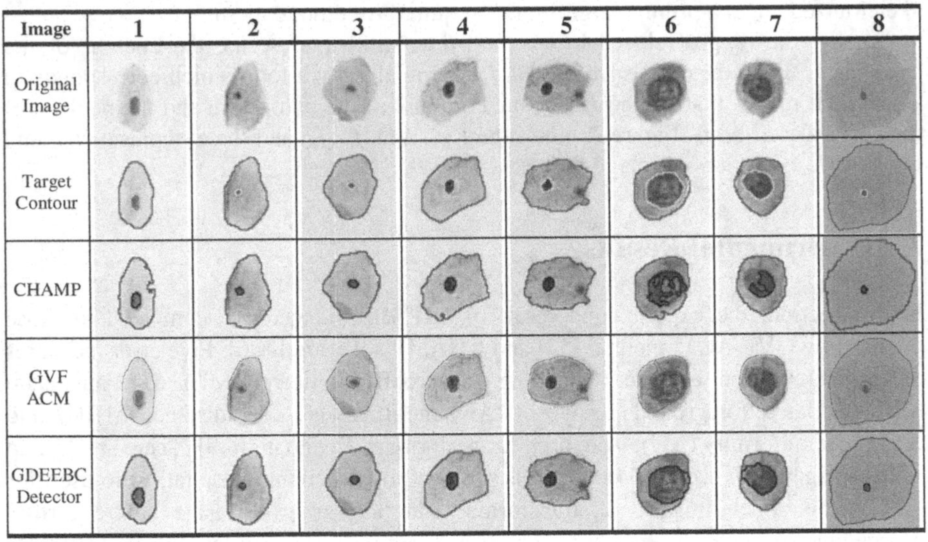

Image	1	2	3	4	5	6	7	8
Original Image								
Target Contour								
CHAMP								
GVF ACM								
GDEEBC Detector								

Fig. 5. Comparisons of nucleus and cytoplasm segmentation using CHAMP software, detector, GVF-ACM method, and GDEEBC Detector

Table 1. Comparisons of average errors using different measures

Method	Objects	ME	EMM	NU	RAE	MHD
GVF-ACM	Nucleus	0.0149	0.6812	0.0146	0.3545	1.2603
	Cytoplasm	0.0785	0.5537	0.1005	0.1244	1.4356
CHAMP	Nucleus	0.0107	0.2993	0.0106	0.2493	0.5124
	Cytoplasm	0.0578	0.4156	0.1429	0.1062	0.7574
GDEEBC	Nucleus	0.0016	0.0634	0.0160	0.0360	0.0954
	Cytoplasm	0.0061	0.0363	0.1098	0.0184	0.1191

4 Conclusions

This paper proposes an automatic method, namely gradient direction edge enhancement based contour (GDEEBC) detection, to segment the nucleus and cytoplast from a cervical smear image. A trim-meaning filter is proposed to remove the noise in a cervical smear image, which can efficiently remove impulse as well as Gaussian noise and meanwhile preserve the edge sharpness of the objects. This paper also proposes a bi-group enhancer to separate the object pixels from the background pixels which are close to the object contours. A gradient direction weighting (GDW) enhancer is also given for efficiently suppressing the gradients of pixels corrupted by noise and to brighten the gradients of object contours.

According to the experimental results, the GDEEBC detector is demonstrated to have an impressive performance in object segmentation than GVF-ACM method and CHAMP software. In addition to cervical smear images, these proposed techniques can be employed to segment objects from other kinds of images as well.

References

1. Davies, E.: Machine Vision: Theory, Algorithms and Practicalities, vol. 5. Academic Press, London (1990)
2. Gonzalez, R., Woods, R.: Digital Image Processing. Prentice-Hall, Englewood Cliffs (2002)
3. National Health Insurance.: Cause of Mortality Report 2004. Health and National Health Insurance statistics information (2004), http://www.doh.gov.tw/statistic/
4. Martin, E.: Cervical smear Classification. Master's thesis, Technical University of Denmark: Oersted-DTU, Automation (2003)
5. Mat-Isa, N.A., Mashor, M.Y., Othman, N.H.: Seeded Region Growing Features Extraction Algorithm; Its Potential Use in Improving Screening for Cervical Cancer. Int. J. Computer, the Internet and Management 13(1), 61–70 (2005)
6. Norup, J.: Classification of Cervical smear Data by Transductive Neuro-Fuzzy Methods. Master's thesis, Technical University of Denmark: Oersted-DTU, Automation (2005)
7. Otsu, N.: A Threshold Selection Method from Gray-Level Histograms. IEEE Transactions on Systems, Man, and Cybernetics, 9(1), 62–66 (1979)
8. Russo, F., Lazzari, A.: Color Edge Detection in Presence of Gaussian Noise Using Nonlinear Prefiltering. IEEE Transactions on Instrumentation and Measurement 54(1), 352–358 (2005)
9. Sezgin, M., Sankur, B.: Survey Over Image Thresholding Techniques and Quantitative Performance Evaluation. J. Electronic Imaging 13(1), 146–165 (2004)
10. Wu, H.-S., Gil, J., Barba, J.: Optimal Segmentation of Cell Images. IEE Proc. Online-Visual Image Signal Processing 145(1), 50–56 (1998)
11. Walker, R.F.: Adaptive Multi-Scale Texture Analysis with Application to Automated Cytology. Department of Electrical and Computer Engineering, University of Queensland, Dissertation (1997)
12. Xu, C., Prince, J.L.: Snakes, Shapes, and Gradient Vector Flow. IEEE Transactions on Image Processing 7(3), 359–369 (1998)
13. Yin, L., Basu, A., Chang, J.K.: Scalable Edge Enhancement with Automatic Optimization for Digital Radiographic Images. Pattern Recognition 37(7), 1407–1422 (2004)

Three Dimensional Reconstruction and Dynamic Analysis of Mitral Annular Based on Connected Equi-length Curve Angle Chain

Zhu Lei, Yang Xin, Yao Liping, and Sun Kun

Shanghai Jiao Tong University, Shanghai 200240, P.R. China
{july,yangxin}@sjtu.edu.cn,
itaa2004@sina.com, sunkun@hotmail.com

Abstract. Based on three dimensional echocardiography sequences, a new technique using connected equi-length curve angle chain (CELCAC) model for reconstruction and dynamic analysis of mitral annulus is proposed in this paper. Firstly, the boundary points of mitral annulus of the mitral annulus is extracted by interactive method and ordered according to their positions. Then, the three dimensional mitral annulus visualization model is established based on non-uniform rational B – spline algorithm. Finally, dynamic analysis of mitral annulus presented by the CELCAC model is suggested. The presentation is invariant to rotation, scaling, and translation. Results show that the reconstruction and analysis method proposed in this paper is feasible to assess the geometry and analyze the motion of mitral annulus.

1 Introduction

The mitral annulus has a complex geometry, which can be characterized by an asymmetric elliptic shape with a 3-dimensional saddle structure [1]. Reconstruction and evaluation of the mitral annulus using Non-uniform rational B-Spline (NURBS) algorithm in echocardiographic sequences may provide new insights into the overall function or malfunction of the mitral valve apparatus in human beings.

Extracting boundary points of the mitral annulus is the necessary first step to obtain both qualitative measurements (i.e., the detection of pathological deformation) and quantitative measurements (i.e., parameters about the dynamics). Although there are many extracting methods such as those based on Markov random field [2], artificial neural network [3], mathematical morphology [4] and deformable models [5, 6]. Unfortunately, fully automatic extraction of the mitral annulus in echocardiographic sequences is a difficult task due to poor spatial and contrast resolutions, a high level of speckle noise, the tissue-related textures and dropout inherent to the ultrasonic image formation process [7]. In order to extract the 3-D mitral annulus reliably and correctly, both interactive and computer aided methods are used in our work.

Many works have been reported for giving in-depth analysis about the non-planarity and dynamics of mitral annulus [8-12]. The study [13-15] of tricuspid valve shape, size, and motion over a cardiac cycle also provides reference guide for the study of mitral annulus. In [10], Ormiston measured mitral annulus area at different

D. Zhang (Ed.): ICMB 2008, LNCS 4901, pp. 298–306, 2007.
© Springer-Verlag Berlin Heidelberg 2007

times during the cardiac cycle to examine plastic changes. Watanabe et al. quantified annular circumferences and heights in ischemic mitral regurgitation group in [16]. In [17], Valocik and Kamp defined three novel parameters to describe the size and motion of the mitral annulus throughout the cardiac cycle, namely, the inter-peak distance, the inter-valley distance, and the height of the saddle-shaped mitral annulus. However, these parameters of mitral annulus dynamics was determined by firstly derive a reference plane of least squares fit to minimize the deviation of the annulus points [9, 18], which is a time consuming step. Thus, a convenient method without calculating reference plane—connected equi-length curve angle chain (CELCAC), is needed to descript the shade shape of mitral annulus during the cardiac cycle. In this method, the close annulus is represented as a number of connected equi-length curve segments, and this representation is invariant to rotation, scaling and translation.

This paper is organized as follows. Section 2 presents a computer aided method to study the shape of the mitral annulus from three dimensional echocardiographic sequences. Section 3 gives us the detail of the proposed CELCAC method. Then, we apply this method to descript the mitral annulus and analyze some properties of the proposed method in Section 4. The experimental results are presented in Section 5.

2 Reconstruction of Mitral Annulus

The reconstruction of mitrall annulus consists of the following three steps: At the beginning, the boundary points on the mitral annulus are marked by doctors interactively. Since these marked points are not distributed uniformly and sequentially, it is necessary in a second step to re-arrange these points into a set of sequence ones on a contour of the saddle-shaped mitral annulus. Finally, in order to assess the shape of the 3D mitral annulus, it is described by a 3D non-uniform rational B-spline (NURBS) algorithm.

In order to extract a 3-dimensional closed curve of the mitral annulus, multiple long axis, cross-sectional views are shown sequentially to the medical doctors who mark the points on the mitral annulus interactively in these views (See Fig.1 (a)-(b)). On the cross-sectional views, the boundary points of the mitral annulus are easily recognized and delineated for each frame. Those three dimensional marked points, denoted by P_i, are shown in this coordinate system in Fig.1(c).

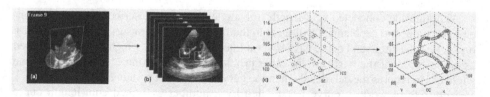

Fig. 1. Schematic diagram of extracted real time 3-dimensional reconstruction of the mitral annulus

The points $P_i(x_i, y_i, z_i), (i = 0, 1, 2, \ldots, N; N = 19)$ marked on the annulus are in general not distributed uniformly and defined in sequence. Therefore, in order to be able to reconstruct the closed contour of the mitral annulus by the non-uniform rational B-spline algorithm, a sort step is needed to re-arrange these marked points as an ordered sequence.

After the marked points are sorted as a sequential chain, a mathematical method for producing a closed three dimensional contour is needed to optimally represent the 3D mitral annulus. As the non-uniform rational B-spline (NURBS) is flexible and smooth enough to depict a closed contour [21], we choose it as our curve model. NURBS splines have the advantage to provide increased flexibility in controlling the shape of a curve. With unequally spaced intervals in the knot vector, we can obtain different shapes for the basis functions in different intervals, and can describe the deformation of the shape of the mitral annulus shapes accurately.

3   Connected Equi-length Curve Angle Chain

In [22], Zhao proposed a curve model named connected equi-length line for closed planar curves representing and encoding. It starts with drawing a circle centered at point H_0 with the radii being R. The intersection point of the curve and the circle along the curve trace H_1, is regarded as the tail of the first cell, and at the same time it is the head of the second cell. Draw another circle centered at with the same radii. The process is iterated until the nth cell $C_n(H_n, H_{n+1})$ is obtained. Fig.2 (a) below illustrates the geometry involved:

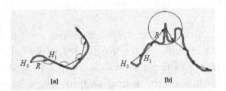 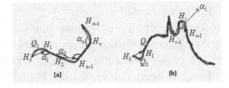

Fig. 2. Curves represented by connected angle chain

Fig. 3. Curves represented by connected equi-length curve angle chain

Although the connected equi-length line angle chain can describe the curve in general situation, two problems it will meet in the following situations as shown in Fig 2(b): one is that the circle and curve have several intersection points, which is should be acted as circle center of the next cell; the other problem is that the connected equi-length line angle chain ignores the cell detail when the curve have high curvature.

In our framework, a curve is modeled by a number of linked equi-length curve segments. Each curve segment has a head and tail, pointing from the head to tail. A sequence of codes using the included angles between a pair of neighboring curve segments is used for representing the curve (See Fig.3(a)). Thus the connected equi-length curve angle chain (CELCAC) able to overcome the exited disadvantages of the

Zhao's method. The CELCAC model extends the curve segment in curve direction, which will not have several intersections with the circle. In addition, with the number of the line segments increases, detailed portions of the curve, such as the dominate points and the smoothing parts, can be described arbitrarily accurate.

A series of orientation difference between neighbor curve segments establish CELCAC is formatted as: the curve Q is divided into n curve segments $\{Q_0, Q_1, Q_2 \ldots\ldots Q_n\}$ with same curve length L, corresponding to the segments ports $\{H_0, H_1, H_2 \ldots\ldots H_n, H_{n+1}\}$ .Then the CELCAC can be presented as $A = (\alpha_1, \alpha_2, \alpha_3, \ldots\ldots \alpha_n)$, where $\alpha_i (i = 1 \ldots\ldots n)$ is the orientation difference between the line connect point H_{i-1}, H_i and the line connect point H_i, H_{i+1} (See Fig.3(b))

$$\alpha_i = \arccos(\frac{\sqrt{d^2(H_{i-1}, H_{i+1}) - d^2(H_{i-1}, H_i) - d^2(H_i, H_{i+1})}}{2d(H_{i-1}, H_i)d(H_i, H_{i+1})}), \tag{1}$$

in which $d(H_{i-1}, H_{i+1}) = |H_{i-1} - H_{i+1}|$.

4 Model Mitral Annulus by the Connected Equi-length Curve Angle Chain

The CELCAC can describe some closed three dimensional curve like mitral annulus. This method has the advantage of the description of the curve with invariance of translation, rotation, scaling and the relative uniqueness of the head point.

4.1 Modeling the Mitral Annulus

Considering three dimensional shape of the mitral annulus, we describe the mitral annulus using the following equation

$$C(t) = (x(t), y(t), z(t)), \tag{2}$$

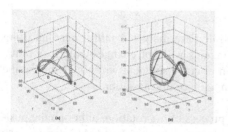

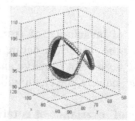

Fig. 4. Mitral annulus represented by equi-length curve angle chain

Fig. 5. Approximation error represented by area principle

in which t is a linear function of the path length ranting over the closed interval$[0,1]$. As the mitral annulus is a closed three dimensional curve, $x(t), y(t), z(t)$ are periodic functions.

4.2 Identifying the Head Point of the First Curve Segment

Identifying the head point of the first curve segment is the necessary first step to describe the closed mitral curve annulus. Firstly, the distance between each pair of points on the curve should be calculated, and the line segment $\overline{AB}$ that has the maximum distance is obtained. For a closed curve as mitral annulus (See Fig.4(a)), the point P has the longest distance to the line conned two port points A and B. The projection of point P on $\overline{AB}$ is point D, and we choose the end point A that is closer to point H_0 as the head of the first curve segment [22].

4.3 Generation of Equa-length Curve Segments

From the section 2, we have obtain the location of every point on the mitral annuls in three dimensional coordinates. Firstly, it starts with the head point H_0 of first curve segment of mitral annulus, extends the curve segment in curve direction. The Lth point H_1 from the head point is regarded as the tail of the first curve segment, and at the same time as the head of the second curve segment. The process is iterated until the Nth point is obtained. Fig.4(b) is an code example of curve presented by equi-Length Curve Angle Chain. Thus, the closed curve can be represented by a number of orientated curve segments of equal length. Each curve segment is attached with an identification vector, which reflects the distribution of the rest of line segments with respect to the current one using orientation difference. A set of orientation difference established the connected equi-length line angle chain.

4.4 Property of Equi-length Curve Angle Chain

Property of relative uniqueness of the head point. Based on the method of identifying the head point of the first curve segment, the head point is unique to each mitral annulus.

Property of invariance of translation. While describing the mitral annulus using CELCAC, the shape and nature of mitral annulus will not change while it is translated. The head point of curve and the length of curve segment will not change at the same time, namely, the chain will keep the invariance of translation.

Property of invariance of rotation. In the process of the rotation, although the positions of overall points on mitral annulus had changed, but the CELCAC chain is also the orientation different of two neighbor curve segments. Therefore, if the number

n of curve segmentation has identified, the CELCAC chain will not change whatever the curve rotate.

Property of invariance of scaling. With the area rule to determine the number n of curve segment, it will have only one CELCAC chain corresponding to the curve. Based on the Property 1 and the method to identify the number of curve segment in section 4, while reduce a curve with arbitrary ratio, the CELCAC chain will not change but the length of curve segment.

5 Experiments and Results

5.1 Study Population

Over a 10-months period, Echocardiographic studies were performed on 11 normal healthy young children (Group ω_N, 6 boys, 5 girls, mean age 4 year ± 3 year), and 10 children with severe mitral regurgitation (MR) (Group ω_{MR}, 6 boys, 4 girl, mean age 5 year ± 3 year). All participants underwent three dimensional echocardiography and filled out an informed consent for the study, which was approved by the Committee for the Protection of Human Subjects in Clinical Research studies at the Shanghai Children's Medical Center.

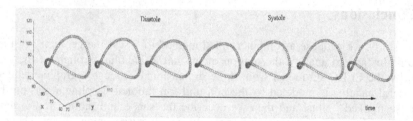

Fig. 6. Dynamics shape of the Mitral Annuls throughout the Cardiac Cycle

5.2 Shape of the Mitral Annulus

The results of the dynamic motion of the mitral annulus throughout the cardiac cycle are presented in both spatial and temporal dimensions (See Fig.6). Extracted 3D images visualize the mitral annulus as though removed from whole image. We obtain results concerning the non-planarity (two high and two low points) configuration of the mitral annulus, which are similar to previously reported studies [23, 24].

5.3 Dynamics of the Mitral Annulus

The dynamic motion of the mitral annulus throughout the cardiac cycle presented by the CELCAC is introduced in Fig.7. In order to facilitate the observation, we enlarge the size of mitral annulus to watch the shape of mitral annulus presented by the CELCAC, which will not affect the description of the curve and the value of CELCAC.

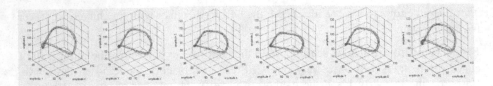

Fig. 7. Mitral annulus represented by CELCAC throughout the cardio circle

From the equation (3), we know that with the number of curve segments increaser, the length of curve segment is shorter, and more accurate of description the shape of mitral annulus; conversely, the longer of curve segment, more rough of description. Therefore, we can adjust the size of area error, namely, the length of curve segments, to meet different requirements in practical applications. The area error is 20 and the number of curve segment is 11 in our work.

The average value of angles between neighbor curve segments, the height, the inter-peak distance, the inter-valley, and the annulus area of the mitral annulus throughout the cardiac cycle have been calculated. From Table.I, the average value of angles between neighbor curve segments is a little smaller in the group of normal young children both end diastole($156^{o} \pm 9^{o}$ vs $162^{o} \pm 8^{o}$, p<0.01) and at end systole($135^{o} \pm 8^{o}$ vs $139^{o} \pm 10^{o}$, p<0.01), than the group of severe MR.

6 Conclusions

In this study, we propose a computer aided method to assess the geometry of the mitral annulus and to analyze the motion of the mitral annulus throughout the cardiac cycle by the CELCAC model from three dimensional echocardiographic sequences. The mitral annulus is modeled by the non-uniform rational **B**-spline algorithm based on those marked points, and then we describe the shape and motion mitral annulus throughout the cardiac cycle using the equi-length curve angle chain. The results show that new CELCAC model is feasible in the evaluation of the configuration and the dynamics of the mitral annulus.

Acknowledgements

This paper has been partially supported by China Natural Science Foundation (60572154) and National Basic Research Program of China (2003CB716104).

References

1. Powel, K., Rodrigruez, L., Patwari, P., et al.: 3-D Reconstruction of Mitral Annulus from 2-D Transesophageal Echocardiographic Images. Comput. in Cardiol., 25–28 (1994)
2. Dias, J., Leitao, J.: Wall position and thickness estimation from sequence of echocardiographic images. IEEE Trans. Med Imaging 15, 25–38 (1996)

3. Kotropolulos, C.: Nonlinear ultrasonic image processing based on signal-adaptive filters and self-organizing neural networks. IEEE Trans. Image Processing 3, 65–77 (1994)
4. Thomas, J., Peters, R., Jeanty, P.: Automatic segmentation of ultrasound images using morphological operators. IEEE Trans. Med. Imaging 10, 180–186 (1991)
5. Hass, C., Ermert, H., Holt, S., et al.: Segmentation of 3-D intravascular ultrasonic images based on a random field model. Ultrasound Med Biol 26, 297–306 (2000)
6. Johan, G., Steven, C., Boudewijn, P.: Automatic segmentation of echocardiographic sequences by active appearance motion models. IEEE Trans. Med. Imaging 21, 1374–1383 (2002)
7. Chen, S., Yang, X., Yao, L., et al.: Segmentation in Echocardiographic Sequences using Shape-based Snake Model Combined with Generalized Hough Transformation. Int. J. Cardiovasc Imaging 22, 33–45 (2006)
8. Saracino, G., Dainion, M., Greenberg, N., et al.: A novel system for the assessment of mitral annular geometry and analysis of 3D motion of the mitral annulus from 3D echocardiography. Comput. in Cardiol. 31, 69–72 (2004)
9. Yamaura, Y., Yoshida, K., Hozumi, T., et al.: Evaluation of the mitral annulus by extracted three-dimensional images in patients with an annuloplasty annulus. Am. J. Cardiol 82, 534–536 (1998)
10. Ormiston, J., Shah, P., Tei, C., et al.: Size and motion of the mitral annulus in man. I. A two-dimensional echocardiographic method and findings in normal subjects. Circulation 64, 113–120 (1981)
11. Ching, Y., Chen, S., Chang, C., et al.: Finding the mitral annular lines from 2-D + 1-D precordial echocardiogram using graph-search technique. IEEE trans. Inf. Technol. Biomed. 8, 1–4 (2004)
12. Wolf, I., Hastenteufel, M., Simone, D., et al.: Three-dimensional annulus segmentation and hybrid visualisation in echocardiography. Comput. in Cardiol., 23–26 (2001)
13. Chandra, S., Powell, K., Breburda, C.: Three dimensional reconstruction (shape and motion) of tricuspid annulus in normals and in patients after tricuspid annuloplasty with a flexible ring. Comput. in Cardiol. 8-11, 693–696 (1996)
14. Tei, C., Pilgrim, J., Shah, P., et al.: The tricuspid valve annulus: study of size and motion in normal subjects and in patients with tricuspid regurgitation. Circulation 66, 665–671 (1982)
15. Tuladhar, S., Punjabi, P.: Surgical reconstruction of the mitral valve. Heart 92, 1373–1377 (2006)
16. Watanabe, N., Ogasawara, Y., Yamaura, Y.: Mitral annulus flattens in ischemic mitral regurgitation: Geometric differences between inferior and anterior myocardial infarction: A real-time 3-dimensional echocardiographic study. Circulation 112, 458–462 (2005)
17. Valocik, G., Kamp, O., Visser, C.: Three-dimensional echocardiography in mitral valve disease. Eur. J. Echocardio. 6, 443–454 (2005)
18. Takemoto, Y., Hozumi, T., Sugioka, K., et al.: Automated Three-Dimensional Analysis of Mitral Annular Dynamics in Patients with Myocardial Infarction Using Automated Mitral Annular Tracking Method. Echocardiography. Journal of Cardiovascular Ultrasound & Allied Techniques 23, 658–665 (2006)
19. Donald, H., Pauline, M.: Computer Graphics with OpenGL, 3rd edn., Beijing, pp. 451–452. Publishing house of electronics industry (2004)
20. Burger, P., Gillies, D.: Interactive computer graphics, Functional, Procedural and Device-level Methods. Addison-Wesley Publishing Co, Reading (1989)
21. Riesenfeld, R.: Berstein-Bezier Methods for the Computer Aided Design of Free-Form Curves and Surfaces. Ph.D. Thesis, Syracuse University (1973)

22. Zhao, Y., Chen, Y.Q.: Connected Equi-Length Line Segments for Curve and Structure. International Journal of Pattern Recognition and Artificial Intelligence 18, 1019–1022 (2004)
23. Levine, R., Robert, A., Marco, O., et al.: The relationship of mitral annular shape to the diagnosis of the mitral valve prolapse. Circulation 75, 751–756 (1987)
24. Tsakiris, A., Bernuth, G., Rastelli, G., et al.: Size and motion of the mitral annulus in anesthetized intact dogs. J. Appl. Physiol. 30, 611–618 (1971)

A Segmentation Method Based on Dynamic Programming for Breast Mass in MRI Images

Jihong Liu[1,2], Weina Ma[1], and Soo-Young Lee[2]

[1] College of Information Science and Engineering, Northeastern University,
Shenyang, 110004 China
[2] Brain Science Research Center, Korea Advanced Institute of Science and Technology,
Daejeon 305-701, Korea
liujihong@ise.neu.edu.cn

Abstract. The tumor segmentation in Breast MRI image is difficult due to the complicated galactophore structure. The work in this paper attempts to accurately segment the abnormal breast mass in MRI(Magnetic resonance imaging) Images. The ROI (Region of Interest) is segmented using a novel DP (Dynamic Programming) based optimal edge detection technique. DP is an optimal approach in multistage decision-making. The method presented in this paper processes the object image to get the minimum cumulative cost matrix combining with LUM nonlinear enhancement filter, Gaussian preprocessor, non-maximum suppression and double-threshold filtering, and then trace the whole optimal edge. The experimental results show that this method is robust and efficient on image edge detection and can segment the breast tumor area more accurately.

1 Introduction

Breast cancer has affected one of every eight women in United States and one of every ten women in Europe[1]. Early diagnoses of breast cancer are important. However, early diagnosis requires an accurate and reliable diagnostic procedure that allows physicians to distinguish benign breast tumors from malignant ones.

The goal of breast mass segmentation is to separate suspected masses from surrounding tissue as effectively as possible. It is extremely important in the diagnostic process, while it is a pre-processing step of Computer Aided Diagnosis (CAD). Over the years researchers have used many methods to segment masses in mammograms or ultrasonic. Petrick et al. [2] used a filtering method called the Density Weighted Contrast Enhancement (DWCE) method. Karssemeijer and Brake implemented a discrete dynamic contour model [3]. Furthermore, many researchers have implemented methods based on maximum likelihood analysis [4,5]. Forbes F et al. [6] proposed an ROI selection method that combines model-based clustering of the pixels with Bayesian morphology. Wismuller A et al. [7] suggested that the minimal free energy vector quantization neural network had the potential to increase the diagnostic accuracy of MRI mammography by improving sensitivity without reduction of specificity. An essential issue for CAD researchers is the ability to properly obtain the boundaries of masses, because these boundaries are often obscured by surrounding breast tissue.

D. Zhang (Ed.): ICMB 2008, LNCS 4901, pp. 307–313, 2007.
© Springer-Verlag Berlin Heidelberg 2007

Image segmentation can be divided into parallel method and serial method. Parallel method based on the check point itself and its neighbors for edge detecting, mainly includes a few of local differential operator, such as Roberts gradient operator, Sobel gradient operator, Laplacian second order difference operator and so on. This method has the advantage of high speed, but the structural information is always discontinuous and fragmentary. Whether the check point is an edge point of image in serial method depends on its surrounding checked points, which is multistage decision process. Thus we can checkout the single-track, consecutive structural information of the ROI. However, the speed of this serial method is slow.

DP (Dynamic Programming) is a powerful tool for image segmentation to solve the optimization of multistage decision process. After examining the local discontinuity of the image, it joins the boundary using serial search method and then the edge detection is achieved successfully. Lie W N et al. [8] proposed a skyline image detection for navigation of mobile vehicles or planes in mountainous environments using DP algorithm can get a fast processing speed. We present a novel DP-based optimal edge detection method to segment the breast tumor in MRI image.

2   A DP-Based Optimal Edge Detection Method

In order to obtain the optimal edge, the whole process presented in this paper is divided into several sections.

2.1   Image Pre-processing

The detecting outcome of the optimal path in DP algorithm highly depends on the quality of the edge image. However, in most medical images as the gray level reflected the body internal structure changes smoothly, the available single filter is rather difficult to satisfy the demands of removing noise while simultaneously enhancing edges.

Edge enhancement and sharpening have traditionally been accomplished using linear techniques. These techniques include Wiener filtering, high-pass filtering, and unsharp masking. The nonlinear filters usually considered are the lower-upper-middle (LUM) filter, the comparison and selection (CS) filter and the weighted majority of samples with minimum range (WMMR) filter. In our study we use LUM filters [9] to avoid many of the shortcomings of conventional linear edge-enhancing filters. In particular, LUM filters can intensively decrease levels of additive noise and remove impulsive-type noise while simultaneously enhancing edges. Furthermore, it does not cause any over-sharp. With an appropriate choice of parameters, LUM filters can function as smoothers. Before presenting the filters, we define some notation as follow:

Consider a discrete sequence $\{ x(n) \}$ where the index $n = [n_1, n_2, ..., n_d]$. Also, consider a moving window that spans N samples at each location n, where N is assumed to be odd. These samples can be indexed and written as a vector $x(n) = [x_1(n), x_2(n), ..., x_N(n)]$. The middle sample in the observation widow is denoted

$x_{(N+1)/2}(n)$ and the filter estimate at this location is denoted $y(n)$. The rank ordered or sorted observation samples are written as

$$x_1(n) \leq x_2(n) \leq ...x_N(n) \tag{1}$$

The output of the LUM filter with parameters k and l is given by

$$y(n) = \begin{cases} x_k & x_{(N+1)/2} < x_k \\ x_l & x_l < x_{(N+1)/2} \leq t_l \\ x_{N-l+1} & t_l < x_{(N+1)/2} < x_{N-l+1} \\ x_{N-k+1} & x_{N-k+1} < x_{(N+1)/2} \\ x_{(N+1)/2} & others \end{cases} \tag{2}$$

Where t_l is the midpoint between x_l and x_{N-l+1} and $1 \leq k \leq l \leq (N+1)/2$. The parameters k and l can be considered tuning parameters that allow the LUM filter to have a variety of characteristics. In the case where $l = (N+1)/2$ and k is varied, the LUM filter acts as a smoothing filter. As k is increased more smoothing can be expected, and if $k = l = (N+1)/2$, then the output of the LUM filter is simply the median. In the case where $k = 1$ and l is varied, the LUM functions as a sharpener. As l is decreased, x_{N-l+1} and x_l move toward the upper and lower extreme values, respectively. This leads to an increased edge enhancing effect. When $1 < k \leq l < (N+1)/2$, sharpening and outlier rejection can be achieved simultaneously. The parameter k can be increased to improve the impulse rejection characteristics of the LUM filter. The parameter l, on the other hand, controls the level of edge enhancement. This parameter is decreased to give more enhancement and increased to reduce enhancement. Finally, the filter performs an identity operation when $k = 1$ and $l = (N+1)/2$.

The image has a significant edge and higher signal-noise ratio after nonlinear filtering. But the false edge of the object image results from the DP algorithm entered the fork in the backward tracking due to the intersection or fork at the edge of image as well as the surplus noise .Therefore, in this paper we use a double-threshold gaussian filter to enhance the edge of low quality image, to reduce the effect of false edge. Based on this, filtering with 3×3 gauss template, the gradient image which includes all information of the edge is calculated.Non-maximum suppression is done on the gradient image to thin the edge.

In order to acquire a more efficient boundary, we propose a double-threshold suppression on the image which is clearly processed by above methods. While the main outline, after processing with double-threshold filtering, is relatively clear, the mixed false edge caused by inhomogeneous gray scale and noise is preferably removed. Then the processed image can be used for iteration of the initial cost matrix in DP algorithm, calculating the minimum cumulative cost matrix. Compared with normal local differential coefficient operator, our experience with proposed methods presents

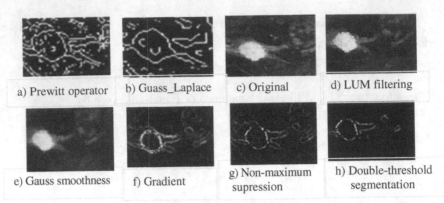

a) Prewitt operator   b) Guass_Laplace   c) Original   d) LUM filtering

e) Gauss smoothness   f) Gradient   g) Non-maximum supression   h) Double-threshold segmentation

Fig. 1. Results gotten from the pre-processing and the traditional methods. a) Prewitt operator. b) Guass-Laplace. c) Original. d) LUM filtering. e) Gauss smoothness. f) Gradient. g) Non-maximum. h) Double-Threshold segmentation.

the more effective and clear results. In Fig.1 a) and b) are gotten by traditional operators, c) to h) are gotten by above pre-processing method in this paper.

2.2 The DP Algorithm for Image Edge Detection

In order to obtain the minimum uncertainty in the final output of medical imaging system, optimal criterion is necessary in edge detection. Especially in some cases it is essential to get the local boundary, and the DP algorithm based on interaction can process the object image perfectly.

When the image edge detection is considered as an optimal problem, it can be formulated in two aspects: (a) The optimal value M of the target function defined as $V = V(x_0, x_1, \ldots, x_N)$, where M is chosen from value of max or min and where $0 \le x_i \le n_i$, $i = 0,1,\ldots,N$. (b) The variable $(\overline{x}_0, \overline{x}_1, \ldots, \overline{x}_N)$ up to optimal target.

When there are different demands on target function and the variable is scattered, the whole problem will include a considerable solution space. Suppose the target function is presented as:

$$V(x_0, x_N) = V_0(x_0, x_1) + V_1(x_1 + x_2) + \cdots + V_{N-1}(x_{N-1}, x_N) \tag{3}$$

Then, the recursion formula of multistage optimization procedure can be applied:

$$f_0(x_0) = 0 \tag{4}$$

$$f_{k+1}(x_{k+1}) = \underset{0 \le x_k \le n_k}{opt} [V_k(x_k, x_{k+1}) + f_k(x_k)] \tag{5}$$

Where $k = 0,1,\ldots,N-1$, and $f_{k+1}(x_{k+1})$ is an intermediate variable. By the end of the recursion we have,

$$M = \underset{x_N}{opt} f_N(x_N) \tag{6}$$

Equation (4) actually is the solution to part(a), and the optimal variable of part(b) is given as follow,

$$\overline{x}_N = m_N = \arg \underset{x_N}{opt} f_N(x_N) \tag{7}$$

$$\overline{x}_k = m_{k+1}(\overline{x}_{k+1}), \qquad k = N-1,\ldots,0 \tag{8}$$

Where, $m_{k+1}(\overline{x}_{k+1})$ denotes the value of $\overline{x}_k$ reaching to optimizing after $\overline{x}_{k+1}$ is given. Hence, through reverse recursion, the optimal variable is obtained.

In DP model for edge detection, the target function is given by the cumulative cost $cum(x_N, y_N)$ from starting point (x_0, y_0) which is the convergence of edge line or has a large curvature with the feature points on edge line to the end point (x_N, y_N). As a result the optimal value is namely the minimum cumulative cost matrix of stop point.

The demands of local gradient information and global edge cumulative cost information are needed in dynamic programming algorithm using for edge detection, which is just the reason that we get the global optimal solution. Using 8-neighbor connective method as an example, Fig. 2 shows the edge image applied DP algorithm after getting the local points.

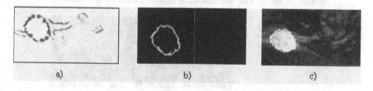

Fig. 2. ROI segmented using DP algorithm. a) Getting points. b) Edge extraction. c) Combination

3 Experimental Results

We tested our algorithm among 120 images of breast MR. Comparing with the traditional edge detection methods, we use above approach to segment abnormal region in breast MRI image and get the similar results with the diagnosis of doctor. One of the experimental results is shown in Fig. 3. It is obvious that this method is particularly helpful when the masses have ill-defined borders.

The threshold segmentation have a good effection on CT slices, simple algorithm and quick calculation, but it must be used according previous experiences or tried time after time, then being adjusted. Comparing with threshold segmentation, the algorithm of interactive segmentation based on DP is good for the object that have a smooth edge, which only need lesser degree to achieve accurate segmentation, although it also must spend time and interactive degree in bad edge image.

Fig. 3 a) is the initial image. Fig. 3 b) and c) show the pre-processing results. In Fig. 3 d) shows a gradient image whose gradient line has more than one pixel. In Fig. 3 e), it only keeps the middle pixels after non-maximum suppression, and accordingly the ridge of single pixel wide is obtained. Fig. 3 f) shows the clear boundary without false edge using double-threshold segmentation. The quality of threshold affects the result of image segmentation directly. However, we can not find a uniform threshold for adjusting due to large and obvious differences existing among the medical imaging, so in processing program the exact threshold is obtained according the user's observation and experience. As in Fig. 3 g), in order to prevent the DP algorithm entering the wrong edge line in backward tracking process, we get several feature points which are in the convergence area of edge line or have a large curvature. The edge points are identified via backward tracking minimum cost path, as it shown in Fig. 3 h). Fig. 3 i) shows the initial image combined with the edge.

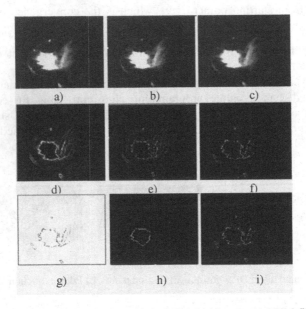

Fig. 3. The experimental results of DP method. a) Original image. b) LUM filtering. c) Guass smoothing. d) Gradient image. e) Non-maximum suppression. f) Double-threshold segmentation. g) Getting points. h) Edge extraction. i) Combined image.

4   Conclusions

We have developed a mass segmentation method that is capable of detecting the edge of the abnormal mass and marking its region. The ROI is segmented using a novel DP-based optimal edge detection technique. Dynamic programming is an optimal approach in multistage decision-making. The method presented in this paper processes the object image to get the minimum cumulative cost matrix combining with LUM nonlinear enhancement filter, Gaussian preprocessor, Non-maximum suppression and Double-threshold segmentation, and then traces the whole optimal edge. The experimental results show that this method is robust and efficient on image edge detection and can segment the breast tumor area more accurately.

References

1. Pandey, N., Salcic, Z., Sivaswamy, J.: Fuzzy logic based microcalcification detection. neural networks for signal processing X. In: Proceedings of the 2000 IEEE Signal Processing Society Workshop 2000, Sydney, NSW, Australia, pp. 662–671 (2000)
2. Petrick, N., Chan, H.-P., Sahiner, B., Wei, D.: An Adaptive Density-Weighted Contrast Enhancement Filter for Mammographic Breast Mass Detection. IEEE Transactions on Medical Imaging 15(1), 59–67 (1996)
3. Brake, G.M., te, K.N.: Segmentation of suspicious densities in digital mammograms. Medical Physics 28, 259–266 (2001)
4. Kupinski, M.A., Giger, M.L.: Automated Seeded Lesion Segmentation on Digtal Mammograms. IEEE Transactions on Medical Imaging 17(4), 510–517 (1998)
5. Kinnard, L., Lo, S.-C.B., Wang, P., Freedman, M.T., Chouikha, M.: Automatic Segmentation of Mammographic Masses Using Fuzzy Shadow and Maximum-Likelihood Analysis. In: Proceedings. IEEE International Symposium on Biomedical Imaging, pp. 241–244 (2002)
6. Forbes, F., Peyrard, N., Fraley, C., Georgian-Smith, D., Goldhaber, D.M., Raftery, A.E.: Model-based region-of-interest selection in dynamic breast MRI. Journal of Computer Assisted Tomography 30(4), 675–687 (2006)
7. Wismüller, A., Meyer-Bäse, A., Lange, O., Schlossbauer, T., Kallergi, M., Reiser, M.F., Leinsinger, G.: Segmentation and classification of dynamic breast magnetic resonance image data. Journal of Electronic Imaging 15 (2006)
8. Lie, W.N., Lin, T.C., Hung, K.S.: A robust dynamic programming algorithm to extract skyline in images for navigation. Pattern Recognition Letters 26(2), 221–230 (2005)
9. Hardie, R.C., Boncelet, C.G.: Gradient-based edge detection using nonlinear edge enhancing profilers. IEEE Trans Image Processing 4(11), 1572–1577 (1995)

A Multi-resolution Optical Flow Based Approach to Respiratory Motion Correction in 3D PET/CT Images

M. Dawood[1,2,3], M. Fieseler[1,3], F. Büther[2,3], X. Jiang[1,3], and K.P. Schäfers[2,3]

[1] Department of Computer Science, University of Münster, Germany
[2] Department of Nuclear Medicine, University Hospital Mnster, Germany
[3] European Institute of Molecular Imaging, Münster, Germany
dawood@uni-muenster.de

Abstract. The problem of motion in PET/CT studies results from the fact that the PET images are formed over an elongated period of time whereas the CT acquisition takes only a few seconds. Additionally, the CT images are also used for attenuation correction of the PET data. The spatial discrepancy between the two sets of images, however, may lead to wrong attenuation and thus to wrong quantification of the radioactive uptake. We present a solution to this problem by respiratory-gating the PET data and correcting the PET images for motion with a multiresolution optical flow algorithm. Our algorithm is based on the combined local and global optical flow algorithm with modifications to allow for discontinuity preservation across organ boundaries and for application to 3D volume sets.

1 Introduction

PET (Positron Emission Tomography) and CT (Computed Tomography) are combined in PET/CT machines to achieve metabolic as well as anatomic images of the patients. Respiratory motion leads to a degradation of PET images of the human thorax because they are acquired over typically several minutes. It leads to two sources of possible artifacts in PET/CT: wrong attenuation correction and image blur. Attenuation correction is the method of correcting the PET data for the effects of photon absorption in the body. Dense tissues, like bones, absorb a larger part of the photons than less dense tissues, like lungs. Therefore PET images without attenuation correction show apparently greater activity in areas with less density. This effect is corrected by scaling the number of photons registered in the scanner in accordance with the density of tissues. In PET/CT scanners the computed tomography (CT) data, which gives information about the densities of tissue, is used for attenuation correction [8]. As the CT is acquired much faster (in seconds) than PET, it represents an almost instantaneous snapshot in comparison to the PET images. Therefore a part of the PET data is not in spatial correspondence with the CT data and will be wrongly corrected for attenuation (e.g. activity from heart may be corrected with lung

D. Zhang (Ed.): ICMB 2008, LNCS 4901, pp. 314–322, 2007.

density). The second disadvantage of motion is image blur. The motion of the source of radioactive emission causes blurring on the PET images proportional to the magnitude of the motion. This leads to loss of contrast. It has been shown that the motion of lungs during the PET acquisition may lead to wrong staging of tumors [5], some tumors even succeed in evading detection [15] and the attenuation correction of PET images with CT may also lead to errors [14].

In addition to the literature cited in [2], it is necessary to mention here some of the recent studies in the field of PET motion correction. Studies which try to estimate the respiratory motion of the organs on gated CT images, e.g. [12],[13],[16], are not of further interest, because they need to gate the CT phase of the scan, which leads to an increase in radiation dose for the patient and is not justifiable for most routine patients. Our study, on the other hand, proposes a PET-images-only based method which does not cause an increase in radiation to the patient and thus is applicable to all patients. One approach proposes to estimate the motion parameters on reconstructed PET images and then induce them in the "Joint estimation" method of reconstruction after the second run [7]. The methodological difference of this approach with our study is that we estimate the parameters and deform the reconstructed images directly, without renewed reconstruction.

The principle applicability of respiratory gating and optical flow algorithms to PET/CT data was already proved in our previous work where the optical flow algorithm by Lucas and Kanade was used to correct the PET images for motion [2]. Advanced optical flow methods were used in a subsequent study to improve the performance of motion correction [4]. These algorithms allowed improvement in case of patients with large respiratory displacements. The aim of the present paper is to solve the problem of large motion in PET/CT data by using a multi-resolution 4D (i.e. 3D+time) implementation of the algorithm presented recently.

2   Methods

Respiratory gating is the technique to divide the PET data into smaller parts, with each part representing only a part of the total respiratory motion [9]. The disadvantage of this method is the loss in image quality due to lower statistics. To retain all information and yet to reduce the motion is necessary. To achieve this, the PET image data can be transformed from the different respiratory gates to one position within the breathing cycle to get a complete dataset with minimum motion.

2.1   Respiratory Gating

The respiratory cycle was divided into eight parts by using a respiratory signal. This signal was acquired from the patient by laying a belt around the patient's waist with a black disc attached to it. The black disc contains a white spot in the center. The position of this spot was tracked with the help of a video camera. The image from the camera is thresholded to segment the white spot. The center of mass of the segmented voxels is then taken as the reference point, whose motion is tracked. The PET data is then sorted based upon the amplitude of the respiratory signal [3]. The eight respiratory phases are then reconstructed individually.

2.2   Optical Flow

Optical flow methods calculate the motion between two image frames. As a voxel with intensity $I(x, y, z, t)$ moves between the two frames, the image constraint equation is given as:

$$I(x, y, z, t) = I(x + \delta x, y + \delta y, z + \delta z, t + \delta t) \tag{1}$$

where x, y, z are the spatial 3D coordinates and t is the time point. Assuming the movement to be small enough and with Taylor expansion:

$$I_x u + I_y v + I_z w = -I_t \tag{2}$$

with u, v, w for the x, y and z components of the velocity or optical flow and I_x, I_y, I_z, I_t for the derivatives of the intensity image in corresponding directions respectively time. To find the optical flow from this equation in three unknowns we need to use some constraints. This is where the different optical flow algorithms come into play. The algorithm by Bruhn et al. [1] estimates the optical flow as follows. Defining:

$$V = \begin{pmatrix} u \\ v \\ w \\ 1 \end{pmatrix}, \quad \nabla I = \begin{pmatrix} I_x \\ I_y \\ I_z \\ I_t \end{pmatrix}, \quad |\nabla V|^2 = |\nabla u|^2 + |\nabla v|^2 + |\nabla w|^2 \text{ and}$$

$$\psi_i(s^2) = 2\beta_i^2 \sqrt{1 + \frac{s^2}{\beta_i^2}}, i \in 1, 2$$

the optical flow may be estimated by minimizing:

$$f_{LG} = \int \psi_1\{k * V^T(\nabla I \nabla I^T)V\} + \psi_2\{\alpha|\nabla V|^2)\}\mathrm{d}x\mathrm{d}y\mathrm{d}z \tag{3}$$

with the smoothing parameter α and the scaling parameters β_i. The first term in this function is dependent upon the image gradient and can be called the data term whereas the second term is the smoothing term. The solution to the minimization problem can be found by using the corresponding Euler-Lagrange equations. The derivatives can be calculated as in [2].

Discontinuity Preserving Optical Flow Algorithm. The smoothing term in the above algorithm also smooths out the flow across the boundaries of the moving objects. To avoid this problem we transform the basic equation by applying a weighting function to the smoothing term:

$$f = \int \{\psi_1(D) + \psi_2(g, S)\}\mathrm{d}x\mathrm{d}y\mathrm{d}z \tag{4}$$

The appropriate weighting function g should reduce the effect of the smoothing term at object boundaries, but retain the effect in areas of homogeneous flow. The smoothing term was weighted in accordance with the image gradient. Thus places where edges are present will be smoothed less than areas inside organs which usually have lesser number of edges and with a lower gradient. This function is given by:

$$\psi_2(g, S) = \psi_2(|\nabla I| * |\nabla V|^2) \tag{5}$$

The convolution in this case is to be understood as applied to the corresponding components. The discontinuity preserving (DP) algorithm uses coupled pairs of equations. The optical flow is calculated iteratively in a double loop. The outer loop updates the ψ variables and the inner loop updates the u, v, w optical flow components. Details can be found in [4].

2.3 Multi-resolution Approach

The algorithm as presented so far is robust enough to be used with noisy images. However, owing to the basic definitions of optical flow i.e the image constraint equation (eq. 2), all optical flow algorithms become inaccurate in estimating the deformations with increasing motion. Thus it is necessary to extend the algorithm to accommodate larger displacements. This calls for a multi-resolution strategy. In this approach the optical flow is calculated by dividing the displacement into parts.

In the first step the images are reduced by half in resolution, thus also reducing the object displacements by half in terms of voxels. The thus reduced images might show artificial edges with high gradients and other artifacts. Therefore smoothing of the reduced images becomes necessary. This was done in our case by applying a Gaussian kernel. The optical flow is then calculated on the reduced resolution images by applying the DP-optical flow algorithm. The deformation vectors thus obtained from the algorithm are magnified by a factor of two by doubling the vectors in number and magnitude to get the original resolution. These vectors are now used to deform the images in original resolution. The remaining part of the motion can be detected by applying the optical flow algorithm to the already deformed images in original resolution, and subsequently correcting for it.

The motion on original images is given as:

$$f(I_o) = f(I_l) + f(I_h) \tag{6}$$

where $f(I_o)$ denotes the motion on original sized images, $f(I_l)$ denotes the motion estimated at the lower resolution, and $f(I_h)$ denotes the *remaining* motion present on the images in original size, already corrected for $f(I_l)$. The number of levels of resolution can be increased to allow estimation of larger displacements. In this study, three levels of resolution were used counting the original images as level one. Further reduction would not be meaningful as the resolution at the lowest level was only 32x32x16 voxels.

2.4   Correction

Once the motion is estimated, it can be removed by inverting the motion vectors at every voxel position and deforming the 3D image accordingly. As the motion vectors are not always integers interpolation has to be employed [10]. Linear interpolation was used for this purpose.

2.5   Patient Data

Eight patients routinely referred to the [18]FDG PET scan were included in this study. PET data was acquired for 20 minutes, 1 hour post injection of [18]FDG (4 MBq/kg). To enhance FDG uptake in the heart, patients underwent a hyper-insulinemic euglycemic clamp technique [17]. The Siemens Biograph Sensation 16 PET/CT scanner (Siemens Medical Solutions) was used for data acquisition. This scanner has a spatial resolution of around 6 mm [6]. The respiratory signal for gating was acquired during the PET acquisition. The patient data was reconstructed with the help of the open-source STIR software package (http://stir.hammersmithimanet.com/). The reconstructed images had a voxel size of 3.375 x 3.375 x 3.375 mm^3.

3   Criteria for Measuring Improvement

Two independent criteria were selected to objectively assess the quality of the motion correction. These are the correlation coefficient and the displacement of the heart on the images. The correlation coefficient was calculated on the whole 3D image volumes. It considers all voxels in the volume and is global in nature. The correlation between the uncorrected images is already high (CC in the range of 0.8) since most voxels in the volume do not move, e.g. those voxels outside the body. As the lungs and the heart move with respiration the correlation between the images decreases. After motion correction the correlation should increase again. The second measure is the displacement of the heart. The heart moves up and down (cranio-caudal) due to respiratory motion. Its displacement should be reduced on the motion corrected images. Due to the usage of the special clamp technique, the heart showed very high uptake in the myocardium. This allows a simple threshold to be used for segmenting the heart on the images. The voxels belonging to the heart are then used to calculate the center of mass of the heart. The maximum distance in the position of this center of mass among all gates is then taken to be the maximum heart displacement. This method takes the 3D aspect of the data into account.

4   Results

The original resolution of the images was 128 × 128 × 64. Each additional level reduced the resolution by half in all three dimensions. The 3D images were motion corrected by using one, two, and three levels of resolution with the help of the algorithm described above. The parameters, such as the smoothing parameter α, the scaling parameters β_i, the number of iterations etc, used for motion correction were optimized for each patient manually. For all experiments with a particular patient dataset, the parameters were kept constant, only the number of levels was varied. The results for a typical patient are shown in Fig 1. The correlation coefficients increase with increasing number of levels. Also better results are achieved for gates closer to the target gate.

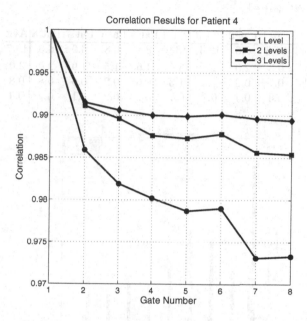

Fig. 1. The results of the Multi-Resolution-DP algorithm for Patient 4

Table 1 gives an overview of all eight patients. In this table only the correlation coefficients for Gate 8, which is the farthest from the target gate, are shown for all patients. Thus, for example, the correlation of Gate 8 with the target gate was 0.9103% for Patient 6 before motion correction. It increased to 0.9789 after motion correction. This result was further improved by using 3 levels of resolution to 0.9928%.

The results for the displacement of the heart criterium are given in Table 2 (see also Fig 2). The results show that the displacement of the heart is reduced significantly when motion correction is applied to the images. In most patients the displacement is further reduced by using the multi-resolution approach to almost 1 mm when two levels of resolution are used and to $\approx$ 0.5 by using three levels.

Table 1. Correlation of Gate 8 with Target Gate [target gate=1]

	Patient 1	Patient 2	Patient 3	Patient 4	Patient 5	Patient 6	Patient 7	Patient 8
Original	0.6422	0.8398	0.8580	0.7337	0.8626	0.9103	0.7926	0.8770
1 Level	0.9040	0.9542	0.9681	0.9733	0.9811	0.9789	0.9634	0.9559
2 Levels	0.9176	0.9740	0.9732	0.9854	0.9838	0.9907	0.9676	0.9637
3 Levels	0.9174	0.9777	0.9739	0.9894	0.9849	0.9928	0.9672	0.9650

Table 2. Maximum Displacement of the Heart with the Multi-Resolution-DP algorithm [in mm, target gate=1]

	Pat 1	Pat 2	Pat 3	Pat 4	Pat 5	Pat 6	Pat 7	Pat 8	Avg
Original	21.6	8.6	12.4	13.6	8.8	6.8	6.9	6.5	10.7
1 level	9.3	2.0	2.8	3.1	1.6	1.5	1.9	2.0	3.0
2 levels	0.7	0.8	1.4	1.3	0.6	0.2	0.6	0.8	0.8
3 levels	0.4	0.4	0.7	0.7	0.2	0.2	0.1	0.2	0.4

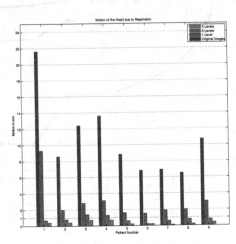

Fig. 2. Results: Motion of the heart due to respiration on different patient datasets

5   Discussion

The results make it clear that the motion correction depends upon the displacements. Thus gates which lay farther from the target gate show lower correlation with the target gate before motion correction. This correlation is increased after motion correction in all gates. However, the results for gates nearer to the target gate are better. The good news is that using the multi-resolution version of the algorithm can resolve this problem to a large extent. Thus the average correlation of all gates with the target gate for patient 4 is not only increased (0.9914, see Fig 1), but also the plotted curve for multi-resolution algorithm with three levels is almost horizontal for Gates 2 to Gate 8. Similar results were seen in all other patients. Table 1 shows that the results mentioned above are not confined to a single patient. For all patients the results are improved by using the multi-resolution based approach. The improvement in the results is not that large as between the original and the motion corrected data. This may be due to the simple reason that the DP-algorithm is robust enough to deal with most of the motion by itself. The incremental benefit seems to vary from patient to patient. It is important to note that the correlation is increased in almost all datasets by using the multi-resolution approach.

Lastly, the results of the heart displacement method show how effective the multi-resolution approach is as compared to the single level application of the DP-algorithm. The motion of the heart was about 10.7 mm on average among the eight patients. This was reduced to around 3.0 mm after application of the single level DP-algorithm. At a voxel resolution of 3.375 mm^3 this means that the motion was reduced to less than a voxel on average. However, we can see that in patients with very large motion (patient 1, 21.6 mm) the residual motion is still large (9.3 mm). In such cases the multi-resolution approach delivers the greatest benefits (residual motion 0.7 mm for two levels). The results are further improved when three levels are used and the residual motion is reduced to less than 0.5 mm. At our voxel resolution, this means a stationary heart. The overall results show that the residual motion is almost reduced by half when an additional level of resolution is used.

6   Conclusions

The discontinuity preserving optical flow algorithm was proposed by the authors for motion correction of PET images. However, residual motion continued to be a problem in some patients with very large respiratory motion. The DP-algorithm was extended to a 4D multi-resolution method to overcome this difficulty. The results on 8 real patient datasets presented in this study show better performance of this algorithm as compared with the previous version.

Acknowledgments

This work was partly funded by SFB 656 MoBil (projects B3 and C2) of the Deutsche Forschungsgemeinschaft (DFG).

References

1. Bruhn, A., Weickert, J., Schnörr, C.: Lucas/Kanade meets Horn/Schunch: Combining local and global optic flow methods. International Journal of Computer Vision 61(3), 211–231 (2005)
2. Dawood, M., Lang, N., Jiang, X., Schäfers, K.P.: Lung motion correction on respiratory gated 3-D PET/CT images. IEEE Trans Med Imaging 25(4), 476–485 (2006)
3. Dawood, M., Büther, F., Lang, N., Schober, O., Schäfers, K.: Respiratory gating in positron emission tomography: A quantitative comparison of different gating schemes. Medical Physics 34(7), 3067–3076 (2007)

4. Dawood, M., Büther, F., Lang, N., Jiang, X., Schäfers, K.P., Jiang, X., Schäfers, K.P.: Respiratory Motion Correction in 3D PET/CT with Advanced Optical Flow Algorithms. Under review
5. Erdi, Y.E., Nehmeh, S.A., Pan, T., et al.: The CT motion quantitation of lung lesions and its impact on PET-measured SUVs. J Nucl Med 45(8), 1287–1292 (2004)
6. Erdi, Y.E., Nehmeh, S.A., Mulnix, T., Humm, J.L., Watson, C.C.: Pet performance measurements for an Iso-based combined pet/ct scanner using the national electrical manufacturers association nu 2-2001 standard. J Nucl Med 45(5), 813–821 (2004)
7. Jacobson, M.W., Fessler, J.A.: Joint estimation of respiratory motion and activity in 4D PET using CT side information. In: IEEE International Symposium on Biomedical Imaging: From Nano to Macro, pp. 275–278 (2006)
8. Kinahan, P.E., Townsend, D.W., Beyer, T., Sashin, D.: Attenuation correction for a combined 3D PET/CT scanner. Med Phys 25(10), 2046–2053 (1998)
9. Lang, N., Dawood, M., Büther, F., Schober, O., Schäfers, M., Schäfers, K.: Organ movement reduction in pet/ct using dual-gated list-mode acquisition. Z Med Phys 16(1), 93–100 (2006)
10. Lehmann, T.M., Gönner, C., Spitzer, K.: Survey: interpolation methods in medical image processing. IEEE Trans Med Imaging 18(11), 1049–1075 (1999)
11. Maeland, E.: On the comparison of interpolation methods. Medical Imaging, IEEE Transactions on 7(3), 213–217 (1988)
12. Mair, B.A., Gilland, D.R., Sun, J.: Estimation of images and nonrigid deformations in gated emission CT. IEEE Trans Med Imaging 25(9), 1130–1144 (2006)
13. Manjeshwar, R., Tao, X., Asma, E., Thielemans, K.: Motion compensated image reconstruction of respiratory gated PET/CT. In: IEEE International Symposium on Biomedical Imaging: From Nano to Macro, pp. 674–677 (2006)
14. Osman, M.M., Cohade, C., Nakamoto, Y., Marshall, L.T., Leal, J.P., Wahl, R.L.: Clinically significant inaccurate localization of lesions with PET/CT: frequency in 300 patients. J Nucl Med 44(2), 240–243 (2003)
15. Papathanassiou, D., Becker, S., Amir, R., Meneroux, B., Liehn, J.C.: Respiratory motion artefact in the liver dome on FDG PET/CT: comparison of attenuation correction with CT and a caesium external source. Eur J Nucl Med Mol Imaging 32(12), 1422–1428 (2005)
16. Qiao, F., Pan, T., Clark, J.W., Mawlawi, O.R.: A motion-incorporated reconstruction method for gated PET studies. Phys Med Biol 51(15), 3769–3783 (2006)
17. Vitale, G.D., de Kemp, R.A., Ruddy, T.D., Williams, K., Beanlands, R.S.: Myocardial glucose utilization and optimization of (18)f-fdg PET imaging in patients with non-insulin-dependent diabetes mellitus, coronary artery disease, and left ventricular dysfunction. J. Nucl. Med. 42(12), 1730–1736 (2001)

Author Index

Lecture Notes in Computer Science

Sublibrary 6: Image Processing, Computer Vision, Pattern Recognition, and Graphics

Vol. 4338: P.K. Kalra, S. Peleg (Eds.), Computer Vision, Graphics and Image Processing. XV, 965 pages. 2006.

Vol. 4319: L.-W. Chang, W.-N. Lie (Eds.), Advances in Image and Video Technology. XXVI, 1347 pages. 2006.

Vol. 4292: G. Bebis, R. Boyle, B. Parvin, D. Koracin, P. Remagnino, A. Nefian, G. Meenakshisundaram, V. Pascucci, J. Zara, J. Molineros, H. Theisel, T. Malzbender (Eds.), Advances in Visual Computing, Part II. XXXII, 906 pages. 2006.

Vol. 4291: G. Bebis, R. Boyle, B. Parvin, D. Koracin, P. Remagnino, A. Nefian, G. Meenakshisundaram, V. Pascucci, J. Zara, J. Molineros, H. Theisel, T. Malzbender (Eds.), Advances in Visual Computing, Part I. XXXI, 916 pages. 2006.

Vol. 4245: A. Kuba, L.G. Nyúl, K. Palágyi (Eds.), Discrete Geometry for Computer Imagery. XIII, 688 pages. 2006.

Vol. 4241: R.R. Beichel, M. Sonka (Eds.), Computer Vision Approaches to Medical Image Analysis. XI, 262 pages. 2006.

Vol. 4225: J.F. Martínez-Trinidad, J.A. Carrasco Ochoa, J. Kittler (Eds.), Progress in Pattern Recognition, Image Analysis and Applications. XIX, 995 pages. 2006.

Vol. 4191: R. Larsen, M. Nielsen, J. Sporring (Eds.), Medical Image Computing and Computer-Assisted Intervention – MICCAI 2006, Part II. XXXVIII, 981 pages. 2006.

Vol. 4190: R. Larsen, M. Nielsen, J. Sporring (Eds.), Medical Image Computing and Computer-Assisted Intervention – MICCAI 2006, Part I. XXXVVIII, 949 pages. 2006.

Vol. 4179: J. Blanc-Talon, W. Philips, D. Popescu, P. Scheunders (Eds.), Advanced Concepts for Intelligent Vision Systems. XXIV, 1224 pages. 2006.

Vol. 4174: K. Franke, K.-R. Müller, B. Nickolay, R. Schäfer (Eds.), Pattern Recognition. XX, 773 pages. 2006.

Vol. 4170: J. Ponce, M. Hebert, C. Schmid, A. Zisserman (Eds.), Toward Category-Level Object Recognition. XI, 618 pages. 2006.

Vol. 4153: N. Zheng, X. Jiang, X. Lan (Eds.), Advances in Machine Vision, Image Processing, and Pattern Analysis. XIII, 506 pages. 2006.

Vol. 4142: A. Campilho, M. Kamel (Eds.), Image Analysis and Recognition, Part II. XXVII, 923 pages. 2006.

Vol. 4141: A. Campilho, M. Kamel (Eds.), Image Analysis and Recognition, Part I. XXVIII, 939 pages. 2006.

Vol. 4122: R. Stiefelhagen, J.S. Garofolo (Eds.), Multimodal Technologies for Perception of Humans. XII, 360 pages. 2007.

Vol. 4109: D.-Y. Yeung, J.T. Kwok, A. Fred, F. Roli, D. de Ridder (Eds.), Structural, Syntactic, and Statistical Pattern Recognition. XXI, 939 pages. 2006.

Vol. 4091: G.-Z. Yang, T. Jiang, D. Shen, L. Gu, J. Yang (Eds.), Medical Imaging and Augmented Reality. XIII, 399 pages. 2006.

Vol. 4073: A. Butz, B. Fisher, A. Krüger, P. Olivier (Eds.), Smart Graphics. XI, 263 pages. 2006.

Vol. 4069: F.J. Perales, R.B. Fisher (Eds.), Articulated Motion and Deformable Objects. XV, 526 pages. 2006.

Vol. 4057: J.P.W. Pluim, B. Likar, F.A. Gerritsen (Eds.), Biomedical Image Registration. XII, 324 pages. 2006.

Vol. 4046: S.M. Astley, M. Brady, C. Rose, R. Zwiggelaar (Eds.), Digital Mammography. XVI, 654 pages. 2006.

Vol. 4040: R. Reulke, U. Eckardt, B. Flach, U. Knauer, K. Polthier (Eds.), Combinatorial Image Analysis. XII, 482 pages. 2006.

Vol. 4035: T. Nishita, Q. Peng, H.-P. Seidel (Eds.), Advances in Computer Graphics. XX, 771 pages. 2006.

Vol. 3979: T.S. Huang, N. Sebe, M. Lew, V. Pavlović, M. Kölsch, A. Galata, B. Kisačanin (Eds.), Computer Vision in Human-Computer Interaction. XII, 121 pages. 2006.

Vol. 3954: A. Leonardis, H. Bischof, A. Pinz (Eds.), Computer Vision – ECCV 2006, Part IV. XVII, 613 pages. 2006.

Vol. 3953: A. Leonardis, H. Bischof, A. Pinz (Eds.), Computer Vision – ECCV 2006, Part III. XVII, 649 pages. 2006.

Vol. 3952: A. Leonardis, H. Bischof, A. Pinz (Eds.), Computer Vision – ECCV 2006, Part II. XVII, 661 pages. 2006.

Vol. 3951: A. Leonardis, H. Bischof, A. Pinz (Eds.), Computer Vision – ECCV 2006, Part I. XXXV, 639 pages. 2006.

Vol. 3948: H.I. Christensen, H.-H. Nagel (Eds.), Cognitive Vision Systems. VIII, 367 pages. 2006.

Vol. 3926: W. Liu, J. Lladós (Eds.), Graphics Recognition. XII, 428 pages. 2006.

Vol. 3872: H. Bunke, A.L. Spitz (Eds.), Document Analysis Systems VII. XIII, 630 pages. 2006.

Vol. 3852: P.J. Narayanan, S.K. Nayar, H.-Y. Shum (Eds.), Computer Vision – ACCV 2006, Part II. XXXI, 977 pages. 2006.

Vol. 3851: P.J. Narayanan, S.K. Nayar, H.-Y. Shum (Eds.), Computer Vision – ACCV 2006, Part I. XXXI, 973 pages. 2006.

Vol. 3832: D. Zhang, A.K. Jain (Eds.), Advances in Biometrics. XX, 796 pages. 2005.

Vol. 3736: S. Bres, R. Laurini (Eds.), Visual Information and Information Systems. XI, 291 pages. 2006.

Vol. 3667: W.J. MacLean (Ed.), Spatial Coherence for Visual Motion Analysis. IX, 141 pages. 2006.

Vol. 3417: B. Jähne, R. Mester, E. Barth, H. Scharr (Eds.), Complex Motion. X, 235 pages. 2007.

Vol. 2396: T.M. Caelli, A. Amin, R.P.W. Duin, M.S. Kamel, D. de Ridder (Eds.), Structural, Syntactic, and Statistical Pattern Recognition. XVI, 863 pages. 2002.

Vol. 1679: C. Taylor, A. Colchester (Eds.), Medical Image Computing and Computer-Assisted Intervention – MICCAI'99. XXI, 1240 pages. 1999.